Blender 3D Basics
Beginner's Guide

The complete novice's guide to 3D modeling and animation

Gordon C. Fisher

BIRMINGHAM - MUMBAI

Blender 3D Basics Beginner's Guide

First published: June 2012

Production Reference: 1130612

Published by Packt Publishing Ltd.
Livery Place
35 Livery Street
Birmingham B3 2PB, UK.

ISBN 978-1-84951-690-7

www.packtpub.com

Cover Image by Gordon C. Fisher (phiinfo@pointhappy.com)

Credits

Author
Gordon C. Fisher

Reviewers
John W. Allie

Allan Brito

Matt Campbell

Roberto Roch

Bryan Tenorio

Willem Verwey

Acquisition Editor
Robin de Jongh

Lead Technical Editor
Dayan Hyames

Technical Editors
Joyslita D'Souza

Vishal D'Souza

Lubna Shaikh

Project Coordinator
Leena Purkait

Proofreader
Bernadette Watkins

Indexer
Rekha Nair

Graphics
Manu Joseph

Production Coordinator
Aparna Bhagat

Cover Work
Aparna Bhagat

About the Author

Gordon C. Fisher got his start in Computer Graphics working with industry pioneers at Information International, Inc. At University of California, Santa Barbara (UCSB) he was the first student to display computer-generated artwork, interactive computer graphics, and computer animation at the UCSB Gallery. Since then, he has made 3D animation for clients including the U.S. Army, Ford Motor Co. the Dallas Cowboys, the Southeastern Conference, and Costco and Southwest Airlines.

He has been using Blender professionally since 2002 and has given classes on using Blender and using Python with Blender at Python conferences in Texas and Arkansas. His short, Land and Sky, made with Blender was shown at the Ozark Foothills Film Fest.

He has garnered two ADDY Citations of Excellence for an animation and an interactive CD. He has been a speaker at Siggraph, describing his work in VRML. His work has been displayed at the National Air and Space Museum.

He is the Creative Director for Point Happy Interactive and spends his spare time as a Bicycling Advocate and Space Activist.

He was the co-author and editor for *Love and Oil*, his grandfather's memoirs of traveling throughout Mexico, prospecting for oil during the Mexican Revolution. He has written articles about 3D modeling and animation for the *American Modeler* magazine and *Digital Video Producer* ezine.

I would like to thank the people without whom this book would not exist.

The staff at Packt; Rachel Gottsch, my English teacher in ninth, tenth, and tenth grades; Gary Demos who encouraged me; Jeffrey Marcus and Gary Brown of UCSB who gave me the access and freedom to do computer graphics; Ton Roosendaal for Blender and Betsy Brown, puppeteer extraordinaire, who got me started in this direction.

About the Reviewers

John W. Allie is an illustrator and writer. He has been using Blender since 1999, when it wasn't even open source. Blender is an important part of his personal and professional work, which includes everything from games to animations. He lives in New Haven, Connecticut, where he is currently working on a graphic novel.

Allan Brito is a Brazilian Architect and a specialist in information visualization, who lives and works in Recife, Brazil. He works with Blender 3D to produce animations and still images for visualization and instructional material. Besides his work with Blender as an artist, he also has a wide experience in teaching and researching about 3D modeling, animation, and multimedia.

He is an active member of the community of Blender users and writes about Blender 3D and its development for websites in Brazilian Portuguese (http://www.allanbrito.com) and English (http://www.blender3darchitect.com and http://www.blendernation.com). Besides his two blogs, he has managed to write three books about Blender in both English and Brazilian Portuguese, covering topics such as architectural visualization, mechanical modeling, and general Blender guides.

To find out more about him visit the website http://www.blender3darchitect.com, where he covers the use of Blender and other tools for architectural visualization.

I want to thank my wife Erica for her support during the review of this book.

Matt Campbell graduated from Conestoga College with a diploma in Mechanical Technology. He has worked in the 3D modeling world since 2007, working mostly with CAD packages. Recently, he has become interested in creating immersive 3D movies.

> I would like to thank my wife Emma and my son Ethan for always being supportive.

Bryan Tenorio studied 3D animation in both high school and in college. He specializes in using Blender as his main tool, and Gimp for most 2D work. He has worked on various freelance jobs. He was on a small team that did previz work for the film *0000*, by *Eddie Alcazar*. He also worked on a few Indie games with (Subli)minal Gaming. Currently he's employed at Rival Theory, a software company that specializes in artificial intelligence for video games.

Willem Verwey is the founder and Chairman of the 3D Animation Network `www.3danim8.net`. The 3D Animation Network introduced children to animation using Blender since 2007.

He has also served on the Blender Foundation Certification Review Board since 2007.

He is the co-owner of Metagon Games and is currently working on *Hidden Object Adventure Games* distributed by *Big Fish Games*.

He technically reviewed *Material Cookbook*.

www.PacktPub.com

Support files, eBooks, discount offers and more

You might want to visit www.PacktPub.com for support files and downloads related to your book.

Did you know that Packt offers eBook versions of every book published, with PDF and ePub files available? You can upgrade to the eBook version at www.PacktPub.com and as a print book customer, you are entitled to a discount on the eBook copy. Get in touch with us at service@packtpub.com for more details.

At www.PacktPub.com, you can also read a collection of free technical articles, sign up for a range of free newsletters and receive exclusive discounts and offers on Packt books and eBooks.

http://PacktLib.PacktPub.com

Do you need instant solutions to your IT questions? PacktLib is Packt's online digital book library. Here, you can access, read, and search across Packt's entire library of books.

Why subscribe?

- ◆ Fully searchable across every book published by Packt
- ◆ Copy and paste, print, and bookmark content
- ◆ On demand and accessible via web browser

Free access for Packt account holders

If you have an account with Packt at www.PacktPub.com, you can use this to access PacktLib today and view nine entirely free books. Simply use your login credentials for immediate access.

Table of Contents

Preface   **1**

Chapter 1: Introducing Blender and Animation   **7**

Welcome to the world of Blender 3D   **8**

Discovering Blender and animation   **9**

    Learning Blender will literally change how you think   10

    Installing Blender   10

    Using Blender   12

Time for action – rendering your first scene in Blender   **12**

Time for action – closing Blender   **15**

Top 10 reasons to enjoy using Blender 3D   **15**

Learning from your animation heros   **16**

    Going back to the year 1922 on an animation field trip   16

Time for action – searching on Felix Turns the Tide + 1922   **17**

    Moving ahead a few years in time, to 1928   18

Time for action – searching on Plane Crazy +1928   **19**

    Arriving in 1938, the animation industry is at a peak   20

Time for action – searching on Goonland + 1938   **20**

Starting to use computers for animation in the 1960s   **21**

    Beginnings of 3D animation in 1963   22

Time for action – searching on Ivan Sutherland + Sketchpad   **23**

    Going to the late 1970s, a few companies are doing 3D animation   24

Time for action – searching on Triple I demo   **24**

Time for action – watching Information International,   **25**

Inc. (Triple I) 1982 demo reel   **25**

    Introducing Pixar – 1984, and everything comes together   25

Time for action – searching for the video of The Adventures of André and Wally B   **26**

    Back to the present time   27

Animation principles	**27**
Using 3D skills, what can you do with them?	**28**
Making 2D animation	29
TV and video	29
Films and pre-visualization	29
Stereoscopic 3D	29
Web animation	29
Games	29
Flight and driving simulators	30
Digital signage	30
Displaying scientific data	30
Legal evidence display	30
Architectural walkthroughs	30
Virtual reality	30
Virtual sets	30
Interactive instruction	31
Showing what can't otherwise be seen	31
Creating a portfolio to get a job	31
Product development and visualization	31
Summary	**31**
Chapter 2: Getting Comfortable using the 3D View	**33**
Exploring the Blender 3D interface	**33**
Setting up Blender the way you want it	34
Using the three basic Blender controllers	35
Using the numeric keypad with Blender	35
Emulating the three-button mouse and Numpad	36
Understanding how to use Blender Windows	36
Time for action – playing with the Blender windows	**36**
Time for action – resizing windows	**38**
Time for action – flipping the window header	**39**
Time for action – maximizing and tiling the window	**39**
Time for action – splitting Blender windows	**40**
Time for action – joining Blender windows	**41**
Exploring the 3D View window, the heart of Blender	**44**
Time for action – discovering your tools	**44**
Looking at the 3D View window, what do you see?	45
Making pictures with computers	47
Making colors with a computer	48
Making millions of colors with just red, green, and blue	48
Measuring things in 3D	49
Navigating in the 3D View	51

Time for action – rotating the scene in 3D View	**51**
Time for action – zooming the scene in 3D View	**52**
Time for action – panning the scene in 3D View	**52**
Using the Numpad to change the angle in the 3D View	53
Time for action – seeing the top view, front view, and right side view	**53**
Time for action – seeing the bottom view, rear view, and left side view	**54**
Time for action – seeing what the camera sees	**54**
Time for action – verifying the Camera View	**55**
Time for action – rotating the view with the Numpad	**56**
Time for action – rotating the view in another direction with the Numpad	**56**
Time for action – zooming with the Numpad	**57**
Time for action – making the camera see what you do	**57**
Understanding Perspective and Orthographic views	59
Time for action – toggling between Perspective and Orthographic views	**59**
Displaying the Quad View and Full Screen	60
Time for action – toggling the Quad view	**60**
Navigating in the 3D View	60
Summary	**62**
Chapter 3: Controlling the Lamp, the Camera, and Animating Objects	**63**
Understanding lamps	**64**
Time for action – moving the lamp	**64**
Time for action – moving the lamp close to the cube	**65**
Time for action – moving the lamp far away	**66**
Time for action – seeing how the lighting looks without rendering	**68**
Adding color to the lamp using the Properties window	69
Time for action – adding color to the lamp	**70**
Using multiple lamps for better lighting	71
Time for action – adding a second lamp	**72**
Light color mixing	73
Saving your work	**75**
Time for action – saving a file	**76**
Always have a backup file	77
Controlling the camera	**77**
Time for action – using the global axis and local axis	**78**
Time for action – moving an object in one plane in global mode	**78**
Time for action – moving an object in one plane in the local mode	**79**
Seeing through the lens	79
Time for action – setting up Blender so you can see what the camera sees	**80**
Using the camera as a canvas	81
Understanding the rules of composition	81
Employing Blender's camera composition guides to make your work look better	83

Understanding the fundamental camera moves 84
Rotating and scaling the camera and other objects 85
Making an animation **85**
Time for action – loading a file **86**
Time for action – making a simple animation with keyframes **87**
Getting a video player so you can play your animation 89
Time for action – downloading the Blender video player **89**
Time for action – installing a video player for Blender **90**
Rendering your animation 91
Time for action – rendering the animation **91**
Controlling motion in the Graph Editor 92
Time for action – exploring the Graph Editor **92**
Introducing the F-Curve 93
Modifying motion with the Bézier curve controls 94
Time for action – working with a Bézier curve **95**
Time for action – adding squash and stretch to the animation **96**
Doing more with the Bézier curve handles 97
Time for action – refining the use of the Bézier curve handles **98**
Selecting which channel to work on 99
Time for action – adding keyframes in the Graph Editor **99**
Time for action – controlling the F-Curves with the Channel Selection Panel **101**
Time for action – controlling channel display with the header **102**
Copying, pasting, and deleting keyframes 102
Time for action – copying and pasting keyframes **102**
Keyframes for properties 103
Time for action – keyframes for lights **103**
Summary **107**

Chapter 4: Modeling with Vertices, Edges, and Faces **109**
Using Object Mode and Edit Mode **109**
Time for action – going into Edit Mode **110**
Investigating vertices, edges, and faces **111**
Time for action – choosing the best display mode **112**
Time for action – working with vertices, edges, or faces **112**
Selecting multiple vertices, edges, and faces 114
Time for action – pressing A to select all **114**
Time for action – pressing B for border selection **114**
Time for action – pressing C for circle selection **115**
Time for action – pressing Ctrl+LMB for lasso selection **116**
Creating Blender's basic objects **117**
Time for action – making a basic object **117**
Understanding what lies behind vertices, edges, and faces **119**
Building vertices, edges, and faces from scratch **120**

Time for action – making faces out of vertices and edges	**120**
Time for action – making a face from an edge	**122**
Summary	**124**
Chapter 5: Building a Simple Boat	**125**
Turning a cube into a boat with box modeling	**126**
Using extrusion, the most powerful tool in box modeling	126
Time for action – extruding to make the inside of the hull	**126**
Using normals in 3D modeling	128
Time for action – displaying normals	**129**
Planning what you are going to make	130
Choosing which units to model in	130
Time for action – making reference objects	**131**
Sizing the boat to the reference blocks	132
Time for action – making the boat the proper length	**132**
Time for action – making the boat the proper width and height	**133**
Time for action – adding curves to the boat's lines by subdividing	**136**
Using clean building methods	140
Time for action – adding a seat to the boat	**141**
Time for action – making the other seat	**143**
Making modeling easier with Blender's layers function	**145**
Time for action – introducing layers	**145**
Time for action – using layers for controlling rendering	**146**
Coloring the boat to add realism	**147**
Time for action – coloring the hull and the gunwale	**147**
Time for action – adding a texture to the seats	**151**
Time for action – naming objects and joining them	**154**
Using Basic Lighting	**155**
Summary	**155**
Chapter 6: Making and Moving the Oars	**157**
Modeling an oar	**158**
Getting scale from an image	158
Making a cylinder into an oar	158
Time for action – making the shaft of the oar	**159**
Time for action – making the grip and guard	**160**
Time for action – making the base of the blade of the oar	**163**
Time for action – making the blade	**164**
Controlling how smooth the surface is	169
Time for action – controlling flat and smooth surfaces	**169**
Making the oarlock	**171**
Time for action – making the oarlock	**171**
Assembling the boat, oars, and oarlocks	**174**

Time for action – loading all of the models together — **175**

Animating the boat — **179**

Time for action – timing a stroke — **179**

Parenting and kinematics — 181

Time for action – animating the oarlock and oar — **182**

Animation cycles — 184

Time for action – copying keyframes to make a rowing cycle — **184**

Moving the boat — 186

Time for action – moving the boat in sync with the oars — **186**

Tracking the boat with the camera — **189**

Time for action – tracking the boat — **189**

Making Stereoscopic 3D Animation — **190**

Summary — **190**

Chapter 7: Planning your Work, Working your Plan — **191**

Using templates for modeling — **192**

Time for action – adding a template — **194**

Time for action – scaling and aligning the template — **195**

Time for action – building the mast — **198**

Modeling with Bezier Curves — **200**

Making an object with a single Bezier Curve — 200

Time for action – making the rudder with a Bezier Curve — **200**

Using multiple Bezier Curves to make an object — 204

Time for action – making the path and the cross-section for the tiller — **204**

Keeping everything organized — **207**

Making an index of your files — 208

Saving your Blender files — 209

Planning your animation — **209**

Discovering the story you want to tell with your animation — 209

Bringing your story to life with storyboards — 211

Making a storyboard — 211

Using animatics to plan the timing of your animation — **214**

Using charts and guides to help you plan your animation — **215**

Staying in TV limits with Safe Title-Action zones and Lower Thirds — 215

Time for action – adding a Safe Title/Safe Action guide to Blender — **216**

Transitioning from Standard Definition TV to High Definition TV — 217

Laying out your motion with Timing — 218

Planning what work must be done to make an animation — 219

Guiding animation production with an audio track — **220**

Time for action – adding an audio track to Blender — **220**

Summary — **224**

Chapter 8: Making the Sloop   225

Modeling with Subdivision Surfaces   225
Time for action – making a simple Subdivision Surface   226
    Using Edge Tools to make modeling easier   227
Time for action – turning a Reference Block into a sloop   228
Time for action – making selection easy with edge loops and edge rings   230
Time for action – creating the shape of the sloop from the top   231
Time for action – giving the hull a hull shape   233
Time for action – flattening the transom   237
Time for action – making the bow sharper   238
Time for action – finishing the hull   239
    Getting the most for your rendering time with Levels of Detail   240
Time for action – making the boat simpler   240
Modeling the hull as a mesh   243
Time for action – converting the surface to a mesh   243
Time for action – making the cockpit   244
Time for action – making the cabin   247
Using Boolean modifiers to cut holes in objects   252
Time for action – detailing the cabin using the Boolean modifier   252
Time for action – applying the Boolean modifier   254
Adding materials and textures to the sloop   255
Time for action – coloring and texturing the sloop hull   256
Time for action – using the same materials for two objects   261
Making the ship's wheel with the Spin tool and DupliVerts   263
Time for action – using the Spin tool to make the rim of the ship's wheel   263
Time for action – making the hub   265
Time for action – making the circle   265
Time for action – making the spoke   266
Time for action – assembling the ship's wheel   269
Summary   271

Chapter 9: Finishing your Sloop   273

Making sure you have the files you'll need in this chapter   273
Finishing the sloop   274
Time for action – setting up the boom and gaff so they swing   274
Time for action – adding the rudder, tiller, and keel   278
Time for action – adding the ship's wheel   281
Time for action – adding the boat name   283
Time for action – using a NURBS surface to make the mainsail   285
Detailing the sloop, adding a door and portals   289
Time for action – adding a line to control the mainsail   289

Time for action – adding the portals   291
Summary   297

Chapter 10: Modeling Organic Forms, Sea, and Terrain   299
Getting ready to make the island   300
Creating the ocean   300
Time for action – making a surface for the water   300
Making an island   303
    Using the ANT Landscape add-on   303
Time for action – using ANT Landscape to make the island   304
    Detailing the island   307
Time for action – understanding the proportional editing control   308
Time for action – using proportional editing to create the port   310
Time for action – building the breakwater   313
Time for action – adding contours to the back side of the island   315
    Painting the island   316
Time for action – painting the island   316
Making the island ready for habitation   322
    Building the pier with just four objects   322
Time for action – creating the pier frame rails with Bezier Curves   322
Time for action – adding planks to the pier with DupliFrames   325
Time for action – using arrays to create the pilings for the pier   327
    Appending the boathouse   329
Time for action – appending the boathouse and building pilings for it   329
    Building modular houses   332
    Creating trees with the Sapling add-on   334
Time for action – adding trees to the landscape   335
    Making rocks   339
    Assembling your world   339
Time for action – using groups to organize your scene   341
Summary   343

Chapter 11: Improving your Lighting and Camera Work   345
Getting ready to do lighting and camera work   345
Using lighting   346
    Lighting with three lights   347
Time for action – introducing the three point lighting system   347
Time for action – lighting with only the key light   348
Time for action – lighting with only the fill light   349
Time for action – lighting with only the back light   350
Time for action – using color to separate what you see   351
Time for action – using cookies   353

Time for action – preparing to adjust falloff   **355**

Time for action – adjusting the falloff   **357**

Time for action – using the Custom Curve to tailor light   **359**

Using the camera to best effect   **363**

  Changing the field of view   363

Time for action – zooming the camera versus dollying the camera   **364**

  Using perspective   367

  Using depth of field   368

Time for action – creating depth of field   **369**

  Getting variety in your camera work   373

    Comparing long and medium shots   374

    Using close-up and two shots   374

    Applying the rule of 180   375

  Using motion blur   375

Planning your animation and making sure it comes out right   **378**

  Storyboarding your ideas   378

  Laying out your animation   379

  Proofing your work   380

    Doing a preview   380

    Using hardware rendering to see the motion   380

    Inspecting details by rendering only part of the frame   381

    Glimpsing what the animation will look like with the quick render   381

Time for action – reducing render times   **381**

  Making corrections   383

Time for action – using the Dope Sheet   **384**

Summary   **387**

Chapter 12: Rendering and Compositing   **389**

  Preparing for Chapter 12   **389**

  Editing with the Video Sequence Editor   **390**

  Time for action – dissolving with the Video Sequence Editor   **390**

  Time for action – editing individual video strips   **395**

  Time for action – using K and Shift+K to make your trims   **397**

  Making stereographic 3D with the Node Editor   **400**

  Time for action – creating the red image for the left eye   **401**

  Time for action – making the right-eye view   **404**

  Rendering your animations   **408**

    Making your computer ready to render   409

    Making rendering more beautiful   409

      Using Anti-Aliasing for more beautiful renderings   409

  Time for action – displaying aliasing   **409**

    Getting realism with subsurface scattering   410

    Putting a sparkle on your animations with ray tracing   410

Time for action – seeing ray tracing   **411**
Choosing the proper number of tiles   412
Using alpha channels   413
Time for action – exploring the alpha channel   **413**
Time for action – using transparency in the Video Sequence Editor   **414**
Choosing the dimensions for your animation   416
Time for action – selecting render presets   **416**
Time for action – seeing what fields look like   **418**
Choosing what gets rendered   420
Selecting the best file format   422
Rendering with the Cycles renderer   **422**
Time for action – simulating the glow of a kiln   **423**
Summary   **428**

Pop Quiz Answers   **429**
Chapter 2, Getting Comfortable using the 3D View   **429**
Chapter 3, Controlling the Lamp, the Camera, and Animating Objects   **430**
Chapter 4, Modeling with Vertices, Edges, and Faces   **430**
Chapter 5, Building and Lighting a Simple Boat   **430**
Chapter 6, Making and Moving the Oars   **430**
Chapter 7, Planning your Work, Working your Plan   **431**
Chapter 8, Making the Sloop   **431**
Chapter 10, Modeling Organic Forms, Sea, and Terrain   **432**
Chapter 11, Improving your Lighting and Camera Work   **432**
Chapter 12, Rendering and Compositing   **432**

Index   **433**

Preface

When researching in preparation to write this book, we discovered that some Blender users try to learn Blender three times and give up twice before they become comfortable with Blender's effective, if unusual, interface. The editors at Packt and I decided that this was a problem that could be solved. The answer is to explain the basics in depth, give you practice so that your hands can learn Blender just as your mind does, and then you build on what you have learned. This isn't just a subject-by-subject reference book. It's a workbook to give you experience.

The theory behind *Blender 3D Basics Beginner's Guide* is to start out simply and delve deeper and deeper into Blender in gradual stages. This book will start with an introduction to Blender and some background on the principles of animation, how they are applied to computer animation, and how these principles make animation better. Then you will be gently guided through the Blender interface, and introduced to using Blender with simple projects that cover the full process of modeling, lighting, camera work, and animation. Then you will continue to practice what you have learned and do more advanced work in all areas. Finally, you will bring it all together with an advanced project covering these subjects and edit animations made in this book; creating a video and a stereoscopic 3D animation.

This may be a workbook, but it's a fun workbook with surprises, humor, and the projects build on each other, so it's not just a random series of exercises. When you are finished, you'll be prepared to show the world your skills.

Let's go!

What this book covers

Chapter 1, Introducing Blender and Animation, will help you to get your first hands-on use of Blender, a brief but very relevant bit of history of animation and computer animation and an overview of the basic principles of animation.

Chapter 2, Getting Comfortable using the 3D View, includes some fun exercises that explore using the Blender window system and the basic elements that are found in the 3D View window.

Chapter 3, Controlling the Lamp, the Camera, and Animating Objects, explains the basics of lights in Blender, good use of the camera, and making your first animation.

Chapter 4, Modeling with Vertices, Edges, and Faces, teaches you the fundamentals of 3D modeling, using Vertices, Edges, and Faces. You'll be introduced to Blender's library of pre-made objects and have fun bending and distorting Blender's lovely mascot, Suzanne.

Chapter 5, Building a Simple Boat, will teach you Box Modeling techniques. You will learn how to use them to make a small johnboat, give it a color, and make wooden seats. Then you will study the different lights that Blender has.

Chapter 6, Making and Moving the Oars, focuses on the oars for the boat. You will use more advanced modeling and animation techniques and discover how to create more complex keyframe animations.

Chapter 7, Planning your Work, Working your Plan, teaches you to create templates to help you plan your modeling. You will get an introduction to modeling with Bezier Curves; take a look at storyboarding and planning an animation as well being introduced to some charts and guides that help you plan your work.

Chapter 8, Making the Sloop, helps you to make the hull of the sloop using Box Modeling and Subdivision Surfaces. You will learn to make holes in objects with Boolean operations and create the Ship's Wheel with Spin Tools and DupliVerts.

Chapter 9, Finishing your Sloop, explains how to use text and fonts in naming your sloop. Then you will assemble all the objects you made in this and the previous chapter, build some sails using NURBS surfaces, and add a few extras that have been provided in your download pack.

Chapter 10, Modeling Organic Forms, Sea, and Terrain, helps you to build and paint an island and the ocean. You make trees for it, and assemble some pre-fab buildings, as well as make a pier from four simple parts.

Chapter 11, Improving your Lighting and Camera Work, focuses on professional lighting and camera techniques. You will also learn more about animation and ways to speed up performing test renders and improve the final rendering quality.

Chapter 12, Rendering and Compositing, covers assembling strips of animated sequences in the Video Sequence Editor to create a completed and edited animation with sound. You will use the Node Editor to assemble a 3D Stereoscopic animation and get introduced to the Cycles renderer, which adds even more realism and possibilities to a Blender scene.

What you need for this book

Of course you need to download a copy of Blender available at `http://www.blender.org/download/get-blender/`. This book was written and tested on Blender 2.63a. It should work with later versions of Blender as well, but we cannot guarantee it.

Who this book is for

This book was written to reduce the frustration that beginning Blender users face, by offering a thorough introduction to the unique Blender interface; starting with simple projects and working up to more complex scenes and animations. It's intended to provide plenty of practice in using Blender, advice on things to keep in mind when doing 3D animation, and an exploration of Blender so that the student, when they finish the book, will have a solid background in using Blender and know enough that they can confidently participate in the world wide Blender community.

This book also takes a peek into some arcane subjects such as the Cycles render engine, so that the reader will not be afraid, and will have a start on how to understand them. The student will have a solid enough basis in using Blender that they can continue and learn all of the higher functions of Blender including the physics engine, game engine, particles, armatures for character modeling, and more.

Conventions

In this book, you will find several headings appearing frequently.

To give clear instructions on how to complete a procedure or task, we use:

Time for action – heading

1. Action 1

2. Action 2

3. Action 3

Instructions often need some extra explanation so that they make sense, so they are followed with:

What just happened?

This heading explains the working of tasks or instructions that you have just completed.

You will also find some other learning aids in the book, including:

Pop quiz – heading

These are short multiple choice questions intended to help you test your own understanding.

Have a go hero – heading

These set practical challenges and give you ideas for experimenting with what you have learned.

You will also find a number of styles of text that distinguish between different kinds of information. Here are some examples of these styles, and an explanation of their meaning.

Code words in text are shown as follows: "For your reference, the file `6907_07_sloop_mast.blend` has the mast started".

New terms and **important words** are shown in bold. Words that you see on the screen, in menus or dialog boxes for example, appear in the text like this: "Click on the **Add Image** button with the *LMB*".

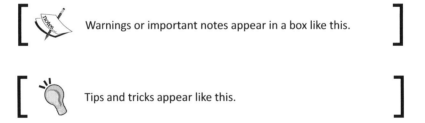

Warnings or important notes appear in a box like this.

Tips and tricks appear like this.

Reader feedback

Feedback from our readers is always welcome. Let us know what you think about this book—what you liked or may have disliked. Reader feedback is important for us to develop titles that you really get the most out of.

To send us general feedback, simply send an e-mail to `feedback@packtpub.com`, and mention the book title through the subject of your message.

If there is a topic that you have expertise in and you are interested in either writing or contributing to a book, see our author guide on `www.packtpub.com/authors`.

Customer support

Now that you are the proud owner of a Packt book, we have a number of things to help you to get the most from your purchase.

Downloading the example code

You can download the example code files for all Packt books you have purchased from your account at `http://www.packtpub.com`. If you purchased this book elsewhere, you can visit `http://www.packtpub.com/support` and register to have the files e-mailed directly to you.

Errata

Although we have taken every care to ensure the accuracy of our content, mistakes do happen. If you find a mistake in one of our books—maybe a mistake in the text or the code—we would be grateful if you would report this to us. By doing so, you can save other readers from frustration and help us improve subsequent versions of this book. If you find any errata, please report them by visiting `http://www.packtpub.com/support`, selecting your book, clicking on the **errata submission form** link, and entering the details of your errata. Once your errata are verified, your submission will be accepted and the errata will be uploaded to our website, or added to any list of existing errata, under the Errata section of that title.

Piracy

Piracy of copyright material on the Internet is an ongoing problem across all media. At Packt, we take the protection of our copyright and licenses very seriously. If you come across any illegal copies of our works, in any form, on the Internet, please provide us with the location address or website name immediately so that we can pursue a remedy.

Please contact us at `copyright@packtpub.com` with a link to the suspected pirated material.

We appreciate your help in protecting our authors, and our ability to bring you valuable content.

Questions

You can contact us at `questions@packtpub.com` if you are having a problem with any aspect of the book, and we will do our best to address it.

1
Introducing Blender and Animation

Welcome, it's a good guess that you are interested in learning how to do 3D animation. You've chosen Blender 3D and you want to learn how to use it. This book is a good choice. We did research on what hurdles new users faced and what their frustrations with other training methods were. So we will go step-by-step, learning how to use Blender comfortably to create animations, do modeling, lighting, camera work, and much more. You will start out with simple steps, get comfortable using the Blender interface, make and animate a rowboat, then a sloop, and create your own private island as shown in the following screenshot:

This first chapter will get us gently into Blender:

◆ We will talk about general animation and look at a few videos. The videos give us a quick introduction to general animation principles.

◆ We will watch some early computer graphics to see how using animation principles benefited early 3D animation.

◆ After that, there will be the top-ten reasons to enjoy Blender.

◆ We will look at what people use 3D for.

◆ And then we'll be ready to focus on the inner workings of Blender itself in the other chapters.

Welcome to the world of Blender 3D

The following is a screenshot made using Blender:

The world of Blender is not an animated world as seen in films like **Big Buck Bunny** as shown previously, or **Sintel** that was made in Blender. It's the amazing community of people all over the world who use Blender. Artists, programmers, professionals, amateurs, teens, and retirees all use Blender and you are one of the newest members of our community.

One thing that makes this community remarkable is the concept that Blender is free, you pay for it by helping out the Blender community. There are many ways to give back. You can recommend Blender to your friends; have fun helping other Blender users at websites such as www.blenderartists.org by critiquing their works or passing along tips that you have learned. Blender is open source. Once you have mastered Blender, you can help create new functions for Blender itself or work with the Blender foundation team to make new cutting edge examples of what Blender can do, such as Sintel. There are as many ways to help as there are Blender users and most important, helping others helps you as a Blender user. Blender is not a solo sport, so join in.

Big Buck Bunny and Sintel are animated films created by the Blender Institute.

They were made with the dual purposes of improving Blender by bringing the best Blender users in the world together to push Blender to its limits, using its full capacity and demonstrating to people what Blender is capable of. You can download Big Buck Bunny and Sintel, or watch them at these locations:

Sintel can be seen at `http://www.sintel.org/`.

Big Buck Bunny can be seen at `http://www.bigbuckbunny.org/`.

Discovering Blender and animation

As Sintel, shown in the following screenshot, learned about her little Dragon, you will be learning a lot about how to use Blender. We will start out with some quick exercises to introduce you to the basics, and as you progress, you will be able to do more and more. As you study and practice, your hands will learn the Blender commands, freeing your mind to let it concentrate on modeling, animation, lights, and camera.

This book is about using Blender 3D, but there is more to animation than knowing which buttons to push while using Blender. Animators who are skilled at using the software, but do not have a broader understanding of animation, do not get the full use of the tools. They don't understand the culture or the history of animation or how animation principles have been used by masters such as Ub Iwerks, Chuck Jones, and Hayao Miyazaki, and therefore cannot profit from them.

So, in this chapter, we will look at animation in general, and then computer animation specifically. After that, we will get a bit closer and apply what we have learned to Blender. As you go through this book, you'll start by making some simple animations, moving the lights and camera in Blender. Once you are confident with this, you'll study the fundamentals of modeling and complete a simple modeling and animation project; and finally, you will work on a more complex scene to expand your skills and get comfortable with the whole Blender production cycle.

There are many excellent books showing how to animate. In this book, we will focus on Blender and include pointers about animation that will help you educate yourself about animation in general and get the most from Blender.

Repetition is important when learning a skill. It takes repeated usage before your arms know what to do when the mind says "Scale this box." So be patient with yourself. Play, learn, and have fun.

Learning Blender will literally change how you think

You'll be able to look at an object and think of several ways to make it. You will perceive everything differently; as you walk down a street you will be imagining how you might model it or render it in Blender.

One thing to remember, there are no buttons in Blender that say "Don't touch".

As long as you back up your files and use the *Ctrl+Z* keys to undo any mistakes, not much is likely to go too wrong.

Now it's time to begin our discovery of Blender. Using Blender is as simple or complex as you want it to be.

Let's begin simply. To start, we will open Blender up and **render** out a scene. Rendering is like taking a picture in Blender. When you take a picture in real life, you have a camera, some light, and something or someone you are taking a picture of.

In a Blender scene, there is also a camera, lights, and something to render. When you render, Blender scans the scene from the camera's point of view. It notes which objects are where, and what lights are available. It then figures out how each object will be lit, what the surface of the object looks like, what part of the object the camera can see, how big it should appear to the camera, and other factors, and then Blender creates a picture. It's pretty amazing.

We'll dip our toe into Blender, just so you can see that using Blender is not difficult and that you can do it. Then we will get a little background on animation so you will understand what animators are trying to accomplish in Blender. Then using what you have learned, you'll be ready to learn more about Blender.

Installing Blender

Go to `http://www.blender.org/` to download Blender for free. There is a **Download** button on the main menu, which will direct you to where you can download Blender for your system. Blender runs on Windows, Mac, Linux, and FreeBSD. Follow the instructions and you should have Blender up and running quickly.

To use Blender, you need to first check that your machine has certain minimum system specifications, so that it is capable of running Blender. Here's where to find your system information:

- On a PC running XP or Vista, press the **Start** button at the lower left of the Windows screen, then find **Programs | Accessories | System Tools | System Information**.

- On a PC running Windows 7, open **System Information** by clicking the **Start** button. When the search box opens, type System Information, and choose **System Information** from the list of results.

- On a Mac, click on the **Finder | Applications | Utilities | System Profiler**.

- On a Linux machine check the **System Settings | System Info**.

The following is what Blender needs in order to be able to run:

- System
    - Windows XP, Vista, or 7
    - Mac OS X 10.5 or later
    - Linux
    - FreeBSD

- Hardware – minimum
    - 1 GHZ Single Core CPU
    - 512 MB RAM
    - 1024 x 768 px Display with 16 bit color
    - three-button mouse
    - Open GL Graphics Card with 64 MB RAM

- Hardware – good
    - 2 GHZ Dual Core CPU
    - 2 GB RAM
    - 1920 x 1200 px Display with 24 bit color
    - three-button mouse
    - Open GL Graphics Card with 256 or 512 MB RAM

- ◆ Hardware – professional
  - ❑ 64 bit, Multi Core CPU
  - ❑ 8–16 GB RAM
  - ❑ Two times 1920 x 1200 px Display with 24 bit color
  - ❑ three-button mouse + tablet
  - ❑ Open GL Graphics Card with 1 GB RAM, ATI FireGL or Nvidia Quadro

Using a three-button mouse and the numeric keypad

In looking at the hardware specs, you may have noticed that Blender is designed to be used with a three-button mouse. Whether you are running a Mac and using a single-button mouse; or you have a laptop with a touchpad or trackpad, this is a great time to go to the store and buy a three-button mouse optical mouse with a mouse wheel. They are not expensive. You shouldn't need anything special. I took one from a PC, plugged it into the USB port of a MacBook Air, running Snow Leopard, and it worked fine. I polled a number of Blender users and they all said that using the three-button mouse was faster and easier than other devices.

If you are using a tablet with a higher end system, check your tablet documentation on how to reproduce right, middle, and left mouse button clicks.

Also, if your computer does not have a numeric keypad built in, treat yourself to an external one. They are not expensive and will add a lot to your enjoyment of Blender, as well as improving your productivity.

Using Blender

Now that you have the latest version of Blender on your system, it's time to try it out.

Time for action – rendering your first scene in Blender

Although Blender is very powerful and has a lot of features, it's easy to get started using it. Blender has a default scene all set up for you to render.

First, start your copy of Blender. You can either click on the **Blender.exe** icon in the directory that you have installed it in, or use a shortcut if you have created one. Blender will even run from a data stick, so you don't need to have it installed on a particular computer.

When you've started it, you should see something like the following screen, but you will also see a splash screen (depending on the version of Blender installed), consisting of an attractive image made in Blender and some links.

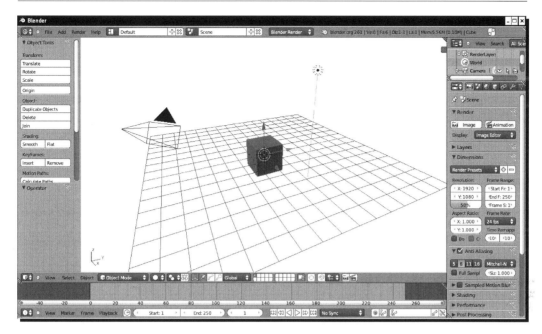

Move the mouse over the big central window. Click the mouse to remove the splash screen.

Then, if you are running Windows or Linux, press the *F12* button on your keyboard.

If you have a Mac, click on where it says **Render** to the left, above the large 3D View window. Select **Render Image** from the drop-down menu. This is because Macs often have the *F1–F12* function keys already mapped to specific functions.

The following are the changes you should make to optimize your Mac for Blender. When you have made these changes, you will be able to use Blender in the same manner as Windows and Linux users, and you will be able to press the *F12* button to start rendering:

◆ Go to the **System Preferences**, Select the **Keyboard** then check **Use all F1, F2, etc. keys as standard function keys**.

◆ Next, in **Keyboard Shortcuts** under **Dashboard & Dock**, uncheck the **Dashboard/F12** checkbox, so you can render by merely pressing *F12*.

◆ Then, uncheck **Exposé Desktop/F11** under **Exposé & Spaces**. Now you will be able to use the *F11* key to bring back your most recent rendered image.

◆ Now, click the left arrow at the top left of the **System Preferences** window to get back to the main **System Preferences** window. Now select the **Exposé & Spaces** symbol in the top row above the **Keyboard**. Select the **Exposé** button. Go down to the **Dashboard** section. Select the button that says **Middle Mouse Button** when the menu pops up, select the dash at the bottom of the pop-up menu. This will enable the middle mouse button for use with Blender.

◆ Finally, click the left arrow at the top left of the **System Preferences** window to get back to the main **System Preferences** window. Select the mouse symbol next to the **Keyboard**. Uncheck where it says **Zoom using scroll wheel while holding**. This will activate the control key while using Blender.

What just happened?

Congratulations, you've now rendered your first scene in Blender. You can see the scene to be rendered in the preceding image. The cube is easy to guess. The dot surrounded by dashed lines is the light. The four-sided cone with a triangle on top is the camera, and there is a reference grid beneath the cube.

When the scene is rendered, as seen in the following screenshot, Blender shows you what the camera would see. The cube is colored gray because you haven't chosen a color. There is only one light in the scene and Blender calculates where the light is, and where the sides of the cube are. The light is not an object like a light bulb, so it is not seen in the rendered image, but its light is used to set the brightness of the scene.

While it's rendering, Blender figures out what portion of the light would bounce off of a particular side of the cube and into the camera. As some sides point away from the light, they appear darker. The sides facing toward the light appear to be brighter. Blender even does a trick that you don't see at all. Blender figures out which parts of the cube the camera does not see and to save itself from additional work, it doesn't render what cannot be seen.

Rendering this image was simple for you to do. Blender doesn't get any more difficult to use, you just learn more things to do with Blender. In future chapters, we will break down using Blender into easy-to-do steps.

Mac users, thank you for making changes to the interface of your Mac. Now you can use the standard Blender commands. This will this pay off by making Blendering much easier and fun. You can still access the Dashboard via the Mac menu bar.

Time for action – closing Blender

Now let's close Blender and study some basics of animation:

1. Press the *Esc* key to close the render window and return you to the 3D View window.

2. Press *Ctrl+Q* to quit Blender. A dialog box will come up asking you to confirm that you want to **Quit Blender**, click on it to quit Blender.

What just happened?

When Blender renders a scene, it brings up a special render window over the 3D window. Pressing the *Esc* button closes this window, returning you to the 3D window. *Ctrl+Q* closes Blender 3D down completely. Congratulations! Everything else about learning Blender is just an elaboration on this.

Top 10 reasons to enjoy using Blender 3D

We all have our reasons for wanting to use Blender. My initial reason was that I wanted to teach a class on 3D animation at my local parks and recreation center. I needed a 3D system that would fit the budget and that students could take home to use. Since then, I've also used it professionally, creating animations for an airline, a national football league team, banks, and more. I made the first animated entry ever into the Film in 48 Hours contest with Blender and one Blender animation of mine was also accepted into the Ozark Foothills Film Festival. So you never know how Blender will come in handy.

Here are the top 10 reasons to enjoy using Blender 3D:

10	It's a fun hobby that will last all of your life.
9	You can use it to make a portfolio to get a job in games, films, advertising, and other fields.
8	You can start a home-based graphics, animation, or game business.
7	Blender has the largest user base and a great world-wide community.
6	You can express your artistic side and make things the way they should be.
5	It's fun to build your own worlds and have God-like power over them.
4	You can make games with the Blender Game Engine and make assets for them.
3	You can learn how to do computer programming with Python.
2	You can impress your friends making animations for your civic social group or favorite team.
1	You can get coffee, a snack, or take a nap while it's rendering and still be productive.

Learning from your animation heros

One of the best ways to learn is to study what others have done; that is no surprise. If you wanted to be a soccer (football) star as a child, maybe you watched Pelé on TV and imagined yourself scoring goals the same way.

Animation is the same. So for the rest of the chapter, we will be looking at what animators learned and what you can learn from them to make lively animation. You will see their early crude animations and how the animations quickly became more dynamic and entertaining. If you know about the 12 principles of animation, and are in a hurry to learn more about using Blender, you can proceed onto the next chapter. But then again, as an animator, you'll probably enjoy watching these animations anyway.

Have a go hero – making a folder of your animation heroes

Think of who your animation heroes are, and make a bookmarks folder in your web browser to store the addresses of websites about your favorite animators, or animations that you have seen. Now go online and look at some works that you know, whether it's Disney's Fantasia, South Park, or Plumiferos (Free Birds), which is the first feature length film made entirely in Blender (you can find out more at http://www.plumiferos.com/). Add a link to your folder whenever you find something you like. You can find quite a number of interesting animations by just looking around on the web. These are some that I found, Nina Paley's "Sita Sings the Blues" is a feature animation done by one person in Flash. It's pretty amazing. I also found "Snow-bo" by Vera Brosgol and Jenn Kluska, and "Kenya" on the Weebl's Stuff website. There are many great Blender animations at www.blenderartists.org.

Your list will be different from mine of course.

Going back to the year 1922 on an animation field trip

We are going to go into the past, back to when animation was young. We are going there because there are general issues that everyone encounters when trying to put graphics into motion. Early animations were simple, so it is easiest to see the fundamental animation techniques done and to see examples of where it wasn't done so we can see the difference.

Back then, like now, animators were under pressure; they had a short time to turn out a completed animation. They ran into issues such as what was required to tell a story believably, what kind of look to give it, how to make it easy to do, and how to get it done before their deadline. They also had to answer questions such as how to tell the story, how to get all the art work done, and how to photograph it with a camera. A lot of the answers they came up with are now universal.

First, we are going to look at a **Felix the Cat** animation called **Felix Turns the Tide** made a few years after World War I. It was a silent animation and cutting edge for its time, but pretty primitive by modern standards, as you can see in the following screenshot. From the thought balloon and text borrowed from newspaper comics you can see that animation hasn't come too far from its roots.

It's a good place to start because they had figured out the mechanics of making an animation, but they were just beginning to learn how to do animation well. In this book, you will learn both the mechanics of Blender animation, and how to do it well. It's a learning experience we will share with these pioneers—so we're in good company!

Time for action – searching on Felix Turns the Tide + 1922

Make a search on the web for the terms **Felix Turns the Tide** + **1922**. YouTube, archive.org, or some other site should have the video. Felix Turns the Tide was made in 1922 and stars Felix the Cat who was the hottest animation star of the time. It was one of 17 different Felix the Cat films made that year, or approximately one animation every three weeks.

Watch it now and enjoy it.

What just happened?

Felix Turns the Tide sure isn't Avatar, but it's surprising how well they used their limited tools and told a story. This was only six years after cel animation had been invented. Cel animation revolutionized early animation because it allowed you to put different parts of an animated frame on different layers, so you didn't have to redraw the entire scene every frame.

Pop quiz – analyzing pioneer animators

There are no right or wrong answers to these questions about the movies. The purpose is to get you to think about the question and come up with your own answers:

1. **Timing:** Are Felix's movements realistic? Or are we given a series of poses and a moment to see each one?

2. **Camera Use:** How would you describe their use of backgrounds? Did they use a variety of distances between the action and the camera? Think of the house where he goes to say goodbye to his girlfriend, or when he hijacks the balloon. How is the camera used? How would you handle either of these scenes?

3. **Producibility:** They made this eight minute movie in a few months without computers; the 14 minute Blender movie Sintel took a year or more. Considering the short deadlines that the animators worked under, imagine some of the compromises the animators made to get the animation out of the door and some of the arguments they might have had about what to do.

4. **Metaphors:** As animation began to move away from the comics section of the paper, it continued to use a lot of the same metaphors that comics did. These are things such as text in balloons for dialog, plants moving along the side of the road to indicate motion, emoticon-like hearts indicating love. What other metaphors do you remember seeing?

5. **Audience expectation:** Think about how the sausages get to the battle. Do you think that modern audiences would accept this? Imagine you are remaking this animation in 3D in Blender for a modern audience, how would you handle getting the sausages to the battlefront?

Moving ahead a few years in time, to 1928

Animators are learning their craft and technology is advancing. **Walt Disney** has lost his main character, **Oswald the Lucky Rabbit**, to Universal Studios. Universal also hired away all of his animators except **Ub Iwerks**, Disney's star animator. This is a serious blow to Disney. So Disney is desperate and he needs something to stay in business. In 1928, Walt Disney and Ub Iwerks make their first Mickey Mouse animation, **Plane Crazy**. It introduces both Mickey and Minnie. But Walt cannot find a distributor for it, so it doesn't get released. His next Mickey Mouse movie, **Steamboat Willie** was the first American animation with sound, and that opened up the market for Mickey. For us, since **Plane Crazy** was made as a silent and retrofitted with sound, it shows how animators had perfected their skills in the period between 1922 and 1928, before the use of sound.

Time for action – searching on Plane Crazy +1928

Make a search on the Web for the terms **Plane Crazy** + **1928**. YouTube, archive.org, or some other site should have the video. This is a good example of silent animation at the dawn of sound. As you watch it, keep Felix Turns the Tide in mind and see how the two are so different.

Watch it now and enjoy it.

What just happened?

Animation has improved quite a bit in those six years. Now, the basic principles of animation were codified and used with good results. Instead of a static, stage-like establishing shot, we enter the scene following a cow, from blackness into a farmyard filled with activity. Let's look at some aspects of this improvement.

Pop quiz – analyzing early animators

Now let's consider how animators improved their skills in eight years and how it changed animation:

1. **Performance:** In one scene, Mickey is primping with a mirror comparing himself to a picture of Charles Lindberg, the first person to fly solo across the Atlantic. Mickey is not that much more complex than Felix visually. But contrast how dynamic the performances are in "Plane Crazy" with "Felix Turns the Tide". Felix has little character, and Mickey is egocentric, impulsive, and just plain crazy. What differences do you see in how the characters move and look, that allowed Iwerks to do more subtle characterization?

2. **Use of Backgrounds:** The backgrounds are softer and more lush in "Plane Crazy" than in "Felix Turns the Tide". They are soft edged pastels while the characters are hard-edged, flat colors, and much simpler visually. Does this accomplish the purpose of highlighting the characters by contrast? How would you decide how much work to put into a given background?

3. **Immersion:** In the scene where Mickey and Minnie fly down the middle of the highway narrowly missing cars and telephone poles, Ub Iwerks is very successful in giving it a three dimensional feel and sweeping you into the action by letting you see the action through Mickey's eyes instead of showing the plane flying along the road. In what ways is "Plane Crazy" visually richer than "Felix Turns the Tide" and how does it help tell the story?

4. **Squash and stretch:** In "Plane Crazy", did you notice how much distortion there was? The first plane swerved and bent back upon itself. The second plane is semi-soft as it flies up and down. Minnie grabs Mickey's head and distorts it terribly. What techniques did Ub Iwerks use to make "Plane Crazy" more dramatic?

5. **Misdirection:** In "Plane Crazy", Iwerks sets you up and then pulls the carpet from under your feet by doing something you don't expect. Mickey and Minnie are taxiing the plane, when it bumps on a rock and knocks Mickey out of the pilot's seat. The animation takes a whole different direction than you were expecting. Are there other places he managed to redirect your expectations so you were fooled, or it helped him to add or remove something without you noticing?

Arriving in 1938, the animation industry is at a peak

The animation industry is mature. Felix ceased production in 1936. Disney released **Snow White and the Seven Dwarfs** in December of 1937 and was beginning production on **Fantasia**. With the popularity of **Popeye, Fleischer Studios** had become the number two animation company and was working on **Gulliver's Travels**. In 1938, Fleischer Studios did the Popeye cartoon **Goonland**. Goonland is a good example of the state of animation then.

Time for action – searching on Goonland + 1938

Make a search on the Web for the terms **Goonland** + **1938**. YouTube, archive.org, or some other site should have the video. According to reviews on imdb.com, this has some of the best artwork of all the Popeyes. Look at it with an eye to what progress has been made since 1930.

Watch it now and enjoy it.

Pop quiz – analyzing what animators had learned in 16 years

Animation was mature by 1938. Studios were busy animating classics such as **Snow White** and **Gulliver's Travels**. Let's examine how they were using their talents:

1. **Secondary motion** can enhance or detract from the main motion. Think of the sails of Popeye's boat and the clouds behind them. The background has become a character. They move in rhythm to Popeye's body and the boat's motion, and when he leaves the wheel, the rhythm changes. And it's subtle enough that you're not likely to notice it at first. Name other places where secondary motion helps the scene.

2. **Arcs** make design and motion more interesting than straight lines. The motion is arced even when Pappy powers up into the air to save Popeye. What places in the animation do they arc the motion to make it more interesting?

3. **Anticipation** and follow through help carry the motion. On his boat, to speed up, Popeye takes a BIG breath in anticipation, he blows the boat onto shore and in follow through the boat goes aft-high when it lands. Are there other places where this principle is used?

4. **Exaggeration.** Popeye blowing the boat along is clearly exaggeration, but we accept it. Are there other places where exaggeration helps the story?

5. Notice how few **metaphors** are used. There are no eye-lines, no text balloons. The fight scene with the goons where it becomes a cloud of arms and fists, seems to be one of the last metaphors. Do metaphors like this still have a place in animation, why or why not?

Have a go hero – studying the masters

You have already made up a library of your favorite animators. It's also good to study the masters; that's one great thing about the Internet, not only can you watch the animations, but you can pause them and scrub back and forth over the best parts, look at how they did it frame by frame, make sketches, and take notes. You see a lot of stuff that way that you would miss if you were just watching it play.

The following are a few recommendations:

- Oswald the Lucky Rabbit, Trolley Troubles
- Felix the Cat, Woos Whoopee
- Popeye the Sailor, The Paneless Window Washer
- Betty Boop, Minnie the Moocher
- Lotte Reiniger, The Adventures of Prince Achmed, made in Germany
- Jiri Trnka, Ruka (The Hand), considered the Walt Disney of Eastern Europe
- Ivan Ivanov-Vano, Blek end Uait, made in Russia, which may be disturbing to some
- Quirino Cristiani, El Mono Relojero, made in Argentina

Please remember that the times and values were different and watch their animation and not their attitudes.

Starting to use computers for animation in the 1960s

The first interactive computer graphics project was carried out using the Whirlwind computer that was used in an attempt to create a flight simulator for the military. Other early adopters were GM and Boeing who tried to use the computer to help them design automobiles and airplanes.

The history of interactive graphics began at the Massachusetts Institute of Technology (MIT) in 1961 with two big projects, one of which was called **Sketchpad**. It's shown in the next image that was provided by MIT. Sketchpad was created by **Ivan Sutherland**, and it was the forerunner of programs such as Blender. You can see Timothy Johnson using it to model what looks like a chair. To use it, he's using a light pen, the box with 40 buttons on it, and all the switches on the panel to his left.

The other project was a game called **Spacewar!**, by **Steve Russell**, which was the first video game to be distributed.

Let's continue our tour. We're going to look at a demonstration of Sketchpad. Then we will look at Triple I, a company founded by three MIT professors to build advanced computer graphics display hardware and we will see what their in-house 3D animation department was learning. Finally, we will look at the first short from Pixar, where the animation and the computer animation industries met.

Beginnings of 3D animation in 1963

It's time to meet Blender's great-great-grandfather. Originally, TV screens were used by computers for short-term data storage, but it wasn't long before people tried to connect the screens to computers especially for making graphics. We're going to look at videos of a few early efforts. The amazing thing about the first one is that one man came up with all of this in 1961. Ivan Sutherland put this system called Sketchpad together. It's the first real-time interactive computer graphics system; all others are descended from it, including Blender.

Time for action – searching on Ivan Sutherland + Sketchpad

Make a search on the Web for the terms **Ivan Sutherland** + **Sketchpad**. YouTube, archive.org, or some other site should have the video. Hopefully, YouTube will have the Ivan Sutherland : Sketchpad Demo (1/2) and Ivan Sutherland : Sketchpad Demo (2/2), but any of them will do. Sketchpad Demo (2/2) is best. Watch it if you can find it. If you watch Ivan Sutherland : Sketchpad Demo (1/2) you can skip the first 3:33 part of the video unless you enjoy 1960s technical jargon.

Watch it now and enjoy it.

What just happened?

We saw the grandfather of all computer animation programs. Similar to early ink animations, it was all done with lines.

Pop quiz – analyzing pioneer computer animators

1. This is like animators are starting all over again. Back to bad animation and black and white line drawings. It's no wonder critics laughed at their efforts and thought that computers would never ever be an animation tool. Part of the problem was that this was done by computer scientists, not animators. They hadn't learned as much as you have about animation principles. But let's think about what they did do.

2. They used a light pen and dozens of switches as their input device. At that time, the mouse was just being invented at the Stanford Research Institute, and the trackball was a military secret. What other input devices do you think would be good for making 3D animation?

3. They spoke about **master drawings** and **instances** of these drawings, and the **data structures** that make them. Given that Blender can use master objects and instances, and organizes everything with data blocks, does it sound to you as though Dr. Sutherland was on the right track for making computer graphics?

4. They showed the Lincoln Labs TX-2 computer used by Ivan Sutherland. As shown in Ivan Sutherland : Sketchpad Demo (1/2), the computer was huge. People used to wonder if a computer like that could take over the world. When you compare how much trouble that computer had in just displaying simple lines, to what your mobile phone can do, which do you think would win in a computing power contest, the TX-2 or your mobile phone? That's right, your mobile phone.

Going to the late 1970s, a few companies are doing 3D animation

A few companies are experimenting with video and film quality computer animation. One of the first was a company called **Information International, Inc.** or **Triple I**. At the time, they were doing some of the best animation in the world, which led to them being one of the teams that made the original Tron. What's amazing looking back is how simple the graphics are.

Time for action – searching on Triple I demo

Make a search on the Web for the term **Triple I demo**. YouTube, archive.org, or some other site should have the video. You want the video Triple I (1976–1979). It is a compilation of two different demo reels. You can tell the change by the soundtrack. But it's also important to see how they used art direction to get the most out of what they were able to do.

Watch it now and enjoy it.

What just happened?

That is quite an improvement over the work in Sketchpad, but still very stiff. Work on color, lighting, and textures was all being done for the first time. What is amazing is that this was a professional demo reel. Now, it might not even get you a job as an intern. Back then it was amazing.

Pop quiz – analyzing early computer animators

1. Just as we saw an improvement between Felix and Mickey, there's been a lot of advancement from Sketchpad to the Triple I demo reel. Let's think about how they are getting better.

2. Did you notice the **teapot** on the table in one of the scenes? The teapot was created in 1975 and is found throughout computer graphics. This was one of the earliest uses of it and in this case it was testing curved surfaces and shading.

3. Did you notice the big boxy machine at the very beginning? You could see something like a movie camera in it. That was the **FR-80** graphics recorder. Yeah it took that whole machine just to make the image back then. No flat panels, screens, or pressing the *Prnt Scr* button for those guys. Then, the camera panned to multi-disk hard drives and several tape back up units. Storing the data and backing it up has always been a problem for computer animators. What are some of the ways you can back up your work?

4. In some of the 3D models such as the ABC logo and the Mercedes Benz logo, you can see the basic geometric structure. You can see that the sides are made of flat panels called polygons. What are some of the ways that they play with these flat polygons to make it more interesting?

5. Compare the animation here with the animation in Felix Turns the Tide. Both are primitive. Are there similarities in how they handle backgrounds? Is Triple I's plastic look equivalent to the line art in Felix in that they did that because they couldn't do better?

6. Although these images are not real-time images, compare them to Ivan Sutherlands Sketchpad images. What changes do you see?

Time for action – watching Information International, Inc. (Triple I) 1982 demo reel

Make a search on the Web for the term **Triple I demo**. You are looking for their Information International, Inc. (Triple I) 1982 demo reel. YouTube, archive.org, or some other site should have the video. It's mostly the same production crew, just a short time later with an art director **Richard Taylor** added. The magician, **Adam Powers** was the first character animation. Note how they pushed their simple geometries farther with the Allied Stars logo, and started to integrate backgrounds to create complete scenes. With their work on Looker and Westworld they also incorporated computer graphics with film. Their modeling has improved so that now they can model an entire human body. Similar to you, their work was simple at first, but it got better.

Watch it now and enjoy it.

What just happened?

In the first demo reel, the animation was pretty much objects floating in space. In the 1982 demo reel, the background becomes an integral part of the scene, and in the Adam Powers section we have a simple character animation, and he has to interact with objects in the scene. The team was the same people, with the addition of an Art Director. So we can see that using principles of graphic design is starting to make a difference.

Introducing Pixar – 1984, and everything comes together

Pixar was the first place that combined computer animation technology with traditional animation techniques. While the modeling and rendering were no better than anyone else at that time, the use of the 12 animation principles revolutionized computer animation. When it was introduced, other animators were in awe.

Time for action – searching for the video of The Adventures of André and Wally B

Make a search on the web for the term **The Adventures of André and Wally B**. YouTube, archive.org, or some other site should have the video. This was Pixar's first animation. It was made in 1984. It was directed by **John Lassiter**, who had been a traditional cel animator at Walt Disney and was familiar with standard animation principles. The modeling is very simple, and the storyline goes right back to the complexity of Felix the Cat. So you can see, even successful and modern companies have learned from the old school, just as you're doing by reading this chapter.

Watch it now and enjoy it.

What just happened?

The Adventures of André and Wally B was a landmark film in a number of aspects. It took ten **VAX-11/750** super-minicomputers and a **Cray X-MP/48** supercomputer to render it out, and it was the first computer animation to use motion blur. But more importantly, it was the first computer animation to have animation principles used seriously. You can see the difference. This was such a breakthrough that the Association of Computing Machinery had John Lassiter write up a paper called Principles of Traditional Animation Applied to 3D Computer Animation for the July 1987 issue of Computer Graphics.

Pop quiz – analyzing mature computer animation

1. You learned about classic animation principles. The Adventures of André and Wally B allows us to see how these applied to computer animation.

2. Notice how all the trees are similar? Is this an application of a master object and instance as invented by Ivan Sutherland?

3. What has John Lassiter done to make Wally B so threatening to André?

4. Lassiter has employed a number of classic animation techniques like anticipation and squash and stretch; the way Wally's feet float as a secondary action is a good example. What are some of the other things Lassiter has done in this that reflect classic animation techniques? Does he use anticipation for Wally's final attack?

5. Compare how dynamic these characters are with Adam Powers by Triple I.

6. Often animations have inside jokes. Did you notice the gloves on André's hands? Which other animated character wore gloves like that?

Have a go hero – educating yourself about animation

There is a lot of great animation to look at. You can never watch too much. If you have time, watch any Pixar shorts you can find. You might also want to check out the following films for a better idea of the range of animation that was happening back then. Do you see differences in the styles of the Americans, the Europeans, and the Japanese?

VintageCG on YouTube has a good collection of early computer animation. Some of the titles are:

- MAGI Synthavision Demo Reel 1982, this was Triple I's main competitor. Both worked on Tron.
- Sogitec Showreel (1985), this is a European competitor. They used some of the equipment that Triple I built, but had their own studios.
- Japan Computer Graphics Lab (1985) shows what the Japanese were doing at that time.
- Stanley & Stella in Breaking the Ice (1987), the first animation with flocking behaviors to control the birds and fish.

Another one you might want to see is:

- Reboot Intro (1994), this was the first half hour TV show that was entirely computer generated.

Your greater understanding of animation will increase your ability to create it.

Back to the present time

So far, we've studied the roots of animation and of computers. It's good to see that the great started humbly, and see how things improved as they practiced. That gives us inspiration. It's the journey we are all on. The changes from Adam Powers to The Adventures of André and Wally B are impressive, as an animation professional moved in and showed the computer boys what using the principles of animation could do for their computer generated animations.

Animation principles

Over time, people have learned techniques that aid the animator in making an interesting and exciting animation. As we saw, it didn't happen overnight, but when everything came together the synergy of the techniques made animation come alive.

The following is a list of techniques to think about and incorporate into your work as you learn to animate in Blender:

Technique	Benefit
Squash and stretch	Makes animated objects like clay. A ball hitting a wall gets taller and narrower as it flattens on the wall momentarily, and then resumes its original shape. This punches up the motion and gives the viewer clues about the weight and rigidity of an object or character.
Anticipation and follow through	Animation is like throwing a ball. You must have a wind up, a pitch, and a follow through to make the action work. You need to build up to an action, and show the results. Anticipation clues the audience that something is going to happen. When Wile E Coyote goes off a cliff when chasing the Roadrunner, he pauses in mid air before falling into a deep canyon, then he falls and then you get a little dust cloud to tell you that he landed.
Staging	How is the action framed by the camera and what part of the area is used? You want to present the action in the clearest and most dynamic manner.
Slow in and slow out	Similar to a drag racing car accelerating or an F1 car stopping in the pits. The rate of motion changes for emphasis and adds to the subtlety that you can express.
Arcs	Arcing motion and curvy lines can be more attractive and powerful.
Secondary action	Motions driven by other motions, like Wally B's floating feet, can add a lot of realism.
Timing	The use of time in animation will affect pacing, characters, and the effect of an action.
Exaggeration	Exaggerating things makes it more interesting and accentuates the things you want to be most important.
Appeal	A character does not need to be as cute as Hello Kitty to have appeal, but the audience must have a way to relate to them and enjoy them. An object should also have appeal, pleasing proportions, and perhaps some sparkle to catch the eye.
Misdirection	Can be used to change the plot, or guide the viewer's eyes magician-like, so that they will not notice entrances, exits, or changes.
Contrast	How much a character or object being animated should stand out from the background.

Using 3D skills, what can you do with them?

There are a lot of different ways to use 3D. The following are a few ways you might want to use your Blender skills.

Making 2D animation

It might seem odd, but if you watch animated shows such as Futurama and American Dad, in outdoor scenes or ones with cars, planes, and rockets moving in them, you can tell that they were originally created in 3D then colored to match the rest of the 2D animation. One director told me that his 2D animated show is all done in 3D, but shot with a camera setting that flattens it out again. He finds it's faster to make it that way than with Flash or other 2D animation packages.

TV and video

This is the market Blender was originally built for, back in the days when it was the in-house system at a Dutch advertising firm called **NeoGeo**. Blender is a good tool for local TV stations and advertisers, because it can do a lot quickly and deliver quality results at a price that even the smallest TV station's manager will appreciate. Networks such as Azteca America have used Blender at some of their studios. Blender is good for schools and universities as well as personal video projects.

Films and pre-visualization

Although there are few films done in Blender, shorts such as Sintel show that Blender has the capacity to do it. Hollywood has been known to use Blender for pre-visualizing a movie before it's made, to figure out how the movie will look when they make it.

Stereoscopic 3D

This is the hot new trend in films. You need to have two cameras render the same scene from slightly different locations, just like your eyes are slightly apart. But the cameras have to work in sync with each other. Think of how your eyes shift if they were to go from threading a needle to looking at mountains in the distance. Blender can do this as well as any other 3D animation package.

Web animation

Blender is good for rendering out complete animations or for making graphics for use in Flash.

Games

Blender has its own **Game Engine**. So it's good for making your own games and showing what you can do. You can also export Blender files for use as assets with other game engines such as **Ogre**, **Unity**, and **CrystalSpace.** You can find out more at sites such as www.blenderartists.org.

Flight and driving simulators

The **Blender Game Engine** and Blender's **physics** packages make it possible to make your own flight and driving simulators.

Digital signage

Nowadays we are seeing digital signs almost everywhere, from HD monitors in McDonalds to the huge signs in Las Vegas. With user-selectable resolution, you can make animations in Blender to whatever size you need, for whatever use. The files can then be uploaded to the Web and distributed to displays all over. This is a quickly growing market for advertising companies.

Displaying scientific data

Because the Python language allows using a scientific data set, anything from weather to a rocket to medial simulations can be animated. NASA uses Blender at some of its locations.

Legal evidence display

With animation for the legal system, the models are often simple though realistic proportions. The clients are paying for accuracy, not fancy graphics. Blender's physics engine can help you make realistic animations. You can make car crashes, track bullets, and help when a crime comes to trial. It's an in-demand way to use your animation talents.

Architectural walkthroughs

Clients of a multi-million dollar project want to see what they are getting before they spend their money. This is a very specialized use of Blender and other 3D animation systems. You can give your clients either a high resolution video walkthrough or use the game engine to make it interactive. You could even use it to plan the remodeling of your basement.

Virtual reality

Blender can output a virtual reality .X3D file to create virtual reality on the Web that can be used interactively on most browsers.

Virtual sets

The set behind the TV personality may not exist at all, it might be a set modeled and rendered in Blender.

Interactive instruction

The Blender game engine can be used, or Blender can provide graphics for Flash or websites.

Showing what can't otherwise be seen

For anything from dinosaurs to the moons of Saturn, 3D is probably the best way to demonstrate what can't be seen directly. This can be used to show others the ideas in your head and the visions you see, taking them to places that are too small, too large, or too dangerous to visit in reality.

Creating a portfolio to get a job

If you do good work and can demonstrate it, many employers don't care what software you use. I know of one animator who perfected his Blender skills while serving in Iraq. He took what he did to the big studios and soon he was working on major Hollywood films.

Product development and visualization

Blender can be used to design and create real objects. Real copies can be made using 3D printers when you export your Blender files in an STL format.

Summary

This first chapter was there to get you ready for Blender 3D.

You dipped your toe into Blender, opening it, rendering a scene, and closing Blender. You looked at the roots of animation, and the techniques that were developed to make animation producible and enjoyable. You got to see into the beginning of computer animation and computer games and understand how the principles of animation apply to computer animation. You've got a top-ten list of cool things about Blender and some ideas on how you can use the skills that you will develop with this book.

In the next chapter, we will get you comfortable working in Blender. We'll discover the secrets behind all those windows, get an explanation of the basic geometry behind 3D animation, and learn how to use the 3D View window where most of the work in Blender is done.

Let's go!

2

Getting Comfortable using the 3D View

Well, in the previous chapter you've had a good introduction to animation and computer animation. You learned a little bit about how to make an animation come alive and discovered that the animation principles are the same whether it's made in the old-fashioned way or with a computer. Now it's time to get into Blender itself.

In this chapter, you will:

- Learn about the idea behind Blender's windowing system
- Investigate how to manipulate and resize the Blender windows
- Discover how computers create and use colors
- Investigate 3D coordinates and measuring in 3D
- Learn how to navigate in the **3D View** window

Exploring the Blender 3D interface

In the early days of Blender the developer's took a different approach to their user interface and time has proven that it is a very productive way to work. Instead of assigning fixed areas for certain tasks or creating a stack of windows, they decided on a flexible system of non-overlapping windows that could be resized interactively to give the user maximum control of their workspace.

When you start your copy of Blender as you did in *Chapter 1, Introducing Blender and Animation*, your screen will show a big central window surrounded by a number of boxes with text and buttons. There are five windows in total. I drew boxes around the windows so that you could see how the default Blender window is organized.

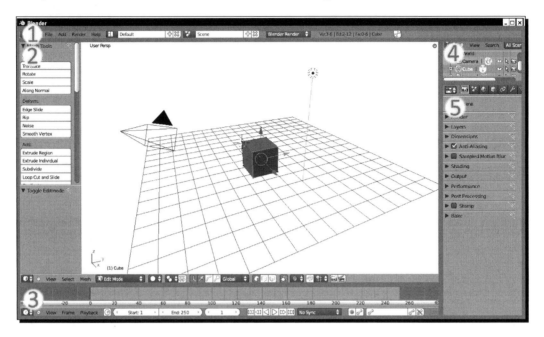

Breaking down the interface bit by bit will make it easy to understand. Remember, you don't have to understand how to use every single control to do a lot of great work with Blender. No one knows it all. You will go through it step by step giving you a strong foundation in using Blender.

You may notice that some of the colors of the 3D View window in the illustrations are different from your copy of Blender. The only difference is that some of the colors were changed so that the screen would show up better on the printed page. There is no change in function.

Setting up Blender the way you want it

You will find the Blender interface to be very flexible. While this may take a little more time at first to feel comfortable with, you will discover that it lets you set up Blender to be just the way you need it at any given moment. For now, most of our focus will be on the Blender windows, but I should mention the Blender **User Preferences**.

The Blender User Preferences facility allows you to remap all the keys and mouse controls. It allows you to change the colors used in the display, the limit on your memory cache, the number of steps that Blender can undo and hundreds of other settings. In this book, I'm going to try to keep changing User Preferences to a minimum so that you will be able to use Blender wherever you find it. But after reading this book, you may want to modify your copy of Blender to reflect your own tastes.

Using the three basic Blender controllers

The three basic Blender controllers are your **Keyboard**, **Numpad**, and **Mouse**. The keyboard is an obvious need. It is best if you have a built-in Numpad or alternate keys that can be used as a Numpad. Blender is designed to work with a three-button mouse. It is a standard Blender convention that the **left mouse button** is abbreviated (*LMB*), the **middle mouse button** is abbreviated (*MMB*), and the **right mouse button** is (*RMB*).

Blender is a two-handed system; meaning that many times you will need to use both the keyboard and mouse at the same time to do an operation. While this may seem a bit different from what you're used to when you started, it's an effective way of working. Pretty soon, your hands will know just what to do. You won't waste time looking for tiny buttons on the edges of your screen every single time you want to change the angle that you are seeing, or zoom into an object. This lets you work faster and maintain your focus on what you are trying to do, rather than getting distracted by the user interface. Practice is the key to using Blender well. Don't be afraid if things are a little slow at first. Have patience. You will soon get a better understanding of Blender and your hands will know which keys to use.

Using the numeric keypad with Blender

Blender uses your computer's numeric keypad or Numpad to control what you see in the 3D View. If your computer does not have a numeric keypad, you have several options:

- Purchase a wireless or USB Numpad to use.

- Look closely and you may see something that looks like a Numpad near the U I O P keys as seen in the next illustration. You'll have to consult your owner's manual to find out how to activate the Numpad instead of the keyboard. In my case, I press the *Fn* button while pressing those keys. For me, the *digits for the Numpad* and the *Fn* button are in blue. Your computer may differ.

♦ However, some computers such as the MacBook Air do not have a keypad at all unless you buy an external one. Blender will let you emulate a Numpad if you set it in the User Preferences. I advise you to get an external keypad if at all possible because Blender already uses the standard number keys for other functions and there are Blender commands using the +, -, and period keys on the Numpad that are harder to perform if you emulate the Numpad. But emulating the Numpad will get you through in a pinch.

Emulating the three-button mouse and Numpad

If you cannot obtain a three-button mouse and a Numpad, Blender does allow you to emulate them. There are checkboxes in the **Input** panel of the **User Preferences** window to emulate the three-button mouse and the keypad.

To emulate the Numpad, move your mouse up to where it says **File**. Click on **File** and scroll down to where it says **User Preferences**. Click on **User Preferences**. At the top of the new window, there is a row of buttons. Select **Input**. On the left, there is a checkbox that says **Emulate Numpad**. Click on it. On the bottom of the window there is a button that says **Save As Default**. Click on it.

On a Mac with a single-button mouse, the mouse button maps to the left mouse button (*LMB*). To simulate the middle mouse button (*MMB*) press the *Alt* key while pressing the mouse. To simulate the right mouse button (*RMB*) press the *command* key while pressing the mouse. Press the key before pressing the mouse.

Emulating the keypad forces the regular numbers to respond as though they were the Numpad numbers. However, you won't be able to use the number keys for their regular functions.

Understanding how to use Blender Windows

As you saw earlier, the main Blender window is divided into five subwindows. There is one major difference between the Blender windows and those of other 3D animation systems. In Blender any window can be any one of the 16 different kinds of editing window. Think of them as tabs in your browser. As you can put any website in any tab, any of the Blender windows can hold any Blender content.

Time for action – playing with the Blender windows

Now we are going to investigate the structure of the windows. Start up your copy of Blender. In the largest Blender window, at the lower-left corner there is a small button that looks similar to the button on the left as shown in the following screenshot. It has a white cube on it. This is the **Current Editor Type** button. Every window has this button, so you can change the type of editor that is in the window.

In the main 3D View window, click on the **Current Editor Type** button with the left mouse button (*LMB*) and the **Editor Type** menu pops up with the 16 different kinds of editors that you can display in that window as shown in the following screenshot:

1. Scroll up the menu shown previously and select **Text Editor**. The window changes and it is now blank. The Text Editor is for you to enter text such as production notes and has other uses.

2. Now go down to the window below it and click the left mouse button (*LMB*) on the **Current Editor Type** button that has a clock on it as shown next. Again the menu pops up. Scroll up the menu and select the **Text Editor**.

There are two windows on the right. Find the **Current Editor Type** buttons in these two windows. They will be at the top of the window. In each window, click the left mouse button (*LMB*) on the window button. Scroll up the menu and select the **Text Editor**. Text editors have their headers at the bottom so you will see the header pop up from the top to the bottom.

What just happened?

In Blender, any window can be any kind of window just like tabs in a browser. You just turned all the windows into text editors. This lets you see the basic structure of the Blender windows as outlined at the beginning of the chapter, without getting confused with all the controls and buttons. The following **image** shows how Blender is laid out initially:

Time for action – resizing windows

Notice the black line between the Blender windows:

1. Move the cursor over one of these lines and you will see a double-headed arrow.

2. While the double-headed arrow is displayed, hold down the left mouse button (*LMB*) and move your mouse perpendicular to the line. The windows on both sides of the line will resize.

What just happened?

You selected the line between two windows and moved it to resize the windows. Blender's windows do not overlap. If you make one bigger, the one next to it gets smaller. Unlike many window-based interfaces, you don't end up with a stack of windows that you have to search through to find which window you were working in.

Time for action – flipping the window header

At the top or bottom of each of the windows there is a bar. It has the **Current Editor Type** button on the left side and some other buttons, as you can see in the following screenshot:

This is called the **Header**. Each of the 16 types of editor windows has different buttons in its header:

1. Click the right mouse button (*RMB*) on an empty area of the **Header**. A menu will pop up that says **Flip to Top**.

2. Select **Flip to Top** with the left mouse button (*LMB*).

What just happened?

The Header can be at the top or the bottom of the window. If it is at the bottom, you can flip it to the top. If it is at the top, you can flip it to the bottom. Set it the way you prefer.

Time for action – maximizing and tiling the window

Blender lets you **maximize** and **tile** the windows:

1. Select the Header again with the right mouse button (*RMB*). The menu also has a selection for **Maximize Area**. Select **Maximize Area** with the left mouse button (*LMB*) now. There's only one window! Don't worry. The others are not gone. The window you maximized is just given the full display.

2. Click the right mouse button (*RMB*) on the Header again; the bottom selection will say **Tile Area**, and clicking on it with the left mouse button (*LMB*) will show all of the windows again.

What just happened?

Blender gives you a lot of flexibility. If you need to, it allows any window to use the entire screen and you can quickly change it back to tiled windows when you are done. This is great when you need an extra big view of the 3D View window to select tiny parts or details.

Time for action – splitting Blender windows

Now you will make new Blender windows. Unlike other systems, you are not limited to a set number of windows or a set layout:

1. Look at any of the windows; you will see three diagonal lines in the lower-left and upper-right corners of the window, as shown in the following screenshot. These control the creation and deletion of the window.

2. Put the cursor over the largest window and move the mouse over the diagonal lines at the lower-left corner of that window. Then, hold down the left mouse button (*LMB*) as you move the mouse horizontally toward the center of the window and release the left mouse button (*LMB*) when you have moved the window edge to replace one third of the old window.

3. Put the cursor over the center window that you just made. Move the mouse to the diagonal lines at the upper-right corner of that window. Then hold down the left mouse button (*LMB*), while you move the mouse horizontally toward the center of the window. Replace another one-third of the original window with the new window and release the left mouse button (*LMB).*

4. Put the cursor over the left-most window. Move the mouse over the diagonal lines at the lower-left corner of that window. Press down the left mouse button (*LMB).* Then move the mouse up towards the center of the window to make a new window vertically. The screen layout should resemble the following screenshot:

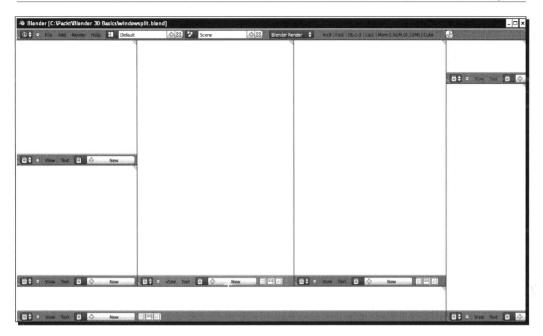

What just happened?

You selected the diagonal lines in the lower-left corner of a window and moved the mouse horizontally. The window was **split** into two windows side by side. The new window is a duplicate of the first. Then you did the same using the diagonal lines in the upper-right corner and created another window. Finally, you discovered that windows can be split vertically as well. This flexibility in window layout gives you complete freedom in setting up Blender for greatest productivity and it can be changed on the fly to reflect your needs at any stage of production. But don't worry, in the next section, you will discover how to join all these windows so you don't have too many.

Time for action – joining Blender windows

Blender windows are easy to remove. Put the cursor over the upper-left window. Move the mouse over the diagonal lines at the lower-left corner of that window. Hold down the left mouse button (*LMB*) while you move the mouse down towards the window below it. The window below becomes darker and there is a light gray arrow pointing into that window.

Continue to hold the mouse down and move the mouse up to the original window; it becomes darker and has an arrow pointing into it as seen in the following image. Whichever window is darker and has the arrow will disappear when you release the mouse button.

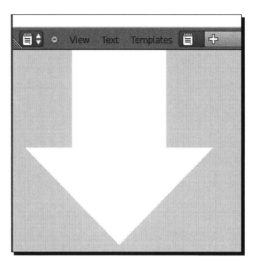

If you find you don't want the window to disappear, just move the mouse into another window besides those two. The arrow will go away and you can release the mouse button without any changes happening.

What just happened?

To **join** two windows, you selected the diagonal lines in the corner of a window and moved the mouse vertically toward the window next to it. Note that for one of the windows to be joined, both windows must share an entire side. If the windows do not share an entire side, you cannot remove one of them. Be assured that no matter what combination of windows you have open, this does not affect the scene that you are working on. No data is lost by closing a window.

Have a go hero – joining windows horizontally

You can now remove windows that are next to each other. See the two windows that you just created in the upper center of the Blender window? Remove one.

Have a go hero – making windows with parallel edges

1. Press the left mouse button (*LMB*) when the cursor is on the edge between the top and bottom windows on the right so you see the double-headed arrow.

2. Move that edge down until it is exactly level with the edge between the two windows in the center and release the mouse button. Now select it again with the left mouse button (*LMB*) and drag it up or down. What happens now?

3. The windows appear to be locked in sync. Make a small window above that line then delete the center window from the bottom window so the window edge on the right moves independently again.

Pop quiz – learning about Blender windows

See, Blender windows are pretty easy. You open them, you close them, and change their size. You can put whatever editor you want in any window. Let's review some basics about Blender windows:

1. The Blender screen has how many windows?

   a. 4

   b. 6

   c. As many as you want

2. How do you make a new Blender window?

   a. Click the left mouse button (*LMB*) on the diagonal lines and drag it toward the window next to it.

   b. Click the left mouse button (*LMB*) on the edge and drag perpendicular to the edge.

   c. Click the left mouse button (*LMB*) on the diagonal lines and drag it toward the center of the window.

Have a go hero – making and removing windows, the secret way

There is a secret method for windows that Blender made to satisfy long-time users of Blender who are used to the old interface that was used in Blender versions 1.0 – 2.4.x. Move the cursor over the edge between two windows so you get the double arrowhead. Press the right mouse button (*RMB*) to get a split/join menu. Move the mouse over the window that you want to split. Play around with it and discover how this method of splitting windows may be more powerful than the standard method.

Exploring the 3D View window, the heart of Blender

Ah, finally it's time to focus on the 3D View as shown in the following screenshot. It's the primary window where you will do most of your work.

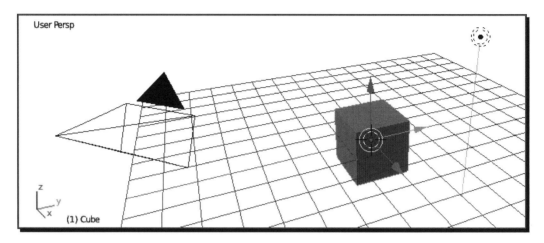

Keep your eye on the cursor. Whatever window the Blender cursor is over is the active window. For example, if you want to work in the 3D View, the cursor must be over the 3D View window; if you want to work in the **Timeline**, the cursor must be over the **Timeline** window.

Time for action – discovering your tools

The 3D View has three major control panels: the **Header**, which we have looked at; the **Tool Shelf** on the left side, which says **Object Tools** at the top; and the **Properties Panel**, which is hidden by default:

1. Close Blender and open it again.

2. With your mouse over the 3D View, press the *N* key. The **Properties Panel** appears. It has controls to change the location, rotation, and scaling of objects.

3. Press the *N* key again. The **Properties Panel** disappears.

4. Press the *T* key. The **Tool Shelf** disappears.

5. Press the *T* key again. The **Tool Shelf** reappears and contains many controls used when building objects.

What just happened?

You looked at the Tool Shelf and Properties Panel as shown in the following screenshot. You also learned how to toggle the Tool Shelf and the Properties Panel on and off.

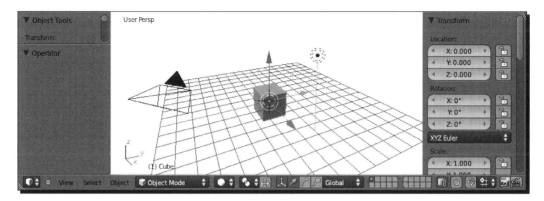

The Tool Shelf gives you control over the current object and the Properties Panel lets you set things like the location of the 3D Cursor and the location, rotation, and scaling of the current object. You will want to toggle them on and off depending on which controls you need and how well you need to see the objects in the 3D View window. It will be easy to remember the *N* and *T* keys, as you will use them frequently.

Looking at the 3D View window, what do you see?

The window looks pretty empty but there is a fair amount in the default screen. It's got everything needed to render a scene. There are three kinds of things; **objects**, **text fields**, and **3D tools**. Blender has eight kinds of objects, which are listed in the table that follows.

There are three **objects** in the default scene:

◆ The cube you see is a 3D mesh in the shape of a cube; you can use it or delete it. When Blender is opened up, the cube is the active object, which means that it is the object currently being worked on.

◆ The four-sided cone with a triangle above it is the camera.

◆ The black dot surrounded by dotted lines with a line hanging down from it is a lamp.

◆ Of these, only the cube will be seen when you render. The camera does not see itself, and the lamps will light the scene, though there is no physical light bulb to be rendered.

The **text fields** are on the left side of the 3D View, as seen in the previous screenshot. They give you current information about the scene:

◆ The upper text field says what the view is. It shows where you are looking from and whether you have a Perspective (**Persp**) view or an Orthographic (**Ortho**) view.

◆ This can be **Top**, **Bottom**, **Front**, **Back**, **right** or **left** if you are looking from one of the major axes. There are also **Camera** and **User** views. **User** is whenever you are not on one of the major axes or taking the Camera's view.

◆ The lower text field has the current frame number in parentheses and says which object is the active object.

There are four **3D tools** as follows:

◆ There is a **reference grid** to help you with orientation and size. It can be scaled and set for as many divisions as you want.

◆ In the lower-left corner there is a graphic with three lines (red, green, and blue) joined at one end and the letters X, Y, and Z nearby. This is the **3D axis indicator**, as shown on the left-hand side of the following graphic. It shows you where you are with respect to the center of the Blender world and gives you an indication of which direction is which.

  ❑ The red line is the X axis.

  ❑ The green line is the Y axis.

  ❑ The blue is the Z axis.

◆ At the origin, the center of the world in Blender, there are two controls, one is the **3D cursor**. It's a red and white dashed circle with four black lines through it as shown in the following screenshot in the center. This marks the location of where a new object can be made. It can be moved wherever you need it, as you'll discover later.

◆ The other 3D control at the origin is the **3D manipulator** as shown in the following screenshot on the right. It's a white circle with red, green, and blue arrows coming out of it, and an orange dot in the center. It gives you control of rotating, translating, and scaling the active object in 3D.

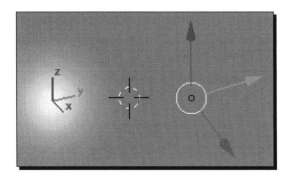

There are eight basic types of objects shown in the Blender screen. You have seen a few already such as the lamp, camera, and mesh. The following table lists the eight types of objects that Blender uses:

Object Type	Definition
Armature	Provides a framework for animating a character or complex model.
Camera	Records the image or animation when you render.
Curve	These are mathematical functions like Bézier curves and NURBS curves that Blender uses to create smooth rounded free-form shapes such as the outline of a logo.
Lamp	Provides the light for a scene.
Lattice	A three dimensional grid that is used to guide the deformation of other objects.
Meta Object	Special spheres, tubes, and cubes that affect each other and can stretch toward each other and appear to merge.
Mesh	These are the standard shapes such as cubes, spheres, cylinders, cones, monkeys.
Surface	These are also mathematical functions, composed of multiple curves that are used together for smooth yet complex shapes like terrain.

Making pictures with computers

Now that you are a little familiar with the 3D View it's good to understand a bit about the 3D world contained within, and how the computer knows what to display.

When you looked at the 3D View, what did you see? A camera? A box? A grid? No, you saw **pixel**s, thousands of them. A pixel is a single little colored rectangle on your computer screen as shown in the magnification of the following picture. Pixels are what digital TVs, mobile phones, and computer screens use to display anything you see. The following picture is 640 pixels wide and 287 pixels tall. The magnified area shows you what an area of 21 pixels width by 16 pixels tall would display. When it is shrunk to the scale of the main picture, they seem to blend together to make a picture.

These pictures are what Blender creates to make animations and still images, and Blender also uses pictures like this as backgrounds and to create textures.

You can see that each pixel is a tiny rectangle of color. But how does a computer know which color to make the rectangle? That's what we'll look at now.

Understanding about how a computer uses color will help you to:

◆ Select colors for objects and lights

◆ Understand how to use colors in combination

◆ Make adjustments to your renderings so that the final colors look exactly right

Making colors with a computer

As you may know, if you dig way too deep into a computer, you will get to a point where everything the computer knows is either a zero or a one. Like a little light switch, it's either on or off. In the computer, each little switch is called a **bit**.

So, imagine you have eight little light switches in a row. Each one can turn on or off as a light. By flipping different switches, you can light them up in 256 different combinations: four lights on, four lights off; or two lights on, three lights off, three lights on, and so on.

In the computer, a group of eight switches is called a **byte**. The computer uses this block of eight switches to store a number between 0 and 255, 256 different numbers. That's why you will see the number 256 popping up a lot. These bytes can be used to store color information and they enable Blender to create millions of different colors.

Making millions of colors with just red, green, and blue

It's also important to understand how your eye works if you want to know why computers display colors the way they do.

Your eyes have two different kinds of receptors; **rods**, which see only black and white but tell you about how bright an object appears to be, and **cones** which tell you how much red, green, or blue light you are seeing. Your brain mixes all this information together, so you think you see shades of yellow, dark magenta, mauve, beige, and raspberry, but it's really just combinations of red, green, and blue light.

Computers were designed to match how your eyes see by telling the display to show red, green, and blue light of differing amounts. Like a box of crayons, the more colors you have, the better you can color. How many colors a given picture can show is called its **color depth**.

The greater the number of colors there are, the greater the color depth a picture will have. Frequently you will see pictures that have two colors, 256 colors, or 16.2 million colors:

- In the simplest pictures (such as the leftmost in the previous screenshot) there would be two colors, black or white.

- More complex ones could have 256 different gray values from black to white such as the second image from the left.

- A simple color picture might have only 256 different colors such as the third image from the left.

- With a true color image, like the one on the right, you can have 256 different shades of red, 256 shades of green, and 256 shades of blue. You mix all of those together and you can display 16.2 million different colors. As the red, green, and blue channels have 8 bits or little switches each, we add them up and call it a 24 bit image. This gives you subtle nuanced colors.

- Some formats such as the JPEG 2000 can have 16 bits per channel, making a 48 bit image, which can display trillions of colors, far more than your eyes can see, but it's useful for applications such as astronomy and medical imaging.

Measuring things in 3D

3D stands for "3 dimensions". Going back to school geometry, those dimensions are called **X**, **Y**, and **Z**. In Blender, X describes width, Y describes depth, and Z describes height. It is displayed as (X, Y, Z). The very center of things is at a point (0, 0, 0) called the **origin**. We describe the location of every object as a set of three values (X, Y, Z) in our Blender world by using numbers to how far to the left or right it is (X), how far to the front or back it is (Y), and mark how far up or down it is (Z). We do this based on the **front view** of the 3D world.

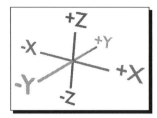

♦ As the value of X gets larger, it goes to the right. As the value of X gets smaller, it goes to the left. The numbers can be positive or negative.

♦ As the value of Y gets larger, it goes further away from you. As the value of Y gets smaller, it goes closer to you.

♦ As the value of Z gets larger, it goes up. As the value of Z gets smaller, it goes down.

♦ This applies to the world in the 3D View as well as the objects in it. The X, Y, Z coordinates in the 3D world are called **global coordinates**. The X, Y, Z coordinates that apply only to one object are called **local coordinates**. The reason for having local coordinates is that it makes it easier for you.

♦ Imagine that you take the default cube and you want to make it twice as wide as it is but unfortunately it's turned at a 53 degree angle with respect to the world. To do that correctly with global coordinates, you'd have to break out your math book and figure out the sines and cosines because global coordinates are stuck to the world and turning something 53 degrees makes it harder to figure out what the scaling would be.

♦ But with local coordinates, Blender remembers that the cube is 2x2x2 in local coordinates. Those coordinates only relate to the cube as it was made. So all you have to do is say okay, now the box is 2x4x2 in local coordinates. Blender will then handle turning it 53 degrees for you.

 Blender uses generic "Blender" units by default, but if you prefer you can specify Metric or Imperial units in the Properties window.

Pop quiz – learning basic computer graphics terms

Now it's time to review some of what you have learned about terms and ideas used in computer graphics:

1. What are pixels?

    a. Employees of Pixar

    b. Colored rectangles that make up a digital picture

    c. Small Celtic fairies

2. How many colors can be displayed in a 24 bit image?

    a. 16.2 Million

    b. 256

    c. 24

3. If a cube is at the location (−5, 5, 0) X, Y, Z, where is it in relation to the origin (0, 0, 0)?

    a. To the right, nearer to you than the origin and below

    b. To the left, nearer to you than the origin and above

    c. To the left, farther away from you than the origin, and at the same height

Navigating in the 3D View

Blender is a two-handed program. You need both hands to operate it. This is most obvious when navigating in the 3D View. When you navigate, you are changing your view of the world, you are not changing the world. There are three ways to navigate, you can **rotate** the scene so you see it from a different angle, **zoom** in or out to get closer or farther away, and **pan**, which is moving up and down and side to side in the scene.

Time for action – rotating the scene in 3D View

When modeling or animating, you frequently want to see differing angles of what you are working on. Rotating your view is often the best way to do this, Try it:

1. Move the cursor over the cube in the 3D View. Press the middle mouse button (*MMB*) and move the mouse left and right.

2. Now try it again, start with the cursor near the center of the screen, and move the cursor up and down.

What just happened?

That isn't too difficult. Pressing the middle mouse button (*MMB*) and moving the mouse revolves your view around the origin.

Time for action – zooming the scene in 3D View

If you need to get a better overview of the scene, or get a closer view, then zooming is what you need:

1. Move the cursor over the 3D View and push the *Ctrl* key.

2. Then press the middle mouse button (*MMB*) and move the mouse up and down.

What just happened?

To zoom in and out of the 3D View you press the *Ctrl* key and hold down the middle mouse button (*MMB*) while you move the cursor up and down over the 3D View.

Time for action – panning the scene in 3D View

The final way to move within the scene is panning, moving your view up and down and right and left. It helps you look at different parts of the scene:

1. Move the cursor over the 3D View then push the *Shift* key. Press the middle mouse button (*MMB*) and move the mouse up and down.

2. Move the cursor over the 3D View then push the *Shift* key. Press the middle mouse button (*MMB*) and move the mouse left and right.

3. Move the cursor over the 3D View then push the *Shift* key. Press the middle mouse button (*MMB*) and move the mouse around as you like.

What just happened?

Pressing the *Shift* key and holding down the middle mouse button (*MMB*) while you move the cursor in the 3D View pans the 3D View. Panning is moving your viewpoint horizontally or vertically. Very good, now you know how to navigate in the 3D View.

Have a go hero – navigating the scene in the 3D View

Now, try and maneuver the cube and grid into different angles. Try for dynamic looking or weird angles, get a close up of the corner, or look along the edges. Use the rotate, zoom, and pan controls.

Have a go hero – navigating for those who have a mouse wheel

Blender loves to give you a choice in how you do things. There is an alternate way to control rotating, zooming, and panning in the 3D View if you have a mouse wheel on your mouse.

Try these:

◆ *Mouse wheel* only: Zooms in and out of the scene

◆ *Shift+mouse wheel*: Pans up and down

◆ *Ctrl+mouse wheel*: Pans side to side

◆ *Shift+Alt+mouse wheel*: Rotates up and down

◆ *Ctrl+Alt+mouse wheel*: Rotates side to side

Using the Numpad to change the angle in the 3D View

The controls we have studied are great for giving you fine control over how you see the 3D View. But sometimes you want to flip from a top view to a side view quickly, or go back and forth. It's also good in case you forget where you are in relation to an object. Knowing which view you are looking from can help you get reoriented, if you've gotten confused.

Blender has some good tools to help. You use the Numpad to activate them. While we will be pressing numbers on the Numpad, note that pressing numbers on the keyboard will not give the same results. You must use the Numpad.

Time for action – seeing the top view, front view, and right side view

You will start by returning Blender to its default setup. To go back to the default scene, you don't have to quit as you did at the start of this chapter. There is another way:

1. Move your cursor to the upper-left corner of the Blender window as shown in the previous screenshot. Click the left mouse button (*LMB*) on **File**. A menu will drop down. Click the left mouse button (*LMB*) on **New**. The default Blender file will be loaded.

2. Press the 7 key on the Numpad.

3. Press the *1* key on the Numpad.

4. Press the *3* key on the Numpad.

What just happened?

You loaded a fresh copy of the default Blender scene and then used the Numpad to control from which direction you were viewing the scene. When you pressed the *7* on the Numpad, Blender displayed the **top view**. When you pressed the *1* on the Numpad, Blender displayed the **front view** and when you pressed the *3* on the Numpad, Blender displayed the **right side view**. Note that these changes are shown by the text field at the upper-left of the 3D View window, which will tell you what direction you are viewing the scene from.

Time for action – seeing the bottom view, rear view, and left side view

Sometimes you also need to look at an object or scene from the bottom, from behind or from the left. These keys will help you:

1. Press the *Ctrl* key, and the *7* key on the Numpad.

2. Press the *Ctrl* key, and the *1* key on the Numpad.

3. Press the *Ctrl* key, and the *3* key on the Numpad

4. Now, alternate pressing the *1*, *3*, and *7* keys on the Numpad, and pressing them with the *Ctrl* key depressed.

What just happened?

You know to use the 1, 3, and 7 keys on the Numpad to change views. To see from the opposing angle of a view, you press the *Ctrl* key and the number for the view on the Numpad. *Ctrl+7* shows the **bottom view**. *Ctrl+1* shows the **back view** and *Ctrl+3* shows the **left side view**.

Time for action – seeing what the camera sees

Unlike some other systems, Blender only renders what a camera sees. You can find out what the camera is seeing by pressing the *0* key on the Numpad.

What just happened?

When you pressed the *0* key on the Numpad, Blender displayed the **Camera View**. It also applied a gray mask called the passepartout to mark the limits of the image that will be created. The following screenshot shows the cube seen through the passepartout on the left and the rendering of that scene on the right.

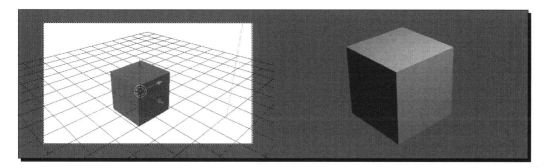

Time for action – verifying the Camera View

It's time to take a look at the Camera View and compare it with what the camera renders. Do you notice any differences?

1. Press the *F12* key to render the scene so you can see it.

2. Press the *Esc* key to close the rendering window.

3. Press the *F11* key to see the previously rendered view.

4. Press the *Esc* key again.

5. Alternate pressing the *F11* and the *Esc* keys and make sure that the Camera View is the same as the rendered scene. Do you notice any difference?

What just happened?

Just to be sure, after pressing the *0* key, you tried doing a test render to compare what is rendered in the camera with the **Camera View**. Of course they looked the same. But you also discovered that if you want to see a previously rendered image, that you press the *F11* key. Did you notice the difference in the shading between the 3D View and the rendering as shown in the previous screenshot? The lamp is to the right side of the camera in the scene. So in the rendered image, the darkest side is on the left as it should be. However, in the 3D View window the darkest side is on the right. This is because the default method of displaying objects in the 3D View is just a quick approximation. But it's good enough for most tasks. You'll discover more accurate displays of lighting in the next chapter.

Time for action – rotating the view with the Numpad

In addition to displaying the scene from particular axes, Blender lets you use the Numpad to revolve around the center:

1. Press the *7* key on the Numpad.

2. Press the *4* key on the Numpad several times.

3. Press the *6* key on the Numpad several times.

What just happened?

Pressing the *7* key, you shifted to the top view. This let you see how pressing the *4* key rotates the view counter-clockwise. Pressing the *6* key rotates the view clockwise. This is useful when you want to inspect an object carefully. It lets you rotate around the scene in 15 degree steps and the motion is repeatable so you can easily return to an earlier angle if you want.

Time for action – rotating the view in another direction with the Numpad

In addition to displaying the scene from particular axes, Blender lets you use the Numpad to revolve around the center:

1. Press the *3* key on the Numpad.

2. Press the *2* key on the Numpad several times.

3. Press the *8* key on the Numpad several times.

4. Press the *1* key on the Numpad.

5. Press the *2* key on the Numpad several times.

6. Press the *8* key on the Numpad several times.

What just happened?

Pressing the *3* key, you shifted to the **right side view**. Pressing the *2* key rotates the view so the front goes up. Pressing the *8* key rotates the view so the front goes down. Pressing the *1* key, you shifted to the **front view**. Pressing the *2* key rotates the view so the front goes up. Pressing the *8* key rotates the view so the front goes down. The *2* and *8* keys are not connected to a particular axis the way the *4* and *6* keys are. Don't worry about memorizing all these. You can always try the numbers on the Numpad to remember what does what and there's a summary table which we'll see later in this chapter.

Time for action – zooming with the Numpad

The Blender Numpad also allows you to control the zoom. But this may not work if you have Emulate Numpad enabled. If you do, skip to the next *Time for action* section.

1. Press the + (plus) key on the Numpad several times.

2. Press the - (minus) key on the Numpad several times.

3. Press the . (period) key on the Numpad.

4. Press the *Home* key on the keyboard (This is not the *Home* key on the Numpad.) Press *fn+Left arrow* if you are using a Mac with no *Home* key.

What just happened?

Pressing the "+" key on the Numpad zooms into the scene by steps and pressing the "-" key on the Numpad zooms out. To fill the view with the active object, you press the "." key on the Numpad, which makes it easy to focus on what you are working on. Pressing the *Home* key on the keyboard lets you see everything in the scene so you can get your bearings, get an overview of the scene, or switch to working on a different object.

If you are emulating the Numpad, the regular plus and minus keys should work to zoom in and out. To equal the function of the Numpad period key, select the **View** from the 3D View header, choose **Align View** and **View selected** from the pop-up menu.

Time for action – making the camera see what you do

As Blender only renders what the camera sees, it's useful to be able to point the camera at what you are working on:

1. Use the keys on the Numpad to move your view to an angle that you like.

2. Press the *Ctrl* key, the *Alt* key, and the *0* key on the Numpad.

 If you accidently press *Ctrl+0* without pressing the *Alt* key and the screen seems to be blank, then press *Ctrl+Z* to undo this command and return to where you were. You just turned the cube into the camera.

3. Press the *7* key on the Numpad.

4. Press the *0* key on the Numpad.

What just happened?

You got a little practice in using the Numpad to move the view. Then, when you press the *Ctrl* key, the *Alt* key, and the *0* key on the Numpad, Blender matches the camera's view to the current view, as seen in the following screenshot. Pressing the *7* key moves you to the top view, so that you can see that when you press the *0* key on the Numpad to get the camera view, that it matches the angle you had selected.

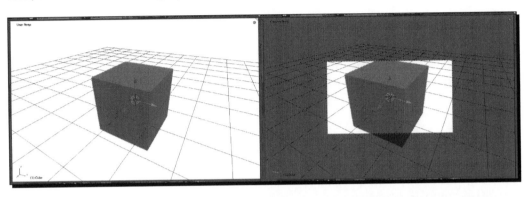

Pop quiz – knowing how to get different views

Now you've gotten a little experience in changing the view and some experience in using the Numpad as it is set up for your computer. Let's see what you remember. As you use Blender more practice will make it easy to remember.

1. Which key do you press to get the front view?

    a. *Home*

    b. *1* on the Numpad

    c. *9* on the Numpad

2. Which key do you press to zoom in on the active object?

    a. *Shift* middle mouse button (*MMB*)

    b. *Ctrl+Alt+0*

    c. . (period) on the Numpad

3. Which key do you press to rotate the view counter-clockwise?

    a. *4* on the Numpad

    b. *6* on the Numpad

    c. *2* on the Numpad

Understanding Perspective and Orthographic views

Blender has two ways to display the 3D View. If you've taken any art courses, you are probably familiar with what perspective is. In **Perspective**, all parallel lines stretch off to the horizon and finally appear to meet at a single point. This is pretty much what our eyes see, and if you look at the left side of the illustration in the following screenshot, you can see what's happening with the grid.

Orthographic is slightly different. It comes from the world of drafting and **CAD**. With Orthographic, all parallel lines are shown as being parallel, as in the right side of the illustration in the following screenshot.

Perspective is what you want to see when you are checking to see how a scene will look in your 3D image or animation. But coming from CAD, the Orthographic view is better when you are modeling an object. When you use a front, side, or top view all parallel points are right behind each other, making it easier to grab them and move them precisely.

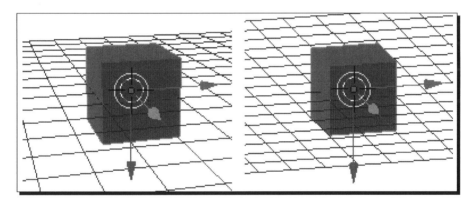

Time for action – toggling between Perspective and Orthographic views

Now you will discover how to change between Perspective and Orthographic view:

1. Press *1, 8, 8, 4, 4* on the Numpad to get a nice angle on the cube.

2. Press the *5* key on the Numpad.

3. Press it again.

What just happened?

When you press the *5* key on the Numpad, the 3D View switches between Perspective and Orthographic views as in the previous illustration.

Have a go hero – playing with Perspective and Orthographic views

Now it's time to play. Using what you have learned about navigating in the 3D view, experiment by finding different angles to view the scene and shifting between Perspective and Orthographic views and see how they compare. Be sure to try views like top, left, and front, as well as using the *2, 4, 6*, and *8* keys to gently rotate the scene. Or you can use the *Alt* key and your mouse if you like.

Displaying the Quad View and Full Screen

You've seen that you can adjust Blender windows just about anyway you want. But, when you are modeling, sometimes it's handy to have a quick way to see several sides of an object at once. Blender has a special view for this called the Quad view.

Time for action – toggling the Quad view

The Quad view is a special view with the camera, front, top, and right side views. I especially like it for setting up lighting:

1. Press the *Ctrl* key, the *Alt* key, and the *Q* key.

2. Press the *Ctrl* key, the *Alt* key, and the *Q* key again.

What just happened?

When you press the *Ctrl* key, the *Alt* key, and the *Q* key, Blender toggles the Quad view on and off. The Quad view gives you three Orthographic views and the Camera view.

Navigating in the 3D View

Following is a handy reference table that you can use while you practice. You've mastered how to navigate in the 3D View window in Blender. This may have been the toughest chapter. Phew! Well done.

Keys	Navigation
Pan, Zoom, Rotate with the mouse	
MMB	Rotate View
Shift+MMB	Pan View
Ctrl+MMB	Zoom View
Ctrl+Alt+Q	Quad View toggle
Pan, Zoom, Rotate with the mouse wheel	
Mouse Wheel only	Zoom In/Out
Shift+Mouse Wheel	Pan up and down
Ctrl+Mouse Wheel	Pan right and left
Shift+Alt+Mouse Wheel	Rotate up and down
Ctrl+Alt+Mouse Wheel	Rotate right and left
Numpad	
Preset viewing angles and stepping views	
0	Camera View
Ctrl+0	Set camera view to current object
Ctrl+Alt+0	Set camera view to current view
1	Front View
Ctrl+1	Back View
2	Rotate front up
3	Right Side View
Ctrl+3	Left Side View
4	Rotate counter-clockwise
5	Perspective/Orthographic toggle
6	Rotate clockwise
7	Top View
Ctrl+7	Bottom View

Keys	Navigation
Numpad zooming commands	
Shift+7	Zoom to fit all objects
8	Rotate front down
-	Zoom out
+	Zoom in
.	Zoom to current object
Home	Display whole scene
Miscellaneous Numpad keys	
9	Redraw
/	Local view and cursor/previous view toggle
*	Local view without moving

Summary

You learned that Blender is not as intimidating as it seemed at first. In this chapter, you learned about the structure of Blender's windows and why they are that way. You learned how to resize them to make them as you want them. You discovered how the computer makes colors. You found out how a computer measures things in a 3D world. You learned to use the mouse, the mouse wheel, the keyboard, and the Numpad to navigate in the 3D View window.

In the next chapter, we're going to have fun. It will be lights, camera, action, as we discover the basics of using light, how to control the camera, and make our first animation.

Let's go!

3

Controlling the Lamp, the Camera, and Animating Objects

You have learned how to use the Blender window and the 3D View window. Now, you will use the principles you have learned about animation, and make use of what you know about modifying windows and navigating in the 3D View.

In this chapter, you will:

- ◆ Study how light affects the scene
- ◆ Practice placing lights in different locations
- ◆ Change the light colors
- ◆ Use multiple lights
- ◆ Learn about using global and local coordinates
- ◆ Discuss composing an image with the camera
- ◆ Move, rotate, and scale the camera
- ◆ Make keyframes for an animation
- ◆ Preview your first animation and render it
- ◆ Use the Graph Editor to improve the animation
- ◆ Learn how to save files and use backup files

The symbols for the camera and the lamp are shown in the following figure. The camera is on the left and the lamp is on the right. First, we are going to look at how to control a lamp, we will learn how its location and color affect the scene. Next, we will investigate the camera, learning how to control it and use it to the best advantage. Finally, we will learn how to make an animation with Blender, how to render it, and save it.

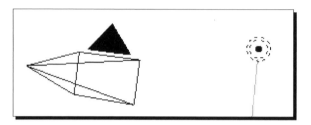

Understanding lamps

Lamps are how Blender controls the light in a scene. There is no physical light bulb or lamp stand needed, so you can put a lamp wherever you want it and it won't be seen in the image, apart from the light it casts. The light of the lamp can be any color.

Time for action – moving the lamp

Up till now, you've just changed your view of the scene. Now it's time to alter it. You'll move the lamp and see how that affects the cube:

1. To start, either open Blender or select **New**. You will see the familiar 3D View.

2. Press *F12* to render the scene.

3. Observe how the cube looks.

4. Press the *Esc* button to close the render window.

5. Put the cursor over the lamp. Hold the *RMB* down and begin to drag the mouse. When the lamp begins to move, you may release the *RMB*. Move the lamp to the left so it is between the camera and the cube. Press the *LMB* to release the object. If you press the *RMB* again, it will cancel the movement.

6. Press *F12* to render the scene.

7. Observe how the cube looks. The left side is much lighter as you can see here.

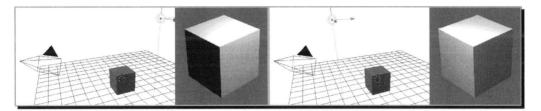

8. Press the *Esc* button to close the render window.

What just happened?

You rendered the cube to see how it looks as shown on the left. Then you used the *RMB* to move the lamp and rendered the cube again, to see how the lighting has changed as seen on the right. You also learned that you can move an object just by grabbing it.

Time for action – moving the lamp close to the cube

Now it's time to use a different method of moving an object. You will demonstrate that the lamp is a point of light radiating out:

1. Press the *1* key on the Numpad to get the front view.

2. Put the cursor over the lamp.

3. Click the *RMB*.

4. Press the *G* key.

5. Move the lamp down until it is level with the cube and right next to it. Click the *LMB* to release it.

6. Press the *7* key on the Numpad to get the top view.

7. Press the *G* key and release it.

8. Move the lamp so that it is next to the cube and level with the center of the cube. Click the *LMB* to release it.

9. Press *F12* to render the scene.

10. Observe how the cube looks.

11. Press the *Esc* button to close the render window.

What just happened?

Earlier, you saw that moving the lamp affects how the scene is lit. This time when you did a render, with the lamp right next to the cube, you created a hotspot that is visible on the cube as seen in the following screenshot. You do not see the lamp itself though. It also shows that you have to be careful where you place the lamp unless you specifically want to show the hotspots, which can look nice adding a highlight to the edge.

You learned another way to move an object. You learned that once you select an object with the *RMB*, in addition to dragging it, you can also use the *G* key (grab) to move it, So once you have selected it, it can be moved repeatedly. I use it often because if the object is close to others, selecting with the *RMB* can sometimes be difficult. If you have already selected it then pressing the *G* key lets you move it without the risk of selecting something else accidently.

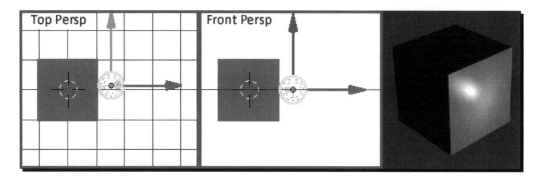

For your reference, the file `6907_03_putting the lamp close to the object 1.blend` which has been included in the download pack, shows the position of the lamp when it is close to the cube. `6907_03_putting the lamp close to the object 2.blend` shows the position of the lamp when it is in level with the cube.

Time for action – moving the lamp far away

There is another way to move an object which you will explore now. Notice the change in how the cube looks when you move the lamp close to the light camera:

1. Press the *1* key.

2. Press the *Home* key. On a Mac without a *Home* key, press the *fn* and Left arrow keys. This will show you all the objects in the scene.

3. Press the *5* key on the Numpad to get the orthographic view.

4. Observe the red and blue arrows that stick out of the lamp.

5. Put the cursor over the blue arrowhead. Hold the *LMB* down and move the lamp up until it is in level with the camera as shown in the left section of the following screenshot. Note that the arrows disappear and are replaced by a line that shows you the direction you can move in. You cannot move the lamp sideways. Release the *LMB* when it's in level with the center of the cube.

6. Press the *7* key on the Numpad to get the top view.

7. Use the red arrowhead and the green arrowhead to move the lamp near the camera as shown in the center section of the following screenshot.

8. Press *F12* to render the scene.

9. Observe how the cube looks.

10. Press the *Esc* button to close the render window.

What just happened?

This time as shown in the following screenshot, the lamp is farther away, so the lighting seems dimmer and the highlights are more muted, as with a real lamp. You switched to the Orthographic view to make it easier to align the lamp and the camera. You also learned a third way to move an object. You learned that once you select an object with the *LMB*, you can use the 3D manipulator to move it. Using the 3D manipulator restricts motion to a single direction. The red handle controls motion in X. The green handle controls motion in Y and the blue handle controls motion in Z.

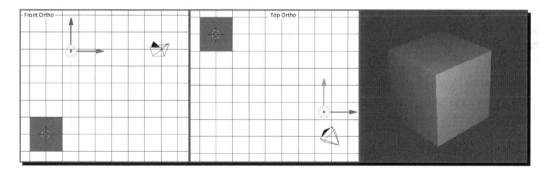

For your reference, the file `6907_03_moving the lamp far away 1.blend` shows the position of the lamp when it is close to the camera. The file `6907_03_moving the lamp far away 2.blend` shows the position of the lamp when it is level with the camera.

Time for action – seeing how the lighting looks without rendering

Sometimes you want to get an idea of how a scene looks without rendering. You can do this with the **Viewport Shading** menu as shown in the following screenshot:

1. On the header at the bottom of the 3D window, there is a blank white circle, as highlighted in the previous screenshot.

2. Click the *LMB* and a menu appears as shown previously.

3. Scroll up to the circle with the checkerboard and the word **Texture**.

4. Press the *LMB*.

5. Press *7* on the Numpad to see the top view.

6. Move the lamp close to one corner of the cube as shown in the following screenshot.

7. Press *1* on the Numpad to see the front view.

8. Move the lamp close to the cube.

9. Press *0* on the Numpad to see the view from the camera.

10. Move the lamp. What happens? The difference is illustrated on the left and right of the following screenshot.

What just happened?

You changed the **Viewport Shading** method from **Solid** to **Texture** and shifted to the **Top View** to move the lamp close to the cube. Then you switched back to **Camera View** so that you could get the camera's view of the lighting changing as you move the lamp around.

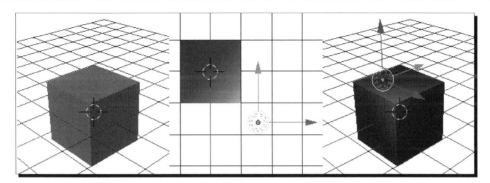

 For your reference, the file `6907_03_see how the lighting looks1.blend` shows the position of the lamp when it is close to the cube and ready to move back and forth. The file `6907_03_see how the lighting looks2.blend` shows the position of the lamp when it has been moved interactively.

Adding color to the lamp using the Properties window

The lower Blender window to the right of the 3D View is currently used as the Properties window. This is different from the **Properties Panel** in the 3D View that is activated with the *N* key. The **Properties** window is the second most used window in Blender. It contains a lot of the controls used for things including:

- Rendering
- Scene
- World
- Object
- Constraints
- Object data
- Material
- Textures
- Particles and physics

Time for action – adding color to the lamp

White light is great, but with a full spectrum to choose from, why restrict yourself? You are going to get your first exposure to Blender's second-most important window, the **Properties** window which has controls for cameras, materials, textures, lights, and so on. Do not confuse this with the 3D View Properties panel which we looked at briefly in the previous chapter. I will always refer to that as the 3D View Properties panel.

1. If the lamp is not selected, select it with the *RMB*.

2. The **Properties** window is the larger window on the right-hand side. Move the mouse over the header of the **Properties** window and select the seventh button from the left with the *LMB* so it is highlighted in blue as in the following screenshot.

3. This is the **Object Data** button. Notice that the buttons in the **Properties** window change when the highlight changes from being on the button with the camera on it to the **Object Data** button.

4. The **Properties** window is divided into panels and subpanels. When you selected the **Object Data** button, you opened the **Object Data** panel. You may have noticed that everything in the **Property** window changed when you clicked on the **Object Data** button. Each panel is divided into a series of subpanels. The subpanels are divided by lines, have a title and a downwards pointing triangle that can be used to close or open the subpanel. Move the cursor down to the third subpanel of the **Object Data** panel. It is labeled **Lamp**. Click on the white box with the *LMB*. A color wheel pops up as shown in the following screenshot:

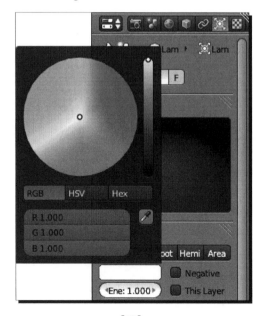

5. Click in the red area of the color wheel with the *LMB*, somewhere near the edge of the circle. Note that the white box just below the color wheel is now a shade of red. Click on an open area within the Lamp subpanel to close the color wheel.

6. Press *F12* to render the cube.

7. Observe how the cube looks.

8. Press the *Esc* button to close the render window.

What just happened?

With the lamp selected, you started using another window, the **Properties** window. Clicking the *LMB* on the **Object Data** button brought up the **Object Data** panel. You opened up the color wheel and changed the color of the lamp to red. In the 3D View window the cube became a red color. When you rendered the cube, the red light colored the cube red. Nothing happened to the color of the cube.

Remember our discussion of colors in *Chapter 2, Getting Comfortable using the 3D View* where we talked about there being 256 levels of Red, Green, and Blue. Look at the digital readout of the RGB colors just below the color wheel. They start at 1.0. For convenience, Blender expresses the 256 levels for a given color for the Red, Green, and Blue channels as percentages of 256. You changed the color from white to red and after you changed it, Red was a value close to 1.0 while Green and Blue were near zero.

The color you see depends on both the color of the object and the color of the light because Blender copies the real world.

For your reference, the file `6907_03_adding color to the lamp.blend` shows the lamp when it has been colored using the **Properties** window.

Using multiple lamps for better lighting

The best way to see the effect of lighting is to have more than one lamp.

Time for action – adding a second lamp

Now you'll learn to copy objects in a Blender scene and see how multiple lamps improve the look:

1. Press *1* on the Numpad to get the front view. Look at the upper left corner of the 3D View to make sure that the 3D View is in **Ortho** mode. Press *5* on the Numpad if it isn't in Ortho mode.

2. Move the lamp to the horizontal grid line above the cube.

3. Press *7* on the Numpad to get the top view.

4. Move the lamp up till it is just to the right of the cube and level with the center of the cube as seen on the left of the following screenshot.

5. Press *F12* to render the cube.

6. Observe how the cube looks.

7. Press the *Esc* button to close the render window.

8. With the lamp selected (Press *RMB* with the cursor over the lamp), press the *Shift* key and the *D* key to make a copy of the lamp.

9. Move the cursor. The new lamp moves while the original stays put. Move this lamp so that it is centered below the cube as shown in the middle of the following screenshot.

10. Press *F12* to render the cube.

11. Observe how the cube looks.

12. Press the *Esc* button to close the render window.

13. Now, go to the **Properties** window and, using the color wheel, change the color of the new lamp to green.

14. Press *F12* to render the cube.

15. Has the cube changed? It should look like the image on the right of the following screenshot:

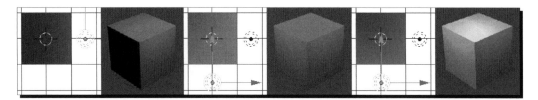

Downloading the example code

You can download the example code files for all Packt books you have purchased from your account at `http://www.packtpub.com`. If you purchased this book elsewhere, you can visit `http://www.packtpub.com/support` and register to have the files e-mailed directly to you.

What just happened?

The previous screenshot shows what you did. You rendered the cube to remind yourself of how the lighting looked. By pressing *Shift+D* (duplicate), you created a copy of the first lamp and moved it. Then you rendered the scene again and you could see that the lighting on the cube was more even. Then you changed the light color of the second lamp to green, and as expected, one side of the cube shows green. But, why is the top of the cube yellow? We'll discover that now.

For your reference, the file `6907_03_adding a second lamp1.blend` shows the lamp when it has been colored and moved into position. `6907_03_adding a second lamp2.blend` shows the position of the lamp when it has been copied and moved. `6907_03_adding a second lamp3.blend` shows the red and green lamps in position.

Now that you are getting into material where color matters, if you don't have the color e-book version, color images of these illustrations are available as a part of the download pack.

Light color mixing

We talked about the three colors that a computer displays, and the 256 levels of each color earlier. The diagram on the left side of the following figure will give you a little better idea of how light colors mix:

◆ When you mix red and blue you get magenta

◆ When you mix blue and green you get cyan

◆ When you mix green and red you get yellow

◆ When you mix red, green, and blue you get white, because white is all colors mixed

In your *Time for action* section, with a red lamp on one side of the cube, that side was colored red. With the green lamp on the second side, it was colored green. Because the top was lit by both lamps, the light was mixed and the color was yellow.

With your 256 shades of each color you can mix light more subtly than that. For example, if you have 100 percent red and 50 percent green, you get orange. The color wheel on the right, here, shows you basic combinations with RGB values written out for use in Blender in the form of (R, G, B). 100 percent becomes 1, 50 percent becomes 0.5, and so on.

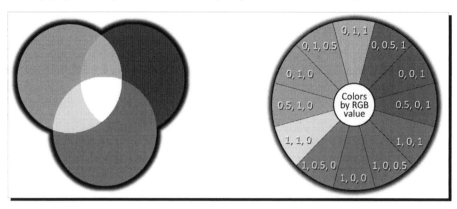

Have a go hero – experimenting with multiple lamps

You now know how to change lamp colors. Play around with moving the lamps and changing the colors.

The following figures show a couple of lighting setups that I came up with and diagrams of where I put the lamps. See what you can do.

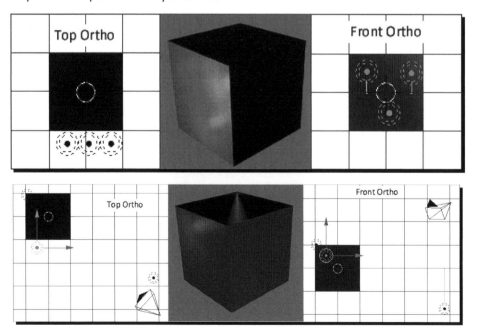

See in what way you can use light to color the different sides of the cube. Does the result look good? Put both lamps on one side of the cube. See what colors you can mix. Try three lamps like the first example.

There are two ways to mix colors in the color wheel. Try them both:

◆ **RGB (Red, Green, Blue)** which adjusts each color channel individually.

◆ There is also **HSV (Hue, Saturation, Value)**. Hue selects the color. Saturation selects how much color is mixed with white. Value selects how dark or light it is.

Spend a little time playing with this. There is a lot you can do. See if you can create a mood just using color.

Some animation professionals, called Lighting Technical Directors, build entire careers just working with lighting color. A quick look through job ads found positions for a 3D Lighting Artist for Games, a Lighting Artist, and a Senior Lighting Artist.

Here, Jeremy Birn, Technical Director at Pixar, discusses what a Technical Director does, `http://www.3drender.com/jobs/TD.htm`.

Here is a link to a good discussion of real world lighting for 3D, `http://en.wikibooks.org/wiki/Blender_3D:_Noob_to_Pro/Understanding_Real_Lights`. You will explore standard lighting methods and setup later.

For your reference, the file `6907_03_experimenting with multiple lamps1.blend` shows the three lamps on one side of the cube as I set them up, and `6907_03_experimenting with multiple lamps2.blend` shows the three lamps on varying sides of the cube.

Saving your work

Now that you are doing more exciting work, it's always a good idea to save what you have done. You will be using this setup more than once, so it will save time to have it saved away.

Time for action – saving a file

Now it's time for the most important command in Blender. Saving the work that you have done:

1. In the upper-left corner of the Blender window, select **File** and choose **Save As** from the drop-down menu. This opens up the **File Browser** as shown in the following screenshot:

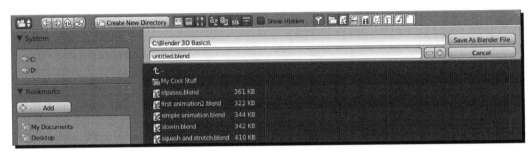

2. Click the *LMB* on where it says **untitled.blend**, as shown in the previous screenshot. The background becomes darker and you can edit the name now. When you have named the file, press *Enter*.

3. If you wish to increment the file name, that is, to have files named `animation1.blend`, `animation2.blend`, and so on, move the cursor over to the right and click on the plus sign. Before you press the **Save As Blender File** button, make sure that you are in the right directory.

4. To go up a directory, click on the up pointed arrow at the top of the list of files. To go into a directory, click on the icon that looks like a cardboard file folder, similar to the **My Cool Stuff** folder in the previous screenshot.

5. Once you are in the right place, press the **Save As Blender File** button.

What just happened?

Blender does not use the computer's filing interface. It has its own. You named the file. You learned about incrementing the name numerically, which is very important for keeping different versions of a project saved in case you have to go back to an earlier version. You learned how to go through the directory structure and save the file.

Always have a backup file

Computers being what they are, it's always good to have a backup file. You have learned to save files on your own, but you wouldn't be the first person to get working in Blender and discover that the hours flew by and you forgot to save the file you are working on. If that should happen, remember the following tip.

The auto backup feature

Blender helps you with this by automatically making a backup file every so often. The default time is every five minutes. These files are tucked away in your `Documents and Settings` folder. The file name is some number with a `.blend` extension. It will be in the directory, `Documents and Settings\"Your user name"\Local Settings\temp`. Of course, Your user name is whatever name the computer has for you as a user. This will be slightly different for Mac and Linux users, so pay attention to where the installation program loads it.

After you have used Blender a little, you may notice files labeled `.blend1` and `.blend2`. These are created by Blender when you save a file that has already been saved. The old copy of the `.blend` file becomes `.blend1` and if there is a `.blend1` copy, it becomes `.blend2`. They can be used by renaming the file to a `.blend` extension. So if you made a mistake and then hit **Save**, `.blend1` and `.blend2` are your friends.

Controlling the camera

Earlier, you discussed the Global *X*, *Y*, *Z* axis and the Local *X*, *Y*, *Z* axis. Using the camera helps us to see the difference in a slightly more vivid way.

Time for action – using the global axis and local axis

We discussed the global and local axes. It's kind of an abstract concept until you use it. Here we can see it:

1. Select **New** in the file menu.

2. With the cursor over the camera, click the *RMB* to select it. Note the 3D manipulator and that the Z axis (in blue) is straight up. You can press *5* to toggle to **Ortho** mode to confirm that the Z axis is pointing up.

3. Move the mouse over the **Orientation** selector in the **3D View** header, outlined in the previous screenshot. Note that it says **Global**. Move the mouse up the **Orientation** pop-up menu and select **Local** with the *LMB*. Note which direction the Z axis is pointing now.

4. Change from **Local** back to **Global** and back several times, noting the change in direction.

What just happened?

By changing the value of the Orientation Selector, you can choose whether you are working with the global or local axes. Why is this important? The global Z axis is up and down. The local Z axis of the camera is almost sideways. In fact, the local Z axis for the camera points toward the lens of the camera and away from the scene. This allows you to move the camera in or out, to get closer or farther from your subject by moving along the camera's local Z axis.

You got a start on moving objects by learning three ways to move the light. Now you will refine your techniques for greater speed and control.

Time for action – moving an object in one plane in global mode

Sometimes you want to move an object freely, and sometimes it's better to move it along one axis. Here's a way to move it, by specifying the axis by letter:

1. Load a new file into Blender.

2. Select the camera with the *RMB*. Press the *G* key to grab it. Now move your mouse.

3. Now press and release (tap) the *Z* key and move the mouse.

4. Now tap the *X* key and move the mouse.

5. Now tap the *Y* key.

6. Press the *RMB* to let go of the camera.

What just happened?

You discovered that you can restrict the axis that you move by pressing the *G* key and then pressing the key of the axis that you wish to move in. This gives us similar control to using the 3D Manipulator.

Time for action – moving an object in one plane in the local mode

We talked about global and local axes. Now you see the difference in action. You tap once to specify moving along a global axis, you tap twice to specify moving along a local axis:

1. With the camera selected, press the *G* key to grab it.

2. Now tap the *Z* key two times and move the mouse.

3. Now tap the *X* key twice and move the mouse.

4. Now tap the *Y* key twice and move the mouse.

5. Press the *LMB* to let go of the camera.

What just happened?

You discovered that when you press the *G* key you can restrict the motion to the global Z plane by pressing the *Z* key once. If you press the *Z* key two times in a row, motion is restricted to the local Z plane. The same applies to the X plane and the Y plane.

Have a go hero – controlling location with numbers

Not only can you control whether you move, rotate, and scale an object, and along which axis with keys, but you can tell Blender what values to do it by. Try it.

Select the cube. Press the *G* key, then the *Y* key, then the *2* key. If you like the change then press the *Enter* key. If you don't like the change, press the *Esc* key and it will go back to where it started. Try it in other axes and with other distances. This is great when you are trying to locate things with precision.

Seeing through the lens

You may have found it frustrating not being able to control the camera when you press render. You're going to fix that now. You'll study the basics of getting the best use of the camera lens and a little bit of the vocabulary of camera motion.

Time for action – setting up Blender so you can see what the camera sees

Quite often, you may need to have more than one view of the scene visible at one time. Blender is great that way because you can break up the 3D View window as you like. In this case, we want to see what the camera is seeing as well as having our standard view of the scene:

1. Select **New** in the **File** menu.

2. Create a new 3D View window as you learned in *Chapter 2, Getting Comfortable using the 3D View*.

3. With the cursor over the right-hand 3D View, press *0* on the Numpad to get the camera view.

4. Press *T* to close the **Tool Shelf** in the right 3D View window. It should look similar to the following illustration.

5. Now save the file to a file named Two 3D Views.blend.

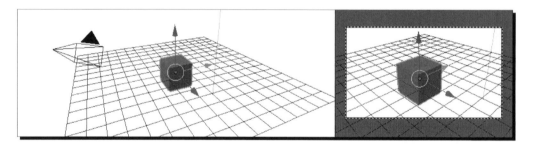

What just happened?

This last exercise was to create a basic Blender file that you can use multiple times. It has the standard 3D View window as well as a 3D View window locked to what the camera sees. This will give you the flexibility of moving around in the scene as you please and you can manipulate things while observing how they appear to the camera.

 For your reference, the file 6907_03_Two 3D Views.blend has the double 3D View setup as shown previously.

Using the camera as a canvas

In *Chapter 1, Introducing Blender and Animation* we discussed how animation progressed from the static posing of Felix the Cat to the lively compositions of Mickey Mouse. You saw how it happened again in the early days of computer animation. These rules enabling good composition were first conceived by painters, amplified by filmmakers, and later applied to animation.

Understanding the rules of composition

There are three basic rules of composition to be aware of:

◆ The rule of thirds

◆ Using positive and negative space

◆ Using a limited palette

Applying the rule of thirds for well balanced scenes

With the rule of thirds, you visually break down an image into thirds vertically and horizontally as done in the left side of the following graphic. A grid has been placed over the left image to show you where the thirds of the image are.

Placing the points of interest along the lines that mark the intersections of the thirds gives you a visual sense of flow that just placing the point of interest in the center of the image would not.

Here, on the left, the subject was posed with the rule of thirds in mind. In the right-hand image the subject was posed in the center. In the left-hand image you are drawn into the scene. You get a stronger feeling of presence. For more information, here is a link that explores the rule of thirds in more depth, `http://www.digital-photography-school.com/rule-of-thirds`.

For your reference, the file `6907_03_rule of thirds.blend` was used to create the left-hand image shown previously.

Using positive and negative space to put the focus on the action

The positive space is the area occupied by the subject of the image. In this case, it is the dancing figure and the red benches. The negative space is everything else. As simple as that is, there is always a delicate dance going on between the two that can add or subtract from the composition. They can compliment or clash, but which of these outcomes you want depends on what you are trying to do. So there is no right or wrong, but you must consider the effect that the background has on the foreground.

In the following photo, the subject is the man looking at the bicycle. Most of the background is flat paving stones, there is little detail in them. This opens up the image, making it simple, but it also contrasts with the amount of detail in the man and the bicycle, and directs your attention to the man. The strip at the edge of the water reinforces the direction of motion of the man and echoes the top tube of the bicycle, so there is a lot of harmonious diagonal motion. But the gondola in the background, while reinforcing the general flow of the image, also provides an important clue about it. It reminds us that the photograph is in Venice. Land vehicles aren't very prominent in Venice, making the loaded bicycle out of place, which may explain why the man is staring at the bicycle.

Scott Mc Cloud investigated this subject well in his book *Understanding Comics*. I recommend reading it. Here is another link that also explores positive and negative space, `http://artinspired.pbworks.com/w/page/13819678/Positive-and-Negative-Space`.

Using a limited palette for better results

A long time ago, painters discovered that using all colors possible didn't work visually as well as having a limited palette of fewer colors. An image should be accomplished with contrast and tone. In the image of the dancer shown previously, all the tones are in the range of reds and blues, there are no yellows or greens. This helps to unify the image. Though often, painters will bend the rules by having one small bit of opposing color or a saturated red (pure red, not mixed with white) to draw your eye to the focal point of the image. The preceding image is a good example. Most of the image is in yellows and oranges. In this case it is the white helmet with the spot of red that draws your attention to the bicycle, similar to the way the man's attention is on the bicycle, and there is only a little blue, that is on the girls in the corner, which helps to set them apart. They are not part of the man's attention though they help with the flow of the image, by counter-balancing the figure in the lower left.

If you watch movies carefully, you may notice that some of the scenes have very limited palettes, where the director wants to use blue to emphasize the coldness of the actions within the scenes, and the next scene may be all oranges or greens. Here is a link to more on limited palettes, `http://channeling-winslow-homer.com/a-rational-palette-index-to-chapters/chapter-one-2/chapter-two-eye-candy-avoiding-monotomy/chapter-three-mixing-convenience/chapter-four-saturation-costs/five-is-the-saturated-palette-what-we-want/six-the-extremely-limited-palette/`.

Pop quiz – composing your scenes

Let's take a moment to review some of what you've learned about composing your scenes:

1. How is color a major clue in the image of the dancer telling the viewer what is positive space and what is negative space?

2. While the image of the dancer obeys the rule of thirds, what might be done to it to improve the visual flow?

   - Put something in the foreground to bridge the gap between the end of the bench and the dancer's foot
   - Show the horizon in the background
   - Make the wall in the background green

Employing Blender's camera composition guides to make your work look better

To help you with your composition, Blender includes a series of camera composition guides including one that outlines the rule of thirds.

Have a go hero – investigating the camera composition guides

We discussed composition. Blender has composition guides to help you that display within the camera's finder.

To find the camera composition guides, first select the camera in the **3D View**. Look in the **Properties** window header and find the image of the movie camera, the seventh button from the left in the **Properties** window header. That is the **Object Data** button for the camera. Click on it with the *LMB*. At the top-right of the **Display** subpanel, there is a pop-up menu button labeled **Composition**. Check out the different composition guides. When you select one, it will be shown in the **Camera** view. You can have several at one time and choose whichever you like. See what kinds there are and do a search on those terms to find out more about them.

Understanding the fundamental camera moves

There are six fundamental camera moves; moving in and out, side to side, up and down, tilting right and left, up and down, and swiveling right and left. They are illustrated in the following figure:

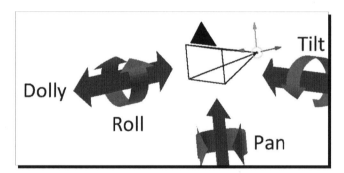

- ◆ **Dolly**: Move the camera towards or away from the scene along its local *Z* axis
- ◆ **Roll**: Turn the camera on its local *Z* axis
- ◆ **Boom**: Move the camera up and down on its local *Y* axis
- ◆ **Pan**: Turn the camera on its local *Y* axis
- ◆ **Truck**: Move the camera sideways along its local *X* axis
- ◆ **Tilt**: Turn the camera on its local *X* axis

Rotating and scaling the camera and other objects

Blender has a very consistent user interface. The commands for manipulating a camera also work on other objects such as the cube or the lamp, except that a lamp doesn't scale. You have got a good idea of the ways to move an object, and that rotating and scaling are almost the same, except you press the *R* key to rotate an object and the *S* key to scale it.

Have a go hero – rotating and scaling objects

You've learned the commands to move, rotate, and scale objects. Have some fun doing it to help train your fingers which commands are which.

Using what you know about the *X, Y,* and *Z* keys, and using the *R* key to rotate an object or the *S* key to scale it, experiment with moving, rotating, and scaling the camera, the cube, and the lamp to make dynamic views of the cube. If you like you can also use the *Shift+D* command to make more cubes. Make compositions that take into account the rule of thirds, positive and negative space, and a limited palette. Take your time. Try it several times.

Making an animation

It's time to make an animation. Animation adds a fourth dimension to 3D. Besides X, Y and Z, there is time. In animation, time is broken into **frames**, a sequence of individual images such as frames of a movie. This is usually expressed as **frames per second**. As a rule of thumb, web animations such as animated gifs, banner ads, and YouTube videos can play at between 7 and 15 frames per second (**fps**); film plays at 24 fps and video plays at 30 fps. Blender renders at 24 fps by default.

Look at the window directly below the 3D window. By default, that is used as the **Timeline window**. The Timeline window lets us know how far along in an animation we are. Look at the following screenshot:

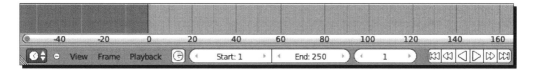

- The three large white buttons give you the most important information.
- By default, Blender allows you 250 frames in which to create an animation. It starts on frame 1, it ends on frame 250, and the third button shows you the frame that Blender is currently on, which by default is frame 1.

◆ To change the frame you can click the *LMB* over the number in the button and type in a different number or use the two small arrows at either end of the button to change the value.

◆ If you look at the top of the image, you see the numbers -40 through 160. There is a little green vertical line just to the right of the 0. This is the **current frame indicator**. It shows you which frame you are on; and you can drag the current frame indicator to change the frame as well.

Earlier, you set up a Blender file with two 3D View windows. Now you need it to do your animation. So let's load the file.

Time for action – loading a file

Loading a file is pretty simple, but essential if you are working on a project that you need to interrupt or make changes to:

1. Loading a file is very similar to saving one. You've made changes in the one you were working on. Save it to a different name from the first file you saved.

2. Select **File** and then choose **Open** from the drop-down menu. The **File Browser** opens and, as you roll the mouse over the files, the one you are over is highlighted. Find **Two 3D Views.blend**.

3. Press the *LMB* to select it. Click the *LMB* on **Open Blender File** as shown in the following screenshot:

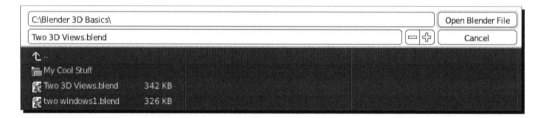

What just happened?

You loaded a file. It's very similar to saving a file. You're saving yourself a little work by reusing the dual 3D View setup that you saved away earlier.

Time for action – making a simple animation with keyframes

In animation, keyframes are the beginning and end of a transition. This transition could be movement, rotation, or scaling of an object. It can also be a change in the color of an object, the brightness of the light, or almost anything that you can set in Blender. The animation is a sequence of keyframes. So let's start by making a simple animation:

1. If the cube is not selected, select it with the *RMB*.

2. With the cursor over the left-hand 3D View window, press the letter *I* key, (I for Insert), to insert a keyframe. A drop-down menu will appear as shown here. Select **Location** and press the *LMB*.

3. In the Timeline window at the bottom of the Blender window, drag the current frame indicator right until it is over the 20. As you do that, the current frame text fields in the lower left of the 3D Views will change, as will the current frame button in the Timeline window.

4. With the cube selected, grab the green 3D manipulator in the left-hand 3D View with the *LMB* and move the cube in the Y axis. Watch in the other 3D View so you can see how it looks to the camera.

5. With the cursor over the left-hand 3D View window, press the letter *I* key. A drop-down menu will appear. Select **Location** and press the *LMB*. Notice that there is an orange line at frame 0. This says that frame 0 has a keyframe.

6. Move the current frame indicator in the Timeline window between 20 and 0 and back to 20 to see the cube's motion. When you do this you can also see an orange line at frame 20, indicating that frame 20 has a keyframe.

7. Select the large button in the Timeline window that is marked **End**. Click where it says **250**. The number will move to the left and you can type in *20* and press *Enter*. Now the animation will end at frame 20.

8. To see a preview of the animation in the 3D View, put the cursor over the 3D View window and press the *Alt* key and the *A* key. Press *Esc* to stop it from playing.

9. Save your file to a unique name so you can remember it.

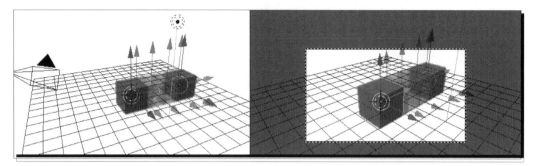

What just happened?

Congratulations. You are now a computer animator! You created a keyframe telling the computer where the cube is on frame one. Then you created another keyframe to tell the computer where the cube is on frame 20. The computer then figured out how to move the cube at frames 2–19 so that it would appear that the cube is moving smoothly.

A keyframe tells the computer what the *state* of an object is on a particular frame. In this example, the first keyframe tells the computer that the state of the cube's location in Y is 0 at frame 1. The second keyframe tells the computer that the state of the cube's location in Y is 5.120 at frame 20. Blender allows us to animate almost any property of the object. A property is any one of the attributes of the object such as location, rotation, scaling, or color, and much more.

Finally, you learned how to preview the animation.

 For your reference, the file 6907_03_a simple animation.blend has our first animation.

This is a pretty simple animation, one cube isn't much for Blender to calculate. But as you go through this book, the models and animations will get more complex. You will get tips and recommendations on how to optimize your rendering and previews.

 Making an animation preview run smoothly

You can preview the animation in the 3D View in any display mode. Remember though, that the computer has to calculate all of this in real time. If in the future, a large scene does not play smoothly as a Texture display, try previewing it as a solid or wireframe display, which Blender can do much faster.

Getting a video player so you can play your animation

You'll render your animation in a moment, but now you need to install a video player so you can see what you rendered. Blender believes that it should not limit your choice of video player, so none is included with Blender.

Time for action – downloading the Blender video player

If you have a favorite one, you may use it, but for the purposes of this book, we shall download the older version of Blender that does have a video player included:

1. Go to `http://download.blender.org/release/Blender2.49a/` to download an older version of Blender.

2. Choose the most appropriate version for your system.

3. Remember where you load it. We will need to refer to that location. Once you have it loaded, we can connect it to Blender.

Linux users take note

I found a bit of a snag when trying to download Blender 2.49 into Ubuntu. If the straight-ahead method fails, it can be done using the Terminal.

You get the Terminal (`terminal.app`) in the Ubuntu Software Center, type in `Terminal` and it will find you one to download.

When you have downloaded it, open the Dash Home and type in `terminal`. It will bring up the Terminal, which is a command-line editor.

1. Open `https://launchpad.net/~irie/+archive/blender` in your Browser.

2. Type in `sudo apt-add-repository ppa:irie/blender` into the Terminal.

3. Enter your password when asked.

4. Press *Ctrl+C* when asked about adding the ppa to your system, as you don't need it.

5. Type in `sudo apt-get update`.

6. Type in `sudo apt-get install blender2.4`.

The Blender file will be in `usr/bin/Blender2.4-bin`. You can scroll up in the Terminal text to double-check the path name. Look for `Blender2.4-bin`.

What just happened?

We just downloaded Blender's old video player from the Internet. It plays a series of frames as an animation. It is recommended that you render frames of an animation out to a series of images rather than as one single video file, just in case your rendering gets interrupted, or you decide to change part of the animation. So this player is right for this use.

Time for action – installing a video player for Blender

To make sure that Blender knows where the video player is, you need to include its location into Blender's User Preferences, which is where Blender stores the information so it can be set up the way that you prefer.

But when you do set the User Preferences, whatever objects, cameras, lights, and so on are in the scene at that moment will also be included as part of the default setup. So, to ensure that the default scene has your standard cube, camera, and lamp, you need to make sure that they are there now:

1. Select **New** in the **File** menu so that we can add this to the default Blender setup. Once a new file is loaded in Blender, select **User Preferences** in the **File** menu. The **User Preferences** menu will appear.

2. There is a row of buttons on the top. With the *LMB*, select the button marked **File** as shown in the following screenshot.

3. On the left-hand side, go down until you see **Animation Player**, as shown at the bottom of the following screenshot:

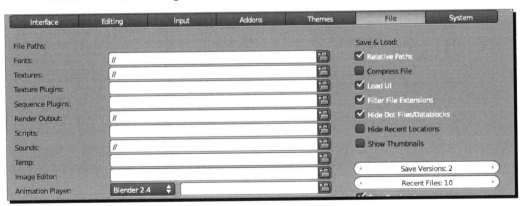

4. Click on the folder symbol to the right of where it says Blender 2.4. Find where you have installed your copy of Blender 2.49a and select it. Click on the **Accept** button.

5. At the bottom-left of the **User Preferences** menu, select the button that says **Save as Default**. Now close the **User Preferences** window.

What just happened?

We just added a new video player to your computer and told Blender where to find it. You also got an introduction to the **User Preferences** window. The **User Preferences** window has controls for many great things, including what color the background of the 3D View window is, special add-ons that give Blender special abilities, and keyboard shortcuts. We will use it more and you can check it out if you want to personalize your copy of Blender.

Rendering your animation

Now it's time to see what you have done. You need to render it so you can see the light, the motion, and the objects. Now is time for that quick snack or cup of coffee I talked about in *Chapter 1, Introducing Blender and Animation*. This is your moment. But hurry right back; the Blender renderer is pretty quick and there isn't much in this scene to render.

Time for action – rendering the animation

You've seen how you can render a single frame by pressing the *F12* key, and look at it by pressing the *F11* Key. Rendering an animation is very similar:

1. Load the animation file that you made just before installing the video player.

2. Press the *Ctrl* key and the *F12* key to start the rendering.

3. Look at the text across the top of the frame where the image is being rendered, as shown in the following screenshot. It tells you which frame is being rendered, how long the last frame took to render, how many vertices and faces there are, how much memory was needed, and other things. This text is for your information only; it doesn't show up in the final images or animation.

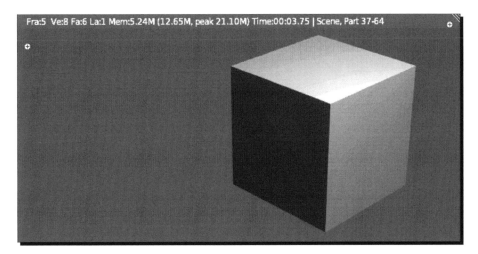

4.   When the animation has finished rendering, press the *Esc* key to close the render window. Then press the *Ctrl* key and the *F11* key. In a moment you should see your animation.

5.   If you don't see anything, go back to the **Blender Video Player** section and make sure you got all the details right.

6.   Press the *Esc* key when you are done looking at your animation.

What just happened?

You learned how to render your animation by pressing the *Ctrl* and *F12* keys, and how to view it using the *Ctrl* and *F11* keys.

Controlling motion in the Graph Editor

Now, let's look at what that motion looks like to Blender, and see how we can control the motion and other transitions using F-Curves.

Time for action – exploring the Graph Editor

The Graph Editor displays the data associated with every single keyframe. It lets you adjust the keyframes and the transitions between them easily:

1.   Move the cursor over the Timeline window and down to the **Current Editor Type** button.

2.   Press the *LMB*, scroll up the menu to the **Graph Editor** and press the *LMB* again.

3.   Move the cursor up to the edge between the Graph Editor and the 3D View till you see the double-headed arrow. Drag the border between the windows up till you can see the curving line as shown in the following screenshot.

4.   Use *Shift+MMB* to move the graphs so that they are centered in the window.

5.   Now, use the *Ctrl+MMB* buttons to scale the display of the graph so it fits comfortably in the window as shown in the following screenshot.

6. Select the vertical green line with the *LMB*. While holding down the *LMB*, move the mouse right and left. The line will move, and if you look in the 3D View, your cube is moving as well.

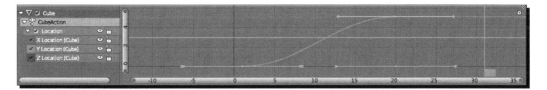

What just happened?

Now the bottom window is the Graph Editor, not the Timeline. It looks similar, but it displays the mathematical curves that control the motion. On the left is a panel that allows you to select which motion curves you are working with. You also discovered that you can use the same commands to navigate in the Graph Editor as in the 3D View.

> For your reference, the file `6907_03_exploring the Graph Editor.blend` shows the curve in the Graph Editor.

Introducing the F-Curve

The curve is called an F-Curve. The orange lines with orange balls on the end are how you control the curve. The center orange dot is the control point. It represents the keyframe. The orange dots at the end are the control handles that you control the curve with. These allow you to control how your object goes from keyframe to keyframe. There are three ways to get from keyframe to keyframe:

◆ One is **Linear interpolation** which goes in a straight line from keyframe to keyframe as seen in the left side of the following screenshot.

◆ The second is **Constant interpolation** which keeps the value constant until the next keyframe as seen in the center of the following screenshot.

◆ The last is **Bézier interpolation**, which gives you the most control because it allows you to control the path between keyframes very flexibly as seen on the right side of the following screenshot. The Bézier (Beh-zee-yay) curve is named after French engineer Pierre Bézier who used them to design automobile bodies for Renault. The Bézier interpolation is the default method in Blender, so, we'll look at that in more detail.

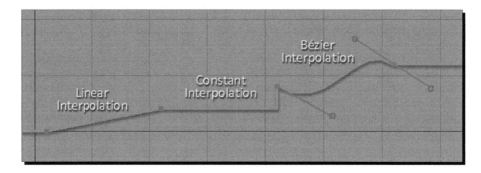

You choose which way you want to interpolate by selecting **Key** on the **Graph Editor** header, then choosing **Interpolation Mode** from the pop-up menu.

For your reference, the file 6907_03_introducing the f-curve.blend shows the three interpolation methods.

Linear interpolation is great when you need nice mechanical transitions between keyframes, say if you were rotating the hands of a clock and want the hands to rotate at a constant speed. Constant interpolation is used when you want to shift from state to state like the escape mechanism that controls the unwinding of a clock spring.

Blender's consistent interface makes it easier for you

The same commands used to move objects in the 3D View can be used to move keyframes in the Graph Editor.

Modifying motion with the Bézier curve controls

As you saw in the preceding illustration, Linear interpolation goes in a straight line from one keyframe to another, without changing the speed of its motion, but the Bézier Interpolation is much more free-form. With the control handles, you can control the rate of acceleration or deceleration of an object as well as its motion.

Time for action – working with a Bézier curve

Bézier curves are very powerful. Blender uses them for modeling as well as for the F-Curves that control animation. Here is how to control them:

1. In the **Graph Editor**, the current frame indicator is a vertical line with a box on the bottom. Move it left and right to scrub along the timeline of the Graph Editor. Watch the motion of the cube in the 3D View.

2. Now, select the left dot on the upper Bézier handle, with the *RMB*, and move it up as shown in the next screenshot. Press the *LMB* to release the handle. The curve will go upwards. Move the current frame indicator back and forth again and watch the motion of the cube. The Bézier handles can be moved with all the same controls as keyframes and objects.

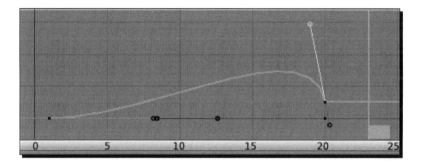

3. With the cursor over either the Graph Editor or the 3D View, press *Alt+A* to play the animation and *Esc* to stop.

What just happened?

You scrubbed the current frame indicator along the timeline of the Graph Editor, to see that the 3D Views reflect how you are controlling the Graph Editor. Then, you modified the motion curve by moving the Bézier handle to change the curve without changing the actual keyframe. This changed the motion of the cube. It now moves farther away from the camera, and comes back. The return is much more dynamic than the trip out and it stops suddenly without much slow out. You can see this reflected in the Bézier curve in the **Graph Editor** window.

For your reference, the file `6907_03_working with a Bezier Curve.blend` shows using the curve handle to change the motion of the cube.

Practice is the only way you will learn all the Blender commands. It may help to write out a list of the commands that you only use occasionally so that you can find them quickly, Here is a list of the keyboard shortcuts for the **Timeline** window.

Moving the Current Frame Indicator with keystrokes

Pressing the Right arrow key goes one frame forward.

Pressing the Left arrow key goes one frame back.

Pressing the Up arrow key goes to the next keyframe.

Pressing the Down arrow key goes to the previous keyframe.

Pressing the *Shift*+Right arrow key goes to the end of the animation.

Pressing the *Shift*+Left arrow key goes to the beginning of the animation.

Pressing the *Shift*+Up arrow key goes 10 frames forward.

Pressing the *Shift*+Down arrow key goes 10 frames back.

Time for action – adding squash and stretch to the animation

We talked about how using squash and stretch adds to how dynamic animation feels. It's easy to do, just taking a little extra time and a keyframe or two:

1. Use the arrow keys to move the current frame indicator in the **Graph Editor** back to frame 1.

2. Place your cursor over the **3D View** window and check that the cube is still selected. If it isn't, select it with the *RMB*. Press *I*. Click the *LMB* on **LocRotScale** to simultaneously create keyframes for location, rotation, and scaling. Look in the **Graph Editor** to see the new curves.

3. Go to frame 20 and make another keyframe in the 3D View with **LocRotScale**.

4. In the **Graph Editor**, move the **Current Frame Indicator** to the frame where the curve is highest. In the 3D View, press *I*. Scroll up the menu to where it says **Scaling**. Make a keyframe for **Scaling** only.

5. Move the current frame indicator two frames ahead. Press *S*, *Y*, and then move the mouse to scale the cube in Y so that it is longer. Press the *LMB* to release the scaling. Press *I* to make a keyframe for **Scaling**.

6. Press *Alt+A* to preview the animation.

7. Save this Blender file. Use the incrementing feature that we discussed earlier to save it to a unique file name.

What just happened?

Using multiple keyframes, you have created your first example of squash and stretch. This may seem a little roundabout way to put in the keyframes, but it was efficient at putting the effect when we wanted it.

First, you modified the keyframes you had already made at frames 1 and 20. This made sure that the **Location**, **Rotation**, and **Scaling** values were locked down as shown in the following screenshot. This let you make further keyframes in the location, rotation, and scaling channels without worrying whether you are altering the starting and ending values.

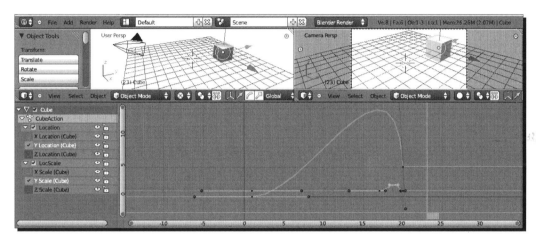

Then, in the middle of the cube's motion, you added a scaling keyframe to keep the scaling constant till you were ready to start the squash and stretch. You went a couple of frames later, when you want the cube stretched to its maximum. You stretched it in Y, and then made a keyframe that recorded how you stretched the scaling. The final keyframe already had the scaling set to be the same as it was originally, so the cube stretches and bounces back. You can see all the keyframes and curves in the preceding screenshot. Note the large curve controlling the motion and the smaller curve controlling the scaling in the preceding screenshot:

 For your reference, the file `6907_03_making the animation more dynamic.blend` shows how squash and stretch was created with the Bézier curves.

Doing more with the Bézier curve handles

The Bézier curve handles are pretty flexible controls. Let's find out more about what they can do.

Time for action – refining the use of the Bézier curve handles

Ironically, you can sometimes get more control by restricting the motion. You'll try limiting the motion of the control handles to a particular axis and you will set the control point so that only one control handle moves at a time:

1. In the **Graph Editor**, zoom into the keyframe where you stretched the cube, select one of the handles with the *RMB*, press the *G* key to grab it, and move it around with the mouse. Press the *Y* key. Move the cursor around and observe how this affects the movement.

2. Press the *X* key. Move the cursor around and observe how this affects the movement. Press the *RMB* to release the curve handle without making a change.

3. Now, select the control point in the center.

4. Press the *V* key. Select **Free** from the drop-down menu as shown in the following screenshot. Pick one of the control handles and move the cursor around and observe how this affects the curve.

What just happened?

You discovered that pressing the *X* or *Y* key locks the handle motion to that direction. Pressing the *V* key and selecting **Free** allows you to control each handle of the control point individually.

> Different handle types give you different control over a control point.
>
> **Free** handles are independent.
>
> **Vector** handles point to the previous or next handle.
>
> **Aligned** handles lie in a straight line and give a continuous curve.
>
> **Automatic** chooses length and direction to ensure the smoothest result.
>
> **Auto Clamped** restores default handle settings.

Here's a page with a lot of good information about using control points and control handles on the F-Curve, http://wiki.blender.org/index.php/Doc:2.6/Manual/Animation/Editors/Graph/FCurves.

Have a go hero – experimenting with control handles to adjust motion

You've seen a lot of ways to set keyframes now. Play with them in both the 3D View and the Graph Editor.

Remember, that not only can you move the control handles in the Graph Editor, but you can move the control points themselves, changing the value and the time of each keyframe. Change values in **Rotation**, **Location,** and **Scaling** of the cube. Try out the **Vector**, **Aligned**, **Automatic**, and **Auto Clamped** settings as well.

Selecting which channel to work on

Things look pretty straightforward right now. But imagine that you have 20 objects all moving at the same time. It's good to be able to control which animation channels you see.

Time for action – adding keyframes in the Graph Editor

The 3D View is not the only place you can add keyframes. The Graph Editor actually gives you much better control over adding and manipulating keyframes:

1. In the 3D View, select the camera.

2. Using the arrow keys, move the current frame indicator to frame 1.

3. With the cursor over the Graph Editor, use *Ctrl+MMB* to zoom the Graph Editor out so that you can see at least -10 to 10 on the vertical scale. Look at the left side of the Graph Editor. It's blank.

4. With the cursor over the 3D View, press the *I* key and make a **Locations** keyframe.

5. In the Graph Editor there are three colored lines, red, blue, and green, just like the 3D axis indicator. Since you have just made a **Locations** keyframe, these are F-Curves for locations in X, Y, and Z. Use *Ctrl+MMB* to zoom in until you can see the red and blue lines clearly.

6. Use the arrow keys to move the current frame indicator to frame 20. Note that you can see orange dots at frame 1 on these lines. They are the keyframes you made.

7. Click on the orange dot on the blue line with the *RMB*. That selects the Z Location F-Curve.

8. In the **3D View** window, Press *G, Z,* and use the mouse to move the camera down. Press the *LMB* to release the camera.

9. With the cursor over the **Graph Editor**, press the *I* key. A menu pops up. Scroll down the menu to choose **Only Selected Channels** as shown in the following screenshot:

10. Click the *LMB* to create a keyframe. Notice that keyframes have only been created on the selected channel, in this case the camera's Z location channel, and they are created on the frame where the **Current Frame Indicator** is.

11. Move the **Current Frame Indicator** to frame 10.

12. In the **3D View** window, Press *G, Y,* and use the mouse to move the camera. Press the *LMB* to release the camera.

13. Scroll the **Current Frame Indicator** back and forth between Frames 1 and 20.

What just happened?

It's always good to think about whether you need a keyframe to control the motion and don't create extra keyframes if you don't need them.

You moved the current frame indicator and made a keyframe for the camera's location as you have done before. Then you moved to the 20th frame and discovered that you could make a keyframe in the Graph Editor. But making keyframes in the Graph Editor gives you different choices from when making them in the 3D View. In the 3D View, if you make a location keyframe, it is automatically made in all three, location X, location Y, and location Z F-Curves. If you choose a single or several curves in the Graph Editor and choose **Only Selected Channels**, a keyframe is made only on the active curve(s).

Then you moved to a different frame, and moved the camera. But when you scrubbed the **Current Frame Indicator** in time, that movement disappeared because you never made a keyframe for it.

If you choose **All Channels**, a keyframe is made on every channel of every object.

Time for action – controlling the F-Curves with the Channel Selection Panel

With several objects and Location, Rotation, Scaling F-Curves for each, the Graph Editor is likely to get cluttered. You need a way to choose which F-Curves you are seeing. It also helps if you can lock an F-Curve so you don't adjust it when you don't intend to:

1. In the **3D View** window, move the cursor over the Cube and select it with *Shift+RMB*. Note that in the Graph Editor, you can see that there are now channels displayed on the left for both the Cube and the Camera, as shown in the following screenshot.

2. On the left side of the Graph Editor, click the *LMB* on the triangle next to the **Location** channel of the Camera so it points down as in the following screenshot.

3. The **X Location**, **Y Location**, and **Z Location** channels appear.

4. Click the eye symbol next to **Z Location** with the *LMB* several times and watch the F-Curve for the **Z location** as you click. Scrub the **Current Frame Indicator** back and forth and watch the **3D View** window. Do it when you can see the eye and do it when you cannot see the eye.

5. Click the eye with the *LMB* so you can see the F-Curve in the Graph Editor. Then, click the *LMB* over the loudspeaker symbol to the right of it. Scrub the **Current Frame Indicator** back and forth and watch the **3D View** window. Do it when you can see the sound out of the loudspeaker and do it when you cannot see sound out of the loudspeaker.

6. Click the *LMB* over the loudspeaker so the F-Curve is not grayed out. Then, click the *LMB* over the lock symbol to the right of the loudspeaker so that the lock is locked. Look at the F-Curve. Set the lock so it is locked.

7. Move the **Current Frame Indicator** to where the Cube's Y motion F-Curve is highest. Press the *I* key to make a keyframe and choose **All Channels** from the menu.

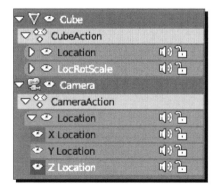

What just happened?

On the left-hand side of the Graph Editor there is a **Channel Selection Panel** as shown in the previous screenshot. It lets you control which channels you can see and work on. The eye controls visibility of the F-Curve. The loudspeaker controls whether the F-Curve is used in the scene. The lock controls whether you can make changes to the F-Curve. And finally, you saw what putting a keyframe on All Channels does. In this case, it made keyframes on every channel for all objects except the Z Location channel, which you had locked.

Time for action – controlling channel display with the header

Sometimes you want to be able to see the channels for all the objects when working on one. There is a button that will let you display the F-Curves for all visible objects:

1. In the **3D View**, click on the **Camera** with the *RMB*.

2. In the **Graph Editor** header there is an arrow button which is highlighted in the following screenshot. Click it with the *LMB*.

3. Do it several times and watch the Graph Editor and the Channel Selection Panel.

What just happened?

The arrow button toggles whether only the F-Curves relating to the current object are displayed or whether the F-Curves for all visible objects are displayed. The ghost next to it allows you to display the F-Curve of objects that are not displayed.

Copying, pasting, and deleting keyframes

In addition to creating and modifying the Bézier curve control points, you can move, copy, paste, and delete them.

Time for action – copying and pasting keyframes

Keyframes like just about everything in Blender can be copied and reused. Here you will learn to copy a keyframe and place it elsewhere in an F-Curve:

1. Darken the arrow button in the **Graph Editor** and select the cube in the 3D View.

2. In the **Graph Editor**, click on the triangle next to **Location**. Click on the word **Y Location** to select the F-Curve. Select the keyframe for the Y Location at frame 20 with the RMB.

3. Press *Ctrl+C* to copy the keyframe.

4. Move the current frame indicator to frame 14. Press *Ctrl+V* to paste the keyframe.

5. Press *X* to delete the keyframe you copied. Press *Ctrl+Z* to undo the deletion.

What just happened?

You discovered how to copy and paste keyframes in the Graph Editor. *Ctrl+C* and *Ctrl+V* are the same commands as PC or Linux machines use to copy and paste. Then you deleted the keyframe. *X* is the key to press to delete things in Blender. And finally you discovered that *Ctrl+Z* undoes the last command.

Keyframes for properties

You can move the lights and camera and make keyframes for them just as you did for the cube. In fact, Blender allows you to set keyframes for almost every property. You sure didn't see them in the drop-down menu, so where are they?

Time for action – keyframes for lights

Next we'll look at making keyframes when in the **Properties** window, ones for light color specifically:

1. Move the Current Frame Indicator to frame 1.

2. Click on the *RMB* to select the lamp in the 3D View. Select the **Object Data** button in the header of the **Properties** window. It's the seventh button from the left with the lamp, as shown in the following screenshot:

3. Down in the **Lamp** subpanel, there is the white box that you used to change the lamp color earlier. Move the cursor over that box and Press *I* to insert a keyframe. There is no menu, but the white box gets a border. In the **Graph Editor** you now see a control curve for the lamp.

4. In the **Graph Editor**, move the **Current Frame Indicator** to **frame 20**.

5. In the **Lamp** subpanel of the **Properties** window, make the light a different color. The white box changes color. With the cursor over the box, press the *I* key to insert another keyframe. You will see the new keyframe appear in the **Graph Editor** as well.

6. If your **3D View** window is set to **Texture mode**, you can see the color change.

7. Press *Alt+A* to preview the animation.

What just happened?

You discovered that not all the keyframes get created in the 3D View or the Graph Editor. You also discovered that many properties can be animated. You learned how to set keyframes for the color of the light and how to observe it while previewing it by putting the 3D View into Texture mode.

For your reference, the file `6907_03_keyframes for lights.blend` shows the keyframes created for changing the light color.

Have a go hero – adding more keyframes

You have done very well. You can control the cube, the camera, and the light. You can make keyframes, you can copy objects, and you can control the length of the animation:

♦ Using these skills make three animations; one of 30 frames, one of 60 frames, and one of 90 frames in length

♦ Use the camera composition guides to help you plan your shots

When you are satisfied with each animation, save the Blender file to a unique name. Take your time and have fun.

Key	Function
Object Manipulation	
RMB	Selects an object.
Shift+RMB	Selects a new item while keeping previously selected items selected.
G	Grabs an object to move it.
S	Scales an object.
R	Rotates an object.
G X	Grabs an object and moves it along the X axis.
G Y	Grabs an object and moves it along the Y axis.
G Z	Grabs and object and moves it along the Z axis.
S X	Scales an object along the X axis.

Key	Function
S Y	Scales an object along the Y axis.
S Z	Scales an object along the Z axis.
R X	Rotates an object around the X axis.
R Y	Rotates an object around the Y axis.
R Z	Rotates an object around the Z axis.
G X 1	Moves an object one unit along the X axis.
S Z 2	Scales an object along the Z axis to twice its former size.
R Y 180	Rotates an object 180 degrees around the Y axis.
X	If tapped while moving, rotating, or scaling, restricts the operation to the X axis.
Y	If tapped while moving, rotating or scaling, restricts the operation to the Y axis.
Z	If tapped while moving, rotating, or scaling, restricts the operation to the Z axis.
Shift+A	Opens up **Add object** menu.
Shift+D	Duplicates an object.

Rendering	
F12	Renders current frame.
F11	Displays last rendered frame.
Ctrl+F12	Renders entire animation.
Ctrl+F11	Displays rendered animation.
Esc	When over a rendered image, closes image display.

Files	
Shift+Ctrl+S	Opens **File Editor** for saving files
F2	Opens **File Editor** for saving files

Graph Editor Commands	
MMB	In Graph Editor it moves the view.
Mouse wheel	In Graph Editor it scales the view.
Shift+MMB	In Graph Editor it moves the view.
Ctrl+MMB	In Graph Editor it scales the view.
Right arrow	Move one frame forward.
Left arrow	Move one frame back.

Key	Function
Up arrow	Go to the next keyframe.
Down arrow	Go to the previous keyframe.
Shift+Right arrow	Go to the end of the animation.
Shift+Left arrow	Go to the beginning of the animation.
Shift+Up arrow	Move 10 frames forward.
Shift+Down arrow	Move 10 frames back.
I	Opens the keyframe menu or creates a keyframe if no menu is needed.
V	Sets keyframe handle type.
V F	Free handles are independent.
V V	Vector handles point to the previous or next handle.
V A	Aligned handles lie in a straight line and give a continuous curve.
V U	Automatically chooses length and direction to ensure the smoothest result.
V C	Restores default handle settings.
Shift+D	Creates a duplicate.
Ctrl+C	Copies.
Ctrl+V	Pastes.
X	Deletes objects, keyframes, and so on.
Delete	Deletes objects, keyframes, and so on.

General	
Ctrl+Z	Undoes last operation.
Home	Zooms to show you all the objects in the Graph Editor or 3D View.
Shift+Alt+LMB	Pans view same as *Shift+MMB*.
Ctrl+Alt+LMB	Zooms view, same as *Ctrl+MMB*.

A more complete list of keyboard shortcuts can be found at `http://blendertips.com/hotkeys.html`.

Summary

Wow, that was quite a chapter. In it, you studied how light affects the scene. You practiced setting the lights in different locations and changed the light colors as well as experimenting with using multiple lights. You learned about using global and local coordinates to control objects and learned to move, rotate, and scale objects. We discussed composing an image within the camera. You learned about keyframes, made several animations, and learned about using the Graph Editor to adjust F-Curves. You also learned how to save your work.

In the next chapter, you will start modeling objects. You will get under the hood and find out what a mesh object is made of. You'll be able to control every last point, edge, and face. You will discover Blender's menu of pre-made objects. You'll meet Suzanne, Blender's very lovely mascot, and have fun stretching and twisting her. You'll learn how to use grouping to make it easy to do what you want and then you'll be ready to start making your own models.

Let's go!

4

Modeling with Vertices, Edges, and Faces

Well, that was quite a chapter. You learned how to control the camera and other objects. You learned the basics of using lights. You created animations by making and adjusting key frames. You learned how to save and load files.

In 3D, every model from futuristic cities to prehistoric dinosaurs depend on what we will study in this chapter. The vertex, the edge, and the face provide the foundation for all the mesh models, and you will be learning how to construct and manipulate them, giving you the background you need to build objects in **Blender**. *You will use your knowledge of operating the 3D View window.*

You will learn about the following topics:

◆ Using **Object Mode** and **Edit Mode** for modeling

◆ Selecting and manipulating vertices, edges, and faces

◆ Blender's basic geometric solids for modeling

◆ Creating vertices, edges, and faces from scratch

◆ Blender's data structure that underlies the model

Using Object Mode and Edit Mode

Until now, when you worked in the 3D View, you were in **Object Mode**. When you moved, rotated, or scaled an object, you did it to the entire object. This chapter is going to focus on **Edit Mode**, working at the sub object level with vertices, edges, and faces. Mesh models are the ones made with vertices, edges, and faces.

Time for action – going into Edit Mode

The difference between **Object mode** and **Edit Mode** is a little confusing at first. You look at the cube, and it's hard to tell which mode is which. But don't worry, you'll get the hang of it quickly enough.

1. Open up Blender, or select **New** from the **File** menu. Zoom into the cube, so that it fills up most of the 3D View. You are going to look at it in more detail.

2. Now press the *Tab* key. Press it several times. Note the changes in the 3D View, and the changes in the 3D View header.

What just happened?

You opened up Blender, and zoomed into the default cube. Then, you pressed the *Tab* key to go into **Edit Mode**. **Edit Mode** lets you modify parts of an object; the vertices, edges, and faces.

Both, **Object Mode** and **Edit Mode**, are shown here. In **Edit Mode**, you see dots at every corner of the cube, and all the edges of the cube are highlighted in orange. In the header, the **Mode Selector** button changes from **Object Mode** to **Edit Mode**, and some of the buttons change. Observe the **Mode Selector** button as seen in the left-hand side of following image, if you get confused about which mode you are in.

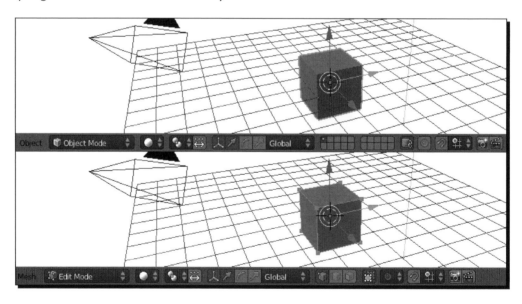

Investigating vertices, edges, and faces

Vertices, edges, and faces are the basic building blocks of the 3D mesh objects. A **vertex** is a point in space. The plural of vertex is vertices, pronounced (ver-tuh-seas), and is used when talking about two or more points in space. You describe a point by the X, Y, and Z coordinates, as we discussed in *Chapter 2, Getting Comfortable using the 3D View*. An **edge** is a line between two vertices. A **face** is the flat area or plane between three or four vertices, outlined by edges that connect between those vertices, as shown here. It is also referred to as a **polygon**. The following graphic shows them all together:

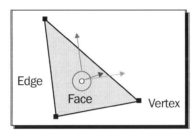

In the next illustration, I will show the default cube, so that you can see how the vertices, edges, and faces are used in a solid object. For illustration purposes, I went into **User Preferences**, and made the vertex and the dot in the center of the face display as large as possible.

On the left-hand side of the image, you can see the vertices and a bordered dot that represents the center of the cube. There are eight vertices. The four lighter ones have been selected. The black ones have not. In the center image, only the edges are shown, and there are 12 of them. Each of the lighter edges goes between the two selected vertices. The faces are shown in the right image. They have a dot in the center of each face, and there are six faces. Only the lighter face with a lighter edge and lighter face dot are associated with all the selected vertices.

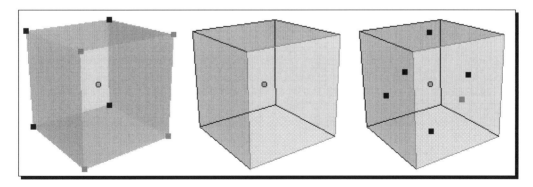

Time for action – choosing the best display mode

The **Viewport Shading** menu is in the header of the 3D View window. It lets you choose between the different methods of shading the objects displayed. While you may want the **Texture** display when you need to show an object's appearance, quite often, the **Solid** and **Wireframe** views will be best for modeling:

1. Use the *Tab* key to get into **Edit Mode** in the 3D View, if you are not already. If you are unsure, look at the button on the header near the left-hand side of the 3D View window. It will say either **Object Mode** or **Edit Mode**.

2. Move the cursor to the **Viewport Shading** menu, as seen in the next image. It's the same one that you used to change the mode to the **Textured** mode, when you were playing with the lighting.

3. Now, select **Wireframe** mode. What is different about the 3D View?

What just happened?

You changed the Viewport Shading in the 3D View to Wireframe. Now, the cube is transparent, and you can see all the vertices and edges. When you are working in **Edit Mode**, this is often the easiest way to work. The differences are deeper than just visual. In **Wireframe**, you can see and select all the vertices, edges, and faces, but the **Solid** mode lets you choose all the vertices, edges, and faces, or just the ones facing you.

Time for action – working with vertices, edges, or faces

In the 3D View header, to the right of where you choose whether you are in the **Global** or the **Local** mode, there are three boxes, as seen in the following screenshot. The left one has an orange dot next to a cube. It is the **Vertex Select Mode** button. The center one has an orange vertical line next to a cube. It is the **Edge Select Mode** button. The right one has an orange parallelogram on a cube. It is the **Face Select Mode** button. They control whether you are selecting vertices, edges, or faces.

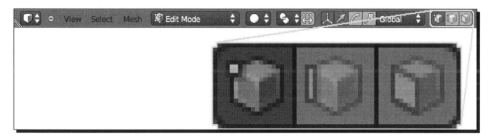

1. Use the *Tab* key to get into **Edit Mode** in the 3D View, if you are not already.

2. In the 3D View window, click on one of the vertices of the cube with the *RMB*. Press the *G* key, and move the vertex. Press the *RMB* to release the vertex where it began.

3. Press the *G* key, and move the vertex. Press the *LMB* to release the vertex where you have moved it.

4. In the 3D View header, click the *LMB* over the **Edge Select Mode** button—the box with the orange vertical line.

5. In the 3D View window, click on one of the edges of the cube with the *RMB*. Press the *G* key, and move the edge. Press the *RMB* to release it where it began.

6. Press the *G* key, and move the edge. Press the *LMB* to release the edge where you have moved it

7. In the 3D View header, click on the *LMB* over the box with the orange parallelogram.

8. In the 3D View window, click on in the center of one of the faces of the cube with the *RMB*, and move the face. Press the *RMB* to release it where it began.

9. Press the *G* key, and move the face. Press the *LMB* to release the edge where you have moved it.

What just happened?

You found out how to control whether you are working on vertices, edges, or faces. You discovered that you can use the same controls to move vertices, edges, and faces that you use to move whole objects.

Have a go hero – rotating and scaling edges and faces

Now, try rotating and scaling the faces and the edges; you can use the same commands. Instead of *G*, press *R* to rotate, or *S* to scale. I did not ask you to rotate or scale vertices because, having no size, they cannot be rotated or scaled.

Selecting multiple vertices, edges, and faces

It's easy to select one vertex. But when you are working with many vertices, you will want tools to make it easier. The following image illustrates some of the selection tools that you'll check out next: the border selection tool, the circle selection tool, and the lasso selection tool.

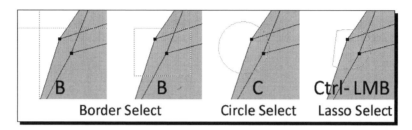

Time for action – pressing A to select all

Pressing the *A* key to select all the vertices is the easiest selection to do. It selects all the vertices, or deselects them if they are all selected. It's often used to clear the current selection, so that you can choose a different set of vertices:

1. Click on the **Vertex Select Mode** button in the 3D View header button with the *LMB*, so that you can work with vertices.

2. Press the *A* key several times.

What just happened?

Pressing the *A* key either selects or deselects everything. You worked with vertices, but this applies to edges, faces, and objects as well. If you look just above the 3D View window on the right as you do it, Blender shows you how many vertices you have selected.

Time for action – pressing B for border selection

The border selection works similar to the **Marquee tool** in Flash or Photoshop, stretching a border around the vertices you want to select:

1. Press the *A* key, once or twice, so that everything is deselected.

2. Move your cursor above and to the left of the cube.

3. Press the *B* key. Notice that the cursor has become dotted—crossed lines as on the left-hand side of the previous illustration.

4. Hold down the *LMB* while you drag the cursor down and to the right. Any vertices within the border will be selected when you release the *LMB*. Just select the vertices on the left side.

5. Press the *B* key again. Make another selection, but start at the bottom-right, and move to the top.

6. Now press the *B* key, move over vertices you have already selected, and press the *MMB* as you drag the cursor.

What just happened?

The *B* key starts the Border selection. You hold down the *LMB* while you drag the cursor. All the vertices within the border box get selected. Each time you do the border selection, vertices are added to the vertices already selected. It doesn't matter which way you go, as long as you create a box around the vertices that you want to select. If you hold down the MMB while doing this, you deselect vertices.

Time for action – pressing C for circle selection

The circle selector gives you a circular cursor to use in selecting vertices, edges, faces, and objects. The selection with the circle selector is cumulative. So, using it adds to the vertices that have been selected:

1. Press the *A* key to deselect everything.

2. Press the *C* key. Notice the circle around the cursor. Click the *LMB* over vertices to select them. You can also hold down the *LMB* as you move the mouse to select more vertices.

3. To stop the selection, either click the *RMB* or the *Esc* key.

4. Press the *C* key again. Hold down the *MMB* while moving over previously selected vertices.

What just happened?

You learned about using the *C* key to initiate the selection of vertices, by holding down the *LMB* and dragging the cursor, or clicking the *LMB*. You learned to press the *RMB* or the *Esc* key when you are done. Pressing the *MMB* instead of the *LMB* after pressing the *C* key deselects vertices.

Time for action – pressing Ctrl+LMB for lasso selection

1. Press the *A* key, once or twice, so that everything is deselected.

2. Press the *Ctrl* button, and hold it down. Hold the *LMB* down, and drag the cursor around the screen. When you have put the border around the vertices you want to select, release the *LMB*.

3. Pres the *Ctrl* button and the *Shift* button, and hold them down. Hold down the *LMB* while you drag the cursor over vertices you have already selected.

What just happened?

You learned to do a lasso selection by holding down the *Ctrl* button and the *LMB*, while moving the cursor around the vertices that you want to select. Pressing the *Shift* button and the *Ctrl* button, while holding down the *LMB*, deselects anything within the lasso area.

A warning about *Ctrl+LMB*

You need to be careful to not hold down the *Ctrl* key, and just click and release the *LMB* without moving the cursor. This will extrude the selected vertices. However, if it happens, you can easily undo it by pressing *Ctrl+Z*.

Pop quiz – making selections

Now, a quick check on what you have learned about selecting vertices.

1. Which key do you press to do a border select?

    a. A

    b. B

    c. C

2. How do you deselect with the Circle selection tool?

    a. *C + MMB*

    b. *C + RMB*

    c. *C + LMB*

Creating Blender's basic objects

You've done well in learning how to select vertices, edges, and faces. As a change up, let's start out by looking at the ready-made objects that Blender has, which you can use as a start for modeling. In *Chapter 2, Getting Comfortable using the 3D View* I listed the different kinds of objects that Blender handles. Now, you will create them yourself. The pre-made ones are called Blender's **Basic Objects**. You make them in the 3D View. They will be created wherever the 3D cursor is.

Time for action – making a basic object

Well, you're not really making it; Blender will make it for you. But now is a good time to briefly look at what is available.

1. Open up Blender, or select **New** from the **File** menu. You already have our first basic object, the cube.

2. Press *Ctrl+MMB*, and use the mouse to zoom in close to the cube, so that you can see it well.

3. Press the *X* key to delete the default cube.

4. Now, you can make a new object. Press the *Shift* key and the *A* key at the same time. The **Add Object** menu will pop up, as seen in the following screenshot. There are quite a few kinds of objects that you can add, from **Meshes** and **Metaballs**, through to **Text** or **Cameras**. So, to start by making a mesh object, move the cursor over **Mesh**, then select **Plane** with the *LMB*.

5. You just made a plane. It can be a building block for a larger object, used as the ground or the surface of the ocean.

6. Press the *X* key to delete the plane.

7. Press *Shift+A* to open up the **Add** menu, and select the circle. The circle has no face, but if you look over on the **Tool Shelf** on the left side of the 3D View, there are buttons that will let you add vertices, and change the size of the circle.

8. Press the *X* key to delete the circle.

9. Press *Shift+A* to open up the **Add** menu, and select the **UV Sphere**. The UV Sphere looks similar to longitude and latitude lines on a globe. In the **Tool Shelf**, you will find buttons to change how many faces the **UV Sphere** has, and its size.

10. Press the *X* key to delete the **UV Sphere**.

11. Press *Shift+A* to open up the **Add** menu, and select the **Icosphere**. The **Icosphere** is a mathematical solid like the cube. With the subdivisions set to 1, it is an icosahedron.

12. Press the *X* key to delete the **Icosphere**.

13. Press *Shift+A* to open up the **Add** menu, and select the **Cylinder**. It can have ends to make a can or column, or no ends to create a tube.

14. Press the *X* key to delete the **Cylinder**.

15. Press *Shift+A* to open up the **Add** menu, and select the **Cone**. Another mathematical solid, its beauty has been admired since the time of the ancient Greeks, and is used in modeling everything from pencils to rockets.

16. Press the *X* key to delete the **Cone**.

17. Press *Shift+A* to open up the **Add** menu, and select the **Grid**. It looks a lot like the plane, but there are buttons in **Tool Shelf** to subdivide it. It's good for making ground with a little more unevenness than a plane and lots of other things.

18. Press the *X* key to delete the **Grid**.

19. Press *Shift+A* to open up the **Add** menu, and select the **Torus**. Another mathematical solid. The **Torus** has more controls than other objects so you can control how the radius of the major and minor dimensions. It's good for making everything from an eyelet earring for a pirate to an old-school space station design from the 1950s; and doughnuts.

What just happened?

You started off by deleting the default cube and using the *Shift+A* command to open up the **Add Object** menu. In this chapter, you are working with the mesh objects, so you went to the Mesh object sub menu. You could see the list of geometric basic objects that come with Blender, including cones, cylinders, spheres, and so on.

> This is just a brief introduction to using vertices, edges, and faces. For an in-depth introduction, I recommend you get the file `6907_04_Making Precise Selections.pdf` from the download pack. It gives you practical exercises in using vertices, edges, and faces and untangling problems you might encounter, advanced methods to do scaling and rotation to achieve better results as well as an introduction to grouping to make modeling easier.

Understanding what lies behind vertices, edges, and faces

You are progressing well. You've learned to navigate in the Blender world. You've learned to translate, rotate, and scale objects in the Blender world. You've learned to open up the object, and translate, rotate, and scale vertices, edges, and faces. You're really digging into Blender.

It's good to have an idea of how Blender sees your scene as well. The following graphic illustrates how the information is arranged in Blender. What you see are little boxes connected together, and that's how Blender is organized.

♦ So, the **Scene** is just a little box of information called a **data block** with a few bits of information about what objects it is connected to. It has a link to each object.

♦ The object is just a box called a data block. It has a little information about which faces, edges, vertices, and other things that it is connected to and links to them.

♦ As you have probably guessed, each face is a data block with a little information about say which texture it is connected to, and a link to the data block of that texture. The process goes on.

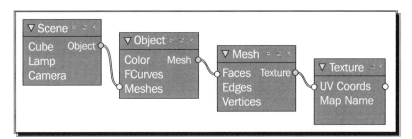

This structure has important benefits. You can make a texture once, and any mesh that needs that texture uses it. When you make a change to the texture, all the mesh objects that use that texture show that change. If you move or rotate an object, it tells all the faces what is happening. You don't have to keep track of it.

Keep this image in mind as you study Blender. It will help you understand Blender, and toward the end of the book, in the Node Editor, you will meet some tools that look much like the connections here.

Building vertices, edges, and faces from scratch

We've played with faces, edges, and vertices. But, sometimes you need to make them yourself, and that's what this section is about. For flexibility and power, nothing can touch this technique, and it introduces you to the methods used to modify and refine your objects.

Time for action – making faces out of vertices and edges

The most fundamental unit of a mesh object is the vertex. So, now you are going to make a vertex, and when you make a second one, the two will be connected by an edge. Then, you continue until you have enough vertices for a face.

1. Load a new file.

2. Press *7* on the Numpad to get the **Top View**.

3. Press the *Tab* key to edit the cube.

4. Press *A* to select all the vertices. Press *X* to delete them.

5. Look in the lower left corner of the 3D View window. It still shows that the active object is the cube. Only the data block of the cube remains. It has no connections to any vertices, edges, or faces. You deleted them. But, to delete the cube itself, you would still need to press *X* while in Object. Don't do that.

6. Click the **3D Manipulator** button in the 3D View header, so that the 3D Manipulator icon does not show up in the 3D View.

7. Hold down the *Ctrl* key, and click the *LMB* somewhere to the left and above the 3D Cursor to create a vertex.

8. Press *Ctrl+LMB* three more times in different locations moving in a clockwise direction around the 3D Cursor. Use the *RMB* and then *Shift+RMB* to select the first and last vertices at the end of your edges. Press *F* to join them.

9. Use the *RMB* and then *Shift+RMB* to select three vertices. Press *F* to make a face, as shown on the left of the following illustration.

10. Press *Shift+RMB* on the vertex that is farthest from the vertex without a face, as seen in the center image. This will deselect it. Select the vertex without a face. Press *F* to make the other face as seen on the right.

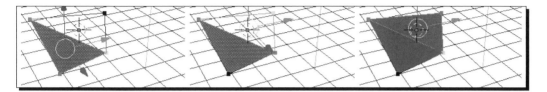

What just happened?

You started with a fresh file, went into **Edit Mode**, and immediately deleted all of the vertices, leaving only the data block as a placeholder. This is because Blender needs an object to toggle between the **Edit Mode** and **Object Mode**, You made four vertices and edges between them using the *Ctrl+RMB* clicks. You controlled how far up and how far over the vertices appeared within the top view. Since you cannot judge the depth from the top view, Blender put them all on the same z depth as the 3D cursor.

Then, you joined the first and last vertices together, by selecting them and pressing the *F* key. Finally, you made a face by selecting three vertices and pressing *F*. The *F* key makes both edges and faces, depending on how many vertices you are connecting. When it does, the front of the face it made is visible to you, and the back of the face is facing away.

Finally, you saved yourself a little selecting work by unselecting one vertex, selecting another one, and then pressing *F*. This was quicker than selecting all the vertices every time you want to make a face.

> For your reference, the file 6907_04_making faces.blend, which has been included in the download pack, has the vertices and one face created.

Time for action – making a face from an edge

This short exercise will introduce you to what some 3D modelers have called the most powerful tool available to modelers, the humble extrusion.

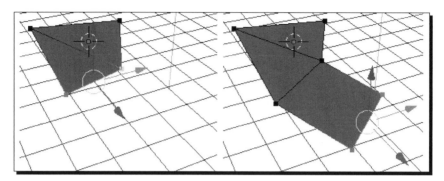

1. Select two vertices along the bottom side of the shape you made, as shown here on the left.

2. Press the *E* key, and use the mouse to create another face as shown on the right.

What just happened?

We discovered that if you press the *E* key when you have two vertices selected in **Edit Mode**, then Blender will create a new face. This is called an **extrusion**. The last two *Time for action* sections seem too simple perhaps. You built a face, and extruded another from it. But, this is often how modelers create objects, such as automobiles, which often have fluid lines and no definite edges for much of their surface. Making faces and extruding them, you can make just about anything.

For your reference, the file 6907_04_making a face from an edge.blend, which has been included in the download pack, has the face being created from an edge.

Key	Function
Mode	
Tab	Toggles between the **Edit Mode** and the **Object Mode**.
Ctrl+Tab	When you are in **Edit Mode**, this opens the **Mesh Select Mode** menu, allowing you to choose to work in vertex, edge, or face mode.
Selection	
A	Select/deselect all.
B	Border select, use *LMB* while selecting.
B	Border deselect, use *MMB* while deselecting.
C	Circle select, use *LMB* while selecting.
C	Circle deselect, use *MMB* while deselecting.
Ctrl+LMB	Lasso select.
Ctrl+Shift+LMB	Lasso deselect.
+	Plus sign used while doing circle select increases size of circle.
-	Minus sign used while doing circle select decreases size of circle.
H	Hides selected vertices.
Alt+H	Redisplays hidden vertices as selected vertices.
Shift+H	Hides unselected vertices.
L	Selects linked vertices.
Transformation controls	
Shift	When used with the *G, R,* or *S* keys, it limits the transformation to small increments.
Shift+Ctrl	When used with the *G* key, it limits the movement to increments of 0.1.
Shift+Ctrl	When used with the *R* key, it limits the rotation to steps of 1 degree.
Shift+Ctrl	When used with the *S* key, it limits the scaling to steps of 0.01.
Ctrl	When used with the *G* key, it limits the motion to steps of 1.
Ctrl	When used with the *R* key, it limits the rotation to steps of 5 degrees.
Ctrl	When used with the *S* key, it limits the scalings to steps of 0.1.
Shift	Press the *S* key, then *Shift+X*, and you can scale on both the Y and Z axes at the same time.
Shift	Press the *S* key, then *Shift+Y*, and you can scale on both the X and Z axes at the same time.

Key	Function
Shift	Press the *S* key, then *Shift+Z*, and you can scale on both the X and Y axes at the same time.
Shift	Choosing manipulators on the 3D View Edit Mode header allows you to display more than one manipulator in the 3D View at one time.
Shift	Choosing vertex, edge, and face selection on the 3D View Edit Mode header allows you to select several edit modes at once, that is, faces and vertices.
Shift+S	Brings up the **Snap** menu.

Faces	
F	When two vertices are selected, it creates an edge, and when three or four vertices are selected, it creates a face.
E	Extrudes a face from two vertices or an edge, and it can be used on multiple edges as well.

Summary

That was good. You learned a lot about the basic skills needed for creating and working with vertices, edges, and faces. You will be using these skills in the following chapters for building quite a variety of objects. You learned the difference between the Object Mode and Edit mode, and learned to select and manipulate multiple vertices, edges, and faces. You were introduced to Blender's basic geometric primitive objects. You got a bit of experience in troubleshooting a model, and learned how to group vertices, edges, and faces. You discovered the basic structure of Blender, and learned how to make vertices, edges, and faces from scratch.

You have covered the basics. You understand the tools, and it's time to get started applying what you have learned to a real project. Much thought has gone into choosing a good project. It seems that since the world is two-thirds ocean, and everyone has a river, lake, or sea near them, that a nautical theme would be appropriate. So, in the next chapter, you'll begin by building yourself a seaworthy little boat, launch it, and sail it through various kinds of light.

Let's go Mateys.

5
Building a Simple Boat

It's time to get out your hammers, saws, and tape measures, and start building something. In the previous chapter, you focused on the basics of building objects: how to adjust vertices, edges, and faces, how to make edges and faces from vertices, different ways to select vertices, edges, and faces, and how to group vertices, so that you can organize your work.

In this chapter, you're going to put your knowledge of building objects to practical use, as well as your knowledge of using the 3D View to build a boat. It's a simple but good-looking and water-tight craft that has three seats, as shown in the next screenshot.

You will learn about the following topics:

- ◆ Using box modeling to convert a cube into a boat
- ◆ Employing box modeling's power tools – extrusion and subdividing edges
- ◆ Joining objects together into a single object
- ◆ Adding materials to an object
- ◆ Using a texture for greater detail

Turning a cube into a boat with box modeling

You are going to turn the default Blender cube into an attractive boat, similar to the one shown in the following screenshot. First, you need to know a little bit about boats. The front is called the **bow**, and sounds like bowing to the Queen. The rear is called the **stern** or the **aft**. The main body of the boat is the **hull**, and the top of the hull is the **gunwale**, pronounced "**gunnel**".

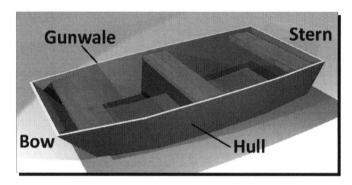

You will be using a technique called **Box Modeling** to make the boat. Box modeling is a very standard method of modeling. As you might expect from the name, you start out with a box, and sculpt it like a piece of clay to make whatever you want. There are three methods that you will use in most of the instances for box modeling: **extrusion**, **subdividing edges**, and **moving vertices**, **edges**, and **faces**.

Using extrusion, the most powerful tool in box modeling

Extrusion is similar to turning the dough into noodles, by pushing them through a die. It's very similar to how you made a face out of an edge in the previous chapter. Blender pushed out the edge, and connected it to the old edge with a face. In extruding a face, the face gets pushed out, and gets connected to the old edges by new faces.

Time for action – extruding to make the inside of the hull

The first step here is to create an inside for the hull. You will extrude the face without moving it, and shrink it a bit. This will create the basis for the gunwale:

1. Create a new file, and zoom into the default cube.

2. Select **Wireframe** from the **Viewport Shading** menu on the header, as discussed in the previous chapter.

3. Press the *Tab* key for **Edit Mode**.

4. Choose **Face Selection** mode from the header. It is the orange parallelogram, as discussed in the previous chapter.

5. Select the top face with the *RMB*.

6. Press the *E* key to extrude the face, then immediately press *Enter*.

7. Move the mouse away from the cube. Press the *S* key to scale the face with the mouse. While you are scaling it, press *Shift+Ctrl,* and scale it to 0.92. Watch the scaling readout in the 3D View header. This will be forming the hull of the boat.

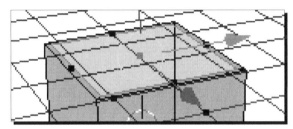

8. Press *Numpad 1* to change to the **Front view**, and press *5* on the Numpad to show the **Ortho view**. Move the cursor a little above the top of the cube.

9. Press *E*, and Blender will let you now move the new face up or down. Move it down. When you are close to the bottom, press the *Ctrl+Shift* buttons, and move it down until the readout on the 3D View header is -1.92. Click the *LMB* to release the face.

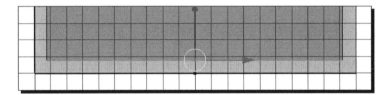

What just happened?

You just made a simple hull for your boat. It's going to look better, but at least you got the thickness of the hull established. Pressing the *E* key extrudes the face, making a new face and sides that connect the new face with the edges used by the old face. You pressed *Enter* immediately after the *E* key the first time, so that the new face wouldn't get moved. Then, you scaled it down a little to establish the thickness of the hull. Next, you extruded the face again. As you watched the readout, did you notice that it said **D: -1.9200 (1.9200) normal**? When you extrude a face, Blender is automatically set up to move the face along its normal, so that you can move it in or out, and keep it parallel with the original location.

For your reference, the file `6907_05_making the hull1.blend`, which has been included in the download pack, has the first extrusion. `6907_05_making the hull2.blend` has extrusion moved down. `6907_05_making the hull3.blend` has the bottom and sides evened out.

Using normals in 3D modeling

What is a normal? The **normal** is an unseen line that is perpendicular to a face. This is illustrated in the following image by the red line:

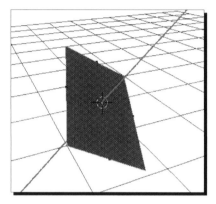

Blender has many uses for the normal.

◆ It lets use Blender to extrude a face, and keep the extruded face in the same orientation as the face it was extruded from

◆ This also keeps the sides straight, and it tells Blender in which direction a face is pointing

◆ Blender can also use the normal to calculate how much light a particular face receives from a given lamp, and in which direction lights are pointed

Modeling tip

If you make a 3D model, it seems perfect except that there is this unexplained hole where a face should be. You may have a normal facing backwards. To help you, Blender can display the normals for you.

Time for action – displaying normals

Displaying the normals does not affect the model, but sometimes it can help you in your modeling to see just in which way your faces are pointing.

1. Press *Ctrl+MMB*, and use the mouse to zoom out, so that you can see the whole cube.

2. In the 3D View, press *N* to get the **Properties Panel**.

3. Scroll down in the **Properties Panel** till you get to the **Mesh Display** subpanel.

4. Go down to where it says **Normals:**.

5. There are two buttons like the edge select and face select buttons in the 3D View header. Click on the button with a cube and an orange rhomboid, the **Face Select** button to choose selecting the normals of the faces. Beside the **Face Select** button, you can adjust the displayed size of the normal, as shown in the following screenshot. The displayed normals are the blue lines. Set the **Normal Size** to 0.8. In the following image, I used the cube as it was just before you made the last extrusion, so that it displays the normals a little better.

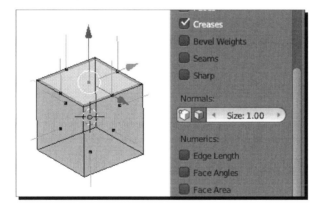

6. Press the **MMB**, use the mouse to rotate your view of the cube, and look at the normals.

What just happened?

To see the normals, you opened up the **Properties Panel**, and instructed Blender to display them. They look like little blue lines, and you can make them whatever size works best for you. Normals, themselves, have no length, but just a direction. So, changing this setting does not affect the model. It's there for your use when you need to analyze the problems, with the appearance of your model. Turn off the normal display now, if you like. To do that, just click on the **Face Select** button in the **Mesh Display** subpanel again.

For your reference, the file `6907_05_displaying normals.blend` has been included in the download pack. It has the cube with the first extrusion, and the normal display turned on.

Planning what you are going to make

It always helps to have an idea in mind of what you want to build. You don't have to get out calliper micrometers, and measure every last little detail of something you want to model, but you should at least have some pictures as reference, or an idea of the actual dimensions of the object that you are trying to model. There are many ways to get these dimensions, and we are going to use several of these as we build our boats.

Choosing which units to model in

I went on the Internet and found the dimensions of a small jonboat for fishing. A boat like this is often carried or towed by larger boats. You are not going to copy it exactly, but knowing what size it should be will make the proportions that you choose more convincing. As it happened, it was an American boat, and the size was given in feet and inches.

Blender supports three kinds of units for measuring distance: **Blender units**, **Metric units**, and **Imperial units**. Blender units are not tied to any specific measurement in the real world as Metric and Imperial units are. To change the units of measurement, go to the **Properties** window, as shown in the following image, and choose the third button from the left in the header. It shows a sun, a sphere, and a cylinder. It is the **Scene** button. In the second sub panel down, the **Units** sub panel lets you select which units you prefer. But, rather than choosing between **Metric** or **Imperial**, I decided to leave things in the default Blender units.

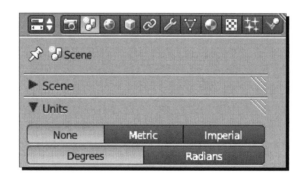

Since the measurements that I found were Imperial measurements, I chose to interpret the Imperial measurements as Blender measurements, equating 1 foot to 1 Blender unit, and each inch as 0.083 Blender units. If I have an Imperial measurement that is expressed in inches, I just divide it by 12 to get the correct number in Blender units.

The boat I found on the Internet is 9 feet and 10 inches long, 56 inches wide at the top, 44 inches wide at the bottom, and 18 inches high. I converted them to decimal Blender units or 9.830 long, 4.666 wide at the top, 3.666 wide at the bottom, and 1.500 high.

Time for action – making reference objects

One of the simplest ways to see what size your boat should be is to have boxes of the proper size to use as guides. So now, you will make some.

1. In the 3D View window, press the *Tab* key to get into **Object Mode**. Press *A* to deselect the boat.

2. Press *Numpad 3* to get the side view.

3. Create a cube. Press *Shift+A*, and choose **Cube** off the menu. You will use this as a reference block for the size of the boat.

4. In the 3D View window **Properties** panel, **Transform** sub panel, click on the **Dimensions** button, and change the dimensions for the reference block to 4.666 in the X direction, 9.83 in Y, and 1.5 in the Z direction. You can use the *Tab* key to go from X to Y to Z, and press *Enter* when you are done.

5. Move the mouse over the 3D View window, then press *Shift+D* to duplicate the block. Then press *Enter*.

6. Press *Numpad 1* to get the front view.

7. Press *G* and *Z* to move this block down, so it's top is in the lower-half of the first one. Press *S*, *X*, and then the number 0.79, then *Enter*. This will scale it to 79 percent along the X axis. Look at the readout. It will show you what is happening. This will represent the width at the bottom of the hull.

8. Press the *MMB*, and rotate the view to see what it looks like.

What just happened?

To make accurate models, it helps to have references. For the boat you are building, you don't need to copy another boat exactly, and the basic dimensions are enough. You got out of **Edit mode**, and deselected the boat so that you could work on something else, without affecting the boat. Then, you made a cube, and scaled it to the dimensions of the boat for the top of the hull to use as a reference block. You then copied the reference block, and scaled the copy down in X for the width of the boat at the bottom of the hull as shown in the following image:

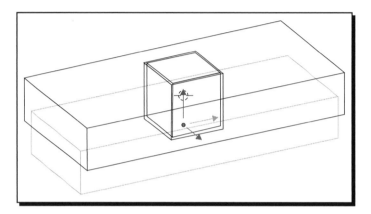

 For your reference, the file `6907_05_making reference objects.blend` has been included in the download pack. It has the cube and the two reference blocks.

Sizing the boat to the reference blocks

Now that the reference blocks have been made, you can use them to guide you when making the boat.

Time for action – making the boat the proper length

Now that you've made the reference blocks the right size, it's time to make the boat the same dimensions as the blocks.

1. Change to the side view by pressing *Numpad 3*, and check in the upper-right corner of the 3D View window to make sure you are in **Ortho mode**. Press *Numpad 5* if you are in **Persp** mode. Use *Ctrl+MMB*, and the mouse to zoom in, until the reference blocks fill almost all of the 3D View. Use *Shift+MMB* and the mouse to re-center the reference blocks.

2. Select the boat with the *RMB*. Press the *Tab* key to go into **Edit Mode**, and then choose the **Vertex Select mode** button from the 3D View header.

3. Press *A* to deselect all vertices. Then, select the boat's vertices on the right-hand side of the 3D View. Press *B* to use the border select, or press *C* to use the circle select mode, or *Ctrl+LMB* for the lasso select, as discussed in the previous chapter. When the vertices are selected, press *G* and *Y* and move the vertices to the right with the mouse till they are lined up with the right-hand side of the reference blocks. Press the *LMB* to drop the vertices in place.

4. Press *A* to deselect all the vertices, select the boat's vertices on the left-hand side of the 3D View, and move them to the left until they are lined up with the left-hand side of the reference blocks, as seen in the following image.

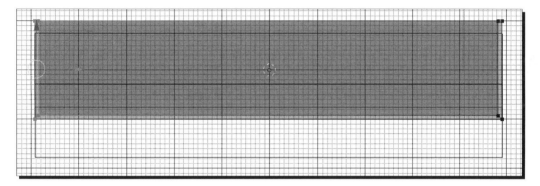

What just happened?

You made sure that the screen was properly set up for working by getting into the side view in **Ortho mode**. Next, you selected the boat, got into **Edit Mode**, and got ready to move the vertices. Then, you made the boat the proper length, by moving the vertices so that they lined up with the reference blocks.

> For your reference, the file `6907_05_proper length.blend` has been included in the download pack. It has the bow and stern properly sized.

Time for action – making the boat the proper width and height

Making the boat the right length was pretty easy. The width and height take a few more steps, but it's very similar.

1. Press *Numpad 1* to change to the front view. Use *Ctrl+MMB* to zoom into the reference blocks. Use *Shift+MMB* to re-center the boat so that you can see all of it.

2. Press *A* to deselect all the vertices and, using any method discussed in the previous chapter, select all of the vertices on the left of the 3D View.

3. Press *G* and *X* to move the left-side vertices in x, till they line up with the wider reference block, as shown in the following image:

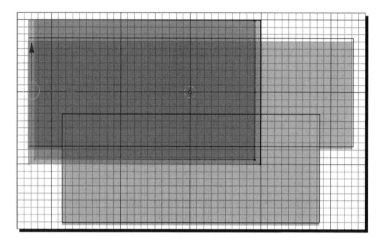

4. Press *A* to deselect all the vertices. Select only the right-hand vertices with a method different from the one you used to select the left-hand vertices, and press *G and* X to move them in x, till they line up with the right side of the wider reference block.

5. Deselect all the vertices, select only the top vertices, and press *G* and *Z* to move them in the Z direction, till they line up with the top of the wider reference block.

6. Deselect all the vertices. Now, select only the bottom vertices, and press *G* and *Z* to move them in the Z direction, till they line up with the bottom of the wider reference block as shown in the following image:

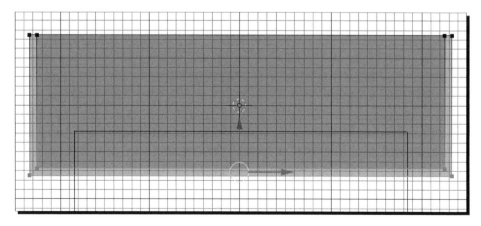

7. Deselect all the vertices. Next, select only the bottom vertices on the left. Press *G* and *X* to move them in X, till they line up with the narrower reference block.

8. Finally, deselect all the vertices, and select only the bottom vertices on the right. Press *G* and *X* to move them in X, till they line up with the narrower reference block, as shown in the following image:

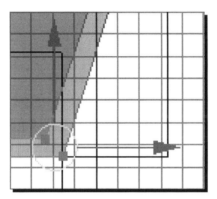

9. Press *Numpad 3* to switch to the **Side** view again. Use *Ctrl+MMB* to zoom out if you need to. Press A to deselect all the vertices. Select only the bottom vertices on the right, as in the following illustration. You are going to make this the stern end of the boat. Press *G* and *Y* to move them left in Y just a little bit, just so that the stern is not completely straight up and down.

10. Now, select only the bottom vertices on the left, as highlighted in the following illustration. Make this the bow end of the boat. Move them right in Y just a little bit. Go a bit further than the stern, so that the angle is similar to the right side, as shown here, maybe about 1.3 or 1.4. It's your call.

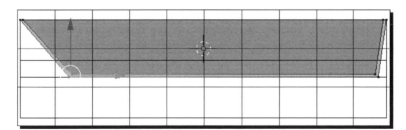

What just happened?

You used the reference blocks to guide yourself in moving the vertices into the shape of a boat. You adjusted the width, the height, and angled the hull. Finally, you angled the stern and the bow. It floats, but it's still a bit boxy.

For your reference, the file `6907_05_proper width and height1.blend` has been included in the download pack. It has both sides aligned with the wider reference block. `6907_05_proper width and height2.blend` has the bottom vertices aligned to the narrower reference block. `6907_05_proper width and height3.blend` has the bow and stern finished.

Pop quiz – figuring out the best way to build the boat

You made the boat by extruding the faces first, then adjusting the vertices to fit your reference blocks. Could you have made the boat by making it the correct size first and then extruding faces to make the inside of the hull? Would it be easier or more difficult?

Time for action – adding curves to the boat's lines by subdividing

You've discovered two of box-modeling's most powerful tools: extrusion and moving vertices. Now, it's time to discover the third one: subdividing. Now, the hull will begin to look like a boat.

1.   Press *A* to deselect all vertices.

2.   Select **Edge Select mode** on the 3D View header.

3.   Press *B* to do a Border select to select the edges of the sides of the boat, but not the bow or the stern, as seen in the following image:

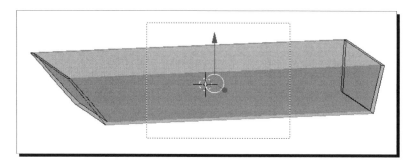

4.   Press *W* to get the **Specials** menu. Select **Subdivide** with the *LMB*.

5. On the left, in the **Tool Shelf**, a sub panel is labeled **Subdivide**. Make sure that the arrow next to the word **Subdivide** is pointing down. Change the **Number of Cuts** to 3. Blender will cut each of the edges into three as shown in the following image:

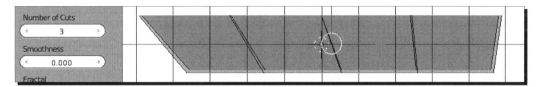

6. Change to **Vertex Select** mode in the 3D View header.

7. Deselect all the vertices. Select the vertices of the bow on the left.

8. Press *Numpad 7* to change to the **Top** view. Use the *Ctrl+MMB*, *Shift+MMB*, and the mouse to zoom and pan, so that you can see the whole boat.

9. Scale the vertices in the X direction, so that the outside of the hull is about as wide as the narrow reference block, as seen in the next illustration.

10. Deselect all the vertices. Now, select the next set of vertices as shown in the following image. Scale them in X to give the boat a bit of curve.

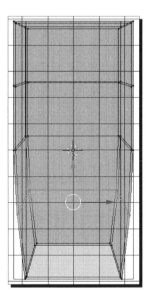

11. Deselect all the vertices. Select the vertices on the top, and scale them a little in X to add a bit of curve to the stern.

12. Press the *Tab* key to get into **Object Mode**. Press *A* to deselect the boat. Press *Numpad 1* to get the front view. Select the two reference blocks with the *RMB* for the first one, and then *Shift+RMB* for the second.

13. Press *M* to bring up the **Move to Layer** menu, as shown in the following image. There are twenty small buttons in groups of five. The upper left square is dark. Click on the LMB on the square to the right of the dark square. This will move the reference cubes to layer two, out of view.

14. Save the file to a unique name.

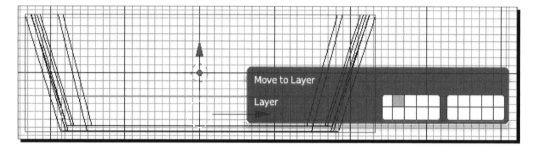

What just happened?

Now, you have put a little art into your modeling. There were no hard measurements to set the width of the boat to, so you just had to use your artistic flair. You subdivided the sides of the hull by 3, and scaled the vertices to give the boat a little curve. You finished off with a discovery about Blender's layers. The Blender layers let you control the visibility of objects.

For your reference, the file `6907_05_adding curve1.blend` has been included in the download pack. It has the sides subdivided. `6907_05_adding curve2.blend` has the sides curved as seen from the top. `6907_05_adding curve3.blend` is the completed hull.

Have a go hero – adding a curve to the profile of the hull

As you can see in the next image, the boat has a little curve in its hull on the bottom and a very subtle one on the top. Try doing that for your boat.

Move the vertices to give it some nice lines similar to the following image. When you are happy with them, be sure to rotate the view, and check the boat from all sides to make sure she looks good from all angles.

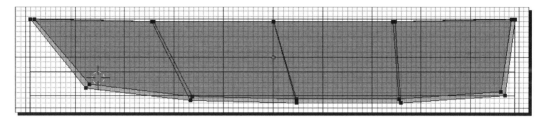

The finished boat should look something similar to the following image. Well done!

1. Press *A* to deselect all vertices.
2. Save the file with a unique name.

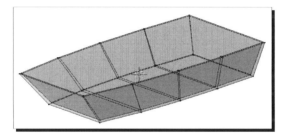

Have a go hero – adding a V-shape to the hull

Now is a chance for you to use the subdivide command to point the bow. The boat will be a little faster if you subdivide the hull end-to-end, add a bit of a "V" shape to the bottom of the hull, and a point to the bow. The next image will give you a hint.

Get the front view, and set the **Mesh Select** mode to **Edge Select**. Select only the edges running across the center of the boat.

1. Press *W* to get the **Subdivide** menu.
2. Change to **Vertex Select mode** in the header.
3. Select and move the vertices.
4. Save the file.

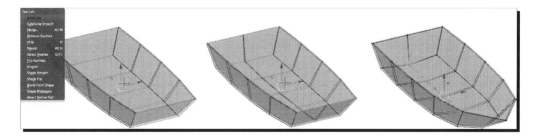

Using clean building methods

The way you built this model was very solid.

◆ Since the hull is a single piece, there are no holes in it. This is known as **water tight**, which is good for a boat.

◆ Objects for 3D printers must be water tight like this.

◆ Since it has no holes, you can use it with the water functions of the physics engine, so the boat will float or it can be filled with water.

◆ It also makes it nice and clean for use in the game engine.

◆ The number of faces was kept to a minimum, so the rendering times will be short.

Choosing between quadrilaterals and triangles

In the previous chapter, we briefly discussed that a face usually has three or four edges. Because of the way you created it, this boat is made entirely of quadrilateral or four-edged faces. Quadrilateral faces are preferred, because they subdivide nicely as you saw when making the sides, and if you are making a model that is controlled by an armature, such as a model of a person or an animal, they deform better.

There is one problem with quadrilateral faces though. You have to take care to make sure that the quadrilateral face is flat.

We talked about normals earlier, and how a normal is a line perpendicular to the face. If you are not careful with a quadrilateral face, it may not be flat. Then Blender won't be able to figure out what the normal for the face is, and won't know how to render it properly.

Imagine a flat floor, and you are trying to sit on a chair that has one leg that is a bit too short. You will always be rocking a bit. Quadrilaterals that are not flat, or non-planar as they are called, are similarly irritating. That's where triangular faces are easier to deal with. Like a three-legged stool, they always sit evenly on a flat surface. What Blender does when it gets a quadrilateral face that is non-planar, is to divide the face into two triangles and calculate the normals for each triangle, sometimes with poor results.

Have a go hero – making a non-planar polygon

Open a new file. Select the upper vertex of the cube nearest to you, move the vertex about half-way down the cube, and a little to the right, then render it. You haven't added any faces to the cube, but what do you notice?

Time for action – adding a seat to the boat

Congratulations, you've made a boat. The next step is to add seats to it. You'll see that you can have an object where the parts are not all in one place.

1. Open up the jonboat file. I'm using the flat bow version, but you can use a flat or pointed bow as you prefer. Press *Numpad 3* to get the side view.

2. Press *Shift+S*, and select **Cursor to Center** from the menu.

3. In the 3D View header, turn off the 3D manipulator display.

4. Use the LMB to move the 3D cursor up, and close to the top of the boat, as shown in the following image:

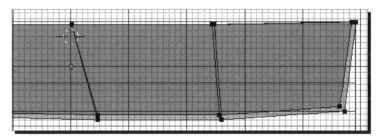

5. Make sure that the boat is in **Object Mode**. Press *Tab* to change it, if it is not.

6. Press *A* to deselect the boat.

7. Use *Shift+A* to make a new cube. Press *N* if the **Properties Panel** of the 3D View is not already open.

8. Press *Numpad 7* to get the **Top** view.

9. In the **Transform** sub panel, look where it says **Dimensions:**. Set the **Y** dimension to 1. Set the **Z** dimension to 0.1666. Use the *Tab* key to go between **Y** and **Z**.

10. Press *S* and *X* to scale the cube in X, till it just meets the inner sides of the boat. The seat I made was 4.320 wide in X.

11. In the **Viewport Shading** menu, select **Solid**.

12. Press the *MMB*, and rotate your view around the boat. Check that the seat is not poking out through the boat, or floating between the inner sides of the hull. If it is, press *S* and *X*, and use the mouse to scale it a little. Press the *LMB* when done.

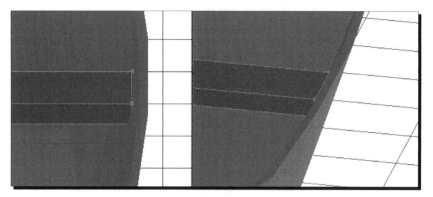

13. Press *F12* to render the boat as I did in this image. The ends of the seat should just touch the inner hull of the boat as seen in this image. Press *Esc* when you are done looking at the boat.

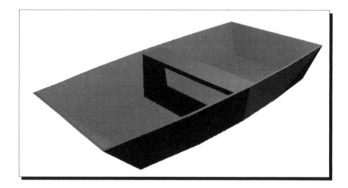

What just happened?

First, you chose a center point for the seat, by moving the 3D cursor. Then, you deselected the boat to begin making a different object. Next, you made a cube and scaled it in the X direction, Y, and Z, so that it became a seat for the boat. Finally, you did a quick sample render to see what you made, as in the previous image.

For your reference, the file `6907_05_boat_adding seat.blend` has been included in the download pack. It has the first seat completed.

Time for action – making the other seat

The first seat was pretty straightforward. The second seat is in the bow, and to fit in it, the front edge of the seat is a little narrower than the back edge. So, you'll copy the first seat, and modify the copy.

1. Change to the **Top** view. Zoom out till you can see the entire boat.

2. Select the **Viewport Shading** menu from the 3D View header, and set the shading to **Wireframe** again.

3. Change to **Edit Mode**.

4. Select all of the vertices.

5. Press *Shift+D* to duplicate them. Move the mouse down, and press the *MMB* to lock the motion to that direction. Move the new vertices to the front section of the boat.

6. Look at how much of a gap you see between the ends of the center seat and the hull. You will want to give the new seat about the same gap between the ends of the seat and the hull. Since the bow is angled first, you will scale the front seat in the X direction, so that the rear edge of the front seat is the proper width. Then, you will scale the front edge of the front seat for proper fit.

7. For best control, move the mouse to the farthest corner of the 3D View, before you start scaling. Press *S* and *X*, and scale the new seat. Make the gap between the seat and the hull about the same as the gap between the center seat and the hull.

8. Deselect all the vertices.

9. Next, you want to make the angle of the side of the front seat match the angle of the hull. Select only the front vertices of the front seat. Press *S* and *X* to scale these in X, so that the sides of the front seat are parallel with the angle of the hull, as shown in the following image:

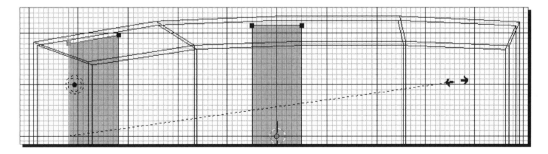

10. In the **Viewport Shading** menu, select **Solid**.

11. Press the *MMB*, and rotate your view around the boat. Check that the seat is not poking out through the boat or floating between the inner sides of the hull. If it is, press *Numpad 7*, and scale the vertices of the front seat again.

12. Press the *Tab* key to exit **Edit Mode**.

13. Press *F12*. Press *Esc* when you have examined the boat.

14. Save the file with a unique name.

What just happened?

Working in **Edit Mode**, you duplicated the seat and moved it to the bow. You also learned that you can move in a certain axis, by starting the motion in that direction, and then pressing the *MMB* to restrict the motion to that axis. You scaled the seat in X, and then scaled the front edge of the seat in X. Since you duplicated the vertices to make the new seat in **Edit Mode**, instead of duplicating the seat in **Object Mode**, both seats are a single object, which will make it easier for you to add textures to it. Well done, you've built a boat similar to the left-side image, and you learned the basics of modeling with Blender at the same time.

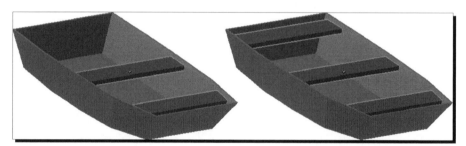

Have a go hero – add a third seat

Add a third seat in the aft of the boat, as shown in the image above on the right.

The steps are about the same as for making the seat in the bow. Then save the file to a unique name.

For your reference, the file `6907_05_boat_making the other seat1.blend` has been included in the download pack. It has the second seat. `6907_05_boat_making the other seat2.blend` has three seats completed.

Making modeling easier with Blender's layers function

A short while ago, you used the **Move to Layer** menu to hide the reference blocks, so you could render the boat. Blender's layers are a powerful tool and something that deserves a bit more study. Perhaps you may have used layers in Photoshop or Autocad. Blender's layers work differently:

◆ In Blender, layers are similar to cubbyholes that you can put objects in, and hide them or show them.

◆ Something on the top layer won't necessarily render on top of something on another layer. You cannot link them together, or move a layer as you can in Photoshop.

◆ An object in a layer that is displayed can be moved, modified, or rendered. An object in a layer that is not displayed, may not.

There are 20 layers in Blender. You can use any number of them. You can select them with the 20 buttons in the 3D View header in **Object Mode** as shown here. They are called the **Layer Visibility Controls**, and they are shown in the next illustration. One half has a yellow border. The button for layer one is on the upper-left. The button for layer 10 is on the upper-right. The button for layer 11 is on the lower left, and the button for layer 20 is on the lower-right. Buttons that are dark show layers that are displayed. Buttons with a dot in the center show layers containing objects. The yellow dot means that the currently active object is in that layer.

Time for action – introducing layers

It's time for a little introduction to using Blender's layers. Here, you will be learning how to use them with the keyboard. If you are using the Numpad Emulator setting, rather than pressing the numbers on your keyboard, use the Layer Visibility Controls as just discussed, and select the layer that corresponds with the keyboard number.

1. Select the **Viewport Shading** menu on the 3D View header, and set the shading to **Solid**.

2. Use the *MMB* to rotate the scene, so you can see the top of the boat. Get into **Object Mode**.

3. Press the 5 key on your keyboard, not on the Numpad. If you are emulating the Numpad, select layer 5 from the Layer Visibility Controls, and do so for the rest of this exercise.

4. Press the *2* key on your keyboard.

5. Press the *1* key on your keyboard.

6. Press the *Alt* key and the *7* key at the same time. Note how the dark color on the Layer Visibility Control shifts to layer 17. Numpad emulators select layer 17.

7. Press *Shift+A*, and make a Monkey.

What just happened?

When you press the number keys on the keyboard, Blender displays the corresponding layer. With key *5* you saw nothing, because there was nothing in the layer. Pressing key *2* showed the reference blocks, which you moved to layer 2. Pressing key *1* gets you back to layer 1, where you have been working. Keys *1* to *10* display layers *1* to *10*. To get layers *11* to *20*, press the *Alt* key and a number key. When you opened up layer 17 with the *Alt* and the *7* key, and made a monkey, a dot appeared in layer 17 to let you know that there was now an object on that layer. The dot is yellow, because the monkey is the active object.

Time for action – using layers for controlling rendering

Layers don't just control what you can see while modeling. They also control what is rendered.

1. Press the *Shift* key, and hold it while you press the *LMB* over the layer 1 box in the Layer Visibility Control.

2. Press *F12* to render the scene. Press *Esc* when you have seen the rendering.

3. Press *Ctrl+MMB*, and zoom back till you can see the lamp. Use the *RMB* to select the lamp.

4. Press *M* to get the **Move To Layer** menu.

5. Select **Layer 5** on the menu with the *LMB*. Then, move the mouse away from the menu.

6. Press *F12* to render the scene. Press *Esc* when you have seen the rendering.

7. Press the number *5*. Numpad emulators select layer 5.

8. Press *M* and *1*.

9. Press *1* and *Shift+Alt+7*. Numpad emulators choose level 1, then *Shift* and choose level 17.

10. Press *F12* to render the scene. Press *Esc* when you have seen the rendering.

11. Use the *RMB* to select the Monkey. Press *X* to delete it.

What just happened?

Just as the *Shift* key lets you select multiple objects, using the *Shift* key when selecting layers lets you select multiple layers to display or render. Pressing the *M* key brings up the **Move To Layer** menu. You can choose which layer to move to by picking the layer off the menu or by pressing the number of the layer on the keyboard. If the lamp(s) are not on an active layer, then they will not illuminate the scene.

Coloring the boat to add realism

The proper use of colors makes an object seem more real. It's time to learn a bit more about how to apply color and textures to the model you have made. There are two kinds of decoration you can do: materials and textures. **Materials** assign a color to faces of an object. They tell Blender how shiny or dull the surface is, how transparent it is, and other qualities. **Textures** allow you to add a design to the surface, and not just colors, but patterns of roughness, bumps, and shapes as well. First, you will add a material to the boat, and then you will add a texture to the seats.

Time for action – coloring the hull and the gunwale

Your boat is a pretty simple object. The entire hull can be one color, but its nice to give the gunwale a different color to accent the top, and provide more definition.

1. Make sure you are working in **Layer 1**.

2. If you have the **Properties Panel** in the 3D View closed, open it with the *N* key.

3. Select the camera with the *RMB*.

4. Press *0* on the Numpad to change to the **Camera** view.

5. Move the camera back by pressing the *G* key, then tapping the *Z* key twice, and move the mouse, so that the camera dollies out along its local Z direction until the whole boat shows up.

6. Change to the **Top** view.

7. Select the lamp with the *RMB*. In the **Properties** pane, set the lamp's location to X= -1.900, Y= -6.800, and Z= 5.900.

8. Press *Shift+D* to copy the lamp. Move it a little with the mouse, so that you can see that you are working on the second lamp. Set the location of the second lamp to X= 4.400, Y= 0.200, and Z= 5.900.

9. Change to the **Side** view, and zoom into the boat.

10. Select the boat with the *RMB*, and press *Tab* to go into **Edit Mode**.

11. Choose **Face Select Mode** on the 3D View header, then choose **Wireframe** in the **Viewport Shading** menu on the header.

12. Press *A* to deselect any faces.

13. Put the cursor below the boat and to the left. Press *B* for border select. Select the bottom and the side faces, but not the top ones.

14. Go to the **Properties** window on the right, and select the materials button in the header, as seen in the previous image. It is the ninth button from the left. When you do, it will become highlighted in blue, as seen in the previous image. You may need to slide the header to the left with the *MMB* to see it.

15. After you have selected the **Material** button, enlarge the **Properties Window** by dragging the edge to the left, until the button with the text **erial** or **terial**, as seen in the following image, becomes **Material**. You will need to enter text into this button. If your **Material** panel is pretty much blank, press the button labeled **New**.

16. In the expanded button labeled **Material**, rename **Material** to Hull, as bordered in yellow in the next image. Click on the word **Material**, type in Hull, then press *Enter*.

17. In the **Diffuse** sub panel of the **Properties** window, click on the white box, and use the color wheel menu to change the color to green. You can use the mouse and the color wheel, or type in the values below. I used R=0.015, G=0.24, B=0.054. You can use the *Tab* key to move between the **R**, **G**, and **B** buttons. Then click outside of the menu to continue.

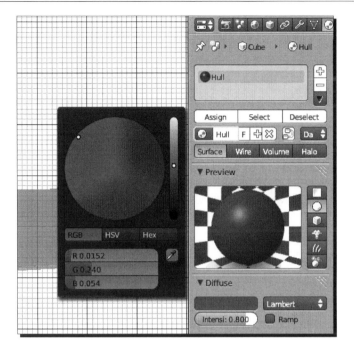

18. Click on the **Assign** button. It is located at the top of the **Material** panel, just above where you entered the word Hull to assign the color to the selected vertices. If you do not see it, make sure that you are in **Edit Mode**, and not **Object Mode**. The button is not visible in **Object Mode**.

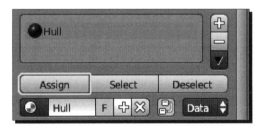

19. Render it. The boat is all green. Press *Esc* to show the 3D View window.

20. Choose **Select** on the 3D View header. Choose **Inverse** from the pop-up menu.

21. In the **Properties** window, add a new material slot, by clicking the *LMB* on the plus sign, across from the word Hull, as seen in the next image.

22. Click on the button that has a plus sign, and the word **New** on it as seen here to create a new material. Name the new material Gunwale.

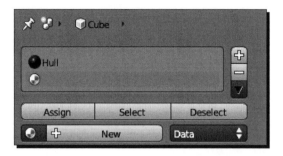

23. Press the *LMB* over the color bar in the **Diffuse** sub panel. The color wheel will appear as seen in the next image. Make the Gunwale material light green. I used R=0.850, G=1.000, and B=0.500.

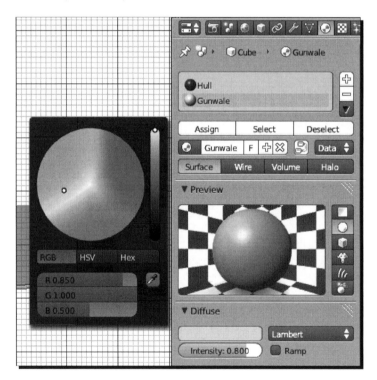

24. Press the *LMB* over the **Assign** button, as seen in the row of three light gray buttons in the preceding illustration, to assign the material to the selected vertices.

25. Now render it. It should look something similar to the following image. Press *Esc* when you are finished looking at it.

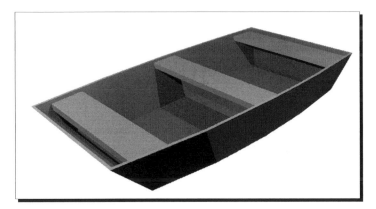

26. Save the file to a unique name.

What just happened?

First, you spent a little time setting up the scene to display the materials well. You moved the camera to where it would see the entire boat, and put modeling lamps on both sides of the boat too, so nothing would be too much in shadow. Then, you selected the faces of the sides and bottom of the hull. You took the default materials slot, made a material for it, and colored the material green. Finally, you assigned that material to the hull of the boat. Next, you inverted the selection, so you had only the faces on the top of the hull. Then, you made a new materials slot, gave it a name and set its color to light green. You assigned that material to only the faces on the top of the hull.

 For your reference, the file `6907_05_boat_color the hull.blend` has been included in the download pack. It has the materials added to the hull and gunwale.

Time for action – adding a texture to the seats

Now, you've added a material to the boat. Next, you will add a wood texture to the seats and learn a new panel in the **Properties** window.

1. Press *Tab* to go into **Object Mode**, and select the seats with the *RMB*.

2. Add a new material slot just like you did when you made the `Hull` material. Name it `Seats`.

3. Go up to the header of the **Properties** window, and select the **Textures** button. It has a red and white checkerboard on it, and it is next to the **Materials** button. It's highlighted in blue, as seen at the top of the next image.

4. Add a new texture by clicking on the button called **New**, as shown at the bottom of the following screenshot:

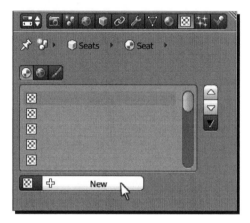

5. Where the **New** button was, it now says **Texture**. Click on the word **Texture**, and change it to `Seat Texture`. Press *Enter* when you are done.

6. Just below where you named the texture, it says **Type:**, as seen in the following graphic. Click on the dark button to the right of **Type:**. A menu comes up. Select **Image** or **Movie**.

> The way I organized the files for this book is pretty simple. Each chapter has its own directory. Within each chapter are three sub directories, Blender Files, Images, and Audio. This is the way all the files in your download pack will be organized. It will make it easier if you emulate this on your own hard drive.

7. Go to the Chapter 5/Images directory of the download pack, and choose 6907_05_37.png. It is a wood texture. Copy the file to your Image directory.

8. A sub panel appears that is labeled Image. At the bottom of the sub panel, it says **Open**, as seen in the previous graphic. Select the **Open** button, and you will get the Blender file browser. Find 6907_05_37.png in your Images directory.

9. In the **Properties** window header, select the **Materials** button.

10. Press *F12* to render the scene. Your boat now has wooden seats.

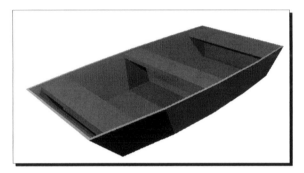

11. Save the file to a unique name in your Blender Files directory.

What just happened?

You added a textured material to the boat seats. First, you created a new material slot, and a material to put into it. Then, you opened up the texture editor to create the texture. You chose an **Image** or **Movie** texture, and chose a wood-grain texture from the download pack. Since you added the material to the entire object, you did not have to get into **Edit Mode** to assign the texture.

> For your reference, the file 6907_05_boat_add texture to seats.blend has been included in the download pack. It has the materials added to the hull and gunwale, and the texture added to the seats.

Time for action – naming objects and joining them

Next, you will select the seats, and then add the boat to your selection. Then you can join them.

1. On the header of the **Properties** window, select the **Object** button. It has the orange cube. It is the fifth button from the left.

2. Use the button shown at the bottom of the following graphic, in the **Properties** window, to change the name to Seats. You can type it in and move the cursor away, or press *Enter* when you finish.

3. Select the boat. Change the name to Boat.

4. Save the Blender file.

5. Select the seats again with the RMB. Now press the *Shift* key when selecting with the *RMB* to also select the boat. Be sure to select the seats first.

6. Press *Ctrl+J*.

7. The seats and the boat are now a single object. Now look at what the name is.

8. Look at the **Material** panel in the **Properties** window. Note that the properties of all three materials are listed, since both objects have been joined.

9. Save the file to a unique name.

What just happened?

You selected the seats and named them. Then, you selected the boat, named it, and saved the file.

Then you selected both the seats and the boat and used the command *Ctrl+J* to join the two objects. The first object selected is joined into the last object selected. Finally, you saved the finished boat to its own file.

For your reference, the file `6907_05_boat_naming objects.blend` has been included in the download pack. It has the boat completed and named.

Using Basic Lighting

In addition to building your boat, you really want to display it in its best light. As a bonus, I have provided a special section that focuses strictly on using the array of lights that Blender provides and helps you understand the basics of how to use them. They will be covered again in this book in greater detail, but I recommend you check out `6907_05_Lighting a Small Boat.pdf`.

It will add another layer to your learning and help you in later chapters.

Key	Function
Z	Toggles between **Wireframe** and **Solid** mode in **Viewport Shading**.
Alt+Tab	In **Edit Mode** brings up the **Mesh Select Mode** menu.
Ctrl+Tab	In **Edit Mode** brings up the **Mesh Select Mode** menu.
Tab	In three part buttons, such as X, Y, Z locations or R, G, B colors, it can be used to jump from one button to the next.

Summary

In this chapter, you put your knowledge of building objects to a practical use, and built a boat. It was also good practice in using the controls of 3D View; keyboard shortcuts and buttons, including the buttons on the header, in the Tool Shelf and in the Properties panel.

You studied box modeling to create the boat from the default cube, and used box modeling's most powerful tools: extrusion, subdividing edges, and moving vertices to reshape the cube into a hull. You learned about joining objects together, so that the boat and the seats can be used as a single object. You got your first taste of creating a material to make the boat look more realistic, and added a wood texture to the seats.

In the next chapter, you will make some oars and oarlocks to move the boat with. You will extend your ability with more powerful modeling techniques. You will animate the boat, the oars, and the oarlocks as a coordinated unit, so that the oars appear to propel the boat.

Let's go!

6

Making and Moving the Oars

In the last chapter, you put your knowledge of building objects to a practical use as well as what you knew of how to use the 3D View. You made a small boat and added textures, and then explored different ways of lighting.

In this chapter you will expand on your modeling skills and what you have learned about animation to take things to the next level. You'll learn some cool modeling techniques, and animate the boat and the oars.

You will explore:

- ◆ Creating oars and oarlocks to move the boat
- ◆ Controlling the smoothness of a surface
- ◆ Appending objects to the scene to reuse previously made objects
- ◆ Creating child-parent relationships, to group objects for animation
- ◆ Using kinematics to organize animation
- ◆ Employing animation cycles to save work
- ◆ Using camera tracking to follow the boat's motion

Let's start by making the oar.

Modeling an oar

We'll do a little more precise modeling with the oar. We'll be flipping groups of vertices exes around to make rich details while keeping the polygon count as low as possible. First you need to know more about what you are making.

Getting scale from an image

It's good to be able to make an object the size you want it to be. As I used a real boat for the basis to build the boat model, a picture of an oar will help make a realistic oar, and as you'll see, you can get quite a bit of information from it.

For a reference image I went to a website and grabbed an image of an oar similar to the one here. Here's what I did to figure out the size of the oar.

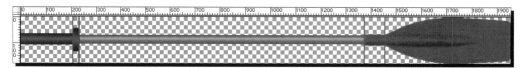

The specs on the website had the length of the paddle and the width of the blade, which was enough information for me to scale things in the image and get some basic measurements:

- I trimmed down the image until it was just the oar and got an image that was 1954 x 178. I knew that the paddle was six inches long. So, I divided six by 1954 and got a scaling factor of 0.003. That means every pixel was 0.003 Blender units long.

- Then, all I had to do was measure the length of a part in pixels and convert that to Blender units. It's easy to measure the pixels in an image using the rulers and guides in a paint program as seen in the previous illustration.

- For example, the grip, which was 195 pixels long in the image, got multiplied by 0.003 and that meant that the grip was 0.6 units long.

- I measured them all and made a list of my measurements. I also took note that, on the website, one customer complained that the shaft of the oar was just a bit too small for his oarlocks. So, in my measurements, I boosted up the radius of the shaft a bit.

Making a cylinder into an oar

Once all the measurements are made, it's time to begin. The shaft itself is simple, so there are two basic parts that need the most work, the grip and the blade.

Time for action – making the shaft of the oar

Starting the oar is pretty easy. In *Chapter 4, Modeling with Vertices, Edges, and Faces* you looked at the basic shapes Blender has available, that's where you will begin:

1. Open Blender.

2. Press *X* to delete the default cube.

3. Press *Shift+A* and select cylinder from the pop-up menu.

4. In the **Tool Shelf**, set **Add Cylinder** for **12 Vertices**, **0.083 Radius**, and **4.2 Depth**. This will make the oar handle and shaft as seen in the following screenshot. You can use the *Tab* key to jump between the **Vertices**, **Radius**, and **Depth** buttons.

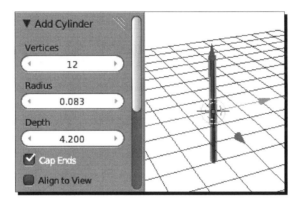

5. Now you have the handle to the right length.

6. Press the *Tab* key to get into **Edit Mode**.

7. Press *Numpad 1* and *Numpad 5* to set the view to **Front Ortho**.

8. Zoom into the cylinder.

9. Make sure that the **Limit selection to visible** button is light gray in the **3D View header**, as shown in the following screenshot, so that you select all edges and not just the visible ones:

10. Choose **Edge Select** mode from the **3D View header**, it's the highlighted button with the cube and the vertical line shown in the previous screenshot.

11. Press *A* to deselect all the edges. Press *B* and then draw the marquee border across the middle of the cylinder. Do not select the ends. If you have questions about using the border select, check *Chapter 4, Modeling with Vertices, Edges, and Faces* to refresh yourself.

12. Press *W* to get the **Specials** menu, choose **Subdivide**. In the **Tool Shelf**, set the number of cuts to **2** as shown in the following screenshot:

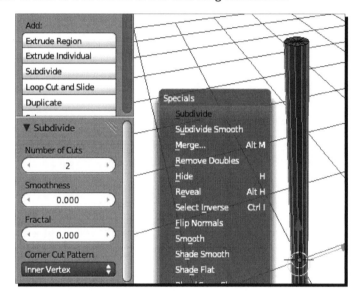

What just happened?

You created a cylinder, modified it to be the correct size, and divided it into thirds to create the edges you will need to make the grip and guard.

Time for action – making the grip and guard

Now you are going to use those box modeling tools, moving vertices, scaling, and subdivision to create the grip and guard for the oar:

1. Press *A* to deselect all the edges. Press *B* for a Border Select. Select the upper set of the horizontal edges that you just created.

2. Zoom in so that the edge that you selected is at the bottom of the **3D View** and that the top of the cylinder is at the top of the **3D View** window, as seen on the left side of the next screenshot. Move the mouse so it is level with edges.

3. The reference grid in the background will help you judge how far to go. Each section of the main grid in the background is 0.1 in Blender units. So, you will want to move the edges so they are six boxes from the top.

4. Press *G,* and use the mouse to move the edges up. When you start moving the edge, press the *MMB* briefly to lock the motion to the *Z* axis. Move them until they are 0.6 units or six boxes from the end of the oar, as seen on the left of the following screenshot. For best control, press the *Ctrl* key while you move. Press *LMB* to release it.

5. Deselect all the edges.

6. Press *Ctrl+MMB* and use the mouse to zoom out so you can see the lower set of horizontal edges that you just created. Select the edges. Put your cursor on the edges.

7. Press *G,* and move the edge back up. Press *MMB* briefly as you move them up to lock the motion to the *Z* axis. Press *LMB* to release it.

8. Move them close to the upper set of edges. Hold the *Ctrl* key while moving them. Move it up until it is one grid mark below the upper edge you just moved.

9. Zoom in until the smaller grid appears.

10. Press *G.* Press *MMB* briefly as you move the edges up to lock the motion to the *Z* axis, and using the reference grid in the background, use the mouse to move the edges until they are four small boxes below the upper set of edges. Hold the *Ctrl* key while moving them for precise control. Press *LMB* to release it.

11. Now you have the edges in the right place to make the grip. Next you will make the guard.

12. Zoom in and recenter the 3D View on the area between the edges you just moved.

13. Press *A* to deselect all the edges. Press *B* and use the Border Select to select only the vertical edges that are between the two edges that you just created and moved; as in the center of the following screenshot.

14. Press *W* to get the **Specials** menu, and choose **Subdivide**. Set the number of cuts to **2**.

15. Press *A* to deselect all the edges. Press *B* and use the Border Select to select the horizontal edges that you just made with the **Subdivide** command and the vertical edges between them.

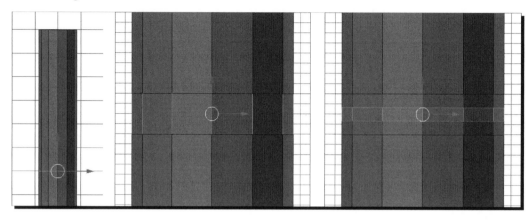

16. Move the mouse away from the cylinder for best control. Press *S* and use the mouse to scale the edges until the guard section is 0.07 larger in radius than the main oar shaft, as seen on the left of the following screenshot, that is seven of the small grid units. Press *LMB* to release it.

17. Press *S, Z,* and use the mouse to scale them in *Z*. Scale them up until they cover the first set of edges you made, as seen in the right of the following screenshot. Press *LMB* to release it.

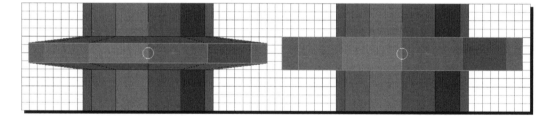

What just happened?

You got started with making the oar. First you made a cylinder and gave it the proper length and radius. Twelve sides were chosen, and because these oars will not be seen very closely, this is enough detail. Then the side edges were subdivided to make some vertices to create the grip guard with. They were moved into position, and then you subdivided that space again to make the guard itself. Then the guard was scaled out to the proper radius and scaled in Z so that the side walls of the guard were parallel. Also you learned another way to control motion; by starting to move edges in one direction and then pressing MMB to lock the motion to the most similar axis. It works with edges, vertices, sides, and objects.

For your reference, the file 6907_06_Oar Grip1.blend has the cylinder with the first two subdivisions. 6907_06_Oar Grip2.blend has the vertical edges selected. 6907_06_Oar Grip3.blend has the next two subdivisions. 6907_06_Oar Grip4.blend has the guard scaled up. 6907_06_Oar Grip5.blend has the guard scaled in *Z*.

Time for action – making the base of the blade of the oar

Now you need to make the plastic part of the oar. This will take more detail, so you will be using both extrusion and subdivision to make this transition between parts of the oar:

1. Zoom out so you can see most of the oar.

2. Move to the bottom end of the oar. Rotate the view so you can see the bottom of the oar.

3. Switch to **Face Select** mode in the 3D View header. Select the face on the bottom with the *RMB* and press *X* to delete it. Choose **Faces** from the pop-up menu, as seen in the left of the following screenshot.

4. Change to the **Front Ortho** view. Zoom into the bottom of the oar.

5. Switch to the **Edge Select** mode in the 3D View header. Press *A* to deselect all edges and then select the edges at the bottom of the oar.

6. Press *E* and then *Enter*.

7. Scale the edges so they spread out to the next major grid line, as shown in the center of the following screenshot. This will be the beginning of the oar blade.

8. If you think that you goofed up and need to redo an extrusion, use *Ctrl+Z* to undo the step(s), and be sure to go one step past the extrusion. A double extrusion will add vertices to the model and may cause problems that are hard to figure out.

9. Press *W* to subdivide the edges. Set the number of cuts to **1**. The shaft is simple, but you will need more detail to make the oar blade.

10. Pan the view up so the bottom of the oar is near the top of the 3D View window. Move your cursor to the top as well.

11. Press *E* and move the new extruded edges down three grid sections or 0.3 units as shown on the right of the following screenshot. As you did, a few steps earlier, press *MMB* to lock your motion to the *Z* axis and use the *Ctrl* key as you move it down, so you can see how far you've gone.

12. Note that now, as seen in the following screenshot, the blade has 24 sides around and the shaft has only 12.

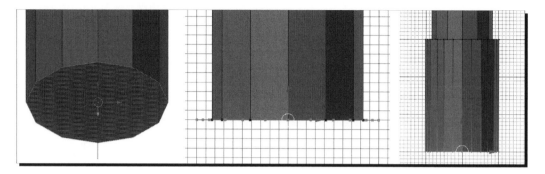

What just happened?

You started making the blade of the oar. The blade of the oar will need more detail than the grip did, so the edges were subdivided. Then the shaft was extruded to the point where the blade of the oar will appear.

For your reference, the file 6907_06_Oar Blade1.blend has the center vertex on the end of shaft being deleted. 6907_06_Oar Blade2.blend has the blade shaft being created by scaling out the vertices. 6907_06_Oar Blade3.blend has the edges moved into place and subdivided. 6907_06_Oar Blade4.blend has the beginning of the blade.

Time for action – making the blade

Now it's time to make the oar blade itself. The modeling will be a little more complex, so pay close attention to the steps:

1. Zoom out a little and move the bottom of the oar to the top of the 3D View. Move the mouse to the top of the 3D View. Have at least eight grids below the bottom of the oar.

2. Press *E*, and move the new edges down 0.8 units, eight of the grid sections. Press *MMB* after starting your motion to restrict the motion to *Z*. Use the *Ctrl* key while moving the edges for more precision.

3. Zoom in to the bottom of the oar. Choose the **Vertex select** mode. Press *A* to deselect all vertices. Press *RMB* to select the left vertex, and then *Shift+RMB* to select the right vertex on the sides at the bottom as seen in the following screenshot:

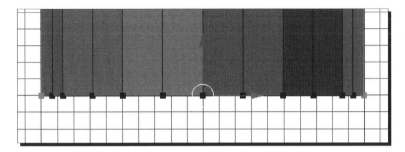

4. You don't need to rotate the view, but after selecting the vertices, zoom back out so you can see three or more large grid lines on either side.

5. Press *S, X,* and use the mouse to scale them in X. Scale them out by one and a half grid units as shown in the next screenshot on the left-hand side. Press *LMB* to release it.

6. Rotate the view so you can see the bottom of the oar.

7. Deselect all the vertices. Select the vertices that are still in a circle, as shown in the right screenshot:

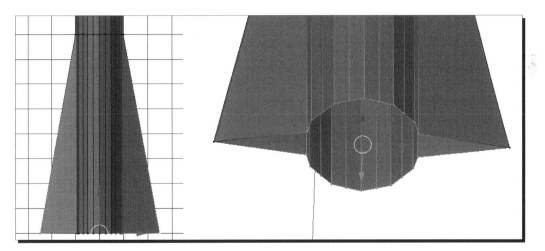

8. Press *S, X, 0.37*, and *Enter* to scale them in X to 37 percent of their original width as shown in the next screenshot:

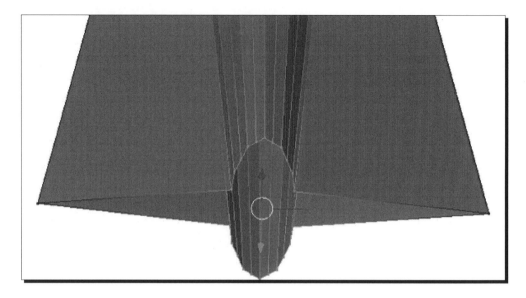

9. Next, the tip of the shaft needs a point. First you will make the right side of the point. Change to the **Right-Side** view.

10. In the **3D View** header, two buttons to the right of the **Edit Mode** button is the **Pivot center** button. Click on the button and select **3D Cursor** from the menu.

11. Press *A* to deselect all the vertices. Press *C* to pick the vertex that is immediately to the right of the center vertex.

12. Press *Shift+S* and choose **Cursor to Selected** from the menu.

13. Select the vertices to the right of the center vertex. This includes the one by **3D Cursor**.

14. Press *R, X, -90*, and *Enter* as seen in the center of the following screenshot.

15. Press *S, Y, 0* (zero), and *Enter*. This ensures that all the vertices are flat with respect to the others.

16. Now you will be making the left side of the point.

17. Press *A* to deselect all the vertices. Use the **Circle** selection to pick the vertex that is immediately to the left of the center vertex.

18. Press *Shift+S* and choose **Cursor to Selected** from the menu.

19. Select the vertices to the left of the center vertex. This includes the one next to 3D Cursor.

20. Press *R, X, 90*, and *Enter*.

21. Press *S, Y, 0* (zero), and *Enter*. This ensures that all the vertices are flat with respect to the others.

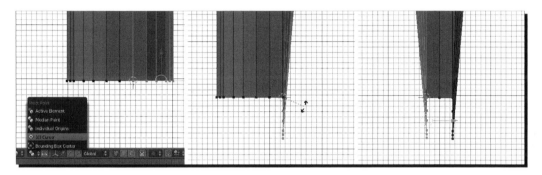

22. Finally, you need to make the bottom edge of the oar.

23. Change to the **Front** view. Move the bottom of the oar to the top of the 3D View.

24. Select all the vertices on the bottom.

25. Place your cursor just above the bottom edge of the oar.

26. Extrude the vertices and move the bottom edge down another eight grid units as seen in the left of the next screenshot. Remember *MMB* and the *Ctrl* buttons.

27. In the 3D View header, set the **Pivot Point** button to **Median Point**.

28. Press *S, Z, 0* (zero), and *Enter* to flatten the bottom of the oar.

29. Press *S, X, 0.85*, and *Enter* to taper the bottom of the oar.

30. Rotate the view so you can see the bottom of the oar.

31. Press *Alt+F* to make faces on the bottom of the oar as shown in the center of the following screenshot. Press *Shift+Alt+F* to make the faces better.

32. Press the *Tab* key to get out of **Edit Mode**. The oar is done. Good work!

33. In the top-right corner of the **Blender** window, above the **Properties Window** is a small window called the **Outliner Window** as seen on the right of the following screenshot. Clicking on **Camera** will select the camera.

34. Press *Numpad 0* to change to the **Camera** view in 3D View.

35. Move the camera so the oar is completely visible.

36. Render it.

What just happened?

You made an oar. Well done! To make the blade, you extruded the end edges. You took two of the vertices at the end to make the blade and scaled them out in X. Then, in a nifty trick, you squeezed the other vertices in X to make them narrower, and then rotated them 90 degrees to make a cool looking point for the oar shaft and flattened them to the surface of the blade by scaling them to zero in Y, so that the point would be flat. After that, you extruded the points again to make the end of the oar and scaled all the vertices to zero in Z so that the bottom end of the oar is flat. Finally, you capped the end of the oar and rendered it out to see what you made.

For your reference, the file 6907_06_Oar Blade5.blend has the blade shaft extruded. 6907_06_Oar Blade6.blend has the blade rotated in the 3D View. 6907_06_Oar Blade7.blend has the two blade vertices selected. 6907_06_Oar Blade8.blend has the blade vertices scaled out. 6907_06_Oar Blade9.blend has the end of the shaft scaled in X. 6907_06_Oar Blade10.blend has the vertices selected to make the pointed tip of the shaft. 6907_06_ Oar Blade11.blend has the pointed tip completed. 6907_06_ Oar Blade12.blend has the blade extruded to the full length. 6907_06_Oar Blade13.blend has the end of the oar flattened.

Controlling how smooth the surface is

As you may have noticed in the render, the grip and the shaft do not look smooth at all. You might want it to look a little nicer. Fortunately, Blender allows you to control how smooth or flat faces appear. By default, the surfaces are flat. You must set them as smooth surfaces if you want them to be smoothed. This tells Blender to consider the normals of the adjacent faces when reading the normal for a particular face.

Time for action – controlling flat and smooth surfaces

By default the surfaces are flat. But you want the rounded surfaces to be smooth. Selecting the faces is the main task. Making them smooth once you have them selected is easy:

1. Press *Numpad 1* and adjust the **3D View** window so you see the grip and the guard.

2. Select the **Oar** and get into **Edit Mode**.

3. Choose **Face Select** mode from the **3D View** header.

4. Press *B* and use **Border Select** to choose the faces of the grip as seen in the left of the following screenshot. Do not select the end of the grip.

5. Next use **Border Select** to select the faces on the perimeter of the grip guard, as shown in the center of the next screenshot. Do not select the faces of the sides.

6. Now select the faces of the oar shaft, the top perimeter of the blade, and where the shaft tapers down within the blade as shown on the right of the next screenshot:

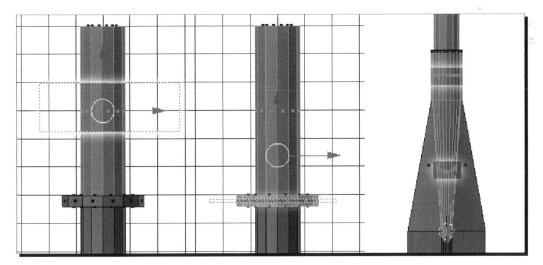

7. Click *LMB* on the **Smooth** button in the **Tool Shelf** on the left side of the **3D View** window.

8. Press the *Tab* key to get into **Object Mode**. Zoom out. Select the lamp. As you changed lamps in the last chapter, change the lamp to a **Hemi** lamp. Press *F12* to render the image.

What just happened?

You selected faces where the surface should be smooth from face to face and assigned them to have a smooth shading.

Other sections of the oar, such as the end of the grip, the flat sides of the grip guard, the end of the oar blade, and the flat sides of the blade, should be flat because they are flat surfaces.

The difference between smooth and flat surfaces is that when calculating a smooth surface, Blender considers the normals of adjacent faces as well as the the normal of the face it is rendering. With flat surfaces, Blender needs only to calculate the normal of the face it is rendering at that moment.

 6907_06_Oar Blade14.blend has the basic oar completed with the surfaces smoothed.

Have a go hero – tidying up details

Modeling, like other arts, is often something where you decide on changes as you go along. Here are some suggestions to improve the oar:

1. The outside edge of the oar blade needs some curve in the top section. Add it.

2. While you did cap the bottom of the oar, Blender offers a better method of capping. Select the bottom vertices. Press *Shift+Alt+F* to improve the placement of the faces. If you are a perfectionist, the best results will come if you make the faces on the bottom yourself as you practiced in *Chapter 4, Modeling with Vertices, Edges, and Faces*.

3. Group the faces for the grip, shaft, and blade.

4. It needs to be colored. Make vertex groups for the grip and guard, the shaft and the blade, and add materials to them as seen to the right of the following screenshot.

5. Find the **Object** button (the orange cube highlighted shown in the following screenshot) in the **Properties Window** header; press it and rename the object to **Oar** in the box, as shown in the following screenshot:

6. Save your `.blend` file with the oar.

 `6907_06_Oar Blade15.blend` has the oar completed with all details tidied.

Making the oarlock

The oarlock is small but important. It connects the oar with the boat and when animated will be used for the rotation keyframes for the *Z* axis. To make it you will start with a torus.

Time for action – making the oarlock

This will be a change. But with some deletion of faces, copying them, moving them, and extruding, them you will soon have an oarlock:

1. Open a new file in Blender.

2. Press *X* to delete the default cube.

3. Make a cylinder. In the **Tool Shelf**, set the radius to **0.083**, like the shaft of the oar as seen in the following screenshot:

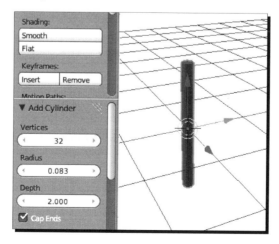

4. Change to the **Top** view, **Ortho** mode, and zoom in to the cylinder.

5. Press A to deselect the cylinder. Press *Shift+A* and select **Mesh** and then **Torus** from the drop-down menu.

6. In the **Tool Shelf** set the **Major Radius** to **0.13**, the **Minor Radius** to **0.035**, **Major Segments** to **18**, and the **Minor Segments** to **12**. This is shown in the following screenshot:

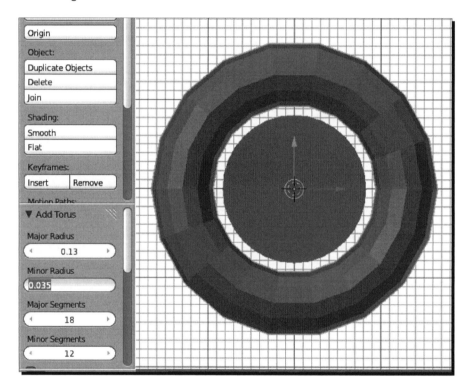

7. Press the *Tab* key to get into **Edit Mode**.

8. Make the **Limit selection to visible** button on the 3D View header light gray so you can select all the vertices.

9. Deselect all the vertices. Press B for Border Select to select the vertices above the center of the torus as shown in the following screenshot.

10. Press X to delete the vertices.

11. Press B for Border Select to select the top ring of vertices. Press E to extrude vertices and start moving them up. Move them up to the next major grid line, or 0.100. Don't forget to use the *MMB* and the *Ctrl* keys.

12. Extrude it again and go up 0.0500 as shown in the center of the following screenshot.

13. Press *Alt+F* to cap them.

14. Press *A* to deselect all the vertices. Press *B* for Border Select to select the edges from one of the ends.

15. Move the cursor up to the top of the torus.

16. Press *Shift+D* to copy it.

17. Move it below the oarlock as shown on the right side of the following screenshot:

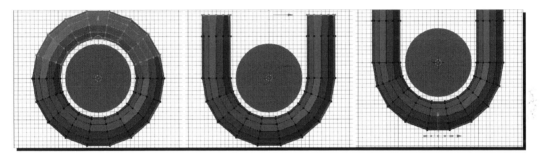

18. Press *E, -0.4,* and *Enter* to extrude the cylinder end into a shaft 0.4 units long as shown in the next screenshot on the left. This will be the oarlock pin.

19. Press *B* for Border Select to select all the edges in the oarlock pin. Make them into a group named **Pin**. This will help if you have to go back to adjust the pin height.

20. Press *G, Y,* and use the mouse to move the pin up in Y until it is in level with the center of the metal of the oarlock as shown in the center of the next screenshot. Press *LMB* to release it.

21. Press *A* to deselect all edges. Press *B* for Border Select to select only the edges at the top of the oarlock on the left side.

22. Press *S, X, 0.5,* and *Enter.*

23. Press *G, X,* and use the mouse to move the selected vertices in X so that the left-hand side is vertical as shown on the right side of the following screenshot. Press *LMB* to release it.

24. Press *A* to deselect all the edges. Press *B* for Border Select to select only the edges at the top of the oarlock on the right side.

25. Press *S, X, 0.5,* and *Enter.*

26. Press *G, X*, and use the mouse to move the selected edges in X so that the right-hand side is vertical. Press *LMB* to release it.

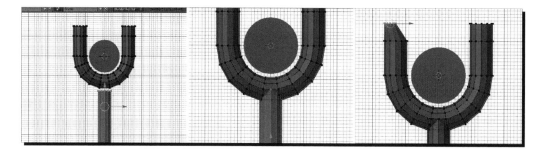

27. In the **Properties** window, select the **Object** button (orange cube) in the header. In the subpanel below, rename the object to **Oarlock**.

28. Save the file.

What just happened?

To make the oarlock, you started by making a torus that would fit around the oar's shaft. Then you removed half of it and extruded the ends up to create a U shape. You duplicated one of the ends and moved it below the torus to create the oarlock pin. You grouped the extrusion to avoid having to search for the vertices if you ever need to work on the oarlock in the future, and then you moved the oarlock pin up so that both pieces appear to be one. Finally, you shrank the top ends of the oarlock to make it easier for the oar to be located into the oarlock.

For your reference, the file 6907_06_Oarlock1.blend has the torus with the top half removed. 6907_06_Oarlock2.blend has the top of the oarlock extruded. 6907_06_Oarlock3.blend has the shaft started. 6907_06_Oarlock4.blend has the shaft in place. 6907_06_Oarlock5.blend has the oarlock completed.

Assembling the boat, oars, and oarlocks

Well done. You've made the boat, an oar, and an oarlock. Now it's time to assemble everything and animate them all. We'll open the boat and then add the oar and oarlock by appending them to the file.

Time for action – loading all of the models together

You have the boat, the oar, and the oarlocks all done. Now it's time to assemble them together:

1. Load the final version of the boat you built, or if you want, you can load `6907_05_boat_test the lights.blend` from the download pack.

2. Press *A* to deselect everything.

3. Select **Layer 3** by pressing *3* or using **Layer Visibility Controls**.

4. Choose **Wireframe** from the **Viewport Shading** menu on the **3D View** header.

5. Select the **File** menu, and go to **Append**.

6. Find the directory that you stored the oarlock in, or you can use `6907_06_ Oarlock5.blend` from the download pack. Select the file with *LMB*. **Object** from the next menu. and then select **Oarlock** from the final menu. Press **Link/Append** from the **Library** button in the upper-right corner of the window.

7. Name the Oarlock, **Oarlock–R**. Press *Enter* after naming.

8. Find the directory that you stored the oar in, or you can use `6907_06_Oar Blade15.blend` from the download pack. Select the file with *LMB*, Select **Object** from the next menu, and then select **Oar** from the final menu. Press **Link/Append** from the **Library** button in the upper-right corner of the window.

9. Name the Oar, **Oar-R**. Press *Enter* after naming.

10. Press *R, Z, 90,* and *Enter* to rotate the oar so that the blade is parallel to the oarlock shaft, as shown on the left side of the following screenshot.

11. Zoom in so you can see the oarlock.

12. Press *Shift* and *RMB* to also select the oarlock. Press *Ctrl+P* to parent the oarlock to the oar. Choose **Set Parent to Object** in the pop-up menu.

13. Select only the oarlock, move it around to check that the oar moves when you move the oarlock. Press *Esc* or *RMB* to let it go in the original position. If the oar doesn't move with the oarlock, go back a step and try to parent the oarlock to the oar again.

14. Press *R, X, 90,* and *Enter* to rotate the oarlock and the oar into the correct orientation as seen on the right side of the following screenshot:

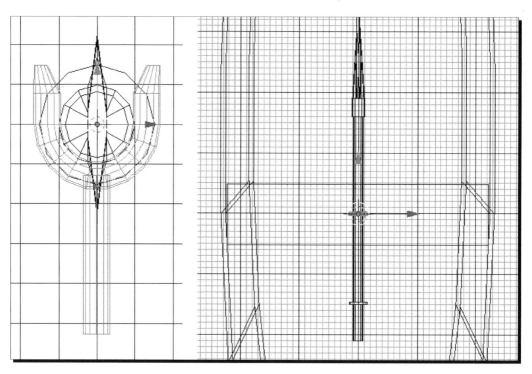

15. Press *Shift+1* to display both layer 3 and layer 1. Or use *Shift+LMB* over layer 1 in **Layer Visibility** Controls.

16. Change to the **Side** view.

17. Press *G, Z,* and then move the oarlock up with the mouse so that the top of the oarlock pin is above the gunwale. Press *LMB* to drop it in place.

18. Press *G* and *Y* to move the oarlock 1.200 units to the right, so it is about half-way between the seat and the end of the face, as shown on the right side of the following screenshot. Press *LMB* to release it.

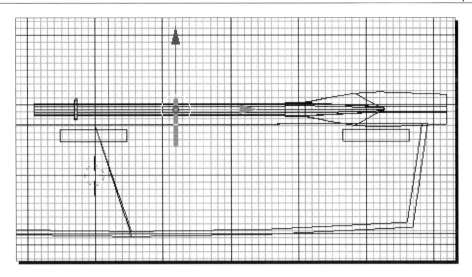

19. Set the **3D View Viewport Shading** button to **Solid**.

20. Press *Numpad Ctrl+1* to change to the **Rear** view, Press *G* and *X* and use the mouse to move the oarlock to the right of the gunwale. Make sure it doesn't stick through the boat to the outside, as shown on the left side of the following screenshot. Press *LMB* to release it.

21. Press *R, Z, 90*, and *Enter* to rotate the oarlock and oar.

22. Press *Shift+RMB* to select the oar in addition to the oarlock.

23. Press *Shift+D* to and then press Enter duplicate them. Use the mouse to move the duplicates to the opposite side of the boat, press *MMB* to keep motion to the X axis. Move it till it pokes out at the side of the boat, then move it back a little so it doesn't show.

24. Select the oar you just made with *RMB* and name it **Oar-L**. Press *Enter* after naming.

25. Select the oarlock you just made, with *RMB*. Name it **Oarlock-L**. Press *Enter* after naming.

26. Press *R, Z, 180*, and *Enter* to rotate the oarlock as shown on the right side of the following screenshot.

27. Now, select the boat in addition to the oarlock. Press *Ctrl+P* to parent the boat to the oarlock. Choose **Set Parent to Object** in the pop-up menu.

28. Select the other oarlock with *RMB* and then the boat with *Shift+RMB*. Press *Ctrl+P* again.

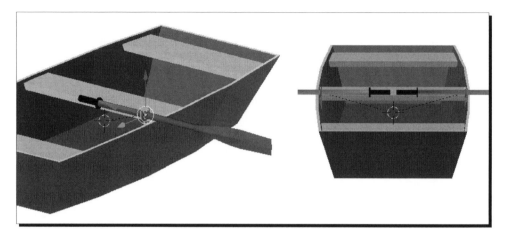

29. Select the boat only with *RMB* and test rotate it to make sure all the parenting is correct and that the oar locks and oars follow the boat. Press *Esc* or *RMB* to release the boat back to its original position.

30. Select **Layer 3**. Press *B* and select the oars and oarlocks. Press *M* and move them to **Layer 1**. Select **Layer 1**.

What just happened?

You just loaded the boat, the oar, and the oarlock into a single file. You made some minor adjustments to the oar and oarlock. You parented the oarlock to the oar, and then moved the oarlock into place and rotated it properly. After duplicating them, you parented the boat to both oarlocks. Notice that when you copied both the oarlock and the oar that the parenting relationship between the objects was copied as well. Well done. If the parenting did not succeed, just press *Ctrl+Z* to undo what you did, and retry it.

For your reference, the file 6907_06_boat_assembled1.blend has the boat, oar, and oarlock in one file. 6907_06_boat_assembled2.blend has the oarlock parented to the oar and oar properly oriented. 6907_06_boat_assembled3.blend has the oarlocks in position. 6907_06_boat_assembled4.blend has the boat parented to the oarlocks and oars.

Have a go hero – adding some blocks to put the oarlock in

You put the oarlocks in the proper place, but to look the best, it would help if there were wooden blocks around the oarlock pin. Open up the boat in the **Edit Mode**, add a block around the oarlock pin, and copy it to the other side. Give the block the same texture as the hull of the boat.

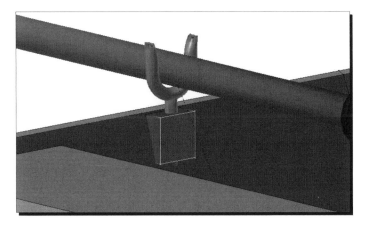

Animating the boat

It's said that "*An animator is an actor with a pencil*". The point remains true even though you are using Blender instead of a pencil. A good animator is also a good actor. This is true even for something as simple as rowing the boat.

Think about rowing the boat. Basically, you dip the oars into the water, move the blades backwards with respect to the boat until the stroke is done, then lift up the oars and move the oars back to the starting position. So how long is that motion going to take?

All animators should own a stopwatch. You can get an inexpensive one on Amazon or at a local store. If you don't have one, you can use a clock or this online stopwatch `http://www.online-stopwatch.com/large-stopwatch/`. But neither is as convenient or as accurate as a stopwatch.

Time for action – timing a stroke

The best way to figure out how long an action takes is to do it and time it. Now you'll do a rowing stroke to see how long the animation should be:

1. Sit where you can lean forward.

2. Hold your arms out and hold your stopwatch in one hand.

3. Start the stopwatch and immediately lean backwards, as though you are pulling oars against the water. This is called the *drive* phase of the stroke.

4. At the end of the stroke, move your hands down to lift the oars out of the water and lean forward. These are known as the *extraction* and *recovery* phases.

5. Then move your hands back up to the starting point to dip the oars back into the water. This is the *catch* phase.

6. Do this three times and then stop the stopwatch. Write down the time it took.

7. Repeat the timing two more times. Hopefully, all three readings are about the same. Take the average of these three readings and then divide that time by three to get the length of time a single stroke cycle takes.

8. Now, start the stopwatch and just pull backward. Stop the stopwatch when you finish pulling backward. Write down the time. Do it three times.

What just happened?

You just did your first bit of acting. By rowing three strokes each time, you got a better average of how long a single stroke should take. By repeating it three times, you know how consistent you are being. My average for the three strokes was 5.8 seconds for three repetitions, or 1.93 seconds for each stroke.

But, you also want a little bit more information about the stroke. That's why you timed just the drive stroke. I was surprised that just the drive stroke was 0.85 seconds. It seemed short, but it leaves 1.08 seconds to raise the oar and move back to the starting position.

Now there is one caveat here

Few of us have a rowboat and a lake at our desk to be sure of our timing. So as an additional reference, I found some rowing videos for you to watch.

Row Exercise: Competitive Rowers
`http://youtu.be/_6JhKZMVL_g`

Tupan: Man rowing a homebuilt skiff in a relaxed manner
`http://youtu.be/6Xc9lLccEf0`

Old Wharf Dory Rowing 1: Maneuvering and turning
`http://youtu.be/Z5wTN0zBFx0`

My Rowing: Man rowing a scull, with comments on improving his form
`http://youtu.be/jPWhTAKSh74`

When I timed the row exercise video, the timing was similar to what I had done, so I was happy with my timing.

Have a go hero – figure out how long it takes you to row the boat

Using the information you got when you acted out rowing the boat, figure out how many frames it will take to do the two parts of the rowing cycle.

 For more information on acting and animating, check out the web page available at http://www.animationarena.com/acting-and-animation.html. It has a lot of good tips on believability, consistency, mood, and personality.

Pop quiz – calculating how long a frame lasts

You can get out your calculators. Here's a basic animation math question.

The default frame speed for Blender is 24 frames per second.

1. If the drive stroke takes 0.85 seconds. How many frames will it need to show it?

2. If the rest of the stroke takes 1.08 seconds, how many frames will it need to show it?

Parenting and kinematics

Earlier you chose the oarlock and parented it to the oar. You also found that you could move the oar around just by moving the oarlock. The oar follows the oarlock just like a child holding their parent's hand.

In *Chapter 3, Controlling the Lamp, the Camera, and Animating Objects* we talked about global axis and local axis. Now each oar has a global axis, a parent boat axis, the parent oarlock axis, and a local axis for the oar itself. It may seem confusing if you describe it, but seeing the boat and the oars, it becomes more intuitive.

Kinematics describes how objects control the motion of other objects. There are two basic kinds that you will use in animation, forward kinematics and inverse kinematics:

◆ **Forward kinematics** is what you will use with the rowboat. The motion of the boat controls the motion of the oarlock, and the oarlock controls the oar.

◆ **Inverse kinematics** is like your hand and shoulder. You focus on moving your hand in relation to your shoulder, and that moves your arm, elbow, and forearm automatically.

Time for action – animating the oarlock and oar

Now that you have the timing, you can animate the oarlock and the oar using the information you got from your timing:

1. Shift to the **Top** view. Drag the **Current Frame Indicator**, the green vertical line in the **Timeline**, as seen seen in the following screenshot, to go to frame **0**.

2. Select the **Oarlock-R**.

3. Press *R, Z, 45,* and *Enter.*

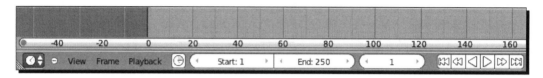

4. Move the cursor over the 3D View and press the letter *I* to set a rotation keyframe at frame **0**. Then move the timeline to frame **58** and set another rotation keyframe. It will look like the left side of the following screenshot. You can either drag the **Current Frame Indicator**, or type in the number of the frame in the button to the right of **End**.

5. Move to frame **26**.

6. Press *R, Z, -90,* and *Enter.* Press *I* to set a rotation keyframe.

7. Repeat this for the other oarlock so that they move in sync with each other. Press the down arrow to go to the previous keyframe at frame **0**. Select **Oarlock-L**, press *R, Z, -45,* and *Enter*, and set a rotation keyframe at frame **0** and frame **58**.

8. Move to frame **26**. Press *R, Z, 90,* and *Enter* and set a rotation keyframe.

9. Shift to the **Side** view.

10. Move to frame **0**.

11. Select **Oar-L**. Press *R, Y, Y, 45*, and *Enter* to dip the oar in the water as shown in the following screenshot. Make a rotation keyframe.

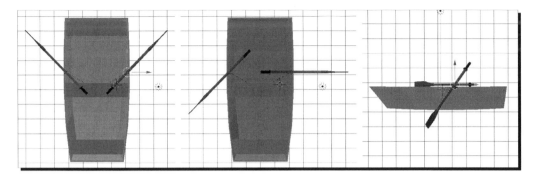

12. Select the other oar. Press *R, Y, Y, 45*, and *Enter* to dip the oar in the water. Make a rotation keyframe.

13. Go to frame **26**. Make rotation keyframes for both oars.

14. Go to frame **58**. Make rotation keyframes for both oars.

15. Go to frame **30**. Select an oar. Press *R, Y, Y, -40*, and *Enter* and make a keyframe for that oar.

16. Select the other oar. Press *R, Y, Y, -40*, and *Enter* and make a keyframe.

17. Go to frame **53**. Select an oar. Press *R, Y, Y, -40,* and *Enter* and make a keyframe for that oar.

18. Select the other oar. Press *R, Y, Y, -40*, and *Enter* and make a keyframe.

19. Scrub the **Current Frame Indicator** in the **Timeline** window to test the animation.

20. Save the file with a unique name.

What just happened?

You set up an animation cycle for the oarlocks and the oars. The oarlocks rotate and move the oars forward and backward by forward kinematics. You set up the drive stroke from frame 0 to frame 26, and the recovery stroke from frame 26 to frame 58. Rotating the oars on their local *Y* axis dips the blades in the water and raises them. First you set up the keyframes at the ends of the drive stroke. Then, you added keyframes for the other extreme of the oar stroke. You placed them a few frames before and after the ends of the drive stroke for the catch and extract phases of the rowing cycle.

For your reference, the file `6907_06_boat_animated1.blend` has all the keyframes for the oarlock and oar.

Animation cycles

In *Chapter 3, Controlling the Lamp, the Camera, and Animating Objects* you experimented with copying keyframes. Here you put that knowledge to use by creating a rowing cycle. As you may have noticed, the keyframes at frame 0 and frame 58 are identical. So you are going to copy the keyframes from frame 26 through frame 58, and move them in time to create a rowing cycle.

Time for action – copying keyframes to make a rowing cycle

Everybody likes to save work. Now that you have made a single rowing cycle, you can just copy it and move the copy down the timeline for a smooth flowing animation:

1. Use the **Current Editor Type** button at the lower left corner of the **Timeline** window, which is below the **3D View,** to change **Timeline** to **Graph Editor** in the window. Open the window up vertically so you can use it more easily. Move **Current Frame Indicator** to frame **84**. You can see what frame you are on in the lower left corner of the **3D View** window.

2. Using the *RMB* and *Shift+RMB* keys, select both oars and both oarlocks.

3. Use *Ctrl+MMB* so you can see all the F-Curves as shown in the next screenshot.

4. With the cursor over the Graph Editor, press *A* to deselect all the keyframes. Use **Border Select** to choose all the keyframes between frame 26 and frame 58 as shown in the following screenshot. You can see that all the keyframes from frame 26 on are highlighted.

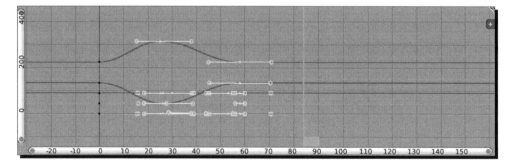

5. Move the Current Frame Indicator to frame 84 in Graph Editor.

6. Press *Shift+D* to copy the keyframes. Move the mouse to the right to start moving the new keyframes, and then press *MMB* to restrict the motion to that direction.

7. Move them until the copies of the keyframes that were at frame 26 are over frame 84. Press *LMB* to release the keyframes as shown in the following screenshot:

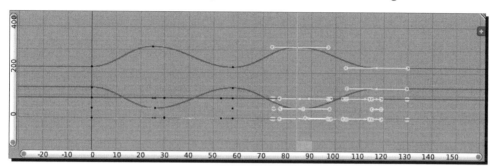

What just happened?

Well done, you made an animation cycle. Did you notice how much less work it took to copy the keyframes than it did to make the original rowing stroke? Animation cycles are a secret that animators have used since Felix the Cat.

The cycle that started at frame 0 finished at frame 58, with identical keyframes; so the rowing cycle is 58 frames long. To repeat the cycle, move copies of the cycle 58 frames farther along the timeline. So when you copied the keyframes from frames 26–58 and moved them, frame 58 became similar to frame 0. Adding 58 to 26 equals 84. So you dragged copies of keyframes at 26–58 and set them down at 84–116 to duplicate the cycle.

Have a go hero – adding more cycles

Make additional cycles by pasting the new frames starting at frame 142 and again at frame 200. You can really start to see the cyclic nature of the motion as shown in the following screenshot. You can see the oscillation of the oarlocks in blue, and the dipping of the paddle in green.

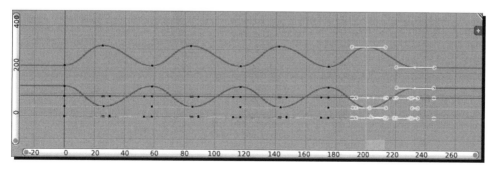

Moving the boat

It looks kind of silly for the boat to stay still while the oars flail quickly. It's time to get your craft moving.

Time for action – moving the boat in sync with the oars

When you row, you dip the oar in the water and push the boat forward using the oar as a lever. The boat coasts while you are moving the oars back. You are going to create a marker to track that motion. When the oar is in the water, the marker will give you a location for the oar tip. When the oar is out of the water, the width of the marker will show you how far to move the boat while it's coasting:

1. Press *Numpad 3* to get the Side view. Make sure you are on frame **0**. Use the **Current Editor Type** button in the lower left corner of **Graph Editor** to change **Graph Editor** to **Timeline**.

2. Move your cursor below the boat. Press *LMB*.

3. Deselect all the objects, and make a cube. Move the cube so the left corner is just below the blade of the oar as shown in the next screenshot.

4. Select the boat and make a location keyframe. Do not make a keyframe for the cube.

5. Move the time to frame **26**.

6. Select the boat and move it in Y so that the oar lines up over the left corner of the cube. Make a location keyframe for the boat as shown in the following screenshot.

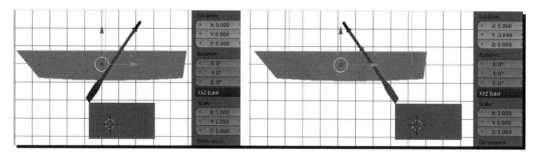

7. Press *N* to open the **Properties** panel. Observe the **Y location** values at frame 0 and frame 26.

8. Mine were **0** and **-3.82**. That's how far the boat moved when being rowed. Assume that it goes about the same distance while coasting, but give it a few frames extra as it will be slower.

9. Select the cube. Change its Y dimension to **3.82**, or the distance your boat went. This is equal to the distance the boat will coast. Move the cube so that the right side of the cube touches the bow of the boat, as seen on the left side of the following screenshot.

10. Go to frame **58**. Select the boat. Move the boat in Y until the bow of the boat touches the left side of the cube, as shown in the following screenshot. Press *LMB* when you are done and make a location keyframe.

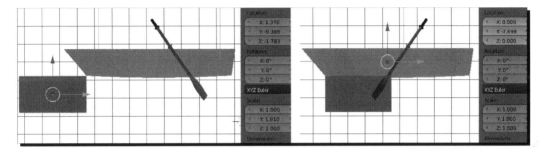

11. Select the cube and move it so the left corner is under the oar again. Don't make a keyframe for the cube. It is just a reference object. If you find you've made a keyframe for the cube, open the Graph Editor, and delete the keyframe. Remember what you learned about selecting particular action channels in *Chapter 3, Controlling the Lamp, the Camera, and Animating Objects* to make it easier. You can use the arrow button next to the **F-Curve Editor** button in the **Graph Editor** header to select active F-Curves.

12. Twenty-six frames past **58** is frame **84**. In the **Timeline**, move to frame **84**. Move the boat again in Y until the oar is over the left corner of the cube, as seen here on the right. It doesn't have to be exact. A little variation is good. It makes it more believable. Make a location keyframe.

13. Go to the frame where the oar dips into the water again. Move the cube so its right side is touching the bow. Move the boat in Y till the bow is touching the left side of the cube. Make a location keyframe. Move the cube so its left corner is by the tip of the oar.

14. Move in the frames until the oar has completed its stroke. Move the boat in Y so the tip of the oar is next to the left side of the cube.

15. Continue this cycle of keyframing the boat's motion as long as your oar strokes continue. Mark the oar when it is in the water and mark the bow when the boat is coasting.

16. Now press *Alt+A* to watch the animation preview. Press *Esc* when you are done watching it.

17. Save the file with a unique name.

What just happened?

With the oar's stroke set, you can know how far the boat should go with each stroke. You started putting in motion keyframes for the boat. Making the keyframes for when the oars are in the water is the easy part. The art is figuring out how long to coast and how far you go when coasting.

If you watched the rowing videos, you know that there is a wide range of expression there. Are you racing, are you purposefully going to a favorite fishing hole, or just enjoying the freedom of being on the water, say with the morning mists curling up from the surface? These would be what you might try to express in a rowing cycle.

 For your reference, the file `6907_06_boat_animated2.blend` has the oarlock, oar, and boat motion.

Have a go hero – rowing your boat

As you saw in the videos, rowing a boat is not just a mechanical motion, it can be very expressive. This is your chance to expand on what you have done.

Modify your rowing cycles and the motion of your boat to express different situations. Here are some suggestions:

- If the cycle seems a bit clumsy, change the timing of when the oar keyframes happen so that the catch and extract phases are smoother. You will want to show only the Y rotations for the oars, and zoom into them so that you can see the rotation.
- Race your boat.
- Make slow, relaxed strokes that let the boat coast a lot.
- Turn the boat in circles.
- Create some buoys in the water and maneuver the boat around them.
- Get cartoony and exaggerate the speed and the rowing; you can even raise the bow up and down in response to the drive strokes.

Tracking the boat with the camera

Now let's follow the boats with the camera. It's pretty easy.

Time for action – tracking the boat

It's pretty natural that if you are watching a boat go by, you turn your head to follow it. The camera is no different. The **Track to Constraint** command lets you do just that:

1. Select the camera with the *RMB*.

2. Press the *Shift* key and the *RMB* to select the boat.

3. Press *Ctrl+T* to get the tracking menu. Select **Track to Constraint**.

4. Press *Numpad 0* to get the camera's view.

5. Press *Alt+A* to preview the animation. Press *Esc* when you are done watching it.

6. Save the file with a unique name.

What just happened?

Tracking is very similar to parenting. Select the camera, then select what you want to track. Press *Ctrl+T* and select **Track to Constraint,** and the camera will follow the object you want to track.

For your reference, the file `6907_06_boat_animated3.blend` has the camera tracking the boat.

Have a go hero – tracking with a light

If you've seen an ice skater, you've probably seen them tracked by a spotlight. Try your hand at tracking an object in motion.

Change the light to a spotlight, and track the boat's motion. The commands are the same as for the camera.

For your reference, the file `6907_06_boat_animated4.blend` has the camera and the spotlight tracking the boat.

Making Stereoscopic 3D Animation

That tracking was pretty cool. But what if you could do it in stereo just like Avatar or Men in Black 3. Blender has got you covered. Check out `6907OS_06_Using Stereoscopic Cameras.pdf` in your download pack. You'll learn how to make two different kinds of stereo camera rigs and use them to record stereo-pairs of images.

Key	Function
MMB	Press it after starting to move, scale, or rotate an object and it locks the motion, scaling, or rotation to the nearest axis.
Ctrl+Z	Undoes a step
Ctrl+Shift+Z	Redoes a previous step undone with *Ctrl+Z*
Alt+F	Makes faces from selected vertices
Shift+Alt+F	Done after using *Alt+F*, this makes a nicer set of faces.
Tab	When using a multi-set button, such as X, Y, Z or R, G, B, it allows you to move quickly between the buttons.
B	Does a border select in the Graph Editor
Ctrl+P	Child a group of selected objects to the last object selected
Ctrl+T	Sets an object(s) to track the last chosen object.
Ctrl+Numpad 0	Sets the active object as the active camera.

Summary

In this chapter you learned how to create oars and oarlocks to move the boat with, and discovered some tricks to make subtle shapes, such as where the shaft tapers into the oar. You found out how to control the smoothness of a surface. You learned to append objects to the scene so you can combine and reuse objects. You created child parent relationships to group objects for animation. You used kinematics to organize your animation. You learned to use animation cycles to save work. You tracked objects in motion with a camera, a spot lamp, and a camera rig.

As you have been making the boat, you may have been wondering how can I plan out my work, how can I use plans from the real world to model, and how can I organize these files to make it easier to work and so I can find them later? That's what the next chapter will help you with, and we'll get started with your main project, creating and animating a nautical scene.

Let's go!

7

Planning your Work, Working your Plan

In the last chapter you increased your understanding of animation. You assembled the boat, parenting the different objects together and animating them. You learned about children, parents, and kinematics. You explored tracking and expanded that knowledge into doing some stereoscopic rendering.

With this good foundation, it's time to take a moment and start planning your big project. You need to understand the conventions that will help you keep track of what you do and where you put what you have done to make it easier for you to achieve what you want.

In this chapter you will examine:

- ◆ Setting up a template in Blender to guide your modeling
- ◆ Using the template to help model the mast, boom, gaff, and bowsprit
- ◆ Using Bezier Curves for modeling the rudder, keel, and tiller
- ◆ Learning better ways to help keep your projects organized:
    - ❏ Planning your animation
    - ❏ Creating a story
    - ❏ Using storyboards to plan what you are going to do
    - ❏ Using animatics to get the timing right before you animate

- Using charts and guides to help you create your animation:
  - ❑ Safe Title/Safe Action/Lower Third guides
  - ❑ Timing diagrams
  - ❑ Exposure sheets and Bar sheets
- Using the sound track to guide animation timing.

Let's get started.

Using templates for modeling

Well, first you have to have a good idea of what you want to make. This is your next project, a comfy little sloop, as shown in the following screenshot:

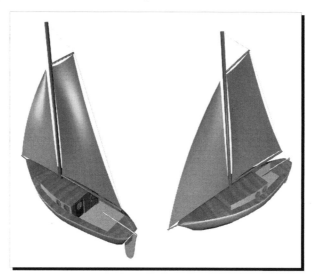

You will need something to tell you what size the object you are building will be. There are many ways to get the measurements you need.

Quite often you can find plans on the net on sites like http://www.boatdesign.net/ plans/index.htm. You could also measure the object itself. Once, to build a model of an electric guitar, I went to the Carvin guitar factory and took my caliper micrometer and rulers to one of their Ultra V guitars and made some accurate drawings to guide my modeling.

In the plans for the sloop, as shown in the next screenshot, you can see a top view, a side view, and to the very right, there is the number 6 between two dashes to indicate the scale of the drawing. In this case the lines above and below the 6 show the scaling for six Blender units. I decided that a front view was not necessary, because all the details can be figured out from the side and top views.

Have a go hero – inspecting the templates

If you are copying from plans, there should be some indication of the scale somewhere on the plans. What you may need to do is take the plans that you find into a photo editing program and adapt them to your needs adding, subtracting, or modifying details. You don't really want details in the plans that you are not going to make.

Sometimes the images that you get on the Web are not necessarily scaled accurately relative to each other. You may need to make sure that the projections are the same scale as each other, so that details in a front view are the same height as they are on a side view; the details for the side view are as long as they are on the top; or the details in the front are as wide as they are in the top view, and so on:

- ◆ Look at the graphics `6907_07_01.png` and `6907_07_02.png` in a paint program.

- ◆ Put the two graphics in a single file and make `6907_07_02.png` semi-transparent.

- ◆ Rotate the top view 90 degrees clockwise. Then move it so that the graphics overlay and you can see how the two views compare. `6907_07_02.png` was originally made so it would lay over `6907_07_01.png`, but then rotated 90 degrees for use in Blender.

All the graphics for templates should be the same width. Blender uses the width of the graphic as a basis for scaling it.

The following illustration has the names of the major components you will be dealing with as you make your sloop in the next three chapters:

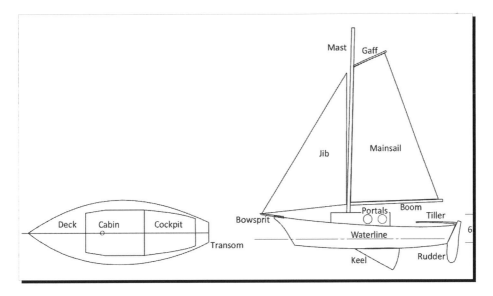

Time for action – adding a template

Now you'll get started by putting up the templates so they can be seen within the 3D View:

1. Open a new file in Blender.

2. Press *Numpad 3* to get the **Right** view in the 3D View. Press *Numpad 5* to make sure it is in **Ortho** mode.

3. Press *N* to display the **Properties** panel in the 3D View.

4. Scroll down to the **Background Images** subpanel of the **3D View Properties** panel as seen in the following screenshot.

5. Click the *LMB* over the triangle that is on the left of the subpanel to open it up.

6. Check the checkbox by the text **Background Images** so that the background image will be displayed.

7. Click on the **Add Image** button with the *LMB*.

8. Click on the **Open** button with the *LMB* and load the image 6907_07_01.png from this chapter's Images directory in the download pack.

9. Click on the black **All Views** button next to **Axis:**, and select **Right** from the pop-up menu.

10. Press *Numpad 7* to see the **Top** view in the **3D View**.

11. Click the **Add Image** button in the **Background Images** subpanel of the **3D View Properties** panel with the *LMB*. Scroll down, you will see the subpanel where you just added the first template. Below it is another subpanel that says **Not Set**, in the upper-left corner. That is the one you want. You will be adding another template.

12. In the **Not Set** subpanel, select the **Open** button with the *LMB* and load the image `6907_07_02.png` from the download pack.

13. In the pop-up menu beside **Axis:** change **All Views** to **Top**. Notice that **Not Set** has been replaced with **6907_07_02.png**.

What just happened?

You just added two templates, one for the **Right** view, and one for the **Top** view. You have also created two new subpanels with quite a few control buttons. It's now time to use them.

Time for action – scaling and aligning the template

The next step is to make sure that the template is properly scaled Blender scene, so that the units marked on the template are the same as an equal number of units in the Blender scene.

To do this, you will set the cube to the size of six Blender units. Next, you will adjust the template until the dimension marks—those two lines above and below the number 6 on the side-view template—align with the top and bottom of the cube.

1. In the **3D View**, select the cube. Scroll to the top of the **3D View Properties Panel** so you can see the **Transform** subpanel. Set the **Dimensions:** to **X: 6.00, Y: 6.00, Z: 6.00**, the same way that you set the dimensions of reference blocks in *Chapter 5*, *Building a Simple Boat*.

2. Press *Numpad 3* to display the **Right** view.

3. Scroll down to the **Background Image** subpanel of the **3D View Properties** panel.

4. Look in the panel where it says **6709_07_01.png**, as shown in the following screenshot.

5. Change the size of the background image by setting the value of **Size:** to **25**. That makes the width of the template 50 units wide, or 25 units on either side of the axis. The height of the template is adjusted proportionately.

6. Below the **Size:** button in the panel as shown in the following screenshot, set the **Y:** value to **18**.

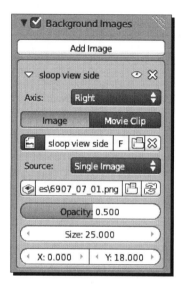

7. Zoom out in the **3D View** until you see the entire image of the sloop.

8. With the cursor over the 3D View, press *G*, then *Z*, then *3*, then *Enter* to move the cube up 3 units in Z. Look at the template. Press *G* and move the cube in *Y* until you reach the number **6** with the two dimensioning marks, above and below, as shown in the following screenshot. Make sure that the top and bottom of the cube lines up with the marks. If they are in line with the mark you can skip the next step.

9. If the marks above and below the number **6** do not match with the top and bottom of the cube, you will need to adjust the **Size:** in the **6709_07_01.png** subpanel until they do. To do this, make an adjustment of the **Size:** then move the cube so it is centered between the dimensioning marks. Repeat this until the dimensioning marks on the template fit the top and bottom of the cube. Then make sure that the cube is selected; and in the **Transform** subpanel of the **3D View Properties** panel, set the cube's Location **Z:** value to **3**. Finally, in the **Background Images** subpanel of the **3D View Properties** panel, adjust the template's **Y:** value until the dimensioning marks once more lay over the top and bottom of the cube. Well done!

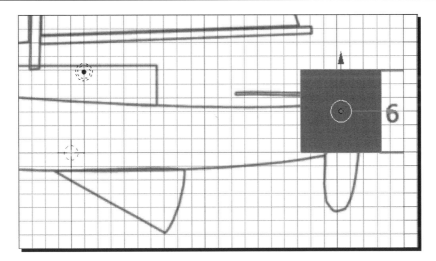

10. In the **Background Images** subpanel of the **Properties** panel, select the subpanel for the **6907_07_02.png** image as shown in the following screenshot.

11. Change **Size:** of the template image to **25** or, if you had to adjust the size, to your final size.

12. Press *Numpad 7* for the **Top** view. You want to make sure that the template is centered. If not, adjust it in **X:** so the centerline of the boat template lays over the *Y* axis.

13. Save the file to a unique name.

What just happened?

By adjusting the size of the background image you scaled it to an object of known size, which in this case is a reference block of six Blender units size. You changed the **Y** offset of the template so that the waterline of the sloop is at the origin of the scene. Then the **Top** view template was scaled to the same size to keep both templates in registration. Now you have two templates to guide you in building the sloop. Well done!

 For your reference, the file `6907_07_templates_set_up.blend` has both templates and the six unit reference block.

Time for action – building the mast

Now it's time to start building the sloop. Since you have the template in the Blender file, you can build each object to the template and be confident that they will all fit together when you are done:

1. Press *Numpad 3* to get the **Side** view. Use *Shift+MMB* to center your view on the mast and *Ctrl+MMB* to zoom into the mast so that the width of the mast in the template covers a third of the 3D View. Press *Shift+S* and select **Cursor to Center** from the menu. This makes sure that the 3D Cursor is centered with respect to the X axis, so your mast will be centered in the sloop. Place your cursor over the center of the mast in the template. Press the *LMB* to put the 3D Cursor there. Press *Shift+A* and select **Mesh**, then **Cylinder** from the menu to make a cylinder.

2. Press *S* and use the mouse to scale the cylinder so that it is about the same diameter as the mast, as shown in the following screenshot. Press the *LMB* to release the scaling.

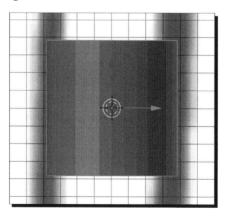

3. Press the *Tab* key to go into **Edit Mode**.

4. Make sure that the **Limit Selection to Visible** button on the 3D View header is light gray so that you select both the front and back facing vertices.

5. Press *A* to deselect all the vertices and then press *B* to start the **Border** select. Select the bottom vertices.

6. Zoom out so you can see the bottom of the mast. If you need help moving the view around within the scene, check out *Chapter 2, Getting Comfortable using the 3D View* to refresh your memory.

7. Press *G* and use the mouse to move the selected vertices to the bottom of the mast. Press the *LMB* to release the move.

8. Press *A* to deselect all vertices. Then, select the top vertices and move them to the top of the mast.

9. Zoom into the top of the mast. Then, press *S* and scale the top vertices in a little to match the template more closely. Press the *LMB* to release the scaling.

10. In the **Properties** window on the right-hand side of the Blender window, select the **Object** button from the header (the orange cube, fifth button from the left). Name the object **Mast** and press *Enter*.

11. With the cursor over the 3D View window, press the *Tab* key to return to **Object Mode**.

12. Press the *Home* key on your keyboard to see the entire scene again. This is not the *Home* key on your Numpad. If you are using a Mac, press *fn+Left arrow*.

What just happened?

Well, you just made the mast. Pretty easy as it turns out. By moving the top and bottom vertices independently, you copied the slight angle of the mast, and then gave it a small bit of taper, like the template.

Have a go hero – making the boom, the gaff, and the bowsprit

Now try it again with different parts. As you make them, make sure that you get into **Object Mode** after making it, and deselect that part before making a new one. Otherwise, the part will be stuck together as part of the same object, just as the seats for the boat were in *Chapter 5, Building a Simple Boat*. It is easiest if you rotate the part so that it is at about the same angle as the object on the template that you are making before you scale it and go into **Edit Mode**:

◆ The boom is the pole at the bottom of the mainsail

◆ The gaff is the pole at the top

- The bowsprit is the pole that sticks off of the bow of the sloop

- Make them and name them

 For your reference, the file `6907_07_sloop-mast.blend` has the mast started. `6907_07_sloop-mast_boom_gaff_bowsprit.blend` has the mast, boom, gaff, and bowsprit completed.

Modeling with Bezier Curves

In *Chapter 3, Controlling the Lamp, the Camera, and Animating Objects* you discussed using Bezier Curves as F-Curves to control motion. Blender uses Bezier Curves for modeling as well. They are good for making objects with smooth curves. One big difference between the curves used for controlling motion and the curves used for modeling is that the ones used for modeling can move along the *X, Y,* and *Z* axes instead of just the timeline axis, so they can be used with much more flexibility.

Making an object with a single Bezier Curve

Much of the time, Bezier Curves are used like cookie cutters to describe a shape which is then extruded. These may even have holes in them so you can make very complex shapes. However you will start with a simple one.

Time for action – making the rudder with a Bezier Curve

The controls for the Bezier Curves work in a similar manner as the controls for the F-Curve. You have a control point that represents a particular location in space and two control handles that control how the curve approaches and departs from the control point. Check *Chapter 3, Controlling the Lamp, the Camera, and Animating Objects* again if you need a reminder on how they work:

1. Select the scaling reference cube. Press *M, 2,* and *Enter* to move it to layer 2 so it won't be in your way.

2. Press *Shift+S* and select **Cursor to Center** from the menu. Use *Shift+MMB* to center your view on the top of the rudder, and *Ctrl+MMB* to zoom into the rudder. Check the diagram earlier in the chapter if you don't remember what the rudder is. Move the 3D Cursor to the top-right corner of the rudder as shown in the following screenshot.

3. Press *Shift+A* and select **Curve** and then **Bezier** as shown in the following screenshot:

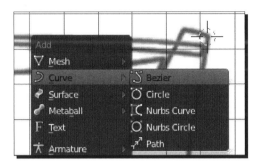

4. By default, the Bezier Curve is facing upwards. Press *R, Y, 90*, and *Enter* to make it face towards you, as seen on the left side of the following screenshot.

5. Press the *Tab* key to get into **Edit Mode**. Use the *RMB* to select the upper control point and then move it to the right-hand top corner of the rudder and click the *LMB* to drop it in place. Move the lower control point down to where the curve in the back of the rudder changes direction, as has been done in the center of the following screenshot.

6. Move the cursor to the bottom of the rudder and press *Ctrl+LMB* to make the new control point. Now make two more control points. Make one where the rudder meets the bottom of the hull and one at the left-hand top of the rudder as shown in the right side of the following screenshot:

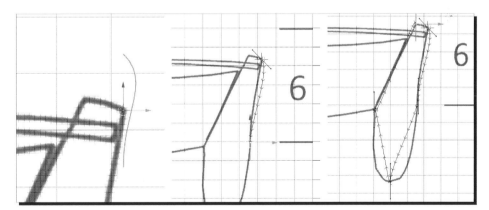

7. The last control point will already be selected. Use *Shift+RMB* to select the first control point at the right-hand top of the rudder as well; then press *F* to close the Bezier Curve.

8. Zoom in and make sure that each control point is over the outline of the rudder in the template. Move the control points if necessary. Don't worry about where the curve goes, just get the control points in place. Zoom back out when you are done.

9. Press the *RMB* to select the lower control handle for the control point at the bottom of the rudder and move the control handles about 90 degrees clockwise, so that the path follows the shape of the rudder more closely. Then, select the other control handle and move it horizontally so that the curve follows the rudder outline, as shown in the left side of the following screenshot.

10. At the place where the rudder contacts the bottom of the hull, select the upper control handle of the control point. Press *V* and select **Vector** from the pop-up menu.

11. Between the top two control points are two control handles, pointing up as seen in the center of the following screenshot. Select both control handles, press *V* and select **Vector** from the menu.

12. Zoom in to the top of the rudder. Press *G* and move the two control handles at the top of the rudder up just a little, so there is a gentle arch on the top of the rudder.

13. Move the lower control handle of the top-right-side control point so that the curve aligns with the outline of the rudder on the template.

14. At the place where the rudder contacts the bottom of the hull, select the control handle that points down and move it so it points straight down, as seen on the right side of the following screenshot:

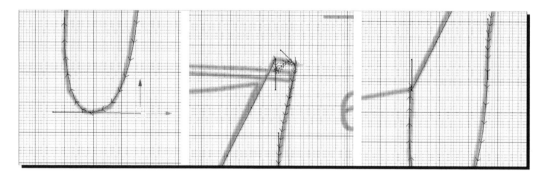

15. Select the left-hand control point at the bottom of the rudder. Move it slightly to the right so that the curve aligns with the outline of the rudder on the template.

16. In the 3D View header set the **Viewport Shading** menu to **Solid**.

17. In the **Properties** window, select the **Object Data** button in the header. It's the eighth button from the left, with the curve and control points on it, as shown in the following screenshot.

18. In the **Shape** subpanel, select the **2D** button with the *LMB* to highlight it in blue as shown in the following screenshot. In the **Geometry** subpanel set the **Extrude:** value to **0.080** as shown in the bottom-left corner of the following screenshot:

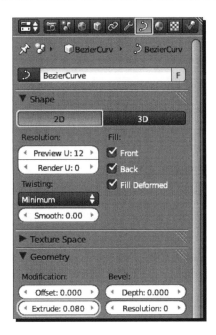

19. Next, select the **Object** panel from the **Properties** window header. It's the fifth button from the left with the orange cube. Name the object **Rudder**.

20. Move the cursor to the 3D View and then press the *Tab* key to get back into **Object Mode**.

21. Save the file to a unique name.

What just happened?

You used the Bezier Curve to create the rudder for the sloop. First you made the control points and then closed the Bezier Curve.

Next, you adjusted the control points and control handles. You discovered that the commands for modeling with a Bezier Curve are the same as the commands for modifying Bezier Curves in the Graph Editor. You may have noticed that when using a Bezier Curve they can be a little messy at the beginning, so you want to use the absolute minimum number of control points possible.

Finally, you made the curve into a solid and made the extrusion 0.080 to make the rudder the right thickness.

> For your reference, the file 6907_07_sloop - bcurve_ rudder1.blend has control points laid in, but not closed. 6907_07_sloop - bcurve_rudder2.blend has the path closed and the top adjusted. 6907_07_sloop - bcurve_ rudder3.blend has the completed rudder.

Using multiple Bezier Curves to make an object

In addition to using Bezier Curves like a cookie cutter, you can also combine them to make objects. One Bezier Curve controls the shape of an object and the other creates a path to follow.

Time for action – making the path and the cross-section for the tiller

First, you will create a path that describes the length of the tiller and then you will create the shape of the cross-section of the tiller:

1. With the cursor over the **3D View**, press *M*, *2*, and *Enter* to move the rudder to Layer 2.

2. Press *A* to deselect all objects.

3. Adjust the 3D View so that you can see the entire length of the tiller on the template (the tiller is the handle that controls the rudder).

4. Move the 3D Cursor to the vertical center of the right end of the tiller.

5. Press *Shift+A* and select **Curve** then **Bezier** from the menus to make a Bezier Curve.

6. Press *R*, *Y*, *90*, and *Enter*.

7. Press the *Tab* key to get into **Edit Mode**. Move the top control point to the left tip of the tiller. Move the other control point to where the 3D Cursor is.

8. Adjust the control handles so that the curve goes along the center of the tiller outline in the template and has a graceful curve.

9. Select the **Object** panel from the **Properties** window header. It's the fifth button from the left with the orange cube. Name the curve **Tiller Path** as shown in the following screenshot, then press *Enter*:

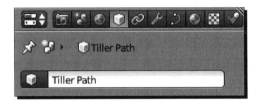

10. With the cursor over the 3D View, press the *Tab* key to change to **Object Mode** and press *A* to deselect everything.

11. Press *Shift+A* and select **Curve** then **Circle** from the menus to make a Bezier Circle.

12. Press *R, Y, 90*, and then *Enter*.

13. Press *S* and use the mouse to scale the circle until it is approximately the same diameter as the base of the tiller on the template, as seen on the left side of the next screenshot. Press the *LMB* to release the scaling.

14. Press the *Tab* key to go into **Edit Mode**, as seen in the center of the following graphic.

15. Press *A* to deselect all the control points and control handles. Press *C* for the **Circle** select. Select the control handles, but not the control points. Press the *RMB* to end the selection.

16. Press *V* and select **Vector** from the menu so that the circle becomes a diamond, as seen on the right side of the following screenshot.

17. Press *A* to select all control points and control handles. Press *R, 45*, and press *Enter*.

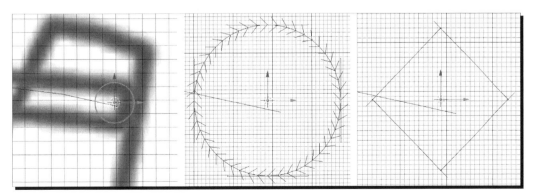

18. Press the *Tab* key to go into **Object Mode**.

19. In the **Properties** window, select the **Object** button from the header (the orange cube, fifth button from the left). Name the object **Tiller Shape**.

20. Select the **Tiller Path** with the *RMB*.

21. In the **Properties** window header, select the **Object Data** button, it's the eighth button from the left, as highlighted in the following screenshot. In the **Shape** subpanel make sure that the **3D** button is highlighted in blue. In the **Geometry** subpanel, click on the box below **Bevel Object:** and select **Tiller Shape** from the menu.

22. Save the file to a unique name.

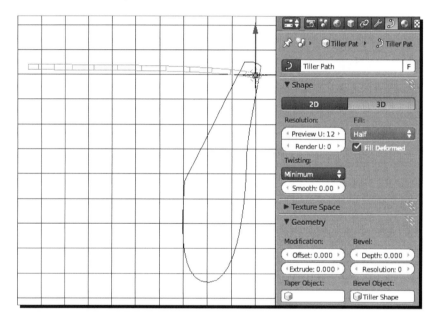

What just happened?

You just discovered another way to build with Bezier Curves, very similar to the way that Pierre Bezier had in mind when he first started to use them. You created a gentle, curving path, and a shape, and put them together to make the tiller. Well done!

For your reference, the file `6907_07_sloop - bcurve_tiller1.blend` has the path for the tiller. `6907_07_sloop - bcurve_tiller2.blend` has shape for the tiller. `6907_07_sloop - bcurve_tiller3.blend` has the completed tiller.

Have a go hero – making the keel

This will be a good exercise in building items using a Bezier Curve. Remember to move the 3D Cursor to the place where you want to begin your keel:

- The keel is the blade on the bottom of the sloop. Use a Bezier Curve to make the keel. It's very similar to building the rudder.

- When it's done, save it to a unique file name.

 For your reference, the file `6907_07_sloop - rudder_tiller_mast_boom_gaff_bowsprit.blend` has all the miscellaneous parts for the sloop.

Keeping everything organized

With all the booms, rudders, oars, and other parts you are creating, you are starting to get quite a collection of 3D objects here. You need to make sure they are well organized so you can find them in the future.

Everybody organizes their files in a slightly different way and there are many good ways to do it. What you need to do is organize your files so that you can find them a year from now, when you've forgotten nearly everything about the project that you are working on. Projects that are hot now can be history in 20 minutes, and then come back in six months. You just never know.

A Blender project won't just be the Blender file. It also includes any graphics that you have used to make textures, special plug-ins for Blender, such as the Bolt Factory which automates making bolts and screws, text and Python language files, as well as the finished files you render out. There's a lot to organize.

There are two ways to specify the locations of files. One is called **absolute addressing**, the other is **relative addressing**. Absolute addressing specifies the address of a file using a specific path such as `C:\blender\graphics\coolgraphic.png`, or `http://www.blender.org/download/get-blender/`. Relative addresses specify where a file is in relation to where they are being called from. This provides flexibility because the root directory is not important, it's just the relationship between any two files that is important.

Pop quiz – organizing Blender files

Blender uses relative addresses for the Blender files that it makes. The addresses are stored relative to where the `.blend` file is stored.

Assume that you save a blender file named `MyBoat.blend` in the `C:\Boat_Project` directory, and you save the textures for the deck in `C:\Boat_Project\Images`:

1. If you copy the `MyBoat.blend` file to a directory named `C:\NewBoat`, where will it look for the textures of the deck?

    a. `C:\Boat_Project\Images`

    b. `C:\NewBoat\Images`

    c. `C:\Blender\Boat Textures`

    d. `http://www.NewBoat.com/Images`

2. By which file name will you be able to best recognize what it was, in six months?

    a. `My new project.blend`

    b. `Boat1.blend`

    c. `Sloop of War_USS Constitution_1854 version.blend`

    d. `Sloop_version 3_done.blend`

3. Which sets of texture files will be easiest to recognize in six months?

    a. `Sloop_texture_deck.png, Sloop_texture_mast.png, Sloop_texture_hull.png`

    b. `deck texture.png, mast texture.png, hull texture.png`

    c. `pine13.png, oak_striated.png, offwhite_pearl.png`

Making an index of your files

Another thing you may want to do is include a text file or spreadsheet file that lets you know what files are needed and which files are which. It can be as simple or complex as you want, but it will pay you back for the time needed to set it up and maintain it many times over. Blender has a text window, which was described in *Chapter 2, Getting Comfortable using the 3D View*. You can use the text window to make a list of all the files you need, and the list will always be handy when you open that Blender file.

Saving your Blender files

In *Chapter 3, Controlling the Lamp, the Camera, and Animating Objects,* you covered saving Blender files and finding out where the backup files are hidden. But saving files is important enough to deserve a little review.

Pop quiz – saving Blender files

1. When is the best time to save your Blender file?

    a. At the end of the work day.

    b. Every couple of hours.

    c. Right now!

2. When saving your Blender file, when do you use the `Increment the filename number` function by pressing the + button before you save the file?

    a. Never

    b. Every time

    c. If I've made a significant change to the file

Planning your animation

Now that you are organized to never lose a frame or element of your animation, you are ready to focus on what you want to do. You want to tell a story.

Discovering the story you want to tell with your animation

Whether you are setting up a game, doing scientific visualization, or making an animation to show on YouTube, odds are that there's a story involved. And I'm sure you want it to be a good one. I can't give you all the rules here. According to Gene Deitch, director of Tom Terrific, Tom and Jerry and Krazy Kat cartoons, you start with a premise, or an idea. The premise breaks down into three parts, a character, a conflict, and a resolution. Think about how your favorite animation breaks down into these three parts.

There are plenty of books and online sources, and the following is a list of a few of those.

Sources for creating stories for animation

Story - What's it All About? available at `http://www.awn.com/ genedeitch/gene-deitch-how-succeed-animation/part- one-how-you-should-do-it/chapter-7-story-whats-it-/ page/1%2C1`

How to Write for Animation available at `http://www.jeffreyscott. tv/HTWFA.htm`

How to Write an Animation Script available at `http://www.ehow.com/ how_2102588_write-animation-script.html`

Animation Scriptwriting: The Writer's Road Map available at `http://www. awn.com/mag/issue5.11/5.11pages/demottanimation.php3`

How To Learn To Write Like An Animator available at `http://www. squidoo.com/writingforanimation`

Robert McKee Story Seminar available at `http://mckeestory.com/`

But we've all been listening to stories, watching stories, and telling stories all our lives. So I'm willing to bet that you can make a good start with what you know now. The issue here is to get your ideas out where you can use them to plan your animation.

Here are a few tips:

◆ Work fast and loose. What you want to do is make a bunch of animations and learn a little more with each one. You're not going to win an Oscar for your first animations, so don't be a perfectionist. Have fun!

◆ Sketch out your ideas on paper. Get a story down, but be willing to let it grow as it will. In *Toy Story*, *Buzz Lightyear* started out as a toy one-man-band character named *Tinny*; *Woody* began as a sarcastic ventriloquist's dummy.

◆ Look around you for inspiration.

◆ Keep it simple, keep it short, keep it so you can make it easily.

◆ Planning is not locking yourself into something. It starts as exploration of the possibilities and morphs into figuring out the best way to present the best of your ideas.

Bringing your story to life with storyboards

Storyboards are like a comic strip where you lay out the sequence of events in quickly drawn panels that let you get an idea of the visual flow of the animations.

Here is how *Sam Chen* tackled the problem when he was planning his short film *Eternal Gaze* which won a *Siggraph Best of Show Award* and a *Student Academy Award*. He drew his storyboard on Post-it® notes. Post-it® notes are about the right size and shape for a storyboard panel, and you can rearrange them any way you want.

Once Sam was happy with the story, he scanned them in to his computer and used the images to create an animatic to guide his animation. His story, *Sam Chen and Eternal Gaze,* available at `http://www.independent-magazine.org/node/156` is an inspiration for the independent animator and is worth your time to read.

Making a storyboard

We are not going to go into depth on how to make great storyboards, but at the most fundamental level, they are an excellent method to think your animation through before you begin it.

Storyboards were first used by millionaire *Howard Hughes* to help him plan the aerial shots in the 1930 movie, *Hell's Angels*, about combat pilots in World War I.

Why do storyboards?

- ◆ They help you think out your shots and experiment before committing yourself to a shot
- ◆ They help you discover continuity problems between shots
- ◆ They help you develop the visual style of your shots
- ◆ They help you communicate to other people just what it is that you intend to do with other people
- ◆ They help you incorporate suggestions from others into your animation without the cost of modeling, animating, rendering, and compositing

Storyboards are notes for your camera work. They can be as simple as rough shapes and stick figures, but you want to give a feeling of scale and how much of the screen an object or character fills. One thing you will notice is that storyboards love incorporating rectangles and arrows.

We discussed camera moves in *Chapter 3, Controlling the Lamp, the Camera, and Animating Objects*. The graphic on the left side shows a camera zoom in. The graphic in the center shows a camera dolly in. The graphic on the right side shows two ways to indicate a pan, you can use an arrow or you can show the starting and ending points of the pan and connect them with smaller arrows.

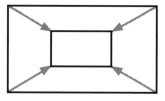 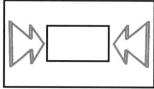 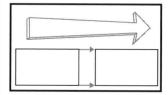

Note that there were two styles of arrows. Stick-like arrows and 3D arrows. The stick-like arrows generally are used to show that the camera is being moved. The 3D arrows suggest motion within the scene. But then again, this is art. There are no hard and fast rules. Do it as you like, but make sure that it communicates your intent. The best way to see how others have done storyboards is to Google the word `storyboards`, and then look at images.

Here are some links for more information on creating storyboards.

Thoughts on drawing for storyboards-PT 1 and Thoughts on drawing for storyboards-PT 2: This is an excellent source on drawing and communicating with drawing available at `http://drawingsfromamexican.blogspot.com/2006/11/thoughts-on-drawing-for-storyboards-pt.html` and `http://drawingsfromamexican.blogspot.com/2006/11/thoughts-on-drawing-for-storyboards-pt_27.html`

Basic Techniques for Drawing Storyboards available at `http://storyboard.cfms.uct.ac.za/`

Storyboards available at `http://accad.osu.edu/womenandtech/Storyboard%20Resource/`

How To Draw Storyboards available at `http://vtkproductions.com/dar_storyboards.htm`

Storyboards and What is a Storyboard Artist? available at `http://www.wildsound-filmmaking-feedback-events.com/storyboards.html`

Post-it®s are good for storyboarding because they come in a variety of sizes and colors. They are cheap and sticky so you will be encouraged to work fast and loose. You will not make your sketch so beautiful that you fall in love with how it looks, and you can include the frame into a storyboard as soon as you finish drawing.

Start by drawing a rectangle that's as wide as the Post-it®. Give the rectangle the proportions your animations will be in, most likely `16:9 HD` or `4:3 Standard` video.

Say you're doing a ghost story involving a boat. All you have in the scene is a boat sitting on the lake. How do you tell the story?

In the establishing shot, the boat is in the middle of a lake, like the first frame of the following storyboard. The camera is far from the boat so that the viewer can see that the boat is isolated, away from the shore, and without an operator.

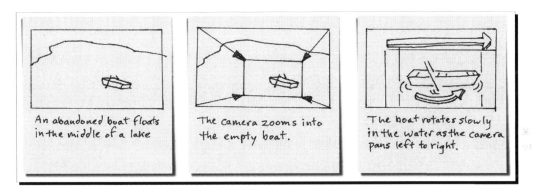

An abandoned boat floats in the middle of a lake

The camera zooms into the empty boat.

The boat rotates slowly in the water as the camera pans left to right.

If you want to show your boat lying idle in the middle of a lake as an opening shot, you will have to draw it so that it only fills a small part of the frame. At the bottom, put a little text that describes the shot.

Next, the boat is obviously the center of interest, so you want to investigate it. You want the camera to zoom into the boat. As shown in the center frame of the preceding storyboard, you draw a similar frame, but you put a rectangle around the area that will be shown at the end of the zoom and you put lines from the edges of the beginning of the zoom to the end of the zoom, and arrowheads on the lines to show which direction the zoom is going, in or out.

Now, observing the boat closely, you see that it is drifting in a slow circle. This tells the viewer that, though the boat is empty, apparently something has happened to cause the boat to move on its own on this placid lake. In the storyboard, the top arrow shows the camera panning, and the two inner frames show where the pan starts and stops. The arrow by the boat shows which direction the boat is turning.

As you make your storyboard, you may want to use a large board or unused wall to tack them all up, from left to right, so that you can see the visual flow of the animation.

Technology changes every day

If you have a graphics tablet and a graphics program that you are very comfortable using, you may want to make your storyboards on your computer. But there are some things to consider. Working completely digitally does allow you to do cleaner work, trace pictures downloaded from the net, and makes creating an animatic very easy.

Using pencil and paper offers you the spontaneity of quick sketches. Being away from the computer encourages you to dip deeper into your imagination. It lets you spread all the images out where you can see them all at once.

Have a go hero – making your own storyboard

There is no better way to understand the power of a storyboard than by making your own. So give it a try. You'll find how flexible this method can be. Drawing skills are not required. But try to make your figures occupy the same amount of room as they will in the camera:

- Get yourself a pad of Post-it® notes.
- Make a storyboard for an animation about a haunted boat. What has just happened? Why and how is the boat haunted? Get creative about the camera angles you use. Could the camera be in the water, about to be run over by the boat? Would the oars become bloody battle axes, or limp and rubbery? How do you use pacing and perspective to tell a story?

Using animatics to plan the timing of your animation

If you read the article about *Sam Chen*, then you know that he scanned his Post-it® notes and made an animatic of his animation from them. Animatics are a combination of slide show, rough animations, and maybe a rough sound track. This gives you a surprisingly good feel for how your animation will work. It will help you establish the pace and timing of the scene before you animate it. The animatic video can even be used as a template for animation. With Blender, you would drop your graphics into the Video Sequence Editor and spread them out over time to give yourself a rough idea of how everything will look after it's animated. You will examine using the Video Sequence Editor to edit animation in a later chapter.

Links about animatics

Using Blender for Animatics available at `http://www.blender.org/features-gallery/testimonials/animatics-for-motion-pictures`

Sintel, the Animatic available at `http://www.sintel.org/news/1st-minute-animatic/`

 Create an Animatic available at `http://www.computerarts.co.uk/tutorials/create-animatic`

Watch these two together, the animatic and the finished animation of Dirty Harry by Gorillaz. See how they changed their ideas between the animatic and final animation.

Gorillaz Dirty Harry Animatic available at `http://www.youtube.com/watch?v=M1uRncKY8DU`

Gorillaz Dirty Harry Finished Animation available at `http://www.dailymotion.com/video/xns26_gorillaz-dirty-harry_music`

Using charts and guides to help you plan your animation

When planning your animation, it's good to make use of guides to help you save time and work. Here are some to help you establish where your animation should happen on screen, how long the actions should take, and plan what work is required to create the animation.

Staying in TV limits with Safe Title-Action zones and Lower Thirds

The **Safe Title zone** and **Safe Action zones** originated in the black-and-white days of television. They were created to make sure that what was put on the screen got seen. The early TV was very imprecise. It was decided that only the inner 80 percent of the image was likely enough to be seen and that it could be trusted to display titles and sponsor logos. Only the inner 90 percent was likely enough to be seen so that any critical action could be shown. The outer 10 percent was not to be trusted at all. Sometimes in local TV ads, you can see text and images chopped off where unskilled artists fail to observe these guidelines.

The **Lower Third** is a convention for advertisers. It reserves about the bottom 1/4 to 1/3 for the sponsor's logo and contact information for ads. This will vary with every sponsor, so contact the station or agency that is in charge of that client if you have any questions.

The following screenshot shows where these areas are. It is included in your download pack as 6907_07_03.png for your use. All of the white area is the **Safe Title** zone. All of the light gray area and the white area is the **Safe Action** zone. All the area in the **Safe Title** zone and under the **Lower Third** line may be used for sponsor logos, and so on.

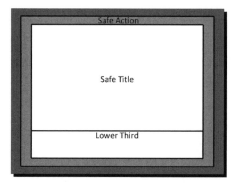

Time for action – adding a Safe Title/Safe Action guide to Blender

Adding the Safe Title/Safe Action guide to Blender is pretty easy. It's just like adding a template. What you will want to watch for is that when you select the presets for NTSC or PAL television, not only do the proportions of the screen change, but the frame rate changes as well:

1. Save and close the Blender file that you were using to make the sloop. Save it to a unique file name that you will remember in six months.

2. Open up a new Blender file.

3. Press *Numpad 0* to get the **Camera** view.

4. The steps for adding a Safe Title/Safe Action guide are the same as those that you used for making the templates.

5. Press *N* in the **3D View** to get the **Properties** panel, as shown in the following screenshot. Scroll down to the **Background Images** subpanel and check the box beside the text **Background Images** as shown in the following screenshot. Press the **Add Image** button. Press the **Open** button to open up the file browser and find the image 6907_07_03.png from the download pack.

6. Change the value of **Axis:** from **All Views** to **Camera**.

7. Now, go to the **Properties** window, as shown in the following screenshot, and press the **Render** button in the header. It is the second button from the left. It has an image of the camera in the header. Select it so that it is highlighted in blue.

8. In the **Dimensions** subpanel, click the **Render Presets** button with the *LMB* and choose **TV NTSC 4:3** or **TV PAL 4:3** depending on which system your country uses. Notice that not only did the **Resolution:** change but the **Frame Rate:** did too, as shown in the following screenshot:

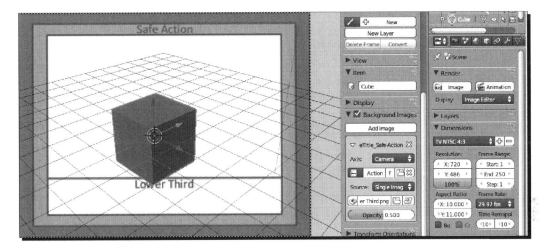

What just happened?

You got set up to render a standard TV image and you put in a guide to help you make sure that any animation that you do will all be within the Safe Title and Safe Action zones for TV. If you are doing an animation for a commercial, you can leave room for the sponsor's logo and contact information.

Transitioning from Standard Definition TV to High Definition TV

Normally, Safe Title zones and Safe Action zones don't apply to HD. Viewers are going to see all of the image. But during the transition from Standard resolution to HD resolution, many studios make ads at HD resolution and also release a Standard resolution version because many TV stations still broadcast at Standard resolution. So the Safe Action/Safe Title zones look like the following image:

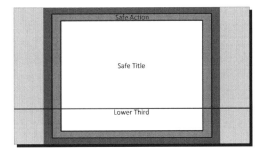

A guide like this will help you if you are in this situation. If you are working in HD resolution, but it will be sent out as Standard resolution, then just put all the important action, titles, and so on within the Safe Action/Safe Title zone. Make sure that your backgrounds extend all the way to the edge of the image.

HD is a much more stable signal. You may need to reserve the lower third for the sponsor's graphics, but you do not need to worry about Safe Action and Safe Title if you are making animation strictly for HD. The preceding graphic is available in your download pack as `6907_07_04.png` and can be used with Dimensions of HD NTSC 1080p or HD PAL 1080p in the same way you just added the Safe Titles for Standard resolution.

For your reference, the file `6907_07_SafeTitle_SafeAction_NTSC_4-3.blend` is set up with the SafeTitle/SafeAction zone templates for a standard NTSC screen. The file `6907_07_SafeTitle_SafeAction_PAL_4-3.blend` is set up with the SafeTitle/SafeAction zone templates for a standard PAL screen. The file `6907_07_SafeTitle_SafeAction_NTSC_HD_16-9.blend` is set up with the SafeTitle/SafeAction zone templates for an HD NTSC screen. The file `6907_07_SafeTitle_SafeAction_PAL_HD_16-9.blend` is set up with the SafeTitle/SafeAction zone templates for an HD PAL screen.

Laying out your motion with Timing

There is just too much to show, but these diagrams will help you to plan out your animation:

- **Animation Bounce Diagrams**: Bounce diagrams are good for analyzing your motion, seeing how it breaks down frame by frame, and how traditional cel animators got their results (`http://www.animationbrain.com/timing-2d-animation-principle.html`).

- **Eadweard Muybridge photographic series**: Eadweard Muybridge invented motion capture and his photographs amazed Victorian audiences. His zoopraxiscope was one of the earliest animation display devices. His Muybridge's Complete Human and Animal Locomotion books are still in print and are valuable references to animators. I used one of his flying bird sequences as the basis for an animation in an encyclopedia (`http://inventors.about.com/od/weirdmuseums/ig/Eadweard-Muybridge/The-Horse-in-Motion.htm`).

- **Walk cycle charts**: As you saw from your rowing examples, there are many ways for a human to do any given action. The first link shows you a page of different walk cycles from *Kit Laybourne's The Animation Book*, a classic which has recently been reissued to include digital animation. The second shows a horse walking, with a diagram describing which feet are on the ground. The final one is a collection of animations of various human motions: `http://minyos.its.rmit.edu.au/aim/a_notes/04_walkcycle_project.html` and `http://blaine901.files.wordpress.com/2011/01/horse-walking600.jpg`.

- **Preston Blair Phoneme Mouth charts**: Preston Blair was the man who animated Mickey Mouse in the *Sorcerer's Apprentice* section of *Fantasia*. His book *Welcome to Cartoon Animation* is a bible for animators and his mouth shape phoneme charts that show the position of a mouth for a certain sound are an animation institution: `http://www.garycmartin.com/mouth_shapes.html`, `http://minyos.its.rmit.edu.au/~rpyjp/a_notes/mouth_shapes_01.html`, and `http://minyos.its.rmit.edu.au/~rpyjp/a_notes/mouth_shapes_02.html`.

Planning what work must be done to make an animation

In addition to helping you plan the exact motions you want to create, there are also guides to help you plan out the whole animation. They are as follows:

- **Exposure sheets**: Exposure sheets, as shown in the following image, are prepared by the animator as a way to plan out their shots and to let the cameraman know what to photograph. However, with the advent of digital methods this has changed a bit. In the action column you can write in what is happening on that frame, for example, oar dips into water. The sound might be "oar splash". You then draw an arrow downward in the column to include any frames that this action includes.

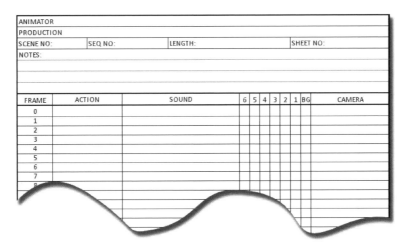

The columns **6**, **5**, **4**, **3**, **2**, **1**, and **BG** originally relate to the layers of cel art. **6** is for the top layer and **BG** stands for background. You can put the frame numbers of the artwork for each particular layer. This is useful when you get to compositing layers in the Video Sequence Editor.

Originally the **CAMERA** column would contain instructions for the cameraman, but now you can use it to mark which camera in Blender you shot a particular sequence with, or what changes you made to the camera's settings.

In the **NOTES** section, you may want to write down the names of the files you are using. You may also want to develop a method that uses the scene number and sequence number to tell you which section of the animation you are working on.

> For your reference, a copy of this Exposure sheet for you to use and modify was included in the download pack as an Excel file named `6907_07_ExposureSheet 30FPS.xls`.

◆ **Bar sheets**: A bar sheet is the audio equivalent of an exposure sheet. They are filled out by the director to tell everyone in the production exactly what is happening on any given frame. But now with digital methods, bar sheets are less commonly used. You should know what they are though, in case a director mentions them. More information is available at `http://www.michaelspornanimation.com/splog/?p=711`.

◆ **Sound as a planning guide**: Since it is now so easy to create the audio track, often animations are made using the sound track itself as the production guide. With an audio track in their 3D program, they can just scrub along the timeline and know where every word or sound begins. More information is available at `http://academic.evergreen.edu/curricular/eat/pdf/Sound.pdf`.

Guiding animation production with an audio track

With the switch to digital animation production, one method that's getting used more and more is to just use the audio track as the basis for the animation. Blender is set up to let you do this. You can drop the audio track into Blender and use the dialog, sound effects, or music to guide your animation.

Time for action – adding an audio track to Blender

Now it's time for an introduction to the Video Sequence Editor, ironically by adding an audio file. You will learn how to position the audio file on the timeline and display a representation of the waveform to help you in timing your animation:

1. Put your cursor on the boundary between the **3D View** and the **Timeline** windows and get the double arrowhead. Press the *LMB* and hold it while you move the boundary up, so that the **Timeline** window is about three times taller than usual.

2. With the cursor over the **Timeline** window, press *Shift+Left arrow* to go to **Frame 0**.

3. Put the mouse in the lower-left corner of the **Timeline** window, over the diagonal lines. Press the *LMB* and drag the mouse up to create a new window.

4. Press the *LMB* over the leftmost button on the upper **Timeline** window header.

5. Scroll up in the **Current Editor Type:** menu and select **Video Sequence Editor** as shown in the following screenshot:

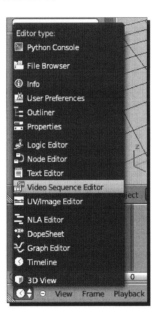

6. In the **Video Sequence Editor** header, select **Add**, then **Sound** from the pop-up menu, as shown in the following screenshot. Get the `6907_07_WalterRoland jookitjookit_excerpt.wav` file from the download pack's `Audio` directory, as shown in the following screenshot. When you have selected the file press the **Add Sound Strip** button in the upper-right corner of the window.

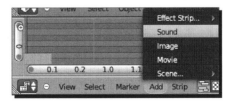

7. With the cursor over the **Video Sequence Editor** window, press *G* to move the audio strip down to layer **1**. Then press *G* again to move the strip so its left side is at Frame **0**.

8. Press *Ctrl+MMB* and scroll the mouse up, to maximize the height of the audio strip. You may want to use *Shift+MMB* to adjust the location of the audio strip.

9. Note that there are a couple of new controls that can be seen in the previous screenshot. On the left and on the bottom of the **Video Sequence Editor** window, there are a couple of scroll bars with gray dots on the ends. The vertical one shows you which layers are displayed. The horizontal one helps you control what portion of the time you see. Both are adjustable. Click on them to slide them. Click on the dot on the end to resize them.

10. With the cursor in the Video Sequence Editor, press *N* to open up the **Properties** panel. Scroll down to the **Sound** subpanel. Check the box marked **Caching** to load the sound into RAM for smooth playback and check the box marked **Draw Waveform**. You should now see the waveform of the audio track within the audio strip as shown in the following screenshot:

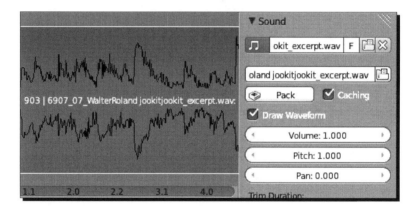

11. Go down to the **Timeline** window header and press the *LMB* to open the **Playback** menu. At the top of the menu, check the **Audio Scrubbing** box as shown in the following screenshot:

12. Now if you scrub the **Current Frame Indicator** along the timeline, or use the **Timeline** window playback controls, or press *Alt+A* over the **3D View** window to preview the animation, the audio track will play in sync with the animation.

13. Save this file to a unique name that you will still remember in six months.

What just happened?

You set up Blender so that you can have an audio file to use to guide you in creating animation. After adding in the audio file, you made it so you can see the audio waveform. Seeing the audio waveform makes it easier for you to know which part you are playing at the present moment. And you set the Caching and the Audio Scrubbing to make it easy for you to hear what is happening.

Have a go hero – animating to a boogie woogie beat

Animating to music is an old tradition going back as far as the *Felix the Cat* cartoons that you studied in *Chapter 1, Introducing Blender and Animation*. It's a good way to see the power that comes from mixing visual and acoustic rhythms:

- This is a Walter Roland tune from 1933, called *Jookit Jookit*. You have the music, now make the cube dance to it. This excerpt is 30 seconds long, so you may change the length of the animation in the timeline as we discussed in *Chapter 3, Controlling the Lamp, the Camera, and Animating Objects*.

- The easiest way to start is to use the controls in the Timeline to play a section and acquaint yourself with a particular phrase of the music. Then, when you have a particular section in mind, use the Current Frame Indicator to scrub the Timeline for frame-by-frame control. The waveform in the audio strip will help you see important points in the audio.

- Once you have a place in the music identified, then create the location, scale, and rotation keyframes to shake, rattle, and roll that cube to the music. If you get inspired, you can add any other objects and animate them as well. Use the Graph Editor if you want. Check in the key function table to refresh your memory of how to move around in the Graph Editor and Timeline. Be sure to stay within the Safe Title zone and Safe Action zone.

- Press *Alt+A* to preview your animation.

 For your reference, the file `6907_07_Audio_Timing_jookit.blend` is set up with *Walter Roland's* song *Jookit Jookit* inserted into the Video Sequence Editor and a sample animation. Also included are `6907_07_WalterRoland jookitjookit_excerpt.wav`.

Well, I hope you enjoyed making that animation, and discovered a new musician at the same time. Here is a table of keyboard commands and their functions:

Key	Function
Home	In the 3D View, it zooms back to display all the visible objects in the scene.
Fn+Left Arrow	On a Mac, in the 3D View, it zooms back to display all the visible objects in the scene.
V	In the 3D View, this brings up the **Set Handle Type** menu for Bezier Curves.
Ctrl+MMB	In the Video Sequence Editor, use this to zoom in and out.

Summary

This chapter covered a lot. You practiced setting up a template in Blender to guide your modeling. You used the template to help model the mast, boom, gaff, and bowsprit. You learned about using Bezier Curves for modeling the rudder, keel, and tiller.

You got tips on planning your animation, creating a story, using storyboards to plan what you are going to do, and using animatics to get the timing of an animation right before you animate.

You looked at some charts and guides that can help you create your animations, including Safe Title/Safe Action/Lower Thirds guides, timing diagrams, exposure sheets, and bar sheets. Finally you had a little fun using a sound track to guide your animation timing.

In the next chapter you will be making the sloop itself. You will use Subdivision Surfaces to model the hull and learn how to optimize the number of faces you create. You will learn to use edge loops and edge rings for more detailed modeling. You will punch holes in your boat with Boolean objects and use Spin tools and DupliVerts to make the ship's wheel.

Let's go!

8

Making the Sloop

In the last chapter you learned a lot to help you make the modeling and animation process easier by planning out what you would do. You created templates for the top view, the front view, and the camera. You also began building your sloop, by modeling some of the parts including the mast, boom, gaff, and bowsprit. You also learned a new use for Bezier Curves, modeling, and you used it to make the rudder, keel, and tiller. And for a change of pace, you finished off by making a short animation to the rumbling piano work of Walter Roland.

In this chapter, you are going to have a chance to really improve your modeling skills by mastering more advanced modeling techniques including:

- ◆ Using Subdivision Surfaces to model the hull and learning how to optimize the number of faces you create
- ◆ Adding details to the model with edge loops and edge rings
- ◆ Punching holes in the sloop's cabin with Boolean objects
- ◆ Using Spin tools and DupliVerts to make the ship's wheel

Let's get started.

Modeling with Subdivision Surfaces

With **Subdivision Surfaces** you start with a regular mesh object, similar to the boat you made, and to use its vertices to control another smoother surface. This makes modeling smoothly curved objects easier and makes animating changes of shape easier, because there are fewer points that need to be modified by you.

Time for action – making a simple Subdivision Surface

Subdivision Surfaces are popular because it makes it easier to make and animate organic objects. It also lets you make shapes that would be difficult with standard box modeling. So try one:

1. Open `6907_08_templates_set_up.blend` from your download pack and load it into your `Blender Files` directory for this chapter. Also, download `6907_08_01.png`, `6907_08_02.png`, and `6907_08_03.png` into the `Images` directory for this chapter.

2. Select the Reference Block that you used to set the scaling of the sloop template in *Chapter 7, Planning your Work, Working your Plan*.

3. Press the *Tab* key to get into **Edit Mode**.

4. In the **Properties** window header, select the **Modifiers** button. It's the seventh button from the left, it has the wrench on it, and is highlighted in blue in the following illustration.

5. In the **Modifiers** subpanel, press the *LMB* on the **Add Modifier** button, scroll down the menu and select **Subdivision Surface.** The Reference Block now looks more like a soccer ball.

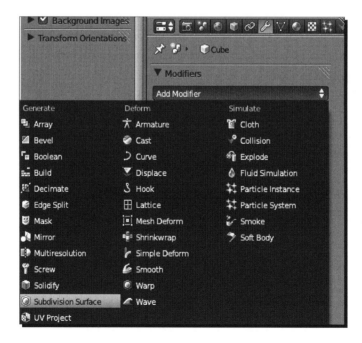

6. Go to the menu below the **Add Modifier** button. Click the *LMB* over the left arrow on the end of the **View:** button. Click down until **View:** is **0** (zero). Click up until **View:** is **6**. Notice how the Reference Block responds as shown here.

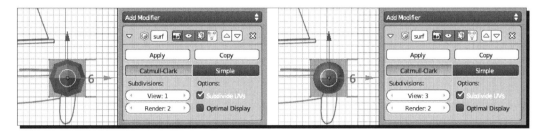

What just happened?

Well, the Reference Block is no longer a block. It is going to become your sloop. The **View:** button controls how many subdivisions there will be when you look at it in the 3D View. As you drop the **Subdivisions** value to **0**, you see a cube. As you raise the **Subdivisions** value to **6**, it becomes a very smooth sphere. The **Render:** button just below it controls how many subdivisions of the Reference Block there will be when you render it. The number of subdivisions changes, but the number of control points doesn't change.

The control points are similar to the control points of the Bezier Curve, but the surface does not have to go right through the control points for a Subdivision Surface. It's similar to a puppeteer controlling a marionette from a distance.

You cannot touch the edges and faces of the Subdivision Surface. The control points are the only thing you can modify. This might seem limiting at first, but it lets you control complex shapes with just a few vertices.

Did you notice the **Catmull-Clark** button. You are using the Catmull-Clark method of Subdivision Surfaces. It was developed by the same Ed Catmull who is now President of Pixar. Woody, Buzz, and Jessie are all just Subdivision Surfaces.

 For your reference, the file `6907_08_templates_set_up.blend` has both templates and the six unit Reference Block.

Using Edge Tools to make modeling easier

Edge Tools is a new tool that you will be exploring. Edge Tools can be used on any mesh object such as the boat or the oars. They provide easier ways to subdivide edges. You will be using them to help you control the form of your Subdivision Surface in this chapter.

Modeling with Subdivision Surfaces is a little like playing with clay. So the modeling here will be a bit more art than science. We will refer to the shape of the Subdivision surface as the surface and the mesh object with all the control points, that controls the surface, as the control object.

Time for action – turning a Reference Block into a sloop

Since you have the templates scaled, you don't need the Reference Block any more. So it's time to recycle it into the hull of the sloop. Using the Edge Tools, you'll stretch and recontour the cube into the sloop:

1. In the **Modifiers** subpanel of the **Properties** window, set the **View:** button to **2**.

2. Make sure that the **Limit Selection to Visible** button in the **3D View** header is light gray so that you are moving all the control points, not just the ones in front.

3. Select the left-hand control points. Press *G, Y,* and use the mouse to move them until the front end of the Subdivision Surface is at the same place as the bow of the sloop in the template, then press the *LMB*.

4. Did you notice that as you moved the left side, the right side also moved a little? When modeling Subdivision Surfaces, you get things close and then work them closer and closer till they are just right.

5. Press *A* to deselect all the control points. Select the right-hand control points. Press *G, Y,* and use the mouse to move them until the rear end of the Subdivision Surface is at the same place as the stern of the boat in the template, as seen here, then press the *LMB*.

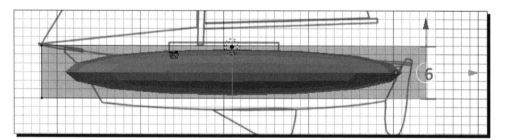

6. Now it's time to establish some key control points.

7. Press *Numpad 7* to get the **Top** view.

8. Now it's time to discover the **Loop Cut** tool. Move the cursor along the top edge of the control object.

9. Press *Ctrl+R*. Now move the mouse across the side edge and back to the top edge several times. Notice that the magenta line appears in the middle. It may be horizontal or vertical. When the magenta line is horizontal, press the *LMB*.

10. The line turns orange and the surface changes shape. Now move the mouse up and down and watch what the surface does.

11. Move the orange line over the front of the cabin area and press the *LMB*. Check the diagram at the start of *Chapter 7, Planning your Work, Working your Plan* if you are unsure of where this is.

12. Now, move the mouse above the orange line and press *Ctrl+R* again. When you get the horizontal magenta line, press the *LMB*. Move the orange line until it is over the rear of the cabin and press the *LMB*.

13. Now repeat this and move the orange line to the rear of the cockpit and press the *LMB*.

14. Move the mouse back to the center of the control object. Press *Ctrl+R*. Select the horizontal magenta line and press the *LMB*. Move the orange line to where the sloop is widest and press the **LMB** as seen in the following screenshot.

15. Now press *Numpad 3* to get the side view. You'll notice that the surface is now longer than the sloop.

16. Press *Ctrl+R* and create a vertical orange line where the bottom of the hull starts to go up to the bow in the template.

17. Press *A* to deselect all control points. Press *B* and use the mouse to select the control points on the left edge. Press *G*, then use the *MMB* to limit the motion to the Y axis. Move the end of the surface back to where the bow is. Press the *LMB* to release the motion.

18. Select just the control points on the right edge and move the end of the surface to where the stern is, as shown in the following screenshot:

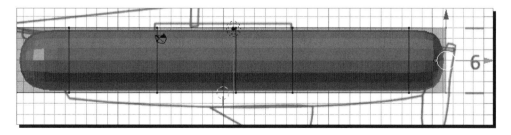

19. Save the file to a name you'll remember in six months.

What just happened?

Well, the sloop is starting to come into shape. You have been using a tool called the Loop Cut. It's pretty simple, but as you can see, very powerful because it allows you to cut a face anywhere along one of the object's edges. But you also notice that it does not just work on one face. It works on what is called a loop of edges. You noticed that the shape tends to move around, but you'll get it to move gently into shape, by making smaller and smaller adjustments.

Time for action – making selection easy with edge loops and edge rings

You've got the sloop to the proper length, and set up the edges you'll need to control the shape of the sloop's hull. Now, you'll learn some new tools that will give you the control you need to complete the job:

1. Use the *MMB* to rotate the view so you see some of the top, side, and end of the control object.

2. Choose **Edge Select Mode** from the **3D View** header.

3. Put the cursor over one of the vertical edges on the side.

4. Press *Alt+RMB* to select **Edge Loop**. It will choose a loop of connected edges, as shown in the following screenshot:

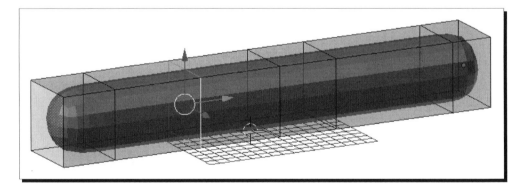

5. Move the mouse over the edge between the top and the side. Now press *Ctrl+Alt+RMB* to select **Edge Ring**. It will select a ring of edges connected by their faces.

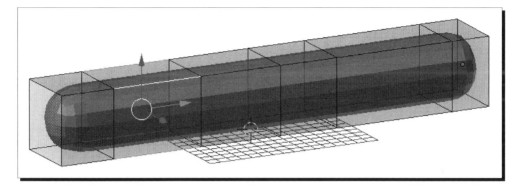

What just happened?

The Edge Loop select and Edge Ring select are handy tools for choosing multiple related edges and can speed up your modeling.

Time for action – creating the shape of the sloop from the top

Now you will learn to use Edge Loop to select the edges and gain experience in adjusting the control points of the Subdivision Surfaces:

1. Press *Numpad 7*.

2. Select **Wireframe** in the **Viewport Shading** menu in the **3D View** header.

3. Move the cursor over the horizontal edges at the widest part of the sloop. Press *Alt+RMB*.

4. Press *S, X,* and use the mouse to scale the surface until it is as wide as the boat in the template, then press the *LMB*. The control edges will be wider than the width of the boat image in the template. For best control of scaling, remember to move the mouse away from the center of the **3D View** before you start scaling.

5. Repeat this with the horizontal edges at the front of the cabin, and where the hull begins to narrow toward the bow, as seen in the following screenshot.

6. The Edge Loop command will not work at the ends of the sloop. Press *A* to deselect the edges, then press *B* and select the edges at the bow.

7. Press *S, X,* and use the mouse to scale the end of the surface inward, until it is as wide as the bow in the template, then press the *LMB*.

8. Repeat this with the horizontal edges in the rear of the sloop, work from the widest section to the stern.

9. Just as the length of the surface changed as you added vertices to the control object, the entire surface changes when you change a vertex. So now that you have the size close to what it should be, look at each of the horizontal edges and scale them in X again as needed. Don't worry about squaring off the stern. Just get the general contours of the sloop correct. Work from the widest portion to the narrowest ends.

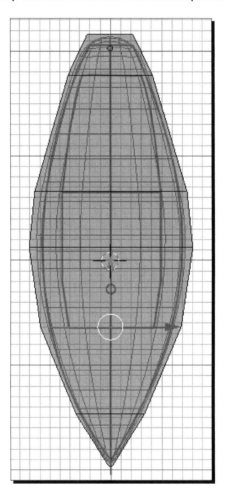

What just happened?

You worked on getting the shape of the sloop correct as seen from the top. You discovered that you can operate on the control object in **Edit Mode** just as you modify any other object. You also discovered that Subdivision Surface is a bit unpredictable, and that you have to gently work the surface into the shape you want. But the cool thing is that you are making the shape of a sloop with only 28 vertices.

Time for action – giving the hull a hull shape

You've got the top view of the hull in good shape. Now it's time to work on the shape as seen from the side:

1. Press *Numpad 1* to get the **Front** view.

2. Notice that the hull is still oval shaped, as seen in the following screenshot on the left. Check that all the control points are level vertically. If any control points are higher or lower than they should be, you can select them and scale them in Z, or move the vertices in Z.

3. Press *Ctrl+R* to activate the **Loop Cut** tool. Select the horizontal magenta line.

4. Move the orange line until it is almost all the way up to the top of the control object as seen in the following screenshot on the right. This will control how tall and curved the deck is. There is an **Edge Slide** readout in the **3D View** header. Move it till the **Edge Slide** is about **-0.85**. Use the *Shift* and *Ctrl* keys to give you better control when sliding.

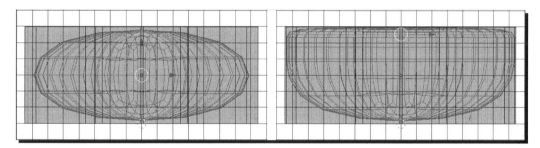

5. Press *Numpad 3* to get the **Side** view and you can see the effect these new control points have all along the length of the shape, as shown in the following screenshot. The top is neatly pinned, and the bottom has a graceful curve at the end.

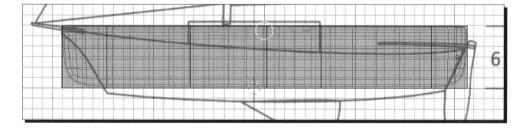

6. Choose **Vertex Select Mode** from the **3D View** header.

7. Press *A* to deselect all vertices.

8. Press *B* and use the mouse to select the top two control points in the center.

9. Press *G, Z,* and use the mouse to move the control points down, so that the lower of the two control points is on top of the deck line in the template, as shown in the following screenshot. Then press the *LMB*.

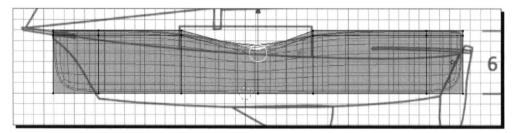

10. Repeat this on the other upper control points until they are aligned with the top of the deck, as shown in the following screenshot:

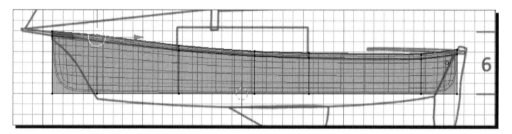

11. Press *A* to deselect all the control points. Press *B* to select all of the control points on the bottom of the hull. Press *G, Z,* and use the mouse to move the bottom control points down until the bottom of the surface is as low as the bottom of the hull, as shown in the following screenshot, then press the *LMB*.

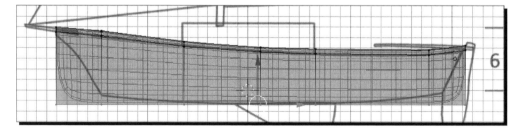

12. Press *Numpad 1* to get the **Front** view.

13. Press *S, X,* and *0.8* to make the bottom of the hull a little narrower, as seen here, then press *Enter*.

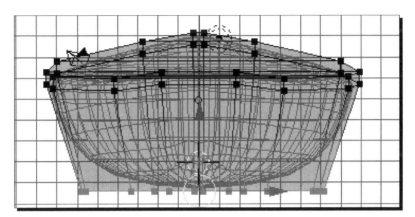

14. Press *Numpad 3* to show the **Side** view.

15. Press *A* to deselect all the vertices.

16. Press *B* and then use the mouse to select the vertices on the stern.

17. Make sure the **Pivot Center** button on the **3D View** header is set to **Median Point**. It's the second button to the right of the **Edit/Object Mode** button.

18. Press *R, X ,*and *-27* to rotate the rear control points so they are parallel with the angle of the stern, then press *Enter*.

19. Press *G, Y,* and move the rear control points so that the stern of the sloop matches the template as closely as possible. Press the *LMB* to release the motion.

20. Press *A* to deselect all the vertices.

21. Press *B* and then use the mouse to select the vertices on the bottom of the stern.

22. Press *G, Z,* and use the mouse to move the vertices up to the bottom of the hull, then press *LMB*.

23. Press *A* to deselect all the vertices.

24. Press *B* and then use the mouse to select the vertices on the bottom of the control points to the right of the stern, as shown in the following screenshot:

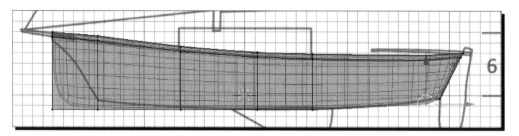

25. Now move the other bottom control vertices up, except the ones on the very left, as shown in the following screenshot:

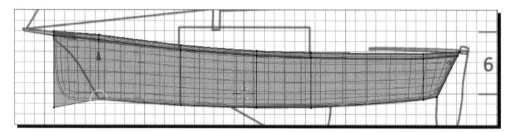

26. Finally select the lower vertices on the left. Press *G* and move them up and over, so that the curve of the bow approximates the curve seen in the template, as shown in the following screenshot, then press the *LMB*:

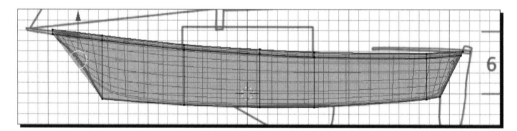

27. Select **Solid** in the **Viewport Shading** menu in the **3D View** header.

28. Press the *MMB* and use the mouse to rotate the hull of the sloop and inspect your work.

29. Press *Numpad 3* to return to the **Side** view.

30. Save the file to a unique name you will remember in six months.

What just happened?

You made the hull. Well done. You learned to gently move the surface into a complex shape by moving and scaling the vertices of the control object. It took a bit of work, but nothing was too difficult. And now you just have a few more steps to finish shaping the surface. You need to flatten the transom, the rear end of the sloop, so you can put a name on the stern. You need to make the bow sharper. You need to finish scaling the width. You need to make sure that the cabin and cockpit will meet where you want them to.

Pop quiz – remembering Edge Tool commands

Now, a quick question to help you remember the Edge Tool commands:

1. Which of the following three statements is false?

    a. To choose edges that are end to end in an Edge Loop, press *Alt+RMB*.

    b. To choose edges that are connected by shared faces in an Edge Ring, press *Ctrl+Alt+RMB*.

    c. To choose edges for a Loop Cut, press *Ctrl+L*.

Time for action – flattening the transom

Now it's time to flatten the transom. By setting control points very close to each other, or even on top of each other, you can make pretty sharp corners. Try it:

1. Press *A* to deselect all vertices. Press *B* and use the mouse to select the control vertices for the transom on the right side of the control object.

2. Press *E* to extrude. Press *Enter*. Press *S, 0.95*, and *Enter*.

3. Press *Tab* to go into **Object Mode**.

4. Press *MMB* and use the mouse to rotate the view so you can see that the transom of the sloop has been flattened.

What just happened?

By extruding the control points and pressing *Enter*, you put two sets of control points in the same place. This flattened out the transom. Then, you scaled in the new points just a little so you could adjust them independently if you ever want to.

Time for action – making the bow sharper

1. Just like you put a corner on the stern by putting the control points close together, you can make the edge of the bow sharper as well.

2. Press *Numpad 3* to see the **Side** view.

3. Press the *Tab* key to get back into **Edit Mode**.

4. Press *A* to deselect all the vertices. Press *B* and then use the mouse to select the control points at the bottom of the bow, as shown in the following screenshot:

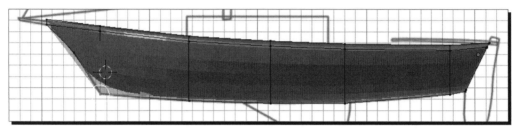

5. Press *Ctrl* and *Numpad 7* to get the **Bottom** view.

6. Press *S, X,* and use the mouse to scale the control points in X until they are as far apart as the other control points in the bow, as shown in the following screenshot, then press the *LMB*.

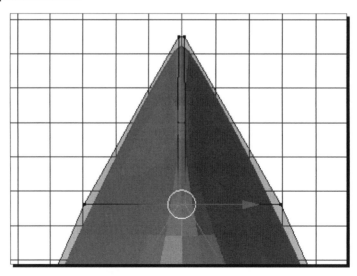

7. Press the *MMB* and use the mouse to rotate the view so you can see that the bow of the sloop is more pointed.

What just happened?

By scaling the control points at the bottom of the bow, you brought the point of the bow down to the bottom of the hull.

Time for action – finishing the hull

The hull is pretty close to its final shape. Now, it's time to check the shape and tighten up the dimensions:

1. Press *Numpad 7* to get the **Top** view.

2. Press *Z* to toggle from **Solid** to **Wireframe**. Press the *Tab* key to go into **Object Mode**.

3. Look carefully at the outline of the sloop as compared to the template, as shown on the left of the following screenshot. The boat is wider than the template shows it should be. Making the hull taller apparently made it a little wider too.

4. Press the *Tab* key again to return to **Edit Mode**. Press *A* to deselect all the control points.

5. Press *B* and then use the mouse to select the three center sets of vertical control points, as shown in the following screenshots:

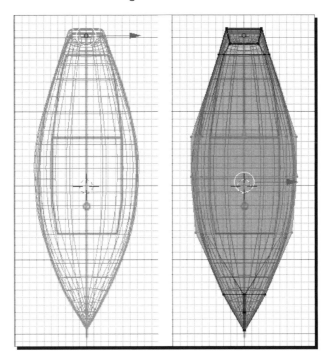

6. Press *S, X*, and use the mouse to scale them to the same width as the template shows the boat should be, then press the *LMB*.

7. Increment the file name and save the file. Note that it is the higher detail version in the file name.

What just happened?

Well done! Making smooth shapes like this is sometimes called organic modeling. It took a little extra care because you are manipulating the control points, not the vertices themselves, but you did it.

Now the surface of the hull is complete.

For your reference, the file `6907_08_Subdivision Surface 1.blend` has the reference block with the subdivision surface applied. `6907_08_Subdivision Surface 2.blend` has the control object with all the vertices. `6907_08_Subdivision Surface 3.blend` has the initial top shape. `6907_08_Subdivision Surface 4.blend` has the initial sides finished with the angling of the bottom of the hull. `6907_08_Subdivision Surface 5.blend` has the bow raised up. `6907_08_Subdivision Surface 6.blend` shows making the cabin cockpit boundary.

Getting the most for your rendering time with Levels of Detail

For games and also for video animation, quite often models are made at different levels of detail. At the beginning of this chapter you looked at how changing the number of **Subdivisions:** changed the detail in the default cube. This allows you to have detail when you need it, or to reduce rendering time by reducing detail when possible. It was good for you to start out with the higher level of detail hull so that you know what the ideal lines will be. But now, to keep the number of polygons down, it's best to make a lower detail version.

Time for action – making the boat simpler

Every time you make a model, you have to decide how much detail you need, and balance that against how many faces and vertices you use. For now, you will make a simpler version:

1. Press *A* to deselect all of the control points.

2. Press the *MMB* and rotate the view so you can see the top and side of the sloop, as shown in the following screenshots. Look at how complex the surface is.

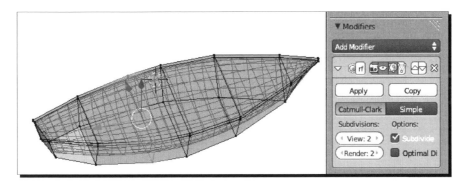

3. In the **Modifiers** subpanel of the **Properties** window, set **Subdivisions: View:** to **1**, as shown in the following screenshot. Note how much simpler the surface is, compared to the preceding screenshot.

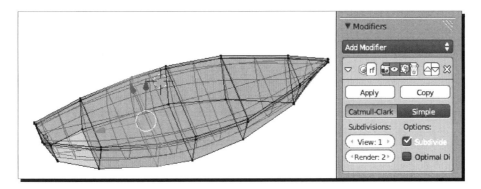

4. As usual, there is a little more massaging to do. The simpler surface does not have a subdivision in the correct place.

5. Press *Numpad 7* to get the **Top** view.

6. Look at where the template shows the edge between the cabin and the cockpit to be, as shown in the following screenshot. You can see that the control points lie over the boundary between the cockpit and cabin, but the edge of the Subdivision Surface itself is a little further up.

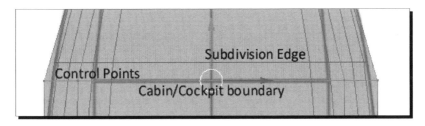

7. Select the control points on the Cabin/Cockpit boundary. Press *G, Y*, and use the mouse to move the control points down so the subdivision edge is on the boundary between the cabin and cockpit, as shown in the following screenshot, then press the *LMB*. It will be easier to see it as you move the control points than in the illustration.

8. Press *S, X*, and use the mouse to make sure that the width of the hull at that point is correct, then press the *LMB*.

9. Press the *Tab* key to go into **Object Mode**.

10. Save the file to a unique name that you will remember in 6 months. Note that it is the lower detail version.

What just happened?

In the beginning of the chapter you looked at the **Modifiers** subpanel of the **Properties** window and what happened to the object when you changed the number of subdivisions. You set the **Subdivisions: View:** value to **2**. That gives great smooth results. But the price to pay is that the hull will have 736 faces after conversion. However, if you set the **Subdivisions: View:** value to **1**, the hull when converted only has 184 faces. For now, this will be enough and will make it easier to continue the project rather than having to hunt through lots of faces and vertices. If you want a prettier version and your computer is fairly powerful, you can come back and redo it with a higher setting for **Subdivisions: View:**.

Have a go hero – adjusting the rear of the cockpit

It's more subtle, but the back of the cockpit in the template does not line up exactly with one of the subdivision edges:

1. You adjusted the front of the cockpit, now adjust the subdivision edge to the rear boundary of the cockpit, and adjust the width of the control points so they match the template, as shown in the following screenshot. Adjust the width in X if needed.

2. Now double check the Cabin Cockpit boundary again and adjust it, if necessary.

3. Look at the stern, and make sure it is the same width as it appears in the template.

4. Save the file.

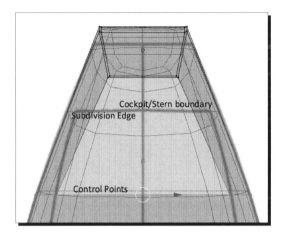

 For your reference, the file `6907_08_Subdivision Surface 7.blend` has the hull ready for conversion from surface to mesh.

Modeling the hull as a mesh

The Subdivision Surface was great for shaping the hull. But now, to create the cabin and the cockpit, you have to change gears. You need some sharper corners and straight edges to define the cockpit and the cabin. For that, you'll shift back to using the extrusion. First you need to convert the surface to a mesh object, then you can create the cockpit, and use the cockpit to build the cabin.

Time for action – converting the surface to a mesh

Now it's time for a big change. Make sure that you saved the file at the end of the previous *Time for action* section. You are going to covert your Subdivision Surface to a mesh object:

1. Make sure you are in **Object Mode**. Rotate the hull so you can see it well.

2. Press *Alt+C* to convert the surface into a mesh object. Select **Mesh from Curve/ Meta/Surf/Text** from the menu with the *LMB* as shown in the following screenshot:

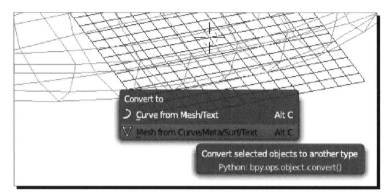

3. Press *Tab* to go into **Edit Mode**. The control points are gone. You now have a boat hull.

4. Press *A* to deselect any selected vertices

What just happened?

This was a short but important step. Objects can be changed from one type to another. You needed to save your work before doing this, because you cannot convert the object back.

Time for action – making the cockpit

Now building the hull will be similar to building the boat because you will be using extrusion and scaling:

1. Press *Numpad 7* to get the **Top** view.

2. Select **Face Select Mode** on the **3D View** header.

3. Press *C* and use the mouse to select the faces over the cockpit and cabin on the template, as shown in the following screenshot. Press the *RMB* to stop selecting.

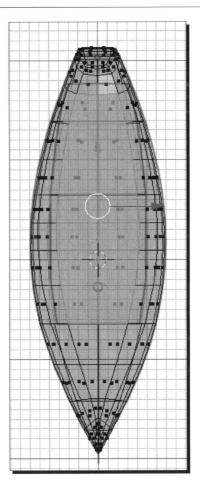

4. Press *Numpad 3* to get the **Side** view.

5. Press *B* and then the *MMB* to deselect the faces on the bottom of the hull that were previously selected, as shown in the following screenshot. Leave only the faces on the top of the hull selected.

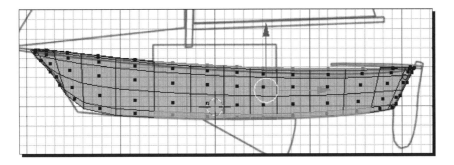

6. Go to the **Properties** window and select the **Object Data** button, which is the eighth button from the left on the header, as shown in the following screenshot. In the **Vertex Groups** subpanel, press the plus sign to create a new vertex group. In the white box to the right of **Name:** name the group **Cockpit**, as shown in the following screenshot, and press *Enter*. Then press the **Assign** button to assign the faces to the group.

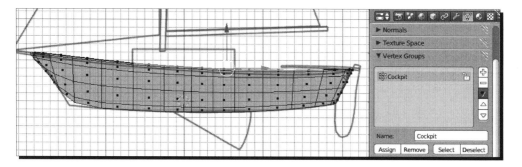

7. Press *E* to extrude the cockpit and use the mouse to move the cockpit floor down, as shown in the following screenshot:

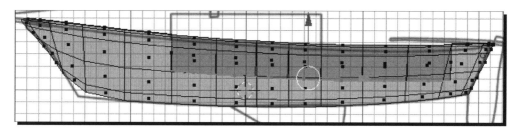

8. Press *S, Z, 0,* and *Enter* to flatten the cockpit floor.

9. Move the cockpit floor up so that the front of the cockpit floor is in level with the edge between the second and third faces from the bottom as seen in the following screenshot:

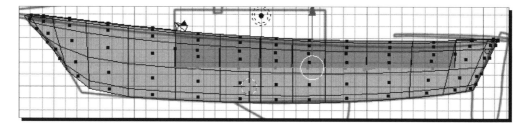

10. Press the *Z* key to toggle the **Viewport Shading** to **Solid**.

11. Press the *Tab* key to go into **Object Mode**.

12. Press the *MMB* and use the mouse to inspect the sloop's hull.

13. In the **Properties** window, select the **Object** button. It's the fifth one from the left. Rename the hull to **Sloop_Hull** and press *Enter*.

14. Save the file to a unique name that lets you know it is the completed hull.

What just happened?

This was very similar to how you created your jonboat. You had a solid hull, you selected the faces and extruded them. Next you are going to use the faces you grouped to create the cabin.

Time for action – making the cabin

The cabin is made with extrusions, as was the boat. By copying faces from the hull as the basis for the cabin, you will make sure that the cabin will fit snugly on the hull:

1. Press *Z* to toggle the **Viewport Shading** to **Wireframe**.

2. Press *Shift + D* to copy the cockpit floor. Press *Enter*. Press *P* to separate the duplicated faces. Choose **Selection** as seen in the following screenshot:

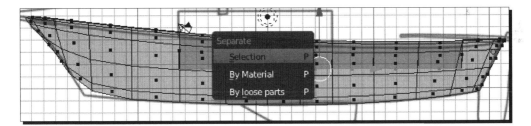

3. Press the *Tab* key to go into **Object Mode**. Press *A* to deselect all objects. Select the copy of the cockpit floor that you have just made with the *RMB*.

4. Press *M*, *2* and then *Enter* to move it to Layer 2.

5. Press *Numpad 3* to return to the **Side** view.

6. Press *2* to go to Layer 2, or use the **Layers** controls in the **3D View** header.

7. Press *Numpad 7* to get the **Top** view.

8. Press the *Tab* key to go into **Edit Mode**.

9. Press *A* to deselect all faces.

10. Press *B* and use the mouse to select the faces that are in the cockpit area and not in the cabin area.

11. Press *X* to delete the selected faces. Choose **Faces** from the pop-up menu as shown in the following screenshot:

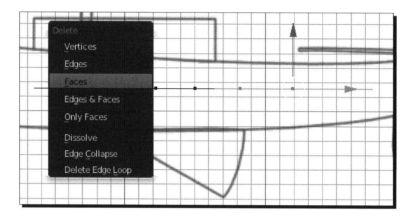

12. Press *A* to select all the faces.

13. Zoom into where the cabin in the template is.

14. Press *E* and extrude the faces up until they are in level with the roof of the cabin in the template.

15. Press *A* to deselect all the faces. Press *B* and use the mouse to select all the faces on the bottom of the cabin.

16. Press the *MMB* and use the mouse to get a better view of the bottom of the cabin, as shown in the following screenshot:

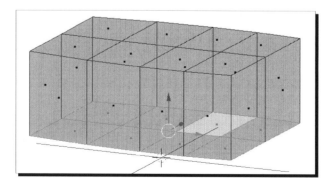

17. In the **3D View**, press *N* and open up the **Display** subpanel of the **Properties** panel. Uncheck **Grid Floor** for a better view of the bottom of the cabin.

18. Press *E* to extrude the bottom face and press *Enter*.

19. Press *S, 0.95*, and then press *Enter*.

20. Press *Numpad 3* for the **Side** view.

21. Press *E*, and move the faces up, so there is an equal gap at the top as at the sides, as shown in the following illustration, then press the *LMB*.

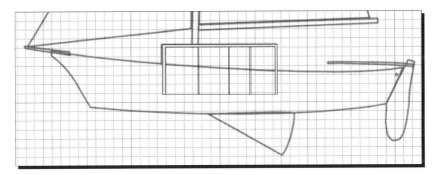

22. Press *Numpad 1* for the **Front** view.

23. Change to **Vertex Select** mode.

24. Press *A* to deselect all the vertices. Select the vertices in the center of the top of the cabin.

25. Press *G, Z*, and use the mouse to raise up the center peak, then press the *LMB*. Move it about **0.6** units up, pressing the *Shift+Ctrl* buttons as you move it. Then press *Enter* to create a peak on the cabin roof, as shown in the following screenshot:

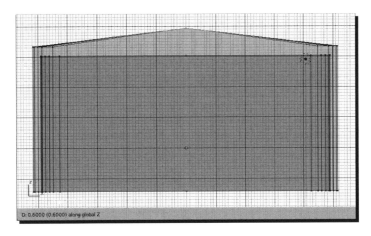

26. Press the *Tab* key to go into **Object Mode**.

27. In the **Properties** window select the **Object** button, it's the fifth one from the left. Rename **Sloop Hull.001** to **Cabin**. Then press *Enter*.

28. With the cursor over the **3D View**, press *A* to deselect the cabin.

29. In the **Layers** buttons in the **3D View** header, select **Layer 1** with the *RMB*, then select **Layer 2** with the Shift + *RMB*. So you can see the hull of the sloop as well as the cabin and that **Layer 2** is the active layer.

30. Press *Numpad 3* for the **Side** view.

31. Press *Shift+S*. Select **Cursor to Center** from the menu.

32. Put the 3D Cursor in the center of the rear panel of the cabin, as shown in the following screenshot:

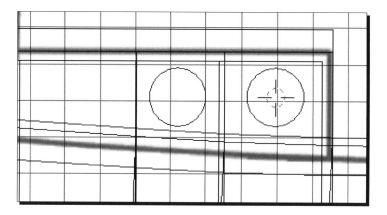

33. Press *Shift+A* and make a cylinder from the **Mesh** menu.

34. In **Tool Shelf**, set the number of **Vertices** to **18**.

35. Press *R, Y, 90, and* then *Enter* to rotate the cylinder so it is properly oriented.

36. Press *S, 0.8*, and then *Enter* to scale the cylinder down in size.

37. Press *S, X, 7*, and then *Enter* to make the cylinder longer than the cabin's width.

38. In the **Properties** window select the **Object** button on the header. It's the fifth one from the left. Rename the cylinder to **Portal Boolean**.

39. With the cursor over the **3D View**, press *Shift+D* to duplicate the Portal Boolean. Press the *MMB* after you start to move it forward to the next panel so it remains at the same height as the original Portal Boolean.

40. Look at whether the portals are centered vertically between the cabin roof and the deck. If you need to center them better vertically, hold the *Shift* key and select the original Portal Boolean so both are selected. Press *G, Z*, and use the mouse to recenter them between the deck and the cabin roof, then press the *LMB*. The positions should be similar to the preceding screenshot.

41. In the **Layers** buttons in the **3D View** header, select **Layer 2**.

42. Press *A* to deselect everything.

43. Press *Shift+A* and select **Mesh** then **Cube** from the menus.

44. Press *S, Z, 3*, and *Enter*.

45. Press *S, X, 1.5*, and *Enter*.

46. Press *Numpad 1* for the **Front** view.

47. Press *G, Z*, and move the cube with the mouse so that the top of the cube is between the Portal Boolean and inner roof of the cabin, as seen on the left in the following screenshot, then press the *LMB*.

48. Press *G, X, 2.500*, and *Enter*.

49. Press *Numpad 3* for the **Side** view.

50. Press *G, Y*, and use the mouse to move the cube so it is centered on the back wall of the cabin, as seen on the right in the following screenshot, then press the *LMB*.

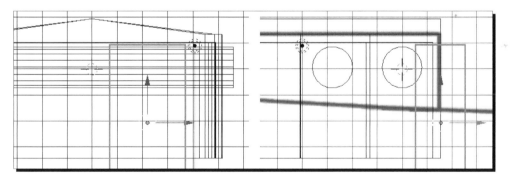

51. In the **Properties** window, select the **Object** button on the header. It's the fifth one from the left. Rename the cube to **Door Boolean**, then press Enter.

52. Save this file, and remember to increment the file number before saving.

What just happened?

All the recent steps should have looked familiar from earlier chapters. You did extrusions, you scaled, you moved vertices. The oddest thing was building the cylinders and cube named Booleans. Next you will discover how to use them. But note that all the objects with Boolean in their name were placed in relation to the cabin so that they cross as few edges of the cabin as possible. That makes the Boolean modifier's work easier.

Using Boolean modifiers to cut holes in objects

Booleans are a 3D extension of the Venn diagrams taught in algebra class. Named after George Boole, Boolean is pronounced Bool-ee-in with emphasis on Bool.

There are three kinds of Boolean operators, **Difference**, **Intersection**, and **Union**. The following figure shows what happens. The **A** circle represents the object to which you add the Boolean modifier. The **B** circle represents the object added by the Boolean modifier.

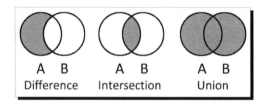

The **Difference** operation leaves all of the **A** object that is not part of the **B** object. With the **Intersection** operation, only what is common to both the **A** and **B** object is left. The **Union** operation combines the two objects.

Time for action – detailing the cabin using the Boolean modifier

You made the cabin, the two portal Booleans and the door Boolean. Now you are going to combine them to make the portals and door openings in the cabin:

1. Select the cabin.

2. Select the **Modifiers** button in the header of the **Properties** window. It's the seventh button from the left, with the little wrench.

3. In the **Modifiers** subpanel, press the **Add Modifier** button with the *LMB*. Then select **Boolean** from the pop-up menu.

4. When the **Add Modifier** subpanel appears, press the button with the cube, below **Object:**. Choose **Door Boolean** from the pop-up menu. Set the **Operation:** to **Difference** as shown on the right of the following graphic.

5. You have just made the door frame.

6. Press the **Add Modifier** button with the *LMB* again. Then select **Boolean** from the pop-up menu.

7. When the second **Add Modifier** subpanel appears, choose **Portal Boolean** as **Object:**. Set **Operation** to **Difference** as shown on the right of the following screenshot.

8. You have just made the rear portals on both sides of the cabin.

9. Press the **Add Modifier** button with the *LMB*. Then select **Boolean** from the pop-up menu.

10. When the third **Add Modifier** subpanel appears, choose **Portal Boolean.001** as **Object:**. Set **Operation** to **Difference** as shown on the right of the following screenshot.

11. You have just made the forward portals on both sides of the cabin.

12. Press *Numpad 7*.

13. Select the **Door Boolean** with the *RMB*. Hold the *Shift* key and use the *RMB* to select **Portal Boolean** and **Portal Boolean.001**. Press *M*, *3*, and *Enter* to move them to **Layer 3**.

14. Press *Z* to toggle **Viewport Shading** to **Solid**.

15. With the *MMB*, rotate the view so you can see the cabin better, as shown in the following screenshot.

16. Increment the file name and save the file.

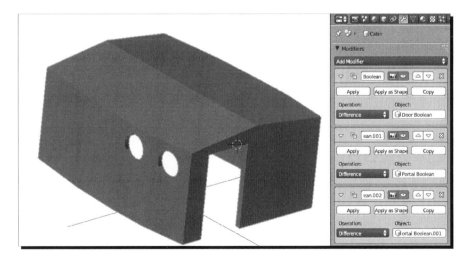

What just happened?

As you can see, creating Boolean modifiers allowed you to use the Door Boolean to punch a hole into the cabin and the same with the Portal Booleans. But you are not quite finished yet. The modifiers have to be applied to the object or they won't show up when you render it.

Time for action – applying the Boolean modifier

This is a pretty easy step. It takes the Booleans you have made and converts the Boolean operations to a mesh model just as you converted the Subdivision Surface to a mesh model:

1. Select the Cabin. In the top **Add Modifier** subpanel, click on the **Apply** button. This will make the Boolean modification permanent.

2. Now, repeat this for the other two **Add Modifier** subpanels.

3. In the **Layers** buttons in the **3D View** header, select **Layer 1** and **Layer 2**.

4. Use the *MMB* to inspect your sloop.

5. Press *1* to move to **Layer 1**.

6. Increment the file name and save the file.

What just happened?

Congratulations, the sloop is well on its way, now that you have finished the hull and the cabin. Making the basic shape of the cabin was very similar to how you made the boat. The big change was using **Boolean** modifiers. They made quick work out of cutting out the portals and the door.

So with your model, the Difference operation left all of the cabin that was not part of the Door Boolean. It also left all of the cabin that was not part of the Portal Booleans. Cutting holes in this manner is probably the most frequent usage of the Boolean modifier.

With the Intersection modifier, you would be able to make the cabin door and the portal windows, because it leaves all of the cabin that is also part of the Door Boolean, or also part of a Portal Boolean.

The Union modifier is not used much because it is usually easier to just join the objects. It would leave all of the cabin and the Door Boolean.

Now the Boolean may seem like a miracle tool, but use it with caution. You'll notice that you used pretty simple shapes, and that the Portal Booleans were centered within the face they were cutting a hole out of.

With more complex Booleans, you may not get the results you were hoping for and it may take a long while. They can be unpredictable and give very bad results when done wrong, which is why you should always save your files before attempting a Boolean. Once I made a spiraled column using Booleans, but I wasn't happy with the look. As a test, I twisted one of the two objects just a few degrees and set the computer for doing the Boolean operation again. Three days later I stopped the operation because it wasn't finished.

Have a go hero – making doors and portal windows

1. Open up the file you saved just before doing the Boolean operations. Make three copies of the cabin object.

2. With one copy of the cabin, add a **Boolean** modifier of **Intersection** and an object of **Door Boolean**. Name the object **Door**.

3. With another copy of the cabin, add a **Boolean** modifier of **Intersection** and an object of **Portal Boolean**. Name the object **Portals_1**.

4. With the third copy of the cabin, add a **Boolean** modifier of **Intersection** and an object of **Portal Boolean.001**. Name the object **Portals_2**.

5. Apply the Modifiers and save the file to a unique name. You can append the door and portals to the sloop later.

 For your reference, the file 6907_08_Subdivision Surface 8.blend has the hull converted to a mesh. 6907_08_Subdivision Surface 9.blend has the cockpit created, and the mesh to build the cabin from, separated. 6907_08_Subdivision Surface 10.blend has the cabin extruded. 6907_08_Subdivision Surface 11.blend has the door and portal Booleans created. 6907_08_Subdivision Surface 12.blend has the Booleans done but not applied. 6907_08_Subdivision Surface 13.blend has the Booleans applied.

Adding materials and textures to the sloop

With the boat in *Chapter 5, Building a Simple Boat* and the oars in *Chapter 6, Making and Moving the Oars*, you're getting to be an old pro at adding textures, so these should be pretty easy.

Blender has a quirk when it comes to creating materials. The default cube comes with a default material. Other objects do not.

Time for action – coloring and texturing the sloop hull

The hull has two textures, a painted texture for the outer hull and the cockpit and a wooden texture for the deck:

1. Reopen the file you just made in the last *Time for action* section, that has the cabin with holes for the door and portals.

2. Press *Numpad 3* to get the **Side** view. Make sure you can see the entire sloop.

3. Select **Layer 1**. Select the hull with the *RMB*.

4. Press the *Tab* key to go into **Edit Mode**.

5. In the **3D View** header choose the **Face Select** mode.

6. Make sure that the **3D View** shading is set to **Solid** in the **Viewport Shading** menu on the header.

7. Make sure that the **Limit Selection to Visible** button is dark gray and that you cannot see through the surface of the sloop.

8. In the **Properties** window, make sure that the **Object Data** button is highlighted in the header. It's the eighth button from the left, with the triangle on it. Make sure that the **Vertex Groups** subpanel is open.

9. In the **3D View**, press *A* to deselect all faces. Now you want to select the faces for the deck. They are the top row of faces as seen from the side.

10. Press *C* and start out by selecting the faces on the top with the *LMB*. Then go back and press the *MMB* to deselect any faces accidently selected. Press the *RMB* when you have the faces on the top selected.

11. Press *Ctrl* and *Numpad 3* to see the other side of the sloop.

12. Press *C* and start out by selecting the faces on the top with the *LMB*. Then go back and press the *MMB* to deselect any faces accidently selected. Press the *RMB* when you have the faces on the top selected.

13. Press the *MMB* and rotate your view of the sloop. Check the bow and stern and select any faces of the deck area that are still unselected. Press *RMB* when you have all of the deck faces selected.

14. Press the *RMB* when you are finished or wish to change the view to get a better angle. Remember that you can use the mouse-wheel to make the selection circle larger or smaller. You may have to zoom in to select the faces at the bow and stern.

15. When you have selected all the faces of the deck, as shown in the following screenshot, create a new vertex group in the **Vertex Groups** subpanel of the **Properties** window. Select the plus sign to create a new group, name it **Deck**, and click on the **Assign** button to assign the selected faces to the group.

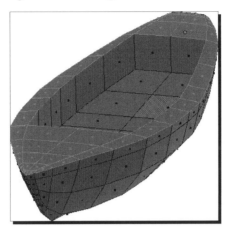

16. With the cursor over the **3D View** window, press *A* to deselect all the faces.

17. In the **Properties** window, in the **Vertex Groups** subpanel, select the **Cockpit** vertex group with the *LMB*, then click on the **Select** button. Are all the faces properly selected? If not, reselect them and reassign them.

18. With the cursor over the **3D View**, press *A* to deselect all the faces.

19. In the **Properties** window, in the **Vertex Groups** subpanel, select the **Deck** vertex group with the *LMB*, then click on the **Select** button. Are all the faces properly selected? If not, reselect them and re-assign them.

20. Now, in the **Properties** window, in the **Vertex Groups** subpanel, select the **Cockpit** vertex group.

21. In the **3D View** header choose **Select**, then choose **Inverse** from the menu.

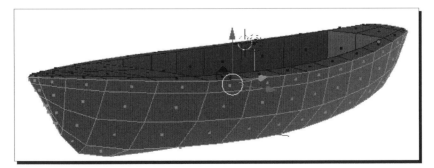

22. Create a new vertex group in the **Vertex Groups** subpanel of the **Properties** window. Name it **Hull** and assign the selected faces to the group.

23. Save the file to a unique name.

24. Select the **Materials** button on the **Properties** window header. It's the ninth button from the left, with the chrome ball on it.

25. In the **Diffuse** subpanel of the **Properties** window, click on the white box and set the diffuse color to **0.5** Red, **0.5** Green, and **1.0** Blue, as shown in the following screenshot. Rename the material to **Hull Material**. You can check *Chapter 5, Building a Simple Boat* if you need to refresh your memory on how to do it. Click on the **Assign** button to assign the **Hull** material to the **Hull** vertex group.

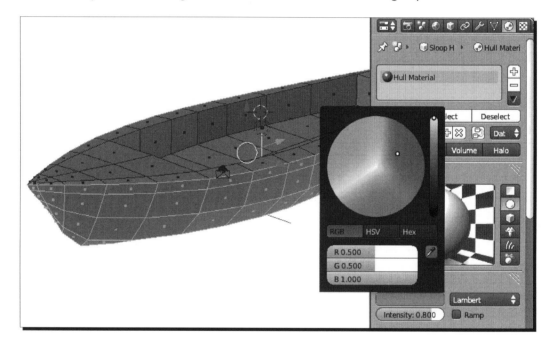

26. In the **Properties** window, make sure that the **Object Data** button is highlighted in the header. It's the eighth button from the left, with the triangle on it. Make sure that the **Vertex Groups** subpanel is open.

27. In the **3D View** window, press *A* to deselect all the faces. In the **Properties** window, highlight the **Deck** vertex group, then click on the **Select** button.

28. Select the **Materials** button on the **Properties** window header. It's the ninth button from the left, with the chrome ball on it.

29. Create a new material by pressing the *LMB* over the plus sign at the top right of the **Material** panel in the **Properties** window. Then press the **New** button.

30. Name the material **Deck Material**. If you need to, you can check back in *Chapter 5, Building a Simple Boat* for more detailed information about creating a material.

31. Select the **Texture** button on the **Properties** window header. It's the tenth button from the left, with the checkerboard pattern on it. Use the *MMB* to slide the header to the left if you don't see it.

32. Press the button labeled **New**. Name the new texture **Deck Texture**.

33. Where it says **Type:**, press the button with the checkerboard and select **Image or Movie** from the menu, as shown in the following screenshot.

34. Go down to the **Image** subpanel. Select **Open** and get the image 6907_08_03.png from the download pack.

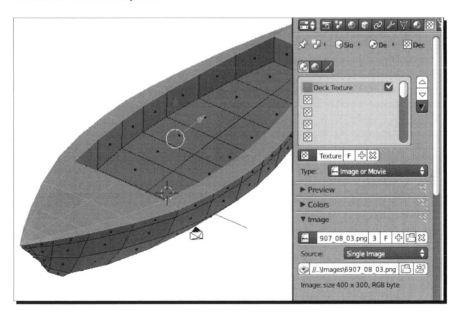

35. Select the **Materials** button from the **Properties** window header.

36. With **Deck Material** highlighted, **Assign** the **Deck Material**

37. In the **3D View** window, press the *Tab* key to go to **Object Mode**.

38. Select the camera.

39. Press *Numpad 0* to get the **Camera** view. Press *G, Z, Z*, and then use the mouse to back the camera up, so you can see the entire sloop, then press the *LMB*.

40. Press *Numpad 7*. Select the lamp and move it nearer to the camera. In the **Properties** window, change the **Lamp** type to **Hemi**.

41. Press *F12* to render the image.

42. Press *Esc* when you are done looking at the image.

43. Select the sloop again with the *RMB*.

44. Press the *Tab* key to go into **Edit Mode**.

45. Press *A* to deselect all the faces.

46. Select the **Object Data** button on the **Properties** window header. It's the eighth button from the left, with the triangle on it.

47. In the **Properties** window, highlight the **Hull** vertex group and select it.

48. In the **3D View** window, if you do not see the **Tool Shelf**, press *T*. Scroll down until you see the button labeled **Shading:**. Choose **Smooth**.

49. Press *F12* to render it. It should look something like the following screenshot. Press the *Esc* key when you are finished looking at it.

50. Save the file to a unique name.

What just happened?

This wasn't too difficult. It was very similar to how you added textures to the boat in *Chapter 5, Building a Simple Boat*. The vertex groups made it easier to make your texture selections. You chose the Cockpit and the Deck vertex groups and then inverted the selection to create the Hull vertex group. Then you used the vertex groups to assign the materials to the parts of the hull.

Have a go hero – creating vertex groups for the cabin

The next step is to add textures to the cabin. You will be using the same textures as you can see in the following screenshot. But you need to create vertex groups for the cabin.

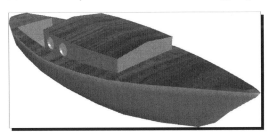

The cabin needs two vertex groups, **Cabin** and **Cabin Roof**. Go to **Layer 2**. Delete the **Cockpit** group left over from separating the cabin from the hull by using the minus sign. Select the faces for **Cabin Roof**, make a group for them, then invert the selection and make the **Cabin** vertex group.

Time for action – using the same materials for two objects

Materials in Blender can be reused. That keeps files smaller and lets you easily modify materials throughout a scene:

1. Select the **Materials** button on the **Properties** window header. It's the ninth button from the left, with the chrome ball on it.

2. In the **Material** panel, notice that **Hull Material** is already there. One clue to why that is can be found next to the box where you input the material's name. Notice that it has the number **2**. That number represents how many objects use that material. Both the **Sloop** and **Cabin** were made from the default cube, and the **Hull Material** started out as the default material. So Blender has already been reusing the materials.

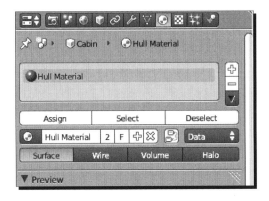

3. With the cursor over the 3D View window, press *A* to deselect all the faces.

4. Select the **Object Data** button on the **Properties** window header.

5. In the **Vertex Groups** subpanel, highlight the **Cabin Roof** group in the menu and press the **Select** button with the *LMB*.

6. Select the **Materials** button on the **Properties** window header.

7. In the **Material** panel, click on the plus sign to the right of the menu that lists **Hull Material**.

8. Press the chrome ball to the left of the **New** button. Select **Deck Material** from the drop-down menu as shown in the following screenshot:

9. Click on the **Assign** button.

10. Press the *Tab* key to get into **Object Mode**.

11. Select both **Layer 1** and **Layer 2** in the **3D View** header.

12. Press *F12* to render the image. Press *Esc* when you are done looking at it.

13. Save the file to a unique name.

What just happened?

Materials in Blender can be used over and over. You took the materials from the hull and applied them to the cabin. Modifying this material will alter its appearance on every object that uses it.

For your reference, the file `6907_08_Subdivision Surface 14.blend` has the cockpit, hull, and deck vertex groups. `6907_08_ Subdivision Surface 15.blend` has the hull and deck materials applied. `6907_08_Subdivision Surface 16.blend` has the cabin and cabin roof vertex groups. `6907_08_Subdivision Surface 17.blend` has the hull and cabin textured.

Making the ship's wheel with the Spin tool and DupliVerts

There are four parts to the ship's wheel; the rim, the hub, the spokes, and a circle to put the spokes on. You will make them in that order. The **Spin tool** is like a 3D lathe and creates circular objects. **DupliVerts** uses the vertices of an object to control the placement of copies of a second object.

Time for action – using the Spin tool to make the rim of the ship's wheel

The Spin tool is a very handy tool for making circular objects. It operates in a similar way to the extrusion, but instead of making a single extrusion in one direction, it creates a series of extrusions around a point. You can specify how many degrees you go around and how many extrusions it takes to do it. You'll start by making the rim of the ship's wheel. Time to give it a try:

1. Select **New** from the **File** menu.

2. Press *Numpad 7* to get the **Top** view. Press *Numpad 5* to get the **Ortho** view.

3. Press *X* to delete the default cube.

4. Press *Shift+A* and select **Mesh**, and then **Plane** from the menu.

5. Press the *Tab* key to get into **Edit Mode**.

6. Press *S, X, 0.125, Enter*.

7. Press *S, Y, 0.08, Enter*.

8. Press the *Tab* key to return to **Object Mode**.

9. Press *N* to open up the **Properties** panel in **3D View**.

10. Press *R, X, 90*, and *Enter*.

11. In the **Transform** subpanel, change the **Location: X:** to **1**, as shown in the following screenshot, to offset the rim away from its center.

12. Use the *MMB* and your mouse to rotate the view similar to what is shown in the following screenshot:

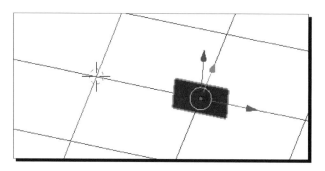

13. Press the *Tab* key to get into **Edit Mode**.

14. If **Tool Shelf** is not visible in the **3D View**, Press *T* to make it appear.

15. In **Tool Shelf**, scroll down to the **Add:** subpanel. Click on the **Spin** button with the *LMB*.

16. In the **Spin** subpanel, set the **Steps** to **18**, set the **Degrees** to **360**, and set the **Axis** to **X: 0.000, Y: 0.000, Z: 1.000**, as shown in the following screenshot. You can use the *Tab* key to move from button to button.

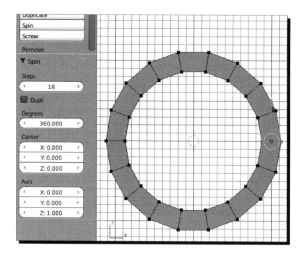

What just happened?

You just used the Spin tool. It's a very powerful tool for making objects. Think of it as a lathe. You moved the plane away from the center and sized it. Then with the Spin tool, you spun it 360 degrees in X around the 0, 0, 0 point, making the rim of the wheel.

Time for action – making the hub

Making the hub is easy. It's a cylinder:

1. Press *Numpad 7* to get the **Top** view.

2. Press the *Tab* key to get into **Object Mode**.

3. Press *A* to deselect all objects.

4. Press *Shift+A* and create a cylinder from the **Mesh** menu.

5. In the **Add Cylinder** subpanel in the lower half of **Tool Shelf**, set the number of **Vertices** to **18**.

6. Press *S, 0.25*, and then *Enter*.

7. Press *M, 2*, and *Enter* to move the hub to **Layer 2**.

What just happened?

That was easy. You put the hub in **Layer 2** so that it won't interfere with your work of making the spokes for the wheel. You will start by making a circle to control the placement of the spokes of the ship's wheel.

Time for action – making the circle

The circle is unseen but important. It is the basis for placing all of the spokes for the ship's wheel:

1. Press *Shift+A* and create a circle from the **Mesh** menu.

2. In the **Add Circle** subpanel of **Tool Shelf**, set the **Vertices** to **8** and the **Radius** to **0.25**.

What just happened

It doesn't look like much, but you will use the circle to control the placement of the spokes of the ship's wheel. There are eight vertices in the circle so your wheel will have eight spokes. Blender has a method called DupliVerts that lets you put a copy of the spoke at each vertex of the circle. These copies are called instances. The difference between regular objects and instances is that whatever change you make to one instance is made to all of them. Next you will be making a spoke for the ship's wheel.

Time for action – making the spoke

There are two stages for making the spoke. In the first, you will make the outline of the shape of the spoke. In the second, you will turn the silhouette into a 3D object using the Spin tool again:

1. Press *A* to deselect all objects.

2. Press *Shift+A* and make a Plane from the **Mesh** menu.

3. Press the *Tab* key to get into **Edit Mode**.

4. Press the *A* key to deselect all the vertices.

5. Press the *B* key and use the marquee to choose the vertices on the left side.

6. Press *X* and select **Delete Vertices** from the menu.

7. In the **Pivot Point** menu in the **3D View** header, select **3D Cursor**.

8. Press *A* to select all the vertices.

9. Press *S*, *X*, *0*, and then *Enter*.

10. Press *W* to subdivide the edge between the vertices. Then, in the **Subdivide** subpanel of **Tool Shelf**, set the **Number of Cuts** to 7.

11. Press *G*, *Y*, and use the mouse to move all of the vertices until the bottom vertex just touches the top of the circle, then press the *LMB* to release the vertices.

12. In the **3D View** header, select **Active Element** from the **Pivot Point** menu.

13. Now you want to set which vertex is the Active Element. Press *Shift+RMB* and select the bottom vertex so it goes black. Press *Shift+RMB* and select the bottom vertex so it goes yellow again. Now all of the vertices are selected but the bottom vertex is now the active element. The **3D Manipulator** shows you which is the **Active Element**.

14. Press *S*, *Y*, and use the mouse until the vertices are scaled down to about 0.7, then press the *LMB*. Don't forget to use the *Shift+Ctrl* buttons for precision.

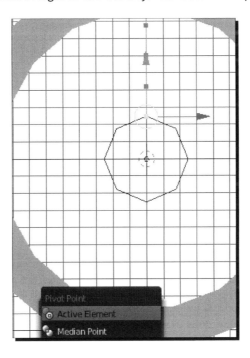

15. Press *A* to deselect all the vertices.

16. Press *B* to border select all the vertices except the top and bottom vertices.

17. Press *G*, *X*, *0.08*, and then *Enter* to move the vertices to the right.

18. Press *A* to deselect all the vertices.

19. Press the *RMB* to select the second to the bottom vertex and then press *Shift+RMB* to select the bottom vertex so it will be the **Active Element**.

20. Press *S*, *Y*, *0*, and then *Enter*.

21. Then, press *G*, *Y*, and use the mouse to move the two vertices down until they are within the circle and press the *LMB*.

22. Select the second to the top vertex with the *RMB*. Press *G*, *Y*, and use the mouse to move the vertex up until it is close to the top vertex and press the *LMB*.

23. Press *Shift+RMB* to also select the third to the top vertex. Press *G*, *X*, *0.02*, and press *Enter*.

24. Select the third from the bottom vertex with the *RMB*. Press *G* and use the mouse to move the vertex down and to the right until the bottom part of the spoke has a nice shape and press the *LMB*, as shown in the following screenshot:

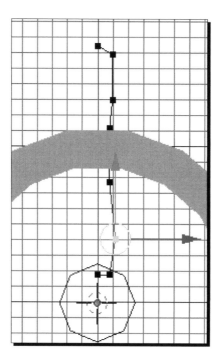

25. Next you need to put the center of the spoke right at the vertex of the circle.

26. Press the *Tab* key to get into **Object Mode**.

27. Select the circle and press the *Tab* key to get into **Edit Mode**.

28. Select the top vertex of the circle with the *RMB*.

29. Press *Shift+S* and choose **Cursor to Selected** from the menu.

30. Press the *Tab* key to go into **Object Mode**.

31. Select the outline of the spoke.

32. In the **3D View** header, select **Object**. Then choose **Transform** and **Origin to 3D Cursor** from the pop-up menus.

33. Press the *Tab* key to get back into **Edit Mode**.

34. Press *A* to select all of the vertices.

35. In the **Add:** subpanel of **Tool Shelf** select **Spin** with the *LMB*.

36. In the **Spin** subpanel of **Tool Shelf**, set the **Steps** to **8**, **Degrees** to **360** (don't move the center), and set the **Axis** to **X: 0.000, Y: 1.000, Z: 0.000**.

37. With the cursor over the **3D View** window, press the *Tab* key to go into **Object Mode**.

38. Press *Shift+S* and choose **Cursor to Center**.

39. Press *Shift+S* and choose **Selection to Cursor**.

What just happened?

You created the outline for the shape of the spoke with the vertices. It turns out that using the Active Element as the center can be a handy way of scaling vertexes, and handier when you are modeling complex surfaces.

When you get to using the DupliVerts, the origin of the spoke will be put at the vertex of the circle. You built the spoke in the place where it would be after using the DupliVert method. Then you made its origin at the location of the circle's vertex. Finally, you moved the spoke so that its origin was at the center of the scene.

You used the Spin tool again with very different results than when you made the rim. This time, the center of the object was within the vertices and, when they were spun, there was no hole in the center. The object looked much more like it was made on a lathe. The Spin tool is great for making table legs, wine glasses, and other round objects.

Now it's time to use DupliVerts.

Time for action – assembling the ship's wheel

When using DupliVerts, Blender starts with a **pattern mesh** object, which in this case is the spoke. It makes an instance of the pattern mesh object and moves the copy to the location of a vertex on the **base object**, in your case, the circle. DupliVerts can also rotate the DupliVerted copy with respect to the center of the base object:

1. Select the circle with the *RMB*.

2. In the **Properties** window header, click on the **Object** button. It's the fifth button from the left.

3. In the **Duplication** subpanel, select the **Verts** button in the center. A **Rotation** checkbox will appear. Check it.

4. Select the spoke with the *RMB*. Then also select the circle again with *Shift+RMB*. Press *Ctrl+P* to parent the circle to the spoke. Choose **Set Parent To Object** in the menu.

5. Now you have all eight spokes, but the original spoke is still there. It can be seen in the following screenshot. Press *F12* and render it, and you will see that the original spoke does not render.

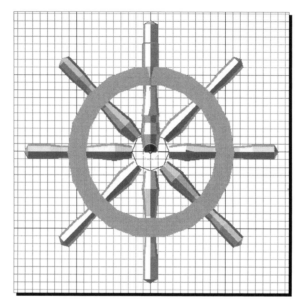

6. In the **3D View** header, select **Layer 2** with *Shift+LMB* so you can see the hub.

7. Press *Numpad 1* to get the **Front** view.

8. Select the hub with the *RMB*. Press *G*, *Z*, and use the mouse to move the hub down until the top of the hub is level with the top of the spokes, as shown in the following screenshot, then press the *LMB*.

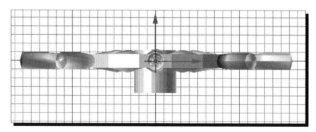

9. Save the file with a unique name.

What just happened?

DupliVerts is a Blender tool that allows you to make multiple copies of an object referred to as the pattern mesh and controls their placement with another object known as the base object. In this case, you had a spoke which was your pattern mesh, and the circle which is the base object.

When you parent the base object to the pattern mesh, and set the duplication mode of the base object to Verts, an instance of the pattern mesh is located at each vertex of the base object. Blender will render all of the instances, but will not render either the base object or the pattern mesh. If you need to make changes to all of the instances, just make the changes to the pattern mesh. And if you want to turn the instances of the pattern mesh into their own objects, you press *Ctrl+Shift+A*.

Well, now you have a sloop and a ship's wheel to steer her with. Here are some of the commands you used:

Key	Function
Ctrl+R	Loop Cut
Alt+RMB	Edge Loop
Ctrl+Alt+RMB	Edge Ring
Z	Toggles between Solid and Wireframe display
Alt+C	Convert a surface to a mesh object
Ctrl+Shift+A	Convert DupliVert instances to independent objects

Summary

In this chapter you learned some advanced modeling techniques. You modeled a sloop with Subdivision Surfaces, and then grabbed some of the geometry to make a cabin that fit precisely together with the hull. You saw how you can control the quality of the model and optimize the number of faces you create depending on your needs. You discovered how to use the loop cut tool, edge loops, and edge rings. You learned how to use Boolean objects to punch holes and shapes in other objects. You made the ship's wheel using Spin tools and DupliVerts.

In the next chapter you will finish the sloop. You will add the boom, mast, spar, bowsprit, gaff, rudder, tiller, and keel that you made. You will make sails for her from NURBS surfaces. You will also focus on text by naming your sloop. You'll use choice of font, letter spacing, shearing, extrusion, and beveling to make it look sharp.

Let's go.

9

Finishing your Sloop

In the last chapter you learned more advanced modeling techniques. You modeled a sloop with Subdivision Surfaces, and then grabbed some of the geometry of the hull to make a cabin that fits precisely together with the hull. You saw how you can control the quality of the model and optimize the number of faces you create depending on your needs. You discovered how to use the Loop Cut tool, Edge Loops, and Edge Rings. You learned how to use Boolean objects to punch holes and shapes in other objects. You made the ship's wheel using spin tools and DupliVerts.

In this chapter, the sloop is going to come together and look great:

- ◆ You will add the boom, mast, spar, bowsprit, gaff, rudder, tiller, keel, and ship's wheel that you made.
- ◆ You'll use NURBS surfaces to make some sails. You'll get a line to control the sails, a door, and a detailed window for the portal in the download pack that you can add to your sloop.

Let's get started.

Making sure you have the files you'll need in this chapter

Make sure you have loaded the following files from your download files into the `Blender Files` subdirectory of this `Chapters` directory:

- ◆ `6907_09_sloop_hull_cabin.blend`
- ◆ `6907_09_sloop_rudder_tiller_mast_boom_gaff_bowsprit.blend`

- ◆ `6907_09_sloop_ships wheel.blend`
- ◆ `6907_09_sloop_Miss Blender Nassau.blend`
- ◆ `6907_09_sloop_line.blend`
- ◆ `6907_09_sloop_door_window.blend`

Make sure you have loaded the following files into the `Images` subdirectory of this chapter's directory:

- ◆ `6907_09_03.png`
- ◆ `6907_09_04.png`

Finishing the sloop

Well, you've done a lot of good work and now it's time to bring it all together. It's time to combine all the bits into a single file and finish your sloop. I have made kits of the parts that have been made so far, plus a few bonus items like sails, a line, a door, and a glass portal. Since your sloop may vary slightly, you can either use what you have made or take parts from the kits. They are in the download pack. Make sure that you download `6907_09_03.png` into the Images directory so Blender will know where to find the wood texture. If you've forgotten any of the names of the sloop's parts, check the illustration in *Chapter 7, Planning your Work, Working your Plan*.

Time for action – setting up the boom and gaff so they swing

Now it's time to assemble the sloop. In addition to just bringing all the parts into the same file there are a couple of other things that need to happen. Some of the parts need to have the materials from the hull and the cabin added to them, and all of the parts must have their relationship to the hull defined. Either they will be joined to the hull to make one solid object or the hull will be parented to them so that it controls their actions. Objects that are fixed, such as the cabin, will be joined to the hull. Objects that move, such as the rudder, will have the hull parented to them. If you wish, you may assemble the parts that you have made in lieu of using the files I have provided:

1. Open `6907_09_sloop_hull_cabin.blend` or the file with your hull and cabin.

2. Select the hull with the *RMB*.

3. Press *Shift+S* and choose **Cursor to Center** from the menu.

4. Select **Object** from the 3D View header and select **Transform** then **Origin to 3D Cursor** from the pop-up menus.

5. Select the cabin with the *RMB*, then select the hull with *Shift+RMB*. Press *Ctrl+J* to join the cabin to the hull.

6. Press *1* to go to Layer 1. If you are emulating the Numpad, you will need to use the layer control in the 3D View header instead.

7. In the **File** menu, select **Append**.

8. Find `6907_09_sloop_rudder_tiller_mast_boom_gaff_bowsprit.blend`, or your file with those pieces.

9. Open the `Object` folder.

10. Select the **Boom**, the **Bowsprit**, the **Gaff**, and the **Mast** with *Shift+LMB* as shown in the following screenshot:

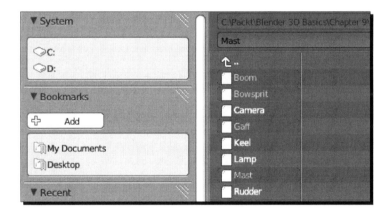

11. Press the *LMB* on the **Link/Append from Library** button as seen here.

12. In the 3D View, press *A* to deselect everything.

13. Use the *RMB* to select the mast.

14. Select the **Material** button in the **Properties** window header. It's the ninth button from the left.

15. Click on the silver ball next to the **New** button, as seen in the following screenshot.

16. Choose the **Deck Material** from the menu, as shown in the following screenshot:

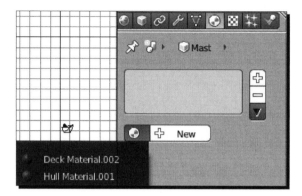

17. Select the boom and repeat the steps to apply the **Deck Material** to it.

18. Select the gaff. It's near the top of the mast. Repeat the steps to apply the **Deck Material** to it.

19. Select the bowsprit and repeat the steps to apply the **Deck Material** to it.

20. Press *F12* to render it. Press *Esc* when you are through looking at it.

21. Select the mast with the *RMB*. Select the bowsprit with *Shift+RMB*. Then select the hull with *Shift+RMB*. Press *Ctrl+J* to join them.

22. Press *Numpad 3* to get the *Side* view and then *Numpad 5* if you need to get into **Ortho** mode.

23. Center your view on the mast, between the boom and the gaff, then zoom in until you cannot see the boom or the gaff, only the mast.

24. Press *Shift+S*, select **Cursor to Center**. With the *LMB*, put the 3D cursor just to the right side of the mast as close as you can.

25. Press *Shift+A* and select **Empty** from the menu.

26. Press *S, 20, Enter* to scale out the axes of the Empty. The long axes make the Empty easier to select.

27. Move the cursor to the outer limits of the 3D View window. Press *R, X*, and rotate the Empty with the mouse, until its Z axis is parallel to the mast as seen here. Press the *LMB* to release it.

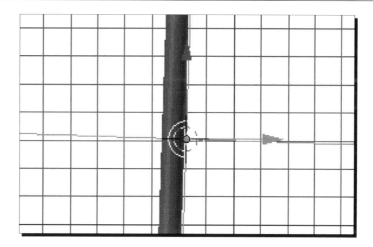

28. Select the mast with *Shift+RMB*. Press *Ctrl+P* to parent the hull to the Empty. Select **Object** from the pop-up menu.

29. Zoom out so you can see both the boom and the gaff.

30. Select the boom with the *RMB*. Select the Empty with *Shift+RMB*. Press *Ctrl+P* to parent the Empty to the boom. Select **Object** from the pop-up menu. You'll see a dotted line between them as seen here.

31. Select the gaff with the *RMB*. Select the Empty with *Shift+RMB*. Press *Ctrl+P* to parent the Empty to the gaff, as seen here. Select **Object** from the pop-up menu.

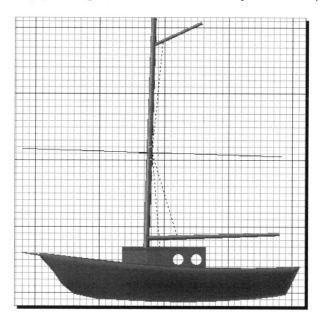

32. Select **Empty**. Press *R, Z, Z* to rotate in the Empty's local axis. Then use the mouse to swing the gaff and the boom back and forth. Press the *RMB* to release **Empty** without disturbing its position.

33. Save the file to a unique name.

What just happened?

A lot of important work happened here. After bringing the hull and the cabin in, you made sure that the center of the sloop was in the right place, then you joined the cabin to the hull. You brought in the mast, boom, gaff, and bowsprit. The mast and bowsprit won't move so they were joined to the sloop. Then you made an Empty. An empty is an object with no vertices, edges, faces, just some visible axes. But it is good for joining one or more things and controlling them. You rotated it so that its local Z axis is parallel with the mast and then parented it to the boom and the gaff. They will swing when it does and they will swing parallel to the mast. Later the mainsail and line will also be added so all will move together.

Time for action – adding the rudder, tiller, and keel

Without the rudder, tiller, and keel, the sloop would drift aimlessly. They are simple objects but they need a little special handling to fit correctly onto the sloop:

1. In the **File** menu, select **Append**.

2. Open the **Object** folder.

3. Select the **Keel**, the **Rudder**, the **Tiller Path**, and the **Tiller Shape** with *Shift+LMB*.

4. Press the *LMB* on the **Link/Append from Library** button.

5. In the 3D View, press *A* to deselect everything.

6. Use the *RMB* to select the tiller. Check to see that the tiller clears the sloop's deck. If it doesn't, move it so it does.

7. Select the **Material** button in the **Properties** window header. It's the ninth button from the left.

8. Click on the silver ball next to the **New** button as seen here.

9. Choose the **Deck Material** from the menu to apply it to the tiller.

10. Select the rudder and repeat the steps to apply the **Hull Material** to it. Select the keel and repeat the steps to apply the **Hull Material** to it.

11. Press *Alt+C* to convert the keel from a Bezier Curve object to a mesh object. Select **Mesh from Curve/Meta/Surf/Text**.

12. Select the hull with *Shift+RMB*. Press *Ctrl+J* to join the keel to the hull.

13. Use *Shift+MMB* and *Ctrl+MMB* to zoom in to the rudder.

14. Select the rudder with the *RMB*. Check to see that there is a little gap between the rudder and the stern of the sloop as seen in the next image. Move the rudder if necessary.

15. Press *Shift+S* and select **Cursor to Center** from the pop-up menu.

16. Choose **3D Cursor** from the **Pivot Point** menu on the 3D View header.

17. Move the 3D Cursor so it is between the rudder and the sloop as seen on the right side of the next illustration.

18. Select the rudder. Choose **Object** from the 3D View header. Choose **Transform** and then choose **Origin to 3D Cursor** from the pop-up menus.

19. Now it's time to do a little trick. You are going to change the local axis of the rudder so that it is parallel with the stern of the sloop. First, you rotate all the control points in one direction, which moves the rudder itself but not the axis. Then, when you rotate the entire object, the axis gets changed and the rudder gets moved back into place. When you made the hull of the sloop in *Chapter 8, Making the Sloop* you angled the stern at 27 degrees. So now you will adjust the local axis of the rudder to match this.

20. Press the *Tab* key to get into **Edit Mode**.

21. Press *A* to select all the control points.

22. Press *R, X, 27, Enter*. It will look like the following illustration on the right.

23. Press the *Tab* key to get into **Object Mode**.

24. Press *R, X, -27, Enter*.

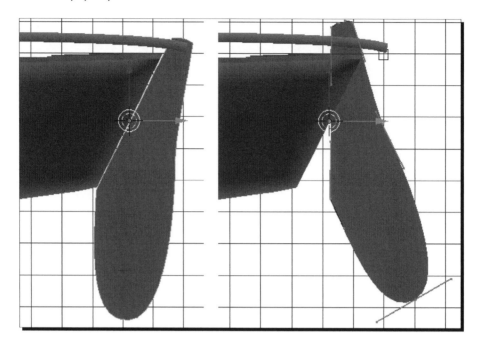

25. Select the tiller with the *RMB* and then select the rudder with *Shift+RMB*.

26. Press *Ctrl+P* to parent the rudder to the tiller and select **Object** from the menu.

27. Select the rudder with the *RMB*. Press *R, X, X*, and use the mouse to test the rotation of the rudder and ensure that the rudder is parented to the tiller. Press the *RMB* to release it without moving it when done.

28. Press *F12* to render it. Press *Esc* when you are done looking at it.

What just happened?

This was very similar to adding the mast, boom, and so on to the hull. But you may have wondered why you opened up the rudder in **Edit Mode**, rotated the control points 27 degrees and then rotated the object -27 degrees in **Object Mode**. Seems kind of redundant, the rudder is right back where it started. But by rotating all the control points in **Edit Mode**, you rotated them without affecting the local axis. Then you got back into **Object Mode** and rotated the entire rudder, so the local axis was rotated by -27 degrees to match the angle of the stern. Now the rudder swings properly in alignment with the stern, instead of just rotating horizontally as it would if you had not done this.

Time for action – adding the ship's wheel

Now it's time to add the ship's wheel. You may be surprised by an after-effect of the DupliVerts as you add materials:

1. Press *2* to go to Layer 2. If you are emulating the Numpad, use the layer controls in the 3D View header instead.

2. In the **File** menu, select **Append**.

3. Find `6907_09_sloop_ships wheel.blend` or the file you saved with the spokes rim and hub still separate.

4. Open the **Object** folder.

5. Press *A* to select all of the objects.

6. Press the *LMB* on the **Link/Append from Library** button.

7. Press the *Home* key to zoom into the spoke. Use the *Fn+Left arrow* if using a Mac without a *Home* key.

8. Use the *MMB* to rotate the view so you can see the ship's wheel better.

9. Use the *RMB* to select a spoke as seen on the left of the following screenshot.

10. Click on the silver ball next to the **New** button.

11. Choose the **Deck Material** from the menu.

12. Use the *RMB* to select another spoke. Note that it already has the deck material. All the spokes are instances of each other.

13. Use the *RMB* to select the rim.

14. Click on the silver ball next to the **New** button.

15. Choose the **Deck Material** from the menu.

16. Use the *RMB* to select the hub.

17. Click on the silver ball next to the **New** button.

18. Choose the **Deck Material** from the menu.

19. Press *B* and use the mouse to select all the parts of the ship's wheel.

20. Press *Ctrl+J* to join them into a single piece.

21. Press the **Object** button in the Properties window header. It's the fifth one from the left. Name the object **Ships Wheel**.

22. Press *M, 1, Enter* to move the ship's wheel to Layer 1.

23. Press *1* to go to Layer 1. If you are emulating the Numpad, use the layer controls in the 3D View header instead.

24. Press *Numpad 3* to get the **Side** view. Press *Ctrl+MMB* and use the mouse to zoom out so you can see the sloop.

25. Press *G* and move the ship's wheel up and to the right so it is over the cockpit. Press the *LMB* to release it.

26. In the 3D View header, select the **Pivot Point** button and choose **Median Point** from the pop-up menu.

27. Press *R, X, -90, Enter* to orient the wheel properly.

28. Press *G* to move the wheel toward the cabin, then press the *MMB* to lock the axis of motion. Put the hub of the wheel touching the cabin as seen here to the right. Press the *LMB* to release it.

29. Press *Ctrl+Numpad 1* to get the **Rear** view.

30. Press *G* and move the wheel to the right side of the cabin. Press the *LMB* to release it.

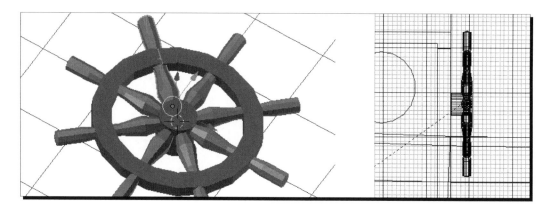

31. Press *Shift+RMB* and select the hull. Press *Ctrl+P* to parent the hull to the ship's wheel. Select **Object** from the pop-up menu.

What just happened?

Adding the ship's wheel was pretty straightforward. The only surprise was that, since you created the spokes by the process called DupliVerts, when you applied the texture to one of them, all of them got the texture applied. This is because the spokes are instances of each other. Remember in *Chapter 1, Introducing Blender and Animation*, where I talked about master objects used by Sketchpad, here is one place where Blender uses them. There is really only one object but Blender uses its object data as many times as is needed.

Naming your boat properly is important. I have chosen the name Miss Blender and made a text object for you. But I'm willing to bet that after all the work you have done to make your sloop, you might want to give her a name of your own choosing.

If so, check out 6907OS_09_Text Blender Style.pdf. It shows you how to create text in Blender with a variety of fonts and materials and gives you tips on how to make it easy to use.

Check it out!

Time for action – adding the boat name

Now it's time to add the boat name and affix it to the stern of the sloop:

1. Press *A* to deselect all objects.

2. Press *Ctrl+Numpad 3* to get the **Left** side view.

3. In the **File** menu, select **Append**.

4. Find 6907_09_sloop_Miss Blender Nassau.blend or the file with your favorite boat name.

5. Open the **Object** folder.

6. Select **Miss Blender Nassau** or whichever name you prefer for your boat with *Shift+LMB*.

7. Press the *LMB* on the **Link/Append from Library** button.

8. Press *G* and move the name to the stern of the boat where you can see it, then press the *LMB* to release it.

9. Press *R, Z, 180, Enter*.

10. Press *S, 0.4, Enter*.

11. Now the name needs to be rotated into the proper orientation. Minus 90 degrees would turn it straight up, but if you remember in *Chapter 8, Making the Sloop,* we angled the stern of the sloop -27 degrees. So add -90 and -27 to get -117. Press *R, X, -117, Enter.*

12. Press *Ctrl+Numpad 1* to get the **Rear** view.

13. Move the name to where you want it on the stern, as seen in the center of the following image.

14. Press *Ctrl+Numpad 3* to get the Left Side view. Move the view so you can see the stern of the sloop.

15. Press *G, Y,* and use the mouse to move the name to the sloop, as seen on the right. Press the *LMB* to release it.

16. If you have used another name than Miss Blender Nassau, make sure it has been converted to a mesh object. Press *Alt+C* if you need to convert it.

17. Press *Shift+RMB* and select the hull. Press *Ctrl+J* to join the name to the hull of the sloop.

What just happened?

You just assembled your sloop, added all the parts you made, and added materials to them. It took a little work, but it was pretty easy. You've handled quite a variety of modeling methods now. Well done.

Time for action – using a NURBS surface to make the mainsail

You have used Subdivision Surfaces to model the sloop's hull and Bezier Curves to make the rudder and keel. Now you will use a NURBS (Non Uniform Rational B Spline) surface to make the mainsail:

1. Zoom out so you can see the whole sloop.

2. Press *Shift+S* and select **Cursor to Center**.

3. Put the cursor between the boom and gaff in the middle of where the sail will be.

4. Press *Shift+A*. Choose **Add Surface** then **NURBS Surface**.

5. Press *R, Y, -90, Enter*.

6. Press the *Tab* key

7. In the **Properties** window select the **Object Data**, it's the eighth button from the left.

8. In the 3D View, select one of the bottom control points of the NURBS Surface with the *RMB*.

9. In the **Properties** window, the **Active Spline** subpanel appears, check the checkboxes for **Endpoint: U** and **Endpoint: V**.

10. Press *C* and select the bottom row of control points. Press the *RMB* to finish the selection.

11. Move the selected control points near to the boom. Press *A* to deselect all of the control points.

12. Select and move each bottom corner control point to its respective end of the boom, as shown on the left side of the next graphic.

13. Space the other two bottom control points evenly between the ends of the boom, as seen in the following graphic on the right.

14. Press *A* to deselect all control points. Press *C* to select the top row of control points. Press the *RMB* to finish the selection.

15. Move the selected control points near to the gaff.

16. Move the top corner control points to the ends of the gaff.

17. Space the other two top control points evenly between the ends of the gaff as seen here on the right.

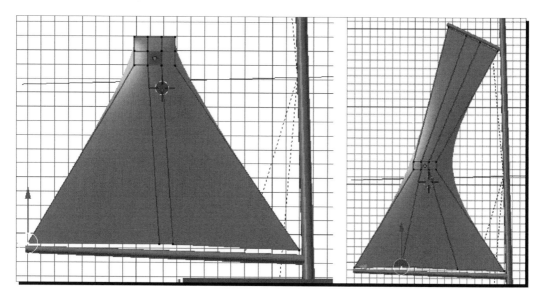

18. Now work with the control points in the center of the sail. Move the right hand ones so they are evenly spaced between the boom and the gaff, by the mast. Move the left hand ones so they are evenly spaced between the tips of the boom and the gaff, as seen here. Then move the center control points so that they are evenly spaced across the mainsail, as seen on the left side of the next image.

19. Press *C* and select all four central control points. Press the *RMB* to complete the selection.

20. Press *MMB* and rotate the view until you can see the curve in the sail as shown here.

21. Press *G*, *X*, and move the control points to -3.000. Then press the *LMB* to release it.

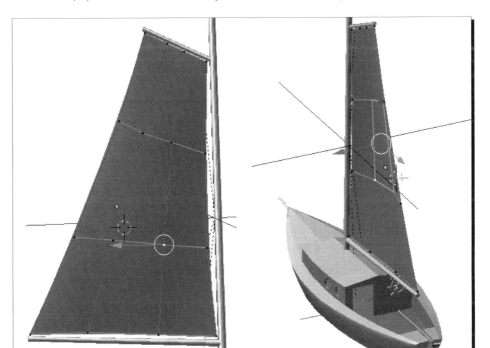

22. Press the *Tab* key to leave **Edit Mode**.

23. In the **Properties** window header, press the **Object** button. It's the fifth button from the left. Name the sail **Mainsail**.

24. Select the **Empty** with *Shift+RMB*.

25. Press *Ctrl+P* to parent the Empty to the mainsail. Select **Object** from the pop-up menu.

What just happened?

The sails are NURBS (Non Uniform Rational B-Spline) curves. They are similar to Subdivision Surfaces in that they use control points to control a surface. They give a little more accurate control but are a little harder to use. Like Subdivision Surfaces you can add control points to extend the surface. And Blender can animate the control points of the sail, so the sail can be filled with wind. The mainsail was parented to the Empty so that it will move along with the boom and gaff.

Have a go hero – making the jib

Making the jib is very similar to making the mainsail, with one little twist, it only has three corners:

1. Add the NURBS surface, rotate it, and check the checkboxes for the end points, just as you did in the last *Time for action*.

2. To make the corner near the bowsprit, grab all the control points on the vertical edge nearest to the bowsprit and scale them all to zero. Then move them near to the end of the bowsprit.

3. Next, move one corner near the mast across from the boom and one corner near the mast across from the gaff.

4. Then adjust all the control points evenly as seen here:

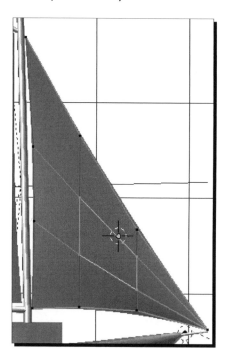

5. Grab the central four control points as seen here and move them in X to put some wind into the sail.

6. Create a material for the jib, then apply it to the mainsail as well.

7. When you are done, parent the hull to the jib.

8. Save the file to a unique name.

Detailing the sloop, adding a door and portals

This book is too short to cover everything. It would be neat to add an interior, an anchor, and other details. But there's is still much to cover. So here are a couple of bonuses for your hard work and persistence; a line for the mainsail which you can copy and use for making other lines for the sloop, the door, the portal window, and a nice brass frame.

For your reference, the file 6907_09_Portal and Door Assembly.blend has the file with parts, textures, and instructions in the Text window on how to create the door, and a glass portal window.

Time for action – adding a line to control the mainsail

You can't control the sail without a line. Made just like the tiller, it shows the flexibility of this technique:

1. Press *A* to deselect all objects. In the **File** menu, select **Append**.

2. Find 6907_09_sloop_line.blend.

3. Open the **Object** folder.

4. Press *A* to select the **Line** and the **Line Shape**.

5. In the **3D View**, select the **Line** as shown in the following screenshot:

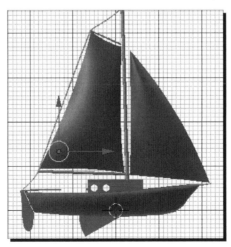

6. Press the *Tab* key to get into **Edit Mode**. You see the control points of the Bezier Curve that creates the line. Press the *Tab* key to re-enter **Object Mode**.

7. In the **Properties** window header, press the **Object Data** button. It's the eighth one from the left. The line is made just the same way as the tiller. In the **Geometry** subpanel you will see **Line Shape** listed as the Bevel Object, as in the following image.

8. Press *Shift+LMB* to select **Empty**. Press *Ctrl+P* to parent the Empty to the line.

9. Select **Empty** and press *R, Z, Z* to do a test rotation. Press the *RMB* when you are done.

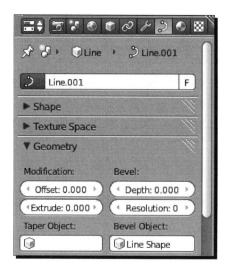

What just happened?

The line was made just the same way that the tiller was, with a Bezier Curve to control the shape of the length and a Bezier circle to control the shape of the cross-section. Like the sail, its control points can be animated.

Have a go hero – adding the door and a portal

Now you will bring in the cabin door and the portal. You will put the cabin door together with the portal window, and separate a copy of the portal window to use on the cabin:

1. Deselect everything. Find `6907_09_sloop_door_window.blend`. Append the Cabin Door and the Portal Window.

2. Make a copy of the Portal Window and move it aside.

3. Move the Door and Window to Layer 2 to work on them. Go to Layer 2.

4. Get the **Side** view. Move the 3D Cursor so it's centered on the door from the side view.

5. Use *Ctrl+Numpad 1* to look at the door as you would from the cockpit.

6. Move the 3D Cursor so it's just to the left of the door, near the center of the hinge. In the 3D View, select **Object** from the header, then **Transform** from the pop-up menu and then **Origin to 3D Cursor** so that the door swings around the 3D Cursor's location.

7. Add the Deck Material to the door. The Portal Window does not need any material.

8. Then, join the Portal Window to the door.

9. Move them back to Layer 1. Go to Layer 1, then parent the hull to the door.

10. Don't join the copy that you made of the Portal Window to the door, though we will use it to cover the other portals in the sides of the cabin.

Time for action – adding the portals

This is the final touch, adding portals to the cabin. The cabin is not rectangular, so you will have to rotate the portals to match the angle of the walls:

1. Press *Numpad 7* to get the **Top** view.

2. In the **Viewport Shading** menu on the 3D View header, select **Wireframe** shading.

3. Select the copy of the portal.

4. Press *R, Z, 90, Enter*.

5. Press *G* and use the mouse to move the portal next to the left side of the cabin. Press the *LMB* to release.

6. Use *Ctrl+MMB* and *Shift+MMB* to zoom in so you see the portal and the portal holes on the left side as well.

7. Press *G* and use the mouse to get the portal aligned up as closely as possible with the forward portal hole. Press the *LMB* to release.

8. Zoom into the forward portal hole. The portal window is a little larger than the portal hole. Aligning the dot that marks the center of the Portal Window with the outside wall of the cabin will help to get started. Then make sure that the sides of the portal window extend on either side of the portal hole.

9. Press *Ctrl+Numpad 3*. Zoom out till you can see both the portal hole and the portal window.

10. Press *G, Z*, and move the portal window down to the portal hole.

11. Use *Ctrl+MMB* and *Shift+MMB* to zoom in so you see the portal and portal hole very well. Press the *G* key and use the mouse to align the portal with the portal hole. The edge of the portal hole will be between the two edges of the portal window as seen in the following illustration. For finer control, press the *Arrow* keys instead of using the mouse. Press *Enter* to release the portal in place.

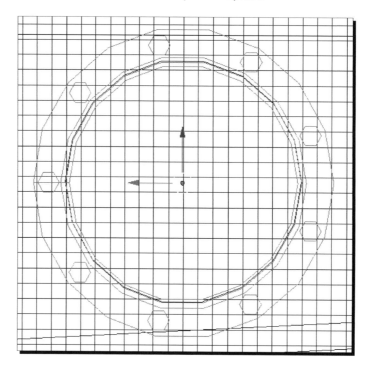

12. Press *Shift+D*, make a copy of the portal and move it to the rearward portal hole. Press the *MMB* when you move to keep it level with the original portal. Press the *LMB* when it is over the portal hole.

13. Press *G* and use the left and right arrow keys to do the final alignment. Press *Enter* to release it.

14. Press *Numpad 7* to get the **Top** view.

15. Press *G, X,* and move the portal next to the portal opening. Use the dot in the center of the Portal Window to guide you. Press the *LMB* to release it.

16. Press *R, Z,* and use the mouse to rotate the portal so it is flush with the side of the cabin, then press the *LMB* to release the rotation, as shown here. The bolt heads should be facing outward.

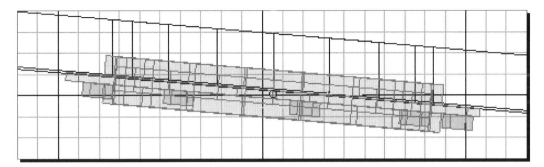

17. Zoom out so you can see both portal windows. Select the forward portal window with the *RMB*.

18. Press *R, Z,* and use the mouse to rotate the portal so it is flush with the side of the cabin, then press the *LMB*. Start with the cursor at the edge of the 3D View for the best control.

19. In the 3D View header, select the **Pivot Point** button and choose 3D Cursor from the pop-up menu.

20. Press *Shift+S* and choose **Cursor to Center**.

21. Press *Shift+D, Enter* to duplicate the portal. Press *S, X -1, Enter*.

22. Select the rear portal with the *RMB*.

23. Press *Shift+D, Enter* to duplicate the portal. Press *S, X, -1, Enter*.

24. Use *Shift+MMB* to move to the other side of the sloop. Make sure you see the portals and the portal holes well.

25. In the 3D View header, select the **Pivot Point** button and choose **Median Point** from the pop-up menu.

26. Press *G, Y,* and move the rear portal window next to the portal opening if it needs it. Press the *LMB* to release it.

27. Press *R, Z,* and use the mouse to rotate the portal window so it is flush with the side of the cabin, as seen in the next illustration, then press the *LMB*.

28. Select the forward portal window with the *RMB*.

29. Press *G, Y,* and move the portal next to the portal opening if it needs it. Press the *LMB* to release it.

30. Press *R, Z,* and use the mouse to rotate the portal so it is flush with the side of the cabin, then press the *LMB*, as seen in the next illustration.

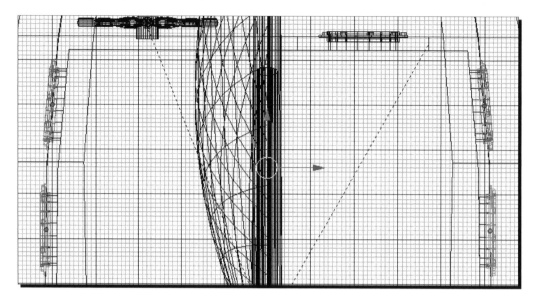

31. Select the four portal windows with the *Shift+RMB*. Select the hull with *Shift+RMB*. Press *Ctrl+J* to join the portal window to the hull.

32. In the **Viewport Shading** menu on the 3D View header, select **Solid** shading.

33. Press the *Home* key so you can see the entire sloop.

34. Press *F12* to render it. Press *Esc* when you are done viewing it.

35. Save the file to a unique name.

What just happened?

Congratulations! You have finished the sloop. That's quite an accomplishment. In this last exercise, the tricky part was getting a tight fit between the portal holes and the portal windows. You learned that the *arrow* keys could be used with the *G* key to move objects in small precise amounts. Just in case you were wondering, the frame of the portal windows were created with the same methods as the ship's wheel; the rim was made with the spin tool, the nuts are DupliVerts and the glass windows were done with a Boolean operation. The door was also a couple of Boolean operations to cut out the door and then a portal hole in the door.

For your reference, the file `6907_09_sloop_build_1.blend` has the hull, cabin, mast, boom, gaff, and bowsprit as separate pieces. `6907_09_sloop_build_2.blend` has the boom and gaff parented to the empty and the cabin, mast, and bowsprit joined to the hull. `6907_09_sloop_build_3.blend` has the rudder, tiller, and keel textured. `6907_09_sloop_build_4.blend` has the keep joined to the hull and the rudder reoriented and parented to the hull. `6907_09_sloop_build_5.blend` has the ship's wheel added. `6907_09_sloop_build_6.blend` has the sails added. `6907_09_sloop_build_7.blend` has the ship's name. `6907_09_sloop_build_8.blend` has the line added. `6907_09_sloop_build_9.blend` has the door and glass portal added. `6907_09_sloop_build_10.blend` has the right-hand portals in place. `6907_09_sloop_build_11.blend` has all the portals in place. `6907_09_sloop_build_12.blend` has the completed sloop.

The following table shows the commands used in this chapter:

Key	Function
A	In the **File Browser** it selects all the files to append.
Backspace	In **Edit Mode** for a Text Object, it deletes a character.
Ctrl+C	Copies Text in the Text Editor, or the Text entry box in the Insert Text subpanel of the Tool Shelf.
Ctrl+V	Pastes Text in the Text Editor, or the Text entry box in the Insert Text subpanel of the Tool Shelf.
Ctrl+M	In the Text Editor, it copies the texts and creates Text Objects in the 3D View.
Left arrow	In **Edit Mode** for a Text Object, it moves the cursor to the left.
Right arrow	In **Edit Mode** for a Text Object, it moves the cursor to the right.
Up arrow	In **Edit Mode** for a Text Object, it moves the cursor up one line.
Down arrow	In **Edit Mode** for a Text Object, it moves the cursor down one line.
End	In **Edit Mode** for a Text Object, it moves the cursor to the end of the line.
Home	In **Edit Mode** for a Text Object, it moves the cursor to the beginning of the line.
Shift+Left arrow	In **Edit Mode** for a Text Object, it selects one character to the left.
Shift+Right arrow	In **Edit Mode** for a Text Object, it selects one character to the right.
Shift+Up arrow	In **Edit Mode** for a Text Object, it selects one row upwards.
Shift+Down arrow	In **Edit Mode** for a Text Object, it selects one row downwards.
Shift+End	In **Edit Mode** for a Text Object, it selects all the characters from the current character to the end of the line.
Shift+Home	In **Edit Mode** for a Text Object, it selects all the characters from the current character to the beginning of the line.
Ctrl+Alt+Numpad 0	Matches Camera View to Current View.
Ctrl+J	Joins two objects together.
Fn+Left arrow	On a Mac without a *Home* key, this accomplishes the Home key command.
Left arrow	After the *G* key is pressed, this moves in small increments to the left, the motion is aligned to the screen.
Right arrow	After the *G* key is pressed, this moves in small increments to the right, the motion is aligned to the screen.
Up arrow	After the *G* key is pressed, this moves in small increments upward, the motion is aligned to the screen.
Down arrow	After the *G* key is pressed, this moves in small increments downward, the motion is aligned to the screen.

Summary

In this chapter, you added the boom, mast, spar, bowsprit, gaff, rudder, tiller, keel, and ship's wheel that you made. You learned how to create a local axis for motion that is not on the global X, Y, and Z axes. You created sails with NURBS surfaces, added a line, a door, and a detailed window for the portal in the download pack.

In the next chapter you will learn how to make organic forms, oceanic surfaces, and terrain. You will populate your world with simple buildings and build a pier for your sloop.

Let's go!

10

Modeling Organic Forms, Sea, and Terrain

In the last chapter, you created several possible names for your sloop. Choosing font, letter spacing, extrusion, Bezier curves, and beveling, you made it look sharp. Then you finished off the sloop. You added the boom, mast, spar, bowsprit, gaff, rudder, tiller, keel, and ship's wheel that you made. You learned how to create a local axis for motion that is not on the global X, Y, and Z axes. You added the bonus sails, line, a door, and a detailed window for the portal in the download pack.

This chapter will help you create a world for the sloop and the boat. You'll learn a lot of cool new ways to model. You will be:

- ◆ Using texturing to create an oceanic surface
- ◆ Using the ANT Landscape add-on to create an island
- ◆ Using proportional editing to finalize the land form
- ◆ Using Blender Paint to color the land form
- ◆ Creating an entire pier with just four objects using arrays, DupliFrames and bevel objects
- ◆ Making trees with the Sapling tree generator add-on
- ◆ Using your organic modeling skills to model rocks and boulders
- ◆ Completing the world by appending houses, rocks, trees, boats, and the sky

Let's get started!

Getting ready to make the island

The following are the files that you should copy from your download pack and into your Chapter 10/Blender Files directory:

- 6907_10_Island_Ocean_Pier.blend
- 6907_10_Port and Breakwater Templates.blend
- 6907_10_House Kit.blend
- 6907_10_Sloop.blend
- 6907_10_Boat.blend
- 6907_10_Tree_Sample_Large.blend
- 6907_10_Tree_Sample_Small.blend
- 6907_10_House Kit_Sample 1.blend
- 6907_10_House Kit_Sample 2.blend
- 6907_10_Five Rocks.blend
- 6709_10_Sky_Cloudy.blend

The following are the image files that you should copy from your download pack into the Chapter 10/Images directory:

- 6907_10_01.png
- 6907_10_02.png
- 6907_10_03.png
- 6907_10_04.png
- 6907_10_06.png

Creating the ocean

First you will create an ocean for the sloop to sail on, using a texture to create a wave-like surface.

Time for action – making a surface for the water

Rather than creating a lot of vertices you will make your surface seem rougher by using a texture map to modify the normals of the face to control the appearance:

1. Create a new file and delete the default cube.

2. Press *Shift+A* and select **Mesh** and then **Plane** from the menus.

3. Press *S*, *Shift+Z*, *800*, and *Enter*. This scales the plane in both the *X* and *Y* axes.

4. Press *S*, *Z*, *1.5*, and *Enter*.

5. In the **Properties** window, select the **Material** button from the header, it's the ninth button from the left with the chrome ball on it.

6. Select the **New** button with the *LMB*.

7. Name the material **Sea Material**.

8. In the **Diffuse** subpanel, click on the white button and set the **Diffuse color** to **R: 0.000, G: 0.0150, B: 0.035**.

9. In the **Specular** subpanel, click on the white button and set the **Specular color** to **R: 0.185, G: 0.500, B: 1.000**.

10. In the **Properties** window, select the **Textures** button from the header, it's the tenth button from the left with the checkerboard on it.

11. Select the **New** button with the *LMB*.

12. Name the texture **Sea Texture**.

13. Set the texture **Type:** to **Clouds**.

14. In the **Clouds** subpanel, click the **Greyscale** button so that it turns blue and set the value of the **Noise:** button to **Hard** by clicking on the **Hard** button so that it turns blue as shown in the left side of the following screenshot.

15. In the **Mapping** subpanel set the **Size** to **X: 100, Y: 100, Z: 1.000** as shown in the following screenshot.

16. In the **Influence** subpanel, uncheck the **Diffuse: Color:** checkbox. Make the **Properties** window wider if you can't tell which checkbox is for **Color:**.

17. Check the **Geometry: Normal:** checkbox and set the value to -0.750.

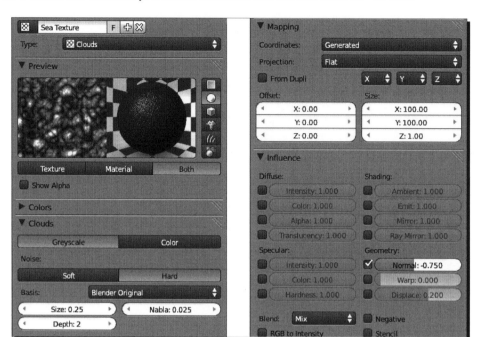

18. In the **Properties** window, select the **Object** button from the header, it's the fifth button from the left with the cube on it.

19. Rename the object from **Plane** to **Ocean**, and then press *Enter*.

20. Select the Lamp with the *RMB*.

21. In the **Properties** window, select the **Object Data** button from the header, it's the seventh button from the left with the sun symbol on it. In the **Lamp** subpanel, change the lamp type to **Sun**.

22. With the cursor over the 3D View, press *Numpad 7* to get the **Top** view. Press *Numpad 5* to get **Ortho** view.

23. Press *R, Z,* and rotate the lamp **125** degrees. Press the *LMB* to release the rotation.

24. Press *F12* to see the surface. It should look similar to the following screenshot. Press *Esc* when you have finished looking at it.

25. Save the file to a unique name.

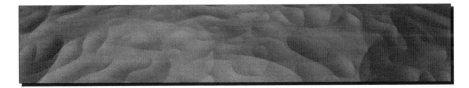

What just happened?

This was pretty simple. We talked about normals in *Chapter 5, Building a Simple Boat*. They show the way that a face is pointing. The plane is flat and there is only one face in a plane and one normal. It figures that it should look flat. All the lumpiness that you see is caused by the texture that you assigned to the Ocean object. It creates more than one normal per face.

When scaling up the plane, in addition to learning a new trick in how to scale in two dimensions at once, you may have wondered, "Wait a minute, this is a plane. It has no thickness, why am I scaling it in Z?". Well, since this is 3D space and not reality, adding scaling in Z to a textured plane makes the waves appear to be higher. It's an optical illusion.

You saw when you made the cloud texture for the Ocean object, that it was shades of gray. Then you set that texture to influence the normals of the face. The darker the shade, the more a normal points one way, the lighter the shade, the more a normal points the opposite way. Blender calculates this for each point in the texture. So instead of one normal per face, there are thousands. Just like the ocean makes waves from a flat surface and the surface of the water tilts one way or another, the texture map is tilting the surface of the face.

Since this will be an outdoor scene, you selected the sun for your lamp type, and it lit all of the Ocean object evenly. The camera is pretty close to the Ocean object, so once you get it into the scene, it will look like fairly smooth water with just a little chop to it.

Making an island

There are several steps toward making your island paradise. First you will create a basic land form with the **ANT Landscape** generator. Next you will edit the finer details to make it the way you want it. Then you will paint it.

Using the ANT Landscape add-on

The ANT Landscape add-on allows you to set factors such as the height and size of a landscape and use other settings to control the contours of the terrain. You can make flat landscapes or spherical planets.

Time for action – using ANT Landscape to make the island

The ANT Landscape uses mathematical algorithms to create an infinite variety of surfaces, but by working in an ordered manner you can achieve the results you want:

1. Select the Ocean with the *RMB*. Press *M* and *2* to move the Ocean to **Layer 2**.

2. In the **File** menu at the upper-left corner of the Blender window, select **User Preferences**, as you did in *Chapter 3, Controlling the Lamp, the Camera, and Animating Objects* to install the animation player. The **Blender User Preferences** window will pop up.

3. Select **Addons** from the Blender **User Preferences** menu. Scroll down and put a checkmark in the box for **Add Mesh: ANT Landscape**. Select **Install Add-on** from the header at the bottom of the menu as shown in the following screenshot:

4. Press the **X** button at the upper right-hand corner of the Blender **User Preferences** window and close the window. If you are using a Mac or Linux, use the red dot on the left-hand corner of the **Blender User Preferences** window.

5. Press *Shift+S* and select **Cursor to Center** from the pop-up menu.

6. If your **Tool Shelf** is not visible in the **3D View**, press *T* to make it visible.

7. Press *Shift+A*. Select **Mesh** and then **Landscape** from the menus.

8. Zoom in to look at the landscape, as shown in the following screenshot. Use the *MMB* to rotate your view so the *X* axis points down and towards the right and the *Y* axis points up and towards the right.

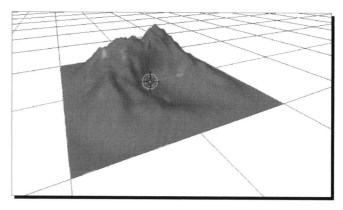

9. In the **Tool Shelf**, put the mouse over the top edge of the **Landscape** subpanel so that you get the double-headed arrow. Move the border of the subpanel up as far as you can.

10. In the second panel within the **Landscape** subpanel, there is a button labeled **Random Seed**. Change the **Random Seed** number from **0** to **5269**.

11. Now, click the arrow on either end of the **Random Seed** button several times and watch the landscape change.

12. Now click the arrow on the other end of the button until you are back to **5269**. The landscape with **Random Seed 5269** will be the basis of your island.

13. In the top panel within the **Landscape** subpanel, set the **Mesh Size:** to **800**.

14. Press the *Home* key on your keyboard to see the entire island again. This is not the *Home* key on your Numpad. If you are using a Mac, press *fn+Left* arrow. It looks flat, this is not surprising, it just got 400 times larger without getting taller. Notice that the ends look a bit cut off.

15. Press *N* to open the **3D View Properties** panel. In the **View** subpanel, set the **Clip: End** to **3000**. The ocean and the islands are bigger models than the sloop. This lets you see them in their entirety.

16. In the **Landscape** subpanel, set the **Height:** to **400**. Not much appears to have changed. That is because there is another button that affects the height.

17. Put the cursor in the center of the **Plateau:** button. Hold down the *LMB* and move the mouse slowly to the right. Watch how the landscape slowly rises as you move the mouse. You can see the Plateau on top where everything gets flattened. If you raise the Plateau above the height, then nothing changes any more.

18. Set the **Plateau:** to **235**. The landscape looks a bit pointy at the moment as seen in the left side of the following screenshot.

19. Set the **Noise Size:** to **400**. The shape looks much more as it did before you enlarged it. The **Noise Size:** button is in the second panel of the **Landscape** subpanel.

20. Scroll down and change the **Offset:** to **-117**.

21. Now set the **Sealevel:** to **-3** so it goes below the Ocean's surface.

22. Use the **Layer Controls** in the **3D View** header. Select Layer 2 with *Shift+RMB*.

23. Press the *MMB* and use the mouse to rotate the view so you can see the island in the Ocean, as shown in the right side of the following screenshot:

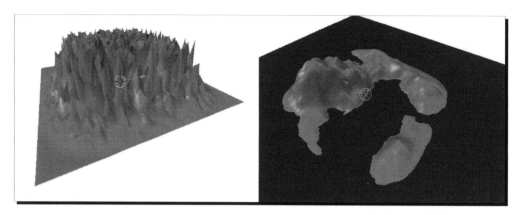

24. Save the file to a unique name.

What just happened?

ANT Landscape is a powerful add-on for creating landforms.

The **Subdivisions** button sets how complex your terrain will be. The setting of 64 makes a 64x64 grid with 4096 vertices. You can change this by selecting more subdivisions for greater detail and a larger file, or fewer subdivisions for a smaller file size with less detail.

The **Mesh Size:** specifies how large the model will be physically.

The **Height:** button specifies the maximum possible height.

The **Plateau:** button flattens any details above a certain height. You might wonder why you have two controls. Setting the height higher places more of the detail higher up. So, a tall height with a low Plateau will create a mesa. The same value Plateau with a lower height might only round off the tallest peak.

The **Noise Size** button controls the size of the noise. As you saw, a value of zero gives very small distances between peaks and valleys, so the landscape is jagged. The larger the value, the more distance between the peaks and valleys, and the more gentle the landscape tends to be.

The **Random Seed:** button, affects the entire shape of the landscape. You try different Random Seeds until you find one that suits your purposes. Your other settings are kept intact when you change the Random Seed values. For instance, the Plateau will always be at the height you set it, no matter what the Random Seed is.

There are 10,000 different Random Seeds so you are likely to find one that will give you the kind of landscape you are looking for. In this case, I was looking for a tall peak with a large low spot that could become a sheltered cove. I also wanted a low set of hills on the far side of the cove. 5269 provided this, and I liked how one of the hills became a separate island. The smaller coves on the back side of the island were a bonus and gave it a nice shape.

Changing the **Offset:** raises or lowers the vertices of the terrain with respect to the **Sealevel:**.

Have a go hero – playing with ANT Landscape

ANT Landscape uses a series of random numbers to create landscape such as objects. It gives you the incredible power to make mountains, hills, and islands in Blender.

Make sure that you have saved the file. Make a new file. Load the ANT Landscape generator again. You didn't save it as a default because you don't need it that often. You can save it as a default if you wish, my philosophy, though, is to keep it simple.

Create a landscape, play with it, and see what you get. Try using the settings you created earlier as a basis and change them. One thing that will help is to keep the scale of your settings consistent. For example, in the default landscape, **Mesh Size** was **2** and **Noise Size** was **1**. When you made the island, **Mesh Size** was **800** and **Noise Size** was **400**.

More subdivisions will give you a better detailed model, but it may slow things down as it takes time to process all that detail. You may even want to back down to 32 subdivisions to speed things up while you play. If you like what you have done, save it for later reference. But also, take notes of what settings you have changed and what values each setting has when you have a terrain you like. You can write it down or type it into the Blender Text editor. Once you finish playing with it, and make a change to the object in the 3D View, and not in the Tool Shelf, the landscape will be turned into a mesh and you will not be able to go back, see what the settings were, or change them.

Detailing the island

Now, it's time to discover the power of proportional editing. With proportional editing, when you move one vertex, the vertices near it are also move to one degree or another. You are going to use this to finish the island. It's nice, but not perfect.

There is no good area for adding buildings, a pier, or trees. You need a **Port** as shown in the following screenshot. The main entrance to the harbor is so large that it offers no protection from large waves. You need a **Breakwater** as shown in the following screenshot. The back side of the island is smooth and square, so it needs to be a little rougher to look more natural.

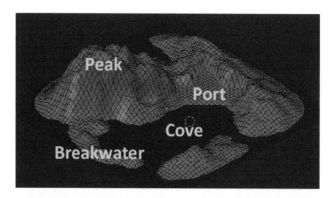

Time for action – understanding the proportional editing control

Proportional editing allows you to move one vertex, and all the vertices around it are also affected to varying degrees. There are seven different falloff patterns that you can choose from depending on your needs. Here you will learn to set up the Proportional Editing controls:

1. Reopen the landscape that you made before the previous *Have a go hero* section.

2. In the **Layers** control in the **3D View header**, select **Layer 1**.

3. Select the island and press the *Tab* key to go into **Edit Mode**.

4. In the **3D View Properties** panel, **Mesh Display** subpanel, click on the **Faces** button under the word **Normals:**. Set the **Size:** button to **10**.

5. Use the *MMB* and the mouse to rotate the island and inspect the normals. Be sure to check the bottom of the island. They will stick through the ocean if they are pointed down.

6. If the normals are pointing downward, press *A* to select all the faces. Then select **Mesh** from the **3D View** header. Choose **Normals** then **Recalculate** Inside from the pop-up menus.

7. In the **3D View Properties** panel, **Mesh Display** subpanel, click on the **Faces** button under the word **Normals:** again to turn the Normals display off.

8. On the right side of the **3D View** header there is a button with a small doughnut and up and down arrowheads next to it. That is the **Proportional Editing** button. Press it with the *LMB* and choose **Enable** from the pop-up menu as shown in the following screenshot.

9. On the right of the **Proportional Editing** button now is the **Proportional Editing Falloff** button. Press it and you will see a pop-up menu of different falloff styles as shown in the following screenshot. For now, the default **Smooth** style is fine.

10. Press *A* to deselect all the vertices.

11. With the *RMB*, select one vertex in the center of the flat area that will become the cove. Press *G Z*, and *60* but don't press *Enter*.

12. Press the *Page Up* key and hold it until you see a circle appear around the vertex as shown in the following screenshot. That circle shows the extent of the proportional editing. Press the *Page Up* and *Page Down* keys and you can see how the sphere of influence grows and shrinks. You can also control this with the mouse wheel. On the Mac, use the *fn+Up arrow* and *fn+Down arrow* keys.

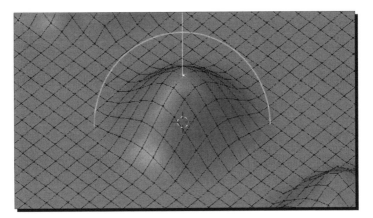

13. Make the circle very large and the whole island will be affected. Make it small again so that only a small area around the vertex is affected. Set the **Proportional size:** to about **72**. You can see the readout in the **3D View** header.

14. Press the *Esc* key or the *RMB* to release the vertex without affecting it.

15. In the **3D View** header, click the **Proportional Editing Falloff** button. Choose **Sphere** from the pop-up menu.

16. Press *G*, *Z*, and *60*, but don't press *Enter*. When you are done looking at the **3D View** press *Esc*.

17. Repeat this with the other settings of the **Proportional Editing Falloff** menu and familiarize yourself with how they affect vertices near the selected one.

18. When you are done, return the **Proportional Editing Falloff** setting to **Smooth**.

19. Press the *Tab* key to return to **Object Mode**.

What just happened?

You found the controls for Proportional Editing. You learned how to change the circle of influence for Proportional Editing and how to change the falloff profile which gives you even more control over how you can move the vertices.

Time for action – using proportional editing to create the port

Now that you have a good basis for your island, it's time to tailor it to your needs. The first step is creating an area for putting houses, trees, and the pier:

1. In the **Layers** control in the **3D View** header, select **Layer 2** with the *RMB* and then select **Layer 1** with *Shift+RMB*.

2. I have provided a template that will help you in selecting the faces for the port and for the breakwater. Append the **Port and Breakwater** object from the file `6907_10_Port and Breakwater Templates.blend` in your Chapter 10/ Blender Files/ download kit.

3. You'll now see two flat objects floating above your island as shown in the following screenshot:

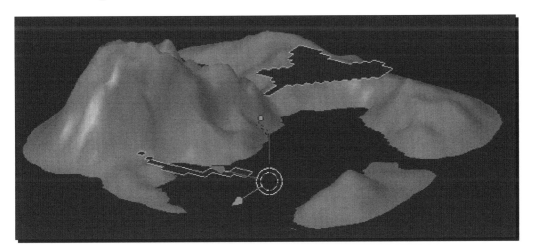

4. Select the island with the *RMB*.

5. Press *Numpad 7* to get the **Top** view.

6. Make sure the **3D View** is in **Ortho** mode.

7. Press the *Tab* key to get back into **Edit Mode**.

8. In the **3D View** header, choose **Face Select** mode.

9. Set the **Limit Selection to Visible** button to a lighter gray.

10. Press *A* to deselect all the faces.

11. Use *Shift+MMB* to center your view on the lower part of the template. Use *Ctrl+MMB* to zoom in so that part of the template fills most of the **3D View**.

12. Press the *C* key and select the vertices you will need to create a flat area to add buildings, trees, and a pier as shown in the following screenshot. This area will be the Port.

13. The template will appear to be flat blue and the unselected faces of the island will be black on gray. The selected faces will be orange lines and dots as shown in the following screenshot, but select all the faces under the blue template area. Use it to guide you. But since the island is the active object, the faces you select will only be faces on the island.

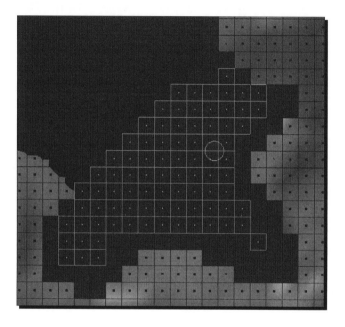

14. Use the *MMB*, and rotate your view so you can see the selected port faces underneath the template.

15. Set the **Pivot Point** menu in the 3D View header to **Median Point**.

16. Press *S*, *Z*, and *0*, but not *Enter*.

17. Press the *Page Up* or *Page Down* keys until the **Proportional Editing** Circle is about **25** according to the readout in the 3D View header.

18. Press *Enter*.

19. Rotate the view with the *MMB* so you can see the distance between the port and the water line well as shown in the following screenshot:

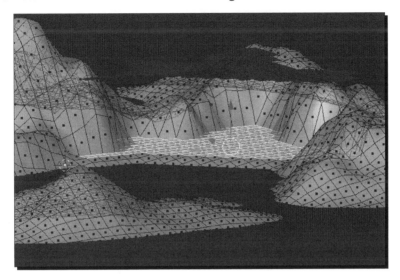

20. Press *G, Z*, and use the mouse to move the selected vertices down about 11 units. Press the *LMB* to release the motion.

What just happened?

Well, you put Proportional Editing to good work now. You used Proportional Editing to ease the transition between the area you were flattening and the surrounding landscape. Now, you have enough room on the island to set up some buildings, some trees, and a pier.

Time for action – building the breakwater

A port needs protection from waves. The opening to the sea is too large, so you will be extending the little jetty and adding contours so that it looks like a natural part of the island:

1. Press *Numpad 7* to get the **Top** view.

2. The breakwater will be at the top of the island. Press *Shift+MMB* and use the mouse to move to the top of the island.

3. Press *A* to deselect all the faces. Press *C* to select the faces for the breakwater using the template as your guide.

4. When you are done, press the *MMB* and rotate around so you can see the faces you've selected.

5. Press *G*, *Z*, and move the selected faces up eight units to create the base of the breakwater. Use the *Ctrl* key to round off the units. Use the *Page Up/Page Down* keys to set the **Proportional size:** to about **25**. Press the *LMB* to release the motion.

6. Deselect some faces as shown in the following screenshot. Press *C* then use the *MMB* to deselect faces. Press the *RMB* to end the selection.

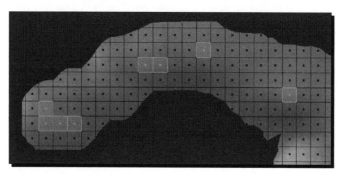

7. Move the remaining faces up eight units to add some hills on the breakwater.

8. Repeat, but deselect the faces so only two remain, as shown in the following screenshot:

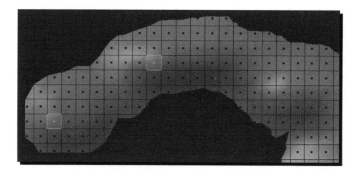

9. Move the remaining faces up eight units to finish off the crests of the hills.

10. Press the *Tab* key to go into **Object Mode**.

11. Select the **Port and Breakwater** template with the *RMB*. Press *X* to delete it.

12. Save the file to a unique name.

What just happened?

In this exercise we built a breakwater, and then kept reducing the number of vertices selected and moving them up a bit to build up a gentle contour.

Time for action – adding contours to the back side of the island

It's a small point, but the back side of the island is too smooth and flat. So next you will add a few contours to make it look more realistic:

1. Select **Layer 2**, then select **Layer 1** while holding the *Shift* key.

2. Select the Island with the *RMB*. Press the *Tab* key to go into **Edit Mode**.

3. In the **3D View** header, choose the **Vertex Select** mode.

4. Press *A* to deselect all of the vertices.

5. Select a vertex in the center of the cove with the *RMB*.

6. Press *Shift+S* and choose **Cursor to Selected** from the menu.

7. In the **3D View** header, set **Pivot Point** to **3D Cursor**.

8. Press *Numpad 7*. Press the *Home* key on your keyboard to see the entire island. This is not the *Home* key on your Numpad. If you are using a Mac, press *fn+Left arrow*. Then use *Ctrl+MMB* to zoom in.

9. The bottom and right sides of the island are unnaturally smooth. You need to put in some small variations to make them look right.

10. Press *C* and select some of the outer edges of the island, as shown in the following screenshot. Yours doesn't have to be an exact copy. Press the *RMB* when done selecting.

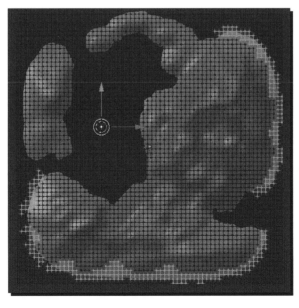

11. Press *S, Z, 0*, and set the **Proportional size:** to about **35**. Then press *Enter*.

12. Save the file to a unique name.

What just happened?

You did just a little final detailing; adding some curves to the coast line. You started out by selecting a vertex from the cove, which is at sea level, and then moved the 3D Cursor to that location. You set the pivot center to the 3D Cursor. That way, when you scaled all of the other vertices that you selected along the edge of the island, they got scaled down to the sea level you had established when you made the island.

Painting the island

Blender has a built-in painting program. While not as fully featured as some dedicated paint programs, it will get you started and allows you to do everything without leaving Blender. By starting the painting in Blender, you can easily match the details of the painting to the details of the object.

Time for action – painting the island

Now it's time for an introduction to using Blender Paint. It takes a while to detail landscape realistically, so here you are going to use some broad brush strokes now just to get an idea of how Blender Paint works. It's good to go online and look at images of islands like the one you want to make, for ideas on how the soil should look, and what the plants and trees should look like. Using the satellite views of Google maps can give you ideas too:

1. Go down to the **Timeline** window below the **3D View** window. Select the **Current Editor Type** button in the lower left-hand corner. Choose **UV/Image Editor** from the menu.

2. Move the mouse to the boundary between the **UV/Image Editor** window and the **3D View** window. When you get the double arrowhead, move the boundary up so you can see the grid background in the **UV/Image Editor**. You can also use *Ctrl+MMB* to zoom out to see the whole grid.

3. If you see a rendered image in the **UV/Image Editor** window, delete it by pressing the **X** to the right of where it says **Render Result** in the **UV/Image Editor** header.

4. With the cursor in the **3D View**, press the *A* key to select all the vertices.

5. Open the **Mesh** menu in the **3D View** header. Select **UV Unwrap** and then **Unwrap** from the menus as shown on the left side of the following screenshot. It may take a moment or two while it does this.

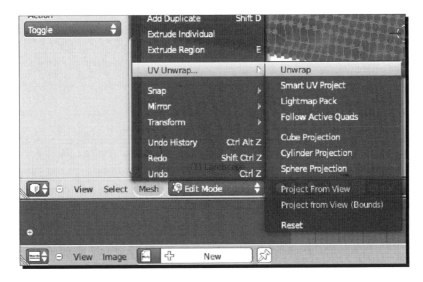

6. In the **UV/Image Editor** header, choose **Image**. Select **New Image** from the pop-up menu. In the **New Image** dialog box, set the name to IslandTexture. Set the **Color** to a nice sandy brown, I used **R 0.350**, **G 0.200**, and **B 0.100**, as shown in the following screenshot. Uncheck the **Alpha** checkbox. Click on the **OK** button.

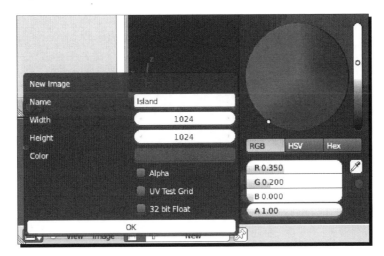

7. In the **3D View** header, click on the button that usually says either **Object Mode** or **Edit Mode**, and select **Texture Paint** from the pop-up menu.

8. Now in the **Tool Shelf** you have the Blender Paint controls.

9. At the top of the **Brush** subpanel there is an image of a yellow swash on a gray background. Put the cursor over the image and press the *LMB*.

10. Choose **FBrush** from the pop-up menu. Set the **Color** to a medium green. I used **R 0.300**, **G 0.600**, and **B 0.300**. Set the **Radius:** to **35**, **Strength** to **0.5**, and **Jitter** to **0.0**.

11. The *LMB* controls your paintbrush. The *MMB* works as usual allowing you to rotate, and with the *Shift* and *Ctrl* buttons, pan and zoom. The *RMB* works as an eyedropper tool, picking up whatever color the cursor is over.

12. Press *Numpad 1* to get the **Front** view and *Numpad 5* to get into **Ortho** mode. Paint the top half to top two thirds of the island green. If you look at the **UV/Image Editor**, you will notice that it records your painting.

13. Press *Numpad 3* to get the **Right Side** view and paint.

14. Press *Ctrl+Numpad 1* to get the **Back** view and paint.

15. Press *Ctrl+Numpad 3* to get the **Left Side** view and paint.

16. Press the *MMB* and rotate the view so you can see from a high angle. You will notice gaps in the painting. Reduce the radius of your FBrush. Touch them up, but not all areas need to be colored green. Look for the valleys, since they collect water they should be more green. Areas where the surface is indented will tend to track the water, so make that a little more green. Imagine the water flowing down the sides of the island as shown in the following screenshot:

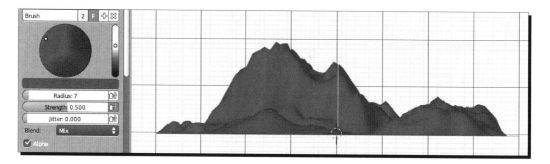

17. Now it's time to add a darker green for areas growing better. In the **3D View Tool Shelf**, change the brush **Color** to a darker green. I chose **R 0.200**, **G 0.400**, and **B 0.200**. The easy way to do this is select the **HSV** button and set the **V** to **0.4**. A brush **Radius:** of **9** is good. Set the **Strength:** to **0.2** so you can build up the darker green in a little bit of time and have a little more variation.

18. Use the brush to fill in the valleys, imagine water running down them watering the plants. Since the **Strength** is **0.2**, you can take several passes making the color more solid with each pass and getting gentle gradations of color.

19. Now paint the Port. In the **3D View Tool Shelf**, change the brush **Color** to **R 0.000**, **G 0.600**, and **B 0.000**. Increase the brush **Radius:** to **15** and increase the **Strength:** to **1**.

20. Use the brush to paint the port as shown in the following screenshot.

21. Choose the **F Smear** brush from the **Brush** menu in the **3D View Tool Shelf**. Set **Strength:** to **0.4** and set **Radius:** to about **25**. Move the brush up or down across the border between the green color of the port and the brown color of the hills above it, as shown in the following screenshot:

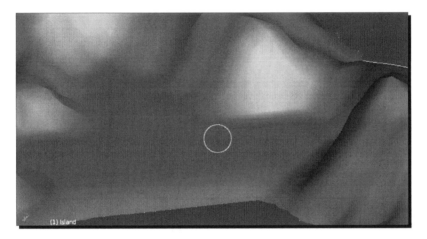

22. Make any changes or touch ups that you want to.

23. When you are done, scroll down to where it says **Texture Paint** in the **3D View** header. Select **Object Mode**. The colors will disappear.

24. In the **3D View** header, select the **Viewport Shading** button and choose **Texture** from the pop-up menu.

25. Use the *MMB* to get a nice view of your island.

26. Go down to the **UV/Image Editor** window and choose the **Image** button on the header. Select **Save As Image** and put the image in your Images subdirectory. Then click on the **Save As Image** button in the upper-right corner of the **File Browser** window. As with saving your basic Blender file, do this frequently while you are painting your terrain. The image file is not saved as part of the Blender file.

27. The image is not automatically added to the texture of your object. You can see it in the 3D View, but if you want it to render you must add the texture to the material in the **Properties** window, just like you have added other textures to materials.

28. In the **Properties** window, select the **Material** button from the header, it's the ninth button from the left with the chrome ball on it.

29. Click on the **New** button and create a new material. Name it **Island Material**.

30. In the **Specular** subpanel, set the **Specular** color to a nice light sandy color. I chose **R 0.500, G 0.400**, and **B 0.200**. Set the **Intensity:** to **0.015**.

31. In the **Properties** window, select the **Textures** button from the header, it's the tenth button from the left with the checker board on it.

32. Click on the **New** button and create a new texture. Name it Island Texture.

33. Select the texture **Type: Image or Movie**.

34. In the **Image** subpanel click on the **Open** button and select the image you saved a few steps earlier.

35. In the **Mapping** subpanel set the **Coordinates:** to **UV**.

36. Press the *MMB* and rotate the view so you can see the scene.

37. Press *Ctrl+Alt+Numpad 0* to set the camera to match the view you are seeing. If the 3D View goes blank, don't worry.

38. In the **Outliner** window at the upper-right of the Blender window, select the **Camera** with the *LMB*.

39. In the **Properties** window, select the **Object Data** button from the header, it's the seventh button from the left with the movie camera on it.

40. In the lower-right corner of the **Lens** subpanel, the lower button below **Clipping:** is the **Clipping: End:** button.

41. Move the cursor from left to right over the button. As the value of the **Clipping: End:** button goes up, the white wall recedes. The **Clipping: End:** saves Blender work, by not displaying anything beyond the far clipping plane as shown in the following screenshot:

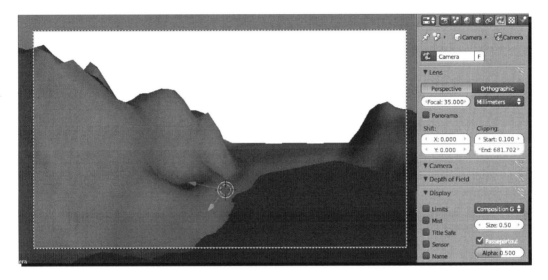

42. Now that you've seen the **Clipping: End:** in action, set **Clipping: End:** to **3000** so it will be out of your way.

43. Press *G, Z, Z*, and use the mouse to zoom out. Press the *LMB* to release the motion.

44. Press *F12* to render the scene.

45. Save the file to a unique file name.

What just happened?

You painted your island. First you created a UV map so that Blender could map a color to a particular part of your island. Then you made a graphic that Blender used to record the painting you made in the **Texture Paint** mode. Next, you painted your island using various brushes similar to programs such as Photoshop or Gimp. And finally, you saved the graphic and made it into your texture map for the island.

Restarting texture painting

If you have to interrupt your Blender activity, and you save the file and close Blender, you may be surprised that when you open it up, your precious hand-painted texture is not there. Unless you have specifically saved the image, it is gone. But we know that you are wise and you saved the image. When you wish to resume work on the texture, in the 3D View window go into **Edit Mode** and select all the vertices. Then open up the **UV Image Editor**, select **Image** on the header, and open the image you were working on. Then in the 3D View choose the **Texture Paint** mode.

Have a go hero – painting your island

Well, the island still looks a little rough. So now, put me to shame and paint the island better. Explore the tools in the Blender Paint Tool Shelf and check out the references I mentioned earlier.

Making the island ready for habitation

The island is looking good, but now you need to add a pier, a boathouse, houses, trees, and rocks so it will be ready for the sloop and the boat.

Building the pier with just four objects

The pier will use tools you learned in the previous chapter, bevel objects, and DupliVerts. You will also use DupliVerts' cousin, DupliFrames.

Time for action – creating the pier frame rails with Bezier Curves

It may be hard to believe that you can make an entire pier with a rectangle, a Bezier Curve, a cube, and a cylinder, but that's what you are going to do next. The first step is to create a frame to carry the planks of the pier:

1. Select **Object Mode** from the **3D View** header.

2. Press *Numpad 7* to get the **Top** view. Press *Numpad 5* to get the **Ortho** mode. Zoom into the edge between the port and the water.

3. In the Layers control in the **3D View** header, select **Layer 1** with the *RMB* and then select **Layer 2** with *Shift+RMB*.

4. Press *Shift+S* and select **Cursor to Center** from the menu.

5. Click the *LMB* over the edge between the water and the port.

6. Press *A* to deselect any objects.

7. Press *Shift+A* and select **Mesh** and then **Cube** from the pop-up menus.

8. Press *S, Y, 60*, and *Enter*.

9. Press *G, Z, 6*, and *Enter*.

10. Press *R, Z, 45*, and *Enter*.

11. Move the cube so it is 2/3 over the water and 1/3 over the port. Center it along the waterfront as shown in the left side of the following screenshot.

12. Zoom into the lower-right corner of the cube, as close as possible.

13. Press the *Tab* key to enter **Edit Mode**. With the *RMB*, select one of the vertices at the lower-left corner of the cube. Press *Shift+S*. Choose **Cursor to Selected**. Press the Tab key to return to **Object Mode**.

14. If the **3D View Properties** panel is not already open, press *N* to open it. In the **3D Cursor** subpanel set the **3D Cursor Location** to **Z: 6.000**.

15. With the cursor over the **3D View** window, press *A* to deselect the cube.

16. Press *Shift+A* and select **Curve** and then **Bezier** from the menus.

17. In the **Properties** window, select the **Object** button from the header, it's the fifth button from the left with the cube on it.

18. Rename the **BezierCurve** to **Pier Railing Path**.

19. Zoom in until you can see the Bezier Curve.

20. Press the *Tab* key to go into **Edit Mode**.

21. Look at the Bezier Curve. There are a series of arrowheads pointing from one Control Point to the other. The left-hand point is the first point. The right-hand point is the last point. The arrowheads point from the first point to the last point.

22. On the **3D View** header, click on the **Proportional Editing** button, that little doughnut, and select **Disable** from the pop-up menu.

23. Select the right-hand control point with the RMB. It's the last control point. Zoom out so you can see the whole length of the cube. Press *G* and move the control point to the lower-left corner of the cube over the water. Press the *LMB* to release the motion. Zoom into the end of the cube over the water. Move the control point as close as you can to the lower-left corner of the cube.

24. Next, go back to the end over the land and select the other control point, the first control point. Press *Shift + S* and choose **Selection** to Cursor.

25. Now, the first control point is at the beginning of the pier, and the last control point is at the end. Don't worry about the control handles, they will add a little curve to the pier, like the curve of lumber.

26. Press the *Tab* key to get into **Object Mode**.

27. In the **3D View** header, select **Layer 2** so that the island is no longer in view.

28. Press *A* to deselect any objects.

29. Press *Shift+A*. Select **Curve** and then **Circle** from the menus.

30. Rename **BezierCircle** to **Pier Railing Shape**.

31. With the cursor over the 3D View, press the *Tab* key to go into **Edit Mode**.

32. Press *V* and select **Vector** from the pop-up menu to make a diamond out of the circle.

33. Press *R, Z, 45*, and *Enter* to rotate it so that the diamond is a square.

34. Press *S, X, 0.12*, and *Enter* to squish the sides.

35. Press *S, Y, 0.35*, and *Enter* to scale the top and bottom, as seen on the right side of the following screenshot:

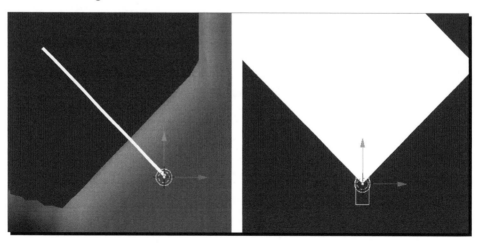

36. In the **3D View** header, set **Pivot Point** to **Median Point**.

37. Press *Shift+D* and then *Enter* to duplicate the control points. Press *G*, *X*, *6*, and *Enter*.

38. Press the *Tab* key to get into **Object Mode**.

39. Press *R*, *X*, *90*, and *Enter*.

40. Press *R*, *Z* ,*45*, and *Enter*.

41. Now to make the Pier Railings as you made the tiller. Select the Pier Railing Path with the *RMB*. You know where it is, keep clicking and watch the bottom-left corner of the **3D View** window until it says **Pier Railing Path**.

42. In the **Properties** window, select the **Object Data** button from the header, it's the ninth button from the left with the curve and control points on it.

43. In the **Geometry** subpanel, select the **Pier Railing Shape** as the **Bevel Object**.

What just happened?

This was very similar to making the tiller, but this time, by duplicating the control points in the Pier Railing Shape and shifting one set to the right by 6 units, you were able to make both rails for the foundation of the pier at the same time.

Time for action – adding planks to the pier with DupliFrames

DupliFrames are the stronger cousin to DupliVerts. It will take one plank and make 100 out of it, and use the same object that you made to control the rails of the pier:

1. Now select the cube you made to establish the length of the pier, with the *RMB*. In the **Properties** window, select the **Object** button in the header. It is the fifth button from the left, with the cube on it. Change the name from **Cube** to **Plank**.

2. In the **3D View Properties** panel in the **Transform** subpanel, set the **Dimensions:** to **X: 8.00, Y: 1.000**, and **Z: 0.150**.

3. Press *Shift+RMB* and select the Pier Railing Path.

4. Press *Ctrl+P* to parent the rails to the plank. Select **Object** from the pop-up menu.

5. Zoom out and select the plank with the *RMB*.

6. Press *G* and move the plank to the land end of the rails.

7. Zoom in to the plank. Move the plank so it is just to the right of the right end of the rails. Center it between the rails as shown on the left side of the following screenshot. Release the motion with the *LMB*. If you need to, press *R, Z*, and rotate it, so it matches the ends of the rails. Release the rotation with the *LMB*.

8. Press *Numpad 1* for the **Front** view. Use *Shift+MMB* and *Ctrl+MMB* to move your view so you can see the plank and the rails.

9. Press *G, Z*, and use the mouse to move the plank up until it rests on top of the rails. Release the motion with the *LMB*.

10. In the **Properties** window, select the **Object** button from the header, it's the fifth button from the left with the cube on it.

11. In the **Duplication** subpanel, press the **Frames** button with the *LMB*. Uncheck the **Speed** checkbox as seen on the right of the following screenshot.

12. Select the **Pier Railing Path** with the *RMB*.

13. Use the *MMB* to rotate the view so you can see the top of the pier.

14. In the **Properties** window, select the **Object Data** button from the header, it's the eighth button from the left with the curve and control points on it.

15. In the **Path Animation** subpanel, put the cursor over the **Frames:** button and use the mouse to change the number of planks on the pier. Watch as the gaps between the planks change. A value for **Frames:** of **93** is good.

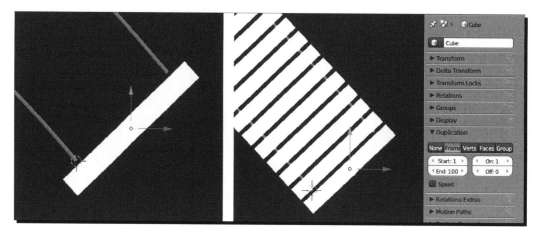

What just happened?

Now you got more use out of the Pier Railing Path. By reusing the cube that you made to measure out the length of the pier, you made one plank for the top and then used DupliFrames to create copies that run the entire length of the pier. The Pier Railing Path has a Path Animation ability, and you used it to control the spacing of the planks.

The DupliFrames method, while similar to the DupliVerts, has some additional power. You may have noted that DupliFrames uses a Bezier Curve for its basis rather than a mesh object as the DupliVerts method does. If you then select the Bezier Curve, Pier Railing Path in this case, and open up the **Object Data** panel, you will see the **Path Animation** subpanel. When you change the number of frames the animation covers, the number of planks changes. A This is more flexible than the DupliVerts object which sets the number of copied objects equal to the number of vertices that its parent mesh had.

If you were to check the **Speed** checkbox in the plank's **Duplication** subpanel, you would see just one plank. But Blender would animate the plank travelling along the Pier Railing Path by making keyframes of the Evaluation Time in the **Path Animation** subpanel of the Bezier Curve.

Think of it like a roller coaster. If you make a Bezier Curve in the shape of a roller coaster track, you can use a Bevel object to create the rails as you did with the pier. If you make a cross tie, you can use parenting and DupliFrames and turn the speed off to make cross-ties to support the roller coaster rails, as you did with the planks on the pier. If you make a roller coaster car and use parenting, when the speed is turned on, your roller coaster car would ride along the rails.

You can freeze the planks into individual objects with the same *Ctrl+Shift+A* command as you did with the DupliVerts to convert the spokes of the ship's wheel. If you are making changes, and you want to clear the parenting with DupliFrames, you must select the child object and press *Alt+P*.

Time for action – using arrays to create the pilings for the pier

Arrays are similar to DupliFrames, and DupliVerts, but instead of depending on objects to control the distribution of copies, arrays use mathematical formulas that list the number of copies and the kind of spacing that is put between copies. They are great for making pier pilings:

1. Press *A* to deselect all objects.

2. Press *Shift+A* and select **Mesh** then **Cylinder** from the menus. Name the cylinder `Piling`.

3. In the **Add Cylinder** subpanel of **Tool Shelf**, set the **Vertices** to **15**.

4. If you do not see the **Add Cylinder** subpanel, look for a small plus sign at the bottom of the **Tool Shelf**. Click on the plus sign and the **Add Cylinder** subpanel will appear.

5. Press *S, 0.650*, and *Enter* to make the cylinder narrower.

6. Press *S, Z, 8*, and *Enter* to make the cylinder taller.

7. Press *Numpad 7* so you get a **Top** view.

8. Press *G, X*, and use the mouse to move the cylinder so it is on the outside of the rail as shown in the left hand side of the following screenshot. Release the motion with the *LMB*.

9. Press *G, Z, -3.5*, and *Enter* to move the piling down with respect to the dock.

10. In the **Properties** window, select the **Object Modifiers** button from the header, it's the seventh button from the left with the wrench on it.

11. In the **Modifiers** subpanel click on **Add Modifier**. Select **Array** from the menu. Set the **Relative Offset X** to **0**. Set the **Relative Offset Y** to **5.7**.

12. Zoom out so you can see both pilings.

13. With the cursor over the 3D View, press *R, Z, 45*, and *Enter*.

14. Zoom out so you can see the entire pier. Press the *MMB* and use the mouse to rotate the view so you see the pilings better.

15. In the Properties window, increase the **Count:** value until the pilings reach the end of the dock as shown in the following screenshot. If they shoot past, then decrease the count.

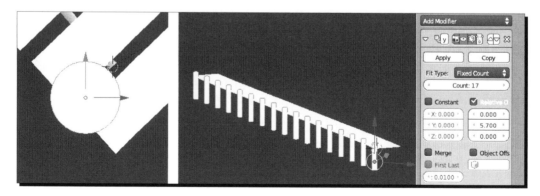

16. In the **Modifiers** subpanel click on **Add Modifier**. Select **Array** from the menu. Move down to the second **Array Modifier** panel. (Not the one that you set to **Y = 5.7**.) Set the **Relative Offset**, **X** to **6.0**. Leave the **Count:** at **2**.

17. Save the file to a unique name.

What just happened?

Well, you just made a pier out of a Bezier Curve, a plane, a cube, and a cylinder. Well done!

The Array is a new technique. The Array Modifier allowed you to take the piling and make copies of it. The modifier took a count of how many copies; how far apart they should be, and in what direction they should go. With the first modifier, you did this to make all the pilings on one side of the pier.

The second modifier modifies the first modifier, not the original object, so it makes a copy of the entire line of pilings that the first modifier created and moves the copy of the line of pilings in the specified direction, in this case, just across the pier. If the second modifier had worked on the original object, there would be only one piling on the other side of the pier.

Appending the boathouse

You learned a lot about appending in the last chapter when you finished the sloop. This will be similar, but the boathouse will need to be fitted to the pier.

Time for action – appending the boathouse and building pilings for it

In addition to bringing the boathouse into the scene, you have to place it and create some more pilings to support the back side of the boathouse:

1. Press *Numpad 7* to get the **Top** view.

2. In the **3D View** header, select **Wireframe** from the **Viewport Shading** pop-up menu.

3. In the **File** menu, select **Append**.

4. Find `6907_10_boathouse.blend`.

5. Open the `Object` folder.

6. Press *A* to select the **Boathouse**, **Door Front**, **Door Garage**, and **Door knob**.

7. Press the *LMB* on the **Link/Append from Library** button.

8. Press *Ctrl+MMB* and zoom out of the scene so you can see the boathouse and the pilings of the pier.

9. Press *G* and use the mouse to move the boathouse to the left side of the pier. Press the *LMB* to release the boathouse.

10. Press *R, Z, 135*, and *Enter*.

11. Press *G* and use the mouse to move the boathouse to near the center of the pier, as seen in the left side of the following screenshot. Press the *LMB* to release the boathouse. Leave room for a boat to dock at the end of the pier before being moved into the boathouse.

12. Zoom in and make sure that the door is located between two pilings as seen on the right side of the following screenshot. Put the right-most corner of the boathouse next to a piling.

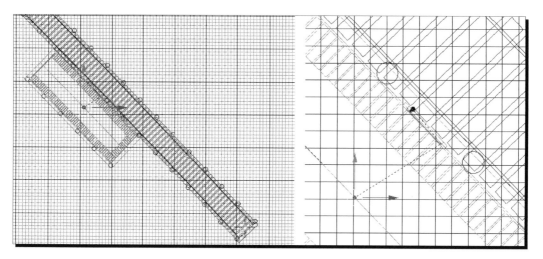

13. Press *Numpad 1* and press *Ctrl+MMB* to zoom into the scene so you can see the bottom of the boathouse and the top of the planks of the pier.

14. Press *G, Z*, and use the mouse to move the bottom of the boathouse until it's in level with the top of the planks of the pier. Press the *LMB* to release the boathouse.

15. Press *Numpad 7* to get the **Top** view.

16. Select the pilings with the *RMB*.

17. Press *Shift+D* to copy the pilings. Move them to the left side of the boathouse. Press the *LMB* to release them.

18. In the **Properties** window, select the **Object Modifiers** button from the header, it's the seventh button from the left with the wrench on it.

19. Under **Add Modifier** there are the two **Array** modifiers that you created. Delete the lower one. Now there is just the one long row of pilings in your copy.

20. Press *Ctrl+MMB* and zoom into the scene so you can see the boathouse and the pilings of the pier well.

21. Press *G*, and move the copy of the pilings so that the first piling is touching the lower back corner of the boathouse. Press the *LMB* to release the motion.

22. In the **Modifier** panel of the **Properties** window, change the **Count:** to **6**.

23. In the **3D View** header, set the **Viewport Shading** mode to **Solid**.

24. In the **3D View** header, press the *Shift* key and select **Layer 1** so you can see **Layer 1** and **Layer 2**.

25. Press the *MMB* and rotate the view so you can see the scene.

26. Press *Ctrl+Alt Numpad 0* to set the camera to the view you are seeing.

27. To select the camera, in the **3D View**, click on the edge between the camera view and the passepartout with the *RMB*.

28. Press *G, Z, Z*, and use the mouse to zoom out. Press the *LMB* to release the motion.

29. Press *F12* to render the scene.

30. If necessary, select the lamp, press *R, Z*, and use the mouse to rotate the lamp as you did when building the Ocean, so you get the light going the way that creates nice shadows.

31. Save the file to a unique name.

What just happened?

This was pretty straightforward. What you should know is that both the door and the garage door are hinged so you can open and close them. The door swings on its *Z* axis. The garage door swings on its local *X* axis.

Copying the piling had interesting results. When you removed the array that created the second row of pilings, you still had a row of pilings that was as long as the original. So you reduced the count of copies until it was just as long as the boathouse.

Building modular houses

Sometimes, you will need to use files that you did not create, and modify them to suit your purposes. In this case, it's a kit that you can make a variety of modular houses with.

Have a go hero – assembling a house from a kit

I included a house kit for you to make houses from to scatter around on the island. The kit is modular. There are eight wall sections that you can mix and match as you like. I used this kit to create the boathouse:

1. The kit is named `6907_10_House Kit.blend`. It's best to open it as a separate file in Blender and save a copy to a unique file name for the particular house you are making, then assemble a house, delete any unneeded parts, and save the file again.

2. Assembling a house is easy. You have eight different walls to choose from. Each wall is in a separate layer. To move a wall to a particular location, just follow the keyboard commands included with the two images of the boathouse that are further down in this *Have a go hero* section.

3. If the wall has a door, select both objects to duplicate them or transfer them from one layer or another.

4. Do not select the door while making the keyboard commands to translate or rotate them. Just select the wall. The door will follow the wall.

5. To make it easy to append your finished house into another file, join as many walls and roof parts as possible into a single object using the *Ctrl+J* command. This is just like making the sloop. If you want a door to work, do not use the *Ctrl+J* command to join the wall to the house. Instead, use the *Ctrl+P* command to parent the house to the wall that has a door in it. Delete any leftover walls and/or doors.

6. When you open the kit, you will find the roof, floor, and foundation in the first layer, and the various walls in other layers as listed in the following table. Each wall section is centered in the house now as shown in the following screenshot. All walls are the same size **X: 12** and **Y: 10**. If you want to make your own wall section, make a copy of the plain wall and move it to an unused layer and do your magic.

7. The roof is in two parts, if you want to resize it, the texture size of the shingle texture can be changed by changing the number in the **Image Mapping** subpanel of the **Texture** panel in the **Properties** window. Just change the **Repeat:** value. There are two Wall tops, a floor, and a foundation. The foundation will let you sink the house down a bit on uneven terrain so the house will not appear to be floating above the surface.

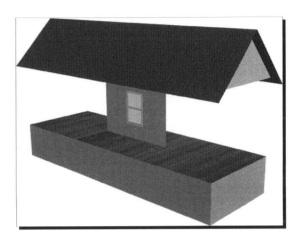

The following table lists which parts are in which layer. Simply select the wall components in a layer, copy them with *Shift+D*, then *Enter*, and press *M*, *1*, and *Enter* to move the copy to **Layer 1**. Next, use the keyboard commands listed in the following screenshot to move the walls into position. Then deselect them and get the next wall.

Layer	Objects on Layer – select all objects on layer before moving them
Layer 1	`Roof_Front, Roof_Rear, Wall_Top Left, Wall_Top Right, Floor, Foundation`
Layer 2	`Wall_Window 1 Center`
Layer 3	`Wall_Window 1 Right`
Layer 4	`Wall_Window 1 Left`
Layer 5	`Wall_Windows 2`
Layer 6	`Wall_Window 1 Large`
Layer 7	`Wall_Front Door, Door_Front, Door_Knob`
Layer 8	`Wall_Garage Door, Door_Garage`
Layer 9	`Wall_Plain`

The following two screenshots contain the keyboard commands to move and rotate any given wall to its proper place depending on where you want it to go. The first screenshot shows the keystrokes for moving walls to the front of the building and the right end. The boathouse is used as the example:

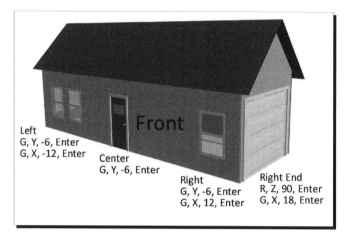

The second screenshot shows the keystrokes for the back of the building and the left end:

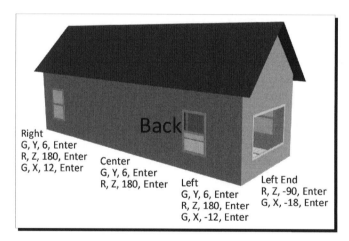

When you are done, delete the extra walls and save your house to a unique name.

Creating trees with the Sapling add-on

Blender has a great add-on for generating trees. Better than the old days when you had to stick every leaf on a tree one by one. Be careful, Sapling can make a lot of faces very quickly. The Info window header at the top gives you a read out of how many vertices, edges, and faces you have. Watch it!

Time for action – adding trees to the landscape

Like the ANT Landscape, Sapling uses mathematical algorithms to create organic forms. You'll step through the menus to make a tree:

1. Create a new Blender file.

2. In the **File** menu at the upper-left corner of the Blender window, select **User Preferences**, as you did earlier in this chapter to use the ANT Landscape add-on. The **Blender User Preferences** window will pop up.

3. Select **Addons** from the **Blender User Preferences** menu. Scroll down and put a checkmark in the box for **Add Curve:Sapling**. Select **Install Add-on...** from the header at the bottom of the menu.

4. Press the **X** button at the upper right-hand corner of the **Blender User Preferences** window and close the window. If you are using a Mac or Linux, use the red dot on the left-hand corner of the **Blender User Preferences** window.

5. Delete the default cube.

6. Press *Shift+A* and select **Curve** and then **Add Tree** from the menus.

7. Press *Numpad 1* to get the **Front** view. Press *Numpad 5* to get **Ortho** mode. Press *Shift+MMB* and move the tree into view. Pull the left side of the **Tool Shelf** to the right so you can see the full text of the buttons. Move the upper border of the **Sapling** subpanel up so you can see all of the **Settings:** subpanel. Watch the tree as you make changes to it.

8. In the **Geometry** subpanel:
   - Check the **Bevel** checkbox.
   - Set the **Ratio:** to **0.02** as seen on the left side of the following screenshot.
   - Click on the **Settings:** button in the **Sapling Add Tree** subpanel, which currently says **Geometry**. Scroll up the pop-up menu and select **Branch Splitting**.

9. In the **Branch Splitting** subpanel:
   - Set **Levels:** to **3**
   - Set **Base Splits:** to **3**
   - Set **Base Size:** to **0.17**
   - Set the top row **Split Angle:** to **20.00**

❏   Set the top row **Split Angle Variation:** to **5.0** as shown in the following screenshot:

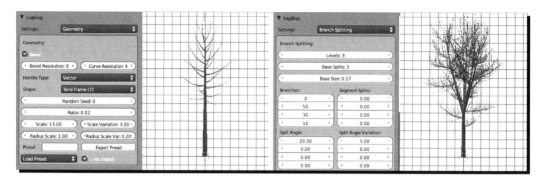

10. Click on the **Settings:** button in the **Sapling Add Tree** subpanel, which currently says **Branch Splitting**. Scroll up the pop-up menu and select **Branch Growth**.

11. In the **Branch Growth** subpanel:

   ❏   Set the second row **Length:** to **0.40**.

   ❏   Set the second row **Length Variation:** to **0.30** as shown in the left side of the following screenshot.

   ❏   Click on the **Settings:** button in the **Sapling Add Tree** subpanel, which currently says **Branch Growth**. Scroll up the pop-up menu and select **Pruning**.

12. In the **Pruning** subpanel:

   ❏   Check the **Prune** checkbox

   ❏   Set **Prune Width:** to **0.30**

   ❏   Set **Prune Width Peak:** to **0.50** as shown in the following screenshot:

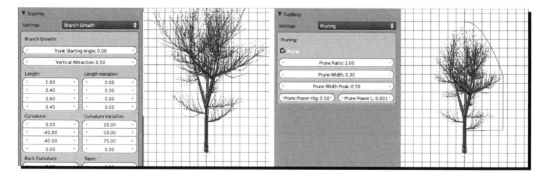

13. Click on the **Settings:** button in the **Sapling Add Tree** subpanel, which currently says **Pruning**. Scroll up the pop-up menu and select **Leaves**.

14. Look at the readout of the number of vertices and faces above the right side of the **3D View** window. **Ve:** shows the number of vertices. **Fa:** shows the number of faces.

15. In the **Leaves** subpanel:

❏ Check the **Show Leaves** checkbox

❏ Look at the number of vertices and faces readout

❏ Set the **Leaf Shape:** to **Rectangular** as seen on the left side of the following screenshot

❏ Look at the number of vertices and faces readout

16. You now have two objects, the Leaves and the Tree.

17. Put the mouse over the 3D View and press *A* twice to finish your tree-making.

18. Select the Leaves with the *RMB*.

19. In the **Properties** window, select the **Material** button from the header, it's the ninth button from the left with the chrome ball on it.

20. Select the **New** button with the **LMB**.

21. Name the material **Leaves Material**.

22. In the **Diffuse** subpanel, set the **Diffuse** color to a dark green. I used **R: 0.0006**, **G: 0.0600**, and **B: 0.000** as shown in the following screenshot:

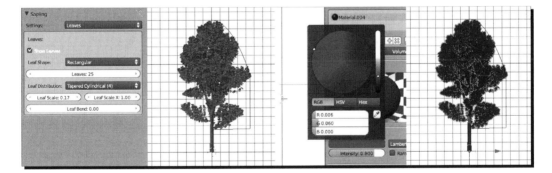

23. Select the Tree with the *RMB*.

24. Select the **New** button with the *LMB*.

25. Name the material **Tree Material**.

26. In the **Diffuse** subpanel, set the **Diffuse** color to a nice reddish brown, I used **R: 0.075, G: 0.0035,** and **B: 0.009**.

27. In the **Specular** subpanel, set the specular **Intensity:** value to **0.030**.

28. Press *Numpad 0* to select the **Camera** view.

29. Select the camera and Press *G, Z, Z,* and use the mouse to back it up so you can see the entire tree through it. Press the *LMB* to release the motion.

30. Press *F12* to render the scene.

31. Press *Esc* when you have finished viewing it.

32. Select the leaves with the *RMB*. Select the Tree with *Shift+RMB*. Press *Ctrl+J* to join the leaves and the tree.

33. Save the file to a unique file name.

What just happened?

Now you're making trees! You added a Bevel to give the tree a little girth and make round branches. The Ratio lets you adjust the diameter of the tree. If you wanted a strange shape for the branches, you could make a shape out of a Bezier Circle and apply it as a Bevel Object in the **Object Data** panel of the **Properties** window instead.

Next you set up the basic branching. The Base Splits controls how many main branches there are and the Base Size controls how tall the trunk is before there are any branches. The Levels control manages the number of times a branch will split into smaller branches, which split into yet smaller branches. Be careful with this control as you can make a lot of branches. Now, with the controls for the Split Angle and Split Angle Variations, there are four rows of buttons. The top row affects the top order branches, the second row affects the second order branches, and so on. Setting a value for the Split Angle Variation adds a little randomness to the angles that they branch at.

In Branch Growth, the Length controls how long a branch grows, and the Length Variation allows for some variation in growth.

Pruning allows you to limit the size of the tree. Prune Width sets some basic boundaries on girth. Prune Width Peak lets you set where the maximum width of the tree will occur, high or low.

With the Leaves, choose rectangular or hexagonal leaves and modify their sizes. I chose rectangular leaves to reduce the number of faces per tree. You could see this difference when you looked at the readout of vertices and faces.

Trees are fairly expensive objects in regard to the number of faces they create and what they do for rendering times. So you want to make them as simple as you can.

Have a go hero – making your own trees

Use the Sapling add-on and make some more trees. Play with the settings and see what you get. Join the Tree to the Leaves for easy use in other scenes.

Making rocks

Rocks might seem mundane, but they have an infinite variety of shapes and sizes and offer great practice in modeling smooth organic forms.

Have a go hero – making rocks with subdivision surfaces

What would an island be without rocks? They are easy to make. Create a cube and apply a subdivision surface modifier, like you did for the hull of the sloop. Use what you learned in *Chapter 8, Making the Sloop* about Edge Tools to add and modify control vertices to create nicely rounded rocks.

Assembling your world

It's time to put all the objects that you have made in separate files onto your island.

Have a go hero – putting your world together

Now it's time to do something that this whole book has been building up to, putting the sloop and the boat into their own world.

Open your island file that you just made or `6907_10_Island_Ocean_Pier.blend` from the download pack.

As you are assembling your world, there are two ways to organize it. You can use groups of objects and you can organize your world by layers.

Initially put each new object on its own layer. Select a layer before appending an object. That will give you best control over selecting objects as you arrange the scene, because if necessary, you can just display one layer and select an object or objects and then select all the layers to see where your selected objects are in relation to the rest of your world. Later, when you have everything in place, you can sort objects into just a few layers.

You can use what you have made, or the following models provided in the *Chapter 10, Modeling Organic Forms, Sea, and Terrain* download pack:

- ◆ `6907_10_Sloop.blend`.

- ◆ `6907_10_Boat.blend`.

- ◆ `6907_10_Tree_Sample_Large.blend`, from the download pack contains the tree made in the exercise. Rotating a tree in *Z* will make it look like a different tree, and you can also scale it.

- ◆ `6907_10_Tree_Sample_Small.blend` contains a lower detail tree. I used it as a bush.

- ◆ `6907_10_House Kit_Sample 1.blend` and `6907_10_House Kit_Sample 2.blend` can be used. `Sample 2` has open doors.

- ◆ `6907_10_Five Rocks.blend` has five sample rocks where the modifier has not been applied yet, so you can further modify them if you want, then apply the modification.

- ◆ `6907_10_Sky_Cloudy.blend` contains a hemisphere with a cloud texture as a background for your world. Add that if you wish.

Save the file after you have added the objects you want. Then position, rotate, and scale them to make your own island paradise.

Here is how my world turned out:

Time for action – using groups to organize your scene

Groups are a good way to organize the objects in your scene. They let you move multiple objects at a time and each object can be a member of more than one group, so you can organize them whatever way you want:

1. Press *A* to deselect everything. Select the sails of the sloop with *Shift+RMB*.

2. In the **3D View header**, choose **Object**, then pick **Group**, and then **Create New Group** from the menus.

3. In the **Properties** window, select the **Object** button from the header, it's the fifth button from the left with the cube on it.

4. In the **Groups** subpanel, under the button that says **Add to Group** is a text entry button. Input **Sail Group** into that button.

5. Now look in the header of the **Outliner** window above the **Properties** window. There is a button that says **All Scenes** or **Current Scene**. Click on it and select **Groups** from the drop-down menu.

6. You will see your new **Sail Group** listed. You can use it to select all the objects of the Sail Group at one time. Click on the **+** (plus) sign to the left of where it says **Sail Group**, and you will see all the objects in the Group listed.

7. Now click on the Line attached to the sloop.

8. In the **Groups** subpanel of the **Properties** window, click on the **Add to Group** button. Select **Sail Group** from the drop-down menu. If you do not see **Sail Group** listed, either scroll with the mouse wheel or start typing in the name **Sail Group** next to the magnifying glass at the top of the menu. Then select it when it appears in the menu.

9. Look in the **Outliner** window again and you will see the Line included in your sail group.

What just happened?

That was a quick introduction to using Groups. You learned how to create a group, and how to add an object to a group. You also learned how to select all the objects of a group, and how to find out which objects are in the group.

Pop quiz – optimizing rendering times

1. What can be done to reduce the number of faces in your final world without hurting the look?

    a. Remove the back sides of the buildings

    b. Remove the faces in the vertex group Ocean Floor

    c. Delete the back sides of the island

Take your time and have fun in building and arranging your world. The possibilities are endless. Don't be afraid to redo or modify any part, no one achieves perfection the on the first try. Back up your world frequently. It's become a very big file and you don't want to lose your work.

Key	Function
O	Turns on proportional editing.
Page Up	Enlarges the proportional editing circle.
Page Down	Shrinks the proportional editing circle.
fn+Up arrow	Enlarges the proportional editing circle on a Mac.
fn+Down arrow	Shrinks the proportional editing circle on a Mac.
Shift+C	Resets 3D cursor position to 0, 0, 0, zooms out to show entire scene.
Shift+X	If used with scaling (*S*) or moving (*G*) it restricts changes to the *Y* and *Z* axes.
Shift+Y	If used with scaling (*S*) or moving (*G*) it restricts changes to the *X* and *Z* axes.
Shift+Z	If used with scaling (*S*) or moving (*G*) it restricts changes to the *X* and *Y* axes.
U	Gets you to the **UV Mapping** menu.
Ctrl+G	Makes a group of the selected objects.
Shift+G	Brings up a dialog box for manipulating groups.

Summary

In this chapter you created a world for the sloop to exist in. You used texturing to create an oceanic surface. You discovered how to use the ANT Landscape add-on to create an island. You used proportional editing to finalize the land form and then painted the island with Blender Paint. With DupliFrames, bevel objects, and arrays you created an entire pier out of four simple objects. You used the Sapling add-on to create trees and subdivision surfaces to make rocks. You built houses from a kit finding creative ways to reuse parts. You appended a boathouse and a sky to complete the scene, and used layers and groups to organize the scene. You're doing some impressive work.

The next chapter will concentrate on lighting and camera use. You'll discover how to do a standard three point lighting setup and use lighting falloffs and shadows. We will discuss camera basics including perspective, lens use, depth of field, clipping, choosing shots, and critiquing them.

Let's go!

11

Improving your Lighting and Camera Work

In the previous chapter you created a world for the sloop to exist in. You created the ocean's surface with texturing. You built an island with the ANT Landscape add-on. You made adjustments to the land form with proportional editing and then painted the island with Blender Paint. You created an entire pier out of four simple objects and used the Sapling add-on to create trees and then you made rocks to practice your skills with Subdivision Surfaces. You built houses from a kit and appended a boathouse and a sky to complete the scene.

In this chapter you will concentrate on lighting and camera use. You'll discover:

- ◆ How to create the standard three point lighting setup
- ◆ Using lighting falloff and shadows
- ◆ Camera use including perspective, lenses, depth of field, clipping, choosing shots, and critiquing them
- ◆ How to animate a scene, and learn ways to make adjustments and do rapid test renderings

Getting ready to do lighting and camera work

The following are the files that you should copy from your download pack and into your `Chapter 11/Blender Files` directory:

- ◆ `6907_11_light test rig_Sintel.blend`
- ◆ `6907_11_Blender Island.blend`

- ◆ 6907_11_Viking ship_subsurface.blend
- ◆ 6907_11_Viking ship_mesh.blend

The following are the image files that you should copy from your download pack into the `Chapter 11/Images` directory:

- ◆ 6907_11_01.png
- ◆ 6907_11_02.png
- ◆ 6907_11_03.png
- ◆ 6907_11_04.png
- ◆ 6907_11_05.png
- ◆ 6907_11_06.png
- ◆ 6907_11_07.png

> If you are reading the printed version of this book, treat yourself by downloading all of the .png files from this chapter's Image subdirectory in the download pack. In this chapter, color is important.

Using lighting

In *Chapter 3, Controlling the Lamp, the Camera, and Animating Objects* and *Chapter 5, Building a Simple Boat*, we looked at the lights and you got a little chance to play around with them. Now we will take a more in-depth look at using light.

Pop quiz – remembering about lighting

Here's a refresher from what you learned in *Chapter 5, Building a Simple Boat* to get your mind thinking of light again:

1. Which light gives the same lighting no matter where the lamp is placed?

    a. Spot

    b. Sun

    c. Area

2. Which lights are dimmer the farther away the lamp is?

    a. Spot and Hemi

    b. Sun and Area

    b. Point and Spot

3. The Spot lamp is like a:

    a. Light bulb

    b. Theatrical light

    c. Fluorescent light

Lighting with three lights

The three point lighting method provides a simple and easy-to-use method of lighting a scene. And when you understand it, you will have a solid foundation for creating more complex lighting.

What the three lights represent are the three stages in setting up the lighting:

♦   Setting up the general lighting level.

♦   Controlling the shadows so everything is well lit. This does not mean bright, but rather that critical details are not lost in shadows.

♦   Adding in highlights to pop the subject of the shot out from the background.

Time for action – introducing the three point lighting system

I've prepared a simple lighting rig. The model is a statue of Blender Foundation's Sintel. The rig has four layers. Layer 1 has the key light. Layer 2 has the fill light. Layer 3 has the back light. Layer 4 has Sintel, the camera, and an empty. Putting the lights on different layers lets you turn them on and off easily. Note that I have set up the 3D View as a QuadView window as discussed in *Chapter 2, Getting Comfortable using the 3D View*. This will let you adjust the lights in all axes without changing the windows:

1. Open the file `6907_11_light test rig_Sintel.blend` from your download pack.

2. Press *F12*. Press *Esc* when you have finished looking at the image.

What just happened?

This rig has three lights. In the 3D View, the lamps are in black. You can see their location on the left side of the following screenshot and the cones of light that are coming from them. The camera is highlighted:

♦   The **Key Light** is placed between 15–45 degrees from the camera. In this case it is on the left of the camera. It provides the main light for a scene.

- The **Fill Light** is placed at about a 90 degree angle to the key light. Here, it is to the right of the camera. It is dimmer and often more diffuse. Its purpose is to fill in many of the shadows created by the key light.

- The **Back Light** is about 180 degrees from the camera. It is used to provide a highlight on the edges of the person or object. You can see the light from all three lamps on the right of the following screenshot:

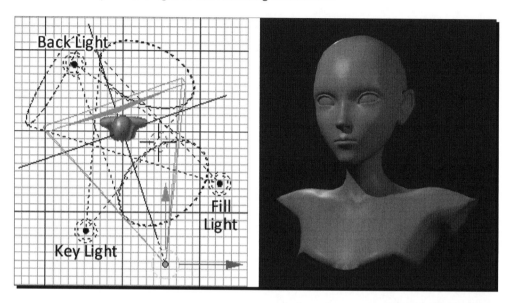

Time for action – lighting with only the key light

The key light is your main light. To know how to use it in combination with other lights, it helps to see how the light appears all by itself:

1. Select **Layer 1**, and then press the *Shift* key while selecting **Layer 4** so that the key light, the camera, and Sintel are visible.

2. Press *F12*. The image should look similar to the following image. Press *Esc* when you have finished looking at the image.

What just happened?

Now you see only the key light, which is to the left of the camera and at a high angle above the Sintel. The shadows are strong. You can see a highlight on her forehead and at the top of her chest as seen on the left side of the following screenshot. The purpose of the key light is to do the main lighting for the scene.

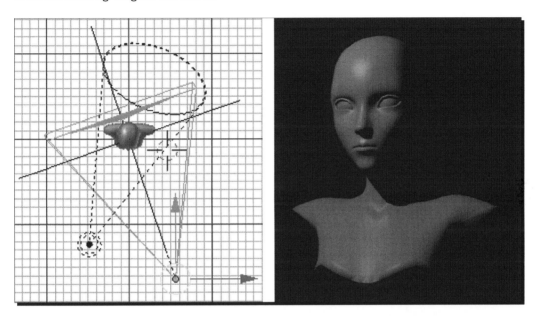

Time for action – lighting with only the fill light

The fill light helps light up areas of the image that the key light does not illuminate. Check out what the fill light can illuminate by itself:

1. Select **Layer 2**, and then press the *Shift* key while selecting **Layer 4**.

2. Press *F12*. The image should look similar to the following image. Press *Esc* when you have finished looking at the image.

What just happened?

Now you see only the fill light, which is to the right of the camera, as seen on the right side of the following screenshot. The light is dimmer, about one half to one quarter the value of the key light. It is also lower, so you see the highlights of the fill light come off the sides of her head and body, as you can see on the right side of the following screenshot. The purpose of the fill light is to fill in the areas that are in shadows created by the key light. You can see that the fill light will give important details about Sintel's left ear and the shape of her neck.

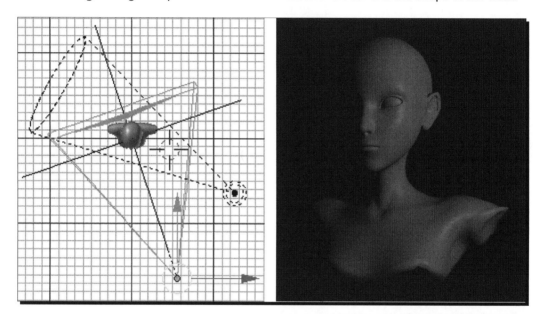

Time for action – lighting with only the back light

The back light adds highlights that help define objects. Without a key and fill light, you can see this more clearly:

1. Select **Layer 3**, and then press the *Shift* key while selecting **Layer 4**.

2. Press *F12*. The image should look similar to the following image. Press *Esc* when you have finished looking at the image.

What just happened?

The back light is about 180 degrees from the camera, as seen on the left side of the following screenshot. With only the back light, you see highlights on the top of the head and the shoulders, as seen on the left side of the following screenshot. Like the key light, the back light is high. Its job is to create highlights that define the subject with a rim of light.

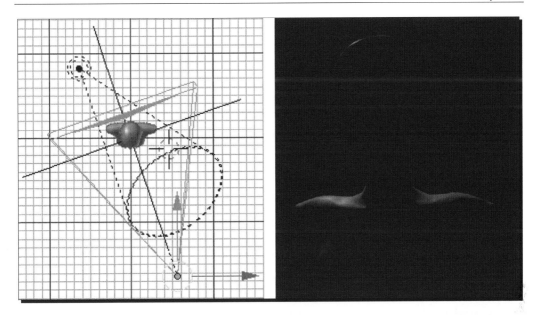

Time for action – using color to separate what you see

You've seen each lamp by itself. Now use color to see how they work together:

1. Select **Layer 1**, and then press the *Shift* key while selecting **Layers 2**, **3**, and **4**.

2. Select the **Spot_Key** lamp, to the left of the camera in the **Top** view, with the *RMB*. In the **Properties** window header, select the **Object Data** button. It's the seventh button from the left. It has a light bulb on it.

3. In the **Lamp** subpanel, select the white **Light Color** button below the row of buttons that define the kind of lamp you are using. In the pop-up color wheel, set **G 0.0000** and **B 0.0000** so that the lamp is red.

4. Select the **Spot_Fill** lamp to the right of the camera with the *RMB*.

5. In the **Lamp** subpanel, select the white **Light Color** button. In the pop-up color wheel, set **R 0.0000** and **G 0.0000** so that the lamp is blue.

6. Select the **Spot_Back** lamp, opposite the camera, with the *RMB*.

7. In the **Lamp** subpanel, select the white **Light Color** button. In the pop-up color wheel, set **R 0.0000** and **B 0.0000** so that the lamp is green.

8. Press *F12.* The image should look similar to the image in the following screenshot. Press *Esc* when you are done looking at it.

9. Save the file to a unique file name.

What just happened?

Now you turned on all three lights at once, but you gave each one a different color, so you could see how the lights interact, as seen in the right of the following screenshot. You studied light color and how it mixes in *Chapter 3, Controlling the Lamp, the Camera, and Animating Objects*. Here, you can see where the key and fill lamps both illuminate Sintel on the left side of her face, because her skin is magenta, not red or blue. The back light is green but the highlight on her neck becomes cyan briefly on her left-hand side where the fill and back light mix. In the center of her right shoulder, the key and back lights mix, making the color a bit more yellow. Under her chin and nose and where her lips meet, there is no light.

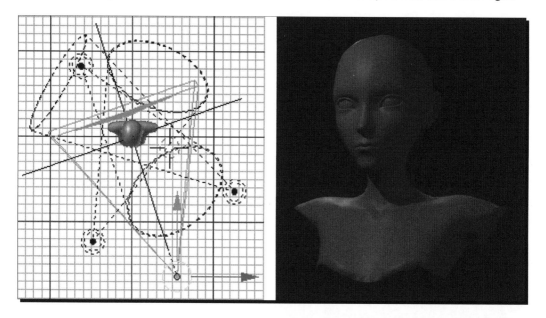

Have a go hero – changing lighting intensity

There is only one good way to know how the intensity of the light affects the scene: try it out. Try these different light intensities.

Open `6907_11_light test rig_Sintel.blend` again. Select **Layer 1** and **Layer 4**. Select the **Spot_Key** lamp. In the **Properties** window, select **Object Data** panel, then **Lamp** subpanel, and set the **Energy** levels of the **Lamp - key** to **0.25**, then render it. Repeat this with **Energy** levels of **0.50**, **1.00**, **2.00**, **4.00**, **8.00**, **16.00**, and **32.00** and note the changes. Look at how, despite the fact that the numbers are doubling each time, the brightness seems to climb steadily.

Time for action – using cookies

Mmmm cookies. Well, not the oatmeal, raisin, chocolate chip, or even the Internet kind. A cookie is a screen put up in front of a lamp to create a pattern within the light:

1. Open the file `6907_11_light test rig_Sintel.blend` from your download pack.

2. In the **3D View** window, select the **Spot_Key** lamp with the *RMB*.

3. In the header of the **Properties** window, select the **Textures** button. It is the eighth button from the left with the checkerboard on it.

4. Press the **New** button to create a new texture.

5. Click on the button to the right of **Type:** Choose **Image or Movie** from the menu.

6. In the **Image** subpanel, click on the **Open** button and select `6907_11_05.png` from the `Images` directory of the `Chapter 11` download pack.

7. Press *F12*.

8. In the **Mapping** subpanel, click the button to the left of **Coordinates:**. Select **Object** from the pop-up menu.

9. Press *F12*.

10. Click on the button to the left of **Object:**. Select **Spot_Key** from the pop-up menu.

11. Set the **X** and **Y** values of **Size:** to **0.50**.

12. Press *F12*.

13. In the **Influence** subpanel, set the **Color:** to **0.250** to provide a softer effect, as shown in the following screenshot:

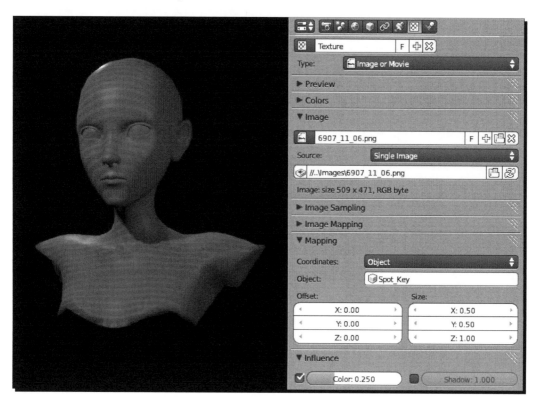

14. Press *F12*. Press *Esc* when you have finished looking at Sintel.

15. Save the file to a unique name.

What just happened?

Just as objects can have textures, lamps can have textures. This can be very handy for suggesting detail, such as a venetian blind that indicates a window, a leaf pattern suggesting a tree, or a stained glass image suggesting a church. You discovered that you can change the size of the image and how strong it is. You can also change the mapping, the default global mapping created a wild pattern. If you chose **View** instead of **Object** in the **Coordinates:** button, the texture would suggest a pattern generated in the camera, not in the lamp.

Time for action – preparing to adjust falloff

Now you are going to prepare a scene to investigate falloff from a light:

1. Open the file 6907_11_light test rig_Sintel.blend from your download pack.

2. Select Sintel with the *RMB*.

3. In the **Properties** window header, select the **Object Modifiers** button, it is the seventh button from the left with the wrench on it.

4. In the **Modifiers** subpanel, select **Add Modifier** and choose **Array** from the menu.

5. In the **Array Modifier** subpanel set the **Relative Offset** to **X: 0.000, Y: 1.300**, and **Z: 0.000**.

6. Set the **Count** value to **7**.

7. Select the camera with the *RMB*.

8. Press *G, X*, and move the camera 15 units with the mouse while pressing the *Ctrl* and *Shift* buttons. Release the move with the *LMB*.

9. Press *G, Y*, and move the camera 5 units with the mouse while pressing the *Ctrl* and *Shift* buttons. Release the move with the *LMB*.

10. Press *R, Z*, and rotate it with the mouse so you can see all the Sintels in the **Camera** view. Release the rotation with the *LMB*. Move the camera in *Z* until you can see all of the Sintels at eye-level, individually, with their shoulders overlapping just a bit in the **Camera Persp** view. Release the rotation with the *LMB*.

11. Select **Layer 1** with the *LMB*. Press *Shift+LMB* and select **Layer 4**.

12. Press *F12*. Do you see all the Sintels? Press *Esc* when you have finished looking at the image.

13. Select the **Spot_Key** lamp.

14. In the header of the **Properties** window, select the **Object Data** button. It is the seventh button from the left with the lamp on it.

15. In the **Spot Shape** subpanel, set the **Size:** to **45** degrees.

16. Press *G, X*, and move the lamp 20 units with the mouse while pressing the *Ctrl* button. Release the move with the *LMB*.

17. Put the cursor over the **Front Ortho** window. Press *G, Z,* and move the lamp 6 units down with the mouse while pressing the *Ctrl* button. Release the move with the *LMB*.

18. Press *R, Z,* and rotate the lamp in the **Top Ortho** view, so that the left side of the cone touches the left side of the first Sintel. Press *R, X,* and rotate the lamp in the **Right Ortho** view so that all the Sintels are within the cone as shown in the following screenshot:

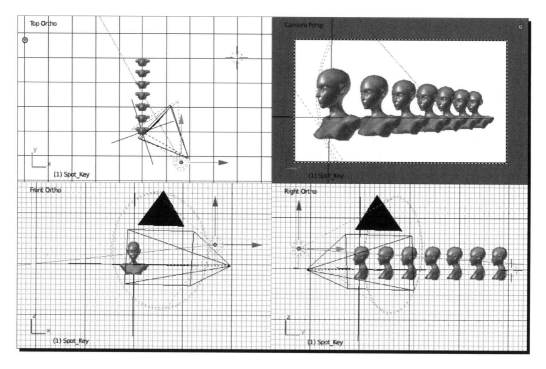

19. Press *F12.* Press *Esc* when you have finished looking at the image.

20. If you don't see all seven Sintels, readjust the lamp.

21. If you don't see the rear-most Sintel, it's likely that the light has been clipped, just the way the camera got clipped in the previous chapter. If so, in the bottom of the **Shadow** subpanel, you can either check the **Autoclip End** checkbox, or set the **Clip End:** button to **100.000**.

22. Press *F12.* Note how the Sintels get darker the farther away they are. Press *Esc* when you have finished looking at the image.

23. Save the file to a unique name.

What just happened?

By setting up a number of Sintels and shining the light along them, you could see what happens as the subject is farther from the light. The light appears to be dimmer.

Time for action – adjusting the falloff

Now that the scene is set, check out how much you can vary the light without ever changing how much energy the light emits:

1. In the **Lamp** subpanel of the **Properties** window, click on the **Sun** button.

2. Press *F12*. No falloff. Sunlight does not get dimmer, only spot lights, point lights, and area lights get dimmer.

3. In the **Lamp** subpanel, click on the **Spot** button.

4. Press *F12*.

5. In the **Lamp** subpanel, change the **Falloff: Distance:** from **25** to **12**.

6. Press *F12*.

7. In the **Lamp** subpanel, set the **Falloff: Distance:** to **50**.

8. Press *F12*.

9. In the **Lamp** subpanel, set the **Falloff: Distance:** to **100**.

10. Press *F12*. Press *Esc* when you have finished looking at the image. Compare what you have seen in the three renders, as shown in the following screenshot:

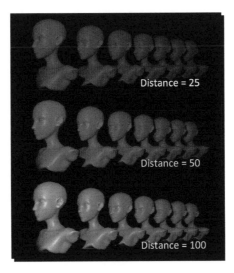

What just happened?

This *Time for action* section brings up a good question. If light can travel distances so far that it takes the light billions of years to get there, why does light get dimmer in just crossing a room? Shouldn't it stay just as bright?

In real life, light gets dimmer because the farther away from the source the light travels, the greater area it is spread over; so there is less light at any particular point.

You can see this in the following diagram. In the diagram, the light source has 90 light rays represented by the lines coming out of the center. There are four cubes, all the same size, but different distances from the light. The closest one gets hit by **19** light rays. The next closest gets hit by **7** light rays. Farther away, the cube only gets hit by **3**, and the farthest only gets hit by **1**. The closest cube will appear 19 times as bright as the farthest cube. Blender mimics that with falloff.

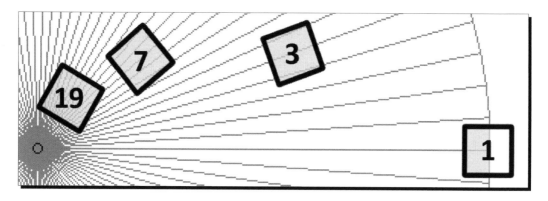

So why does the Sun lamp have no falloff? The diameter of the Sun is 109 times as large as the diameter of the Earth. We are small enough that, for all intents and purposes, the sunlight reaching the Earth is parallel. If the Sun were the size of the orange globe of light in the previous illustration, the Earth would be much smaller than that single line going out to the farthest cube. All of the Earth gets just about the same amount of light.

The falloff distance control specifies the distance at which an object appears half as bright as it is right at the light source.

In my example for the previous *Time for action* section, the front Sintel was 20 units from the lamp. The back Sintel was 43 units from the lamp:

- When the **Distance:** setting was **25**, the front Sintel was a little closer than the halfway point and was about half as bright as it would have been right by the lamp. The last Sintel was almost twice as far as the **Distance:** and the light had dimmed to almost nothing by the time it reached the last Sintel.

- At the **Distance:** setting of **50**, the last Sintel was just ahead of the halfway point, and it is about as bright as the first Sintel was at the **Distance:** of **25**.

- At a **Distance:** of **100**, not much of the falloff has happened in the distance between the lamp and any of the Sintels. They are all brighter.

So you can see that the effect of using the **Distance:** setting is like stretching the brightness of the light as you would a rubber band, one end is still bright and the other is always dark, but you can vary the distance between those points.

Each lamp can have a differing **Distance:** which lets you use the light even more subtly as your key light falls off at a different rate than your fill.

Time for action – using the Custom Curve to tailor light

The Custom Curve allows you to tailor the falloff exactly to your needs:

1. In the **Lamp** subpanel, click the button beneath **Falloff:** look out for **Inverse Square** and select **Custom Curve** from the menu.

2. Set the **Distance:** to **47** in the button below **Custom Curve**.

3. Scroll down to the **Falloff Curve** subpanel.

4. Note that there are three vertical grid lines, and three horizontal grid lines. There is a line that goes diagonally from upper left to lower right. That line is a Bezier Curve. When you click on that line a control point is put there and you can move that control point to change the shape of that line.

5. Move the mouse over the diagonal line. Near the leftmost vertical grid, press the LMB and drag the curve down so the control point is at the intersection of the center horizontal grid and the leftmost vertical grid.

6. Press *F12*.

7. Move the mouse to the right of the control point you just created and press the *LMB* over the line. Drag the point down and over so it is on the center vertical grid at the mid-point between the lowest horizontal grid and the bottom.

8. Press *F12*.

9. Move the mouse to the right of the control point you just created and press the *LMB* over the line. Drag the point up so it is at the center vertical grid and the top horizontal grid.

10. Press *F12*.

11. Move the mouse to the right of the control point you just created and press the *LMB* over the line. Drag the point so it is at the intersection of the top horizontal grid and the right vertical grid.

12. Press *F12*.

13. Move the mouse to the right of the control point you just created and press the *LMB* over the line. Drag the point down so it is just to the right of the intersection of the rightmost vertical grid and the bottom horizontal grid. The complete settings are in the shown in the following screenshot:

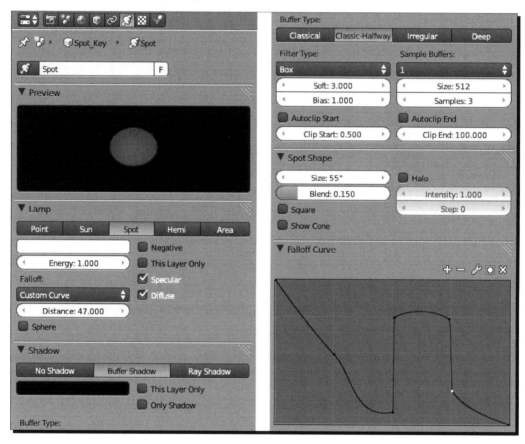

14. Press *F12*. Press *Esc* when you have finished looking at the image. It should look something like the following:

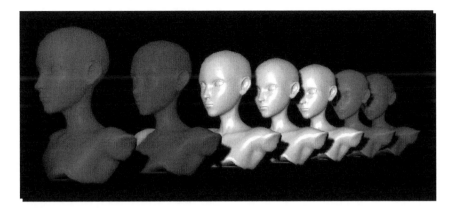

15. Save the file to a unique name.

What just happened?

Finally, the Custom Curve showed that falloff can be fun and that, in Blender, you can control the falloff into shadows exactly as you want, even if real light does not work that way.

Have a go hero – using three point lighting

As I have said, the three point lighting format is just a basis for lighting design. Now try out these variations. Open the file `6907_11_light test rig_Sintel.blend` from your download pack.

Filling in from the key side lighting is an interesting twist on three point lighting. Put both the key and fill lights on the same side at roughly a 45 degree angle from the camera. Put a little space between the key and fill lights, and aim them at different parts of the face. Set the back light to 180 degrees off the key and fill.

Cameo Lighting is used for picking out a particular person in a scene. Set the key light about six Blender units above Sintel's head, shining almost straight down. Turn off the fill and back lights. Set the falloff distance to **50**.

Beauty Lighting is all about highlights. Set the key light directly in front of Sintel at eye level. Set the back light high and above Sintel's head. Turn off the fill light.

Rembrandt Lighting is named after the style of painter Rembrandt van Rijn. This is very similar to three point lighting except that there is no backlight. The goal of Rembrandt Lighting is to create a triangle of light underneath the eye on the darker side of the face. Use **Empty** to rotate the camera so it is directly in front of Sintel. You will want the key light at a high location and the fill about in level with Sintel's face. Try starting out with only the key light and get it into position, then adjust the fill. Do a search on Rembrandt Lighting to see examples.

Film Noir Lighting is used to recapture that gritty 1940s look. Watch the video *How to Light Video Film Noir Style* by *Mark Apsalon* available at `http://www.youtube.com/watch?v=w1gMxT2R9z4`.

The basic idea is to light only what you want the viewer to see. Use a strong key light and minimal fill. Use the back light to create a rim highlight. Adjust the size of the cone, the falloff, and the energy levels. Use extreme camera angles. Use cookies to give the light shapes and cast interesting shadows onto flat walls or light only the eyes. Here's what I did:

Learning more about lighting

Digital Lighting and Rendering, Second Edition by *Jeremy Birn*, New Riders, Berkeley, CA 94710, 2006.

The Complete Guide to Light and Lighting in Digital Photography by *Michael Freeman*, Lark Books, New York, NY 10016, 2007.

The Cinema as a Graphic Art by *Vladimir Nilsen*, Hill and Wang, NY, NY, 1972.

How to Light Video Film Noir Style by *Mark Apsalon*, `http://www.youtube.com/watch?v=w1gMxT2R9z4`.

Using the camera to best effect

The Blender camera can be used much like a film camera. A film camera has three basic controls: the lens, which controls what you see; the aperture, which controls how much light you see; and the shutter, which controls the length of the exposure. Using the aperture and the shutter together, you can control how bright the scene is and how much detail you can see.

Changing the field of view

The **field of view** is the area that can be seen through the camera. This can be thought of as the width of a cone in front of the camera, measured in degrees, as shown on the left side of the following screenshot.

Blender allows you to specify this angle in two ways, in degrees, or as the size of a camera lens that sees a scene of that width.

By default, Blender specifies the field of view as a lens of a certain **Focal Length**, as seen on the right of the following graphic. The focal length is specified in millimeters, in the same way as cameras do. This lets you work more easily with filmmakers.

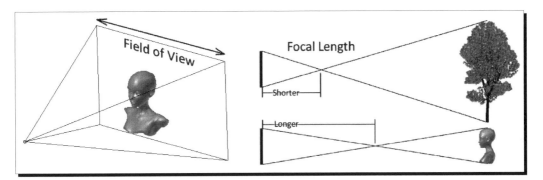

Blender uses the same lens size/field of view ratios as a professional movie camera that uses 35 MM film or a high quality digital camera. Both the film size/sensor size and the lens size are specified in millimeters. From now on we will be talking about lens sizes and assuming 35 MM film.

The following is the same scene rendered from the same view point with three different lens settings. The 28 MM lens shown here is a **wide-angle** lens. The wide-angle lens has a short focal length as shown in the top right of the preceding image. The 50 MM lens is a **normal** lens, and reproduces approximately what people see, and the 135 MM lens is a **telephoto** lens for getting good detail from far away.

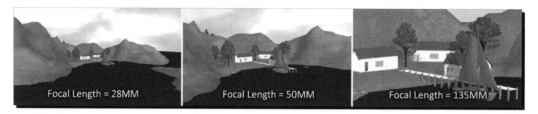

You can find out more about cameras and lenses at `http://www.cambridgeincolour.com/tutorials/camera-lenses.htm`.

Time for action – zooming the camera versus dollying the camera

Say you want to start out with a long shot that transitions into a close-up. Do you zoom or dolly? We studied dollying in *Chapter 3, Controlling the Lamp, the Camera, and Animating Objects*. Dollying moves the camera toward or away from the scene. **Zooming** is making a keyframe with one field of view, and on a different frame making a second keyframe with a different field of view. You can go from a distance to close up to your subject with either lens. Is there a difference in the results? This exercise has two identical cameras, you'll zoom one and dolly the other and see what you think. Check *Chapter 3, Controlling the Lamp, the Camera, and Animating Objects* if you need to review the commands for navigating in the **Timeline Editor**.

1. Open the file `6907_11_Blender Island.blend`. **Camera.Field of View** is selected as the default. It is selected as the active camera in the left-hand **3D View** window.

2. The **Object Data** panel in the **Properties** window will be open. In the **Lens** subpanel, you will see a button labeled **Focal Length: 28**.

3. Move the cursor over that button and push the *I* (letter i) key to create a keyframe. The button will turn yellow as shown in the following screenshot:

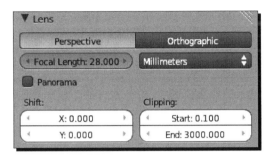

4. With the cursor over the **Timeline** window, press the *Shift+Up Arrow* key twice to move to frame 20.

5. In the **Properties** window in the **Lens** subpanel, change the **Focal Length:** to **135** and with the mouse over the button press the *I* key to create another **Focal Length:** keyframe.

6. With the mouse over the **Timeline** window, press the *Shift+Down Arrow* key twice to move to frame **0**.

7. In the upper-right **3D View** window, click on the camera symbol object until the text in the lower corner of the window changes from **Camera.Field of View** to **Camera.Dolly**.

8. With the cursor over the upper-right **3D View** window, press *I* and then select **Location** from **Insert Keyframe Menu**.

9. In the header of the upper-right **3D View** window, select **View**, then **Cameras**, and then **Set Active Object as Camera** from the menus.

10. Now you are displaying the **Camera.Field of View** in the upper-left **3D View** window and the **Camera.Dolly** in the upper-right **3D View** window. You can use the mouse wheel to make the camera area fill the window.

11. With the mouse over the **Timeline** window, press the *Shift+Up Arrow* key twice to move to frame 20.

12. Move the cursor to the border between **Timeline** and the **3D View** windows and get the double-headed arrow. Move the border between them until both windows are of approximately equal height.

13. Select the diagonal lines at the lower-left corner of the **Timeline** window and move it to the right to create a new window. Divide the windows about 25 percent on the left and 75 percent on the right.

14. Make sure your cursor is not over either of the top **3D View** windows. In the right-side window that you just created, select the **Current Editor Type** menu. Select **3D View**. Press *Numpad 7* to get the Top view in that window. Press *Numpad 5* so that it is an **Ortho** view. Use *Ctrl+MMB* and *Shift+MMB* until you can see the **Camera.Dolly** in the lower-right **3D View**. You can also press the *Home* key to see everything or *fn+left arrow* if you are using a Mac.

15. When you see the **Camera.Dolly** and want to zoom into it, press *Shift+B* and then use the marquee to select the area just around **Camera.Dolly**.

16. In the lower right-hand **3D View** window, press *G, Z, Z*, and move the **Camera.Dolly** towards the house until the view in the upper right-hand **3D View** window is similar to what you see in the upper left-hand **3D view** window as possible. In both cases, the house on the left will be touching the edge of the image. Press the *LMB* to release the move.

17. With your cursor over the lower-right **3D View** window, press *I* and then select **Location** from the **Keyframe** menu.

18. Press the *Left* and *Right Arrow* keys to progress back and forth through the 20 frames and compare the two. Do it several times and compare the two images at each frame. The zoom is on the left, the dolly is on the right. Frame 20 is shown in the following screenshot for comparison:

19. Save the file to a unique name.

What just happened?

This shows a lot about the difference between zoom and dolly. When dollying, I tried to make it match the image area of the zoom motion. In both cases the house on the left touches the edge of the image. The zoom focuses on the house by eliminating part of the area that it sees. The dolly physically moves the lens toward the object.

They have the same image on frame one, but by frame 20 the images are much different. Both images try to cover about the same area. The center of both images is the lower-right corner of the window of the farthest house. The left side is the outer edge of the nearer house. The differences are as follows:

◆ The **Camera.Dolly** is closer to the scene and it has a wider angle lens. Because the camera is closer to the house than the end of the pier is, you only see a part of the sloop's sail instead of the sloop and the pier.

◆ The **Camera.Dolly** image shows more perspective. The boathouse in the foreground is larger and the furthest house is smaller and you can see the tops of the hills in the background.

◆ Because of the angle of the lenses, the distortion is different in each image. In the Zoom image, the left side of the house looks a little smaller than the right side, whereas in the Dolly image, the left side of the house looks a little larger than the right side.

Using perspective

If you took art classes in school, they probably introduced you to perspective. The following image demonstrates classic perspective rules. The two columns of pilings look like they would meet if you extended them out to the horizon in the background. And the planks on the dock get smaller and smaller as they recede in the distance. This provides important clues about the structure of the scene to the viewer. Keep them in mind when placing your camera. And sometimes you can use a smaller structure such as a model of a castle close to the camera, to represent a larger structure far from the camera.

Using depth of field

Depth of field specifies what in the image is in sharp focus, and what is blurred. It uses the **Z-depth**, or how far from the camera an object is, to determine what is in focus. A greater depth of field means more of the scene is in focus. A smaller depth of field means that less of the scene is in focus. By default, Blender renders everything in nice sharp focus. But it has some tricks to fake the depth of field, as shown in the following image, where you can see the people are in focus but objects in the foreground and background are not.

We just studied field of view, it can get confused with depth of field because the terms share two out of three words. Field of view is how wide your field of vision is, depth of field is how deep your field of vision is.

Making your own people in Blender

The two humans I am using were created in an open source program named MakeHuman. It creates fairly realistic men and women who are already rigged, and gives you a wide range of options on their appearance. Using MakeHuman is out of the range of this book, but if you want more information you could go to http://www.makehuman.org/.

Time for action – creating depth of field

Depth of field is a technique borrowed from film cameras to set off what is subject and what is background:

1. Open the file `6907_11_Blender Island.blend`.

2. In the **Outliner** window just above the **Properties** window, select **Camera.Depth of Field** with the *LMB*.

3. In the header of the right-hand **3D View** window, select **View**, then **Cameras**, and then **Set Active Object as Camera**.

4. You can use the mouse wheel to make the camera area fill the window.

5. Look at the **Layers** controls in the **3D View** header. The Sky is in Layer 10. Press *Shift+LMB* over Layer 10 so that all layers with objects will render.

6. Press *F12* to render the scene. It looks similar to the previous image, but without the people. You can use *Ctrl+MMB* and use the mouse to fill the window with the image after it has rendered. Look at it and see how everything in the image is in focus. Zoom into the house so you can see the tiles on the roof. Do not press *Esc* to get rid of the image.

7. In the **Timeline** window, select the **Current Editor Type** button on the left end of the header and choose **Node Editor** from the pop-up menu.

8. In the **Node Editor** window header, there are three buttons on the right side of the word **Node**. Click on the right-hand button. Four checkboxes will appear as seen in the following screenshot. Select **Use Nodes**.

9. Two boxes connected by a cord will appear in the **Node Editor**. They look similar to the illustration of data blocks at the beginning of *Chapter 4, Modeling with Vertices, Edges, and Faces*. Each box represents a data node. The left node is the **Render Layers** node and the right node is the **Composite** node.

10. Move your mouse up to the top of the **Node Editor** window till you see the double-headed arrow. Hold down the mouse button and move the top of the **Node Editor** up so you can make the node boxes bigger. Press *Ctrl+MMB* and use the mouse to zoom into the **Node Editor** window.

11. Select the yellow dot at the right end of the cord between the node boxes. Hold the *LMB* down, move the mouse to the left and the cord detaches as shown in the following screenshot. Release the mouse button and the cord disappears.

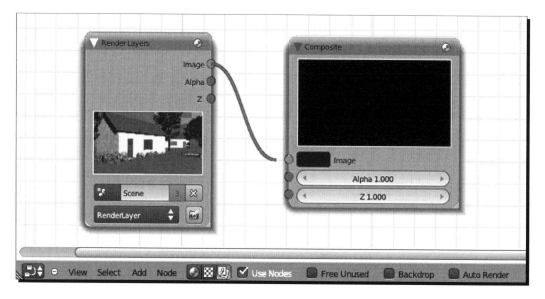

12. In the **Node Editor** header, select **Add**. Choose **Filter** and then **Defocus** from the pop-up menus.

13. Select the **Defocus** node with the *LMB* and hold it down so as you move the **Defocus** node into the center between the other two nodes. Release the *LMB* to release the motion.

14. Move the other two nodes apart so there is a little space between them.

15. Now, connect the nodes. Move the cursor to the yellow dot on the right-hand side of the **Render Layers** node. Hold down the *LMB* and drag the cursor to the yellow dot on the bottom left-hand side of the **Defocus** node. A cord-like connection will be formed.

16. Next, in the **Render Layers** node, select the dot beside the letter **Z**. Hold down the mouse and move it to the gray dot beside the Z button at the bottom of the **Defocus** node as shown in the following screenshot.

17. Click on the **Use Z-Buffer** checkbox in the **Defocus** node.

18. Now connect the **Defocus** node to the **Composite** node on the right. Select the yellow dot on the upper right-hand side of the **Defocus** node. Hold down the *LMB* and move the cursor to the yellow dot on the left-hand side of the **Composite** node.

19. In the **Defocus** node, set the value of **fStop** to **5**.

20. Set the **Max Blur** value to **16**.

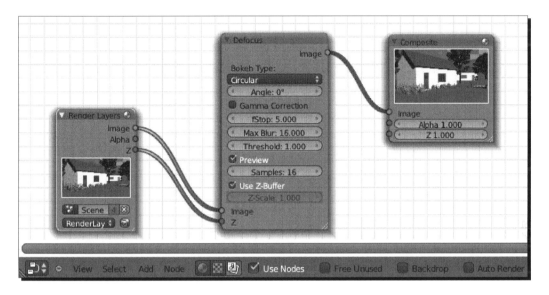

21. Notice that in the **UV/Image Editor** the roof tiles are now blurred.

22. If you want to save the image, with the cursor over the **UV/Image Editor** window, press *F3*.

23. You can decide how far away from the camera the focused portion of the image should be.

24. Look at the **Layers** controls in the **3D View** header. The Sky is in Layer 10. Press *Shift+LMB* over Layer 10 so that Layer 10 is no longer visible.

25. Press *Shift+LMB* twice over Layer 11 to make it the active layer. Layer 11 has the cameras.

26. With the cursor over the left-hand **3D View** window, press *Numpad 7* and use *Ctrl+MMB* and *Shift+MMB* to center on **Camera.Depth of Field** and the house. Move the cursor to where you want the center of the focused area to be. Press the *LMB* to put the 3D cursor there.

27. Once again, if you want to zoom in, you can press *Shift+B* and then use the marquee to select the area that you want to zoom into.

28. With the cursor over the **3D View** window, press *N* to bring up the 3D View **Properties** panel. In the **3D Cursor** subpanel, set the **Z** value to **10**.

29. Press *Shift+A* and select **Empty** from the drop-down menu.

30. Press *S*, *20*, and *Enter*.

31. Select the **Object** button in the **Properties** window header. It's the fifth button from the left.

32. Name the Empty, **Empty.Defocus**.

33. Select **Camera.Depth of Field** in the **3D View** window with the *RMB*, or select it in the **Outliner** window.

34. Select the **Object Data** button in the **Properties** window header. It's the seventh button from the left with the movie camera.

35. In the **Depth of Field** subpanel, below **Focus:**, there is an input box with an image of a cube, as shown in the following screenshot. Click on it and select **Empty.Defocus** from the pop-up menu. If you do not see the name, scroll the mousewheel to see other names or start typing the name into the input box.

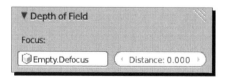

36. Press *F12* to render the scene. Press *Esc* when you have finished looking at it. Move the Empty, closer to the camera or farther away, and press *F12* to re-render the image. Notice the changes.

37. Save the file to a unique name.

What just happened?

Defocusing is how Blender overcomes the difference between the 3D animation camera and a real camera. A real camera is not able to keep everything in focus, but this lets the camera operator decide what the viewer should pay attention to, by giving certain portions of the image less detail.

You set up a shot and rendered it. Then you took your first look at Blender's post-processing capability by opening up the **Node Editor**. By default, when you add nodes in the compositing mode as you did, you get a **Render Layers** node and a **Composite** node. You disconnected them and inserted a **Defocus** node in between. The **Defocus** node uses the Z axis information that it gets from the camera to decide how much to blur any particular part of the image.

The smaller the hole the aperture creates, the less light there is and the longer the shutter has to stay open to get a proper exposure. The longer the shutter is open, the more detail the film can capture, so you get a greater subtlety of tones and colors and more of the image stays in focus. The larger the hole, the faster the light can expose the film, so less time is needed, but it doesn't get as much detail.

You cannot control the aperture directly, but you do it by adjusting the fStop. In a camera, the fStop is the ratio of the focal length divided by the diameter of the aperture. The aperture is the hole that lets light into the camera. The focal length was shown earlier in this chapter. So the larger the number of the fStop, the less light gets to the camera, and with the Defocus node, the less blurring there is. The smaller the number of the fStop the more light gets to the camera and the more blurring there is. You changed the fStop value from 128, down to 5 for a lot of blurring. It works out inversely, the smaller the fStop value, the more depth is blurred, the larger the fStop value, the less depth is blurred.

The Max Blur value sets how much that blurring will be.

Getting variety in your camera work

Unless you are *John Ford*, the director who was famous for using medium shots almost exclusively, so that the editors had to assemble a film just as he shot it, you will probably want to cover your scenes from a variety of distances to provide rhythm and improve the storytelling. There are three basic shots, long, medium, and close up. Anything that is not a close up or a long shot is a medium shot. The following images show a long shot and a medium shot.

Comparing long and medium shots

Long shots are usually used as an introduction to a film or scene. As seen on the left of the following image, they give the viewer the big picture. As a computer animator you are fortunate. You can place your camera anywhere without having to worry about how to hold it up.

The medium shot is a workhorse, often used for action shots. It is close enough to show what is going on, and also has enough room to show where that action is taking place as you can see in the following image on the right side:

Using close-up and two shots

A close up is used to focus the viewer's attention on the subject with little background. Often it may have only one character or a small object in it, as seen on the left side of the following image. A two shot is as it sounds, it has two people in it, as seen on the right. They can be close together or far apart. In *Forrest Gump*, when Forrest was on the park bench with the other characters, even though they sat on opposite ends of the bench, it was still a two shot.

Applying the rule of 180

The rule of 180 helps the viewer keep track of what is happening in a conversational scene. 180 refers to 180 degrees, or a half circle. You want to draw an imaginary line through the two people having a conversation. Then pick one side of that line to stay on. As you can see in the following two images, the camera is always on the side of the woman's left shoulder and always on the side of the man's right shoulder:

Using motion blur

Motion blur can be very effective for conveying motion and gives a more realistic feel to an animation. How much blurring is needed depends on the speed of the object and how close it is to the camera. As a director, you also have to decide what should get blurred; the object that you are interested in or the background. Here, I made an image of the sloop sailing past the pier. I chose to blur the background so that I could show that the woman was piloting the sloop. This also leads the viewer to the expectation that the sloop is the important thing in the shot and that the next shot will show you more about the sloop. If the sloop were blurred and the background still, we might expect that the sloop has sailed off and that next we will turn your attention back to what is happening on the island.

Have a go hero – using motion blur

Motion blur is different than the node based blurring that you just did. With node base blurring, you render a frame and then the node compositor blurs that particular frame and the blurring is based on how far away objects are from the camera.

It's important to remember that a frame of animation is not a single point in time. Rather, it spans a certain period of time, say 1/24th or 1/30th of a second. This is true if you are doing motion blur or not.

If you are not doing motion blur, the camera takes one sample at the starting time of the frame. If you are doing motion blur, then Blender takes a number of samples during the time period covered by that frame, renders them, and then merges them all back together.

There are two controls for sampled motion blur; **Motion Samples** and **Shutter**. The shutter is like a camera shutter. It may open up for the entire duration of the frame or part of the duration of the frame. The motion samples tells you how the time when the shutter is open is divided. If a frame is a whole cake, the shutter says how much of the cake is left, and the motion samples says how many pieces the remaining cake is cut into.

The following image shows you what happens in one frame. In this example, the motion samples are set to six. The shutter setting of 1.0 spreads the six samples evenly over the entire duration of the frame. With a 0.5 setting for the shutter, the six samples are taken from the first half of the duration of the shutter and no samples are taken from the second half. With the 0.75 shutter setting, the six samples are taken from the first three quarters of the duration of the frame and none from the last quarter of the frame.

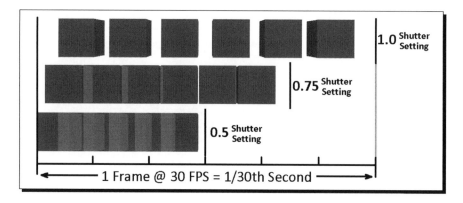

The first thing to do to use sampled motion blur is to deactivate the node based blurring in the **Node Editor**. Set the **fStop** in the **Defocus** node to **128** and set the **Max Blur** to **0**. With node based blurring, parts of the image are blurred based on distance from the camera. The sampled motion blur is based on time.

The sampled motion blur controls are simple. They are in the **Sampled Motion Blur** subpanel of the **Render** panel in the **Properties** window. The **Render** panel button is the second one on the left in the **Properties** window header. It has the still camera on it.

You set the **Motion Samples** button, seen in the next image, to the number of samples of the motion you want in each frame. A higher number will give you better blurring, but it will also take longer to render. If you set it to **1**, the frame will get a single rendering, but no blurring. If you set it to **6**, six samples from the time period covered by the frame will be rendered and then composited together. This is shown in the previous illustration. So it will take six times longer to render.

You can see the sampling in the previous image of the sloop. In the window frames and the overhang of the roof of the boathouse the six different samples are more obvious. But if this were a video and you could only see the image for 1/30 of a second, you might not notice. You'd just see blur.

The **Shutter:** button specifies how much of the time allotted to the frame the blurring covers. If the **Shutter:** is set at **0.500**, then the blurring occurs over half of the time allotted to the frame. The rest of the time of the frame is not recorded as seen in the previous image. From the previous example of the boxes, you might think that you always want a setting of **1.00** for **Shutter**, because it gives a more accurate view. But if you look at the image, you notice that at a setting of **1.00**, the boxes look less like they are blurred together because they do not overlap the way they do at the **Shutter** setting of **0.500**.

In *Chapter 6, Making and Moving the Oars* you learned how to track the boat with the camera.

You can turn the **Node Editor** window back to a **Timeline Editor** window. Now, choose something to move and move it. Set location keyframes for it at two times. Apply a motion blur to the render and see what results you get. Then track the object that is moving to see the background blurred. In the **Timeline** window, set the **End Frame** to the frame with your last keyframe.

Press *F12* to render. Play with the motion samples and the shutter settings and see how this affects what you see. You don't have to use the sloop. If you like, just open up Blender and move the default cube. Put a second object behind it as background.

Planning your animation and making sure it comes out right

You've learned a lot and now it's time to complete your project by animating a scene. You've learned to make keyframes, you've learned how to move objects, how to parent them, and how to change which editors are in which windows. You've studied how to plan an animation and how to time it. You know a lot!

Storyboarding your ideas

First you need an idea. I started off with a question; what if the island got invaded by Viking raiders? I wondered what would be my initial reaction when I discovered what was happening. The following is the storyboard I drew:

Have a go hero – making your storyboard

You can use your island or `6907_11_Blender Island.blend` from the download pack. I made a Viking boat, `6907_11_Viking ship_subsurface.blend` that can be modified, or `6907_11_Viking ship_mesh.blend` which has been turned into a mesh already. Use the sloop, any buildings, or just the haunted boat and the lagoon as we talked about in *Chapter 7, Planning your Work, Working your Plan*.

Laying out your animation

Now that you've got your animation planned, it's time to get back into Blender and lay it out. For me, the first question was what kind of lens should I use for my camera; wide angle, telephoto, or...? I figured that I was trying to represent the hero of the animation, so choosing a camera that shows what a person would see was the best idea. I selected a 55 MM lens. Then it occurred to me that the door to the house was still a part of the house, so I had to go into **Edit Mode**, select the right vertices, press *P* to make them a separate object, and put the pivot point at where the hinges should be.

I took my stopwatch and timed out my reactions. I allowed 22 frames for the explosion sound, 5 frames to run across the room, 3 frames of pause while, out of frame, I supposedly reach for the doorknob, 10 frames for the door to open, 9 frames of dollying the camera towards the boathouse as though I stepped out through the door, and then I rotated the camera over to the boat, ending at frame 70.

I set the sloop adrift, moving it a bit away from the dock and rotating it a little over 90 degrees, starting at frame 1 and ending at frame 120. Then I realize that the main sail should be swinging and the rudder should be flattened to the hull as the boat drifts sideways. I remember that we spent time making the rudder swing along the angle of the hull, so I used the local rotations to get that to work.

The Viking ship is easy. Just lay it out behind the boat house and make a keyframe at the start of the animation. Then move it so it is almost past the breakwater at the end of the animation. Then find the time when it will come closest to the end of the pier, put in a location keyframe so it misses the pier and a rotation keyframe so the Viking ship rotates as it makes the turn.

Have a go hero – laying out the rough animation

Now it's your turn. You can do something like what I'm doing, or go with your own idea. You may find that doing the animation takes more intense use of the 3D View and that two 3D View windows are good to have.

Some things that may help you are:

- Have only the layers you need turned on
- *Right arrow* and *Left arrow* keys go one frame in the **Timeline** or **Graph Editor**
- *Shift+Up arrow* and *Shift+Down arrow* keys go 10 frames
- *Up arrow* and *Down arrow* go to the next keyframe of the active object

Proofing your work

There are four ways to proof your work before doing a full render:

- ◆ You can do a preview
- ◆ You can do a hardware render without textures
- ◆ You can render just a portion of the frame
- ◆ You can tailor your rendering settings to make a quick render

Doing a preview

Once you have the rough animation laid out, it's easy to check your work. Putting the mouse over the 3D View and pressing *Alt+A* is the easiest way. You learned about it in *Chapter 3, Controlling the Lamp, the Camera, and Animating Objects*. You can do it with the **Viewport Shading** set to **Wireframe** or **Solid**. It will play more slowly and erratically the first time it loops through the animation. Watch it several times. Press *Esc* when you are done viewing the proof.

Using hardware rendering to see the motion

Hardware rendering uses advanced OpenGL commands to do a fast render without materials and textures. One unusual thing about this method of rendering is that it is window-based, not camera-based. The normal Blender render always renders what the active camera sees. The hardware render renders whatever is in the active window. One problem though, is that not all computers can do this kind of rendering. If your computer will not, you must load a newer version of OpenGL.

Have a go hero – doing a hardware render

There are two buttons that control hardware rendering. They are on the right end of the 3D View header. Clicking on the camera symbol, as shown in the following screenshot, renders a single frame. Clicking on the clapboard symbol, as shown in the following screenshot, renders an animation.

If your computer cannot do this, Blender will display the error message **Failed to create OpenGL offscreen buffer, unknown**.

- ◆ Try out doing a hardware rendering from different 3D View windows
- ◆ Try rendering a single image or animation from a camera 3D View window
- ◆ To see the rendering, just press *Ctrl+F11*

Inspecting details by rendering only part of the frame

You can save time by not rendering the entire image if you only need to check a part of it.

Have a go hero – rendering only part of the frame

It's pretty easy to render only part of the frame.

Get a camera view in the 3D View window. Press *Shift+B* and use the marquee like the standard border select to choose a portion of the frame in the camera image area. Then press *F12* to render it. To return to rendering the entire window, press *Shift+B* and select the entire camera image area in the 3D View window. It will not change your camera settings if you select some of the passepartout area, you will just get the full camera image.

Glimpsing what the animation will look like with the quick render

You also need to take a peek at the lighting and the textures. You have a couple of options; render selected frames, or do a test rendering of the animation as we did in *Chapter 3, Controlling the Lamp, the Camera, and Animating Objects*. Doing a test rendering of the animation is good. Just press *Ctrl+F12*.

After rendering about two frames though, you may begin to wonder how long it will take to do the whole render. The first frames took about two minutes. Not too bad, but wait... two minutes times 300 frames equals 10 hours of rendering.

So what can you do to make the rendering time shorter?

Time for action – reducing render times

The basic idea here is reducing the work load. You want to turn off everything that you don't need:

1. Move the mouse over the **Timeline** window and go to the **Current Editor type** button in the lower-left corner of the window.

2. Select **Text Editor** from the menu as you learned in *Chapter 9, Finishing your Sloop*.

3. Select **Text** in the **Text Editor** header and choose **Create Text Block** from the pop-up menu.

4. In the **Properties** window header, select the **Render** button. It's the button with the still camera on it, second button from the left.

5. In the **Dimensions** subpanel make sure that the **Resolution:** percentage is no higher than **25%**.

6. In the **Text Editor**, type **Reduced resolution from 100% to 25%**.

7. In the **Properties** window, **Dimensions** subpanel set the value of **Frame Step:** under **Frame Range:** to **2**.

8. Select the **Frame Rate:** button and choose **Custom**.

9. Select the button that says **FPS: 24** and input **12**.

10. In the **Text Editor**, type **Changed Step from 1 to 2, reduced Frame Rate from 24 to 12**.

11. In the **Properties** window, **Anti-Aliasing** subpanel, uncheck the **Anti-Aliasing** checkbox.

12. In the **Text Editor**, type **Unchecked Anti-Aliasing**.

13. If you had the **Sampled Motion Blur** checked, uncheck it and note that in the **Text Editor**.

14. In the **Properties** window, **Shading** subpanel, uncheck the **Shadows**, **Subsurface Scattering** and **Ray Tracing** checkboxes.

15. In the **Text Editor**, type **Unchecked Shadows, Subsurface Scattering and Ray Tracing**.

16. In the **Properties** window, **Performance** subpanel, change the number of **Tiles:** from **8** to **1**.

17. In the **Text Editor**, type **Changed Tiles: 8 to 1**.

18. Save the file to a unique name.

19. Press *Ctrl+F12* to do your test render.

20. When the render is done, press *Ctrl+F11* to watch the animation. If it doesn't play, make sure you have a video player installed as shown in *Chapter 3, Controlling the Lamp, the Camera, and Animating Objects*.

21. Save the file to a unique name.

What just happened?

You conquered quite a hurdle there. What started out as a 10 hour render for 300 frames, ended up taking only 15 minutes and you still got a fairly good representation of what was going on. First, you cut the area rendered to 25 percent of the original size. That cut out 75 percent of the work. The other big thing you did was to render only every other frame and change the frame rate from 24 fps to 12 fps so it will play at the right speed.

That cut down half of the remaining work. So already the work is reduced to 12.5 percent of the original. It also means the animation player can play the animation more easily. Then you turned off a lot of the functions that take up computing time. You removed Anti-Aliasing which makes transitions between pixels smoother. You removed the shadows, subsurface scattering, and ray tracing which all make the final image look better, but aren't needed now.

After you have done all your testing and experimenting and have the animation the way you want it, use the text in the Text Editor to guide you in putting all the settings back to what they were and do the final quality render.

Have a go hero – testing the effect of changing the number of tiles on Rendering speed

Because you are simplifying your render, you turned the number of tiles down to the minimum for speed. Ironically, the usual rule of thumb for getting faster rendering performance is to use more tiles. But from the testing I did, when settings were simplified, a single tile gave the best results.

Once you have all the settings returned to quality levels, do some test renders of individual frames with different numbers of tiles. Use settings of **1**, **2**, **4**, **8**, **16**, or **32** tiles. There is a readout of how long the frame took to render at the top of the **UV/Image Editor** window.

Reducing render times

The following are some sites with good tips on reducing rendering times:

`http://www.blenderguru.com/13-ways-to-reduce-render-times`

`http://www.youtube.com/watch?v=mbZ4PG135FM`

Have a go hero – proofing the animation

After you have your animation finished, do a test render, either a preview, a hardware render, or a quick render. What do you think needs improvement? Write it down.

Making corrections

Well, congratulations, well done! Nobody makes a perfect animation the first time. But the changes you implement will make it better.

You have four basic tools to work with the animation:

+ **3D View window**: It is used to reposition objects and create location, rotation, and scaling keyframes

+ **Timeline window**: It helps you maneuver through the animation timeline

+ **Graph Editor window**: It is good for adjusting the transitions between keyframes by modifying the control points and the control handles as you learned to do in *Chapter 3, Controlling the Lamp, the Camera, and Animating Objects*

+ **Dope Sheet window**: It is the best tool for changing the timing of keyframes

You've studied the first three types of Blender Editors, now it's time for an introduction to the Dope Sheet editor.

Time for action – using the Dope Sheet

You've studied the other three windows, and now we'll look at the Dope Sheet in a little more detail.

The Dope Sheet is descended from the animation timing sheets used by early animators that we talked about in *Chapter 7, Planning your Work, Working your Plan*. You can move, subtract, and add keyframes, but unlike the Graph Editor, you have no control of the Bezier Curves that control the motion. The window controls are the same as the Graph Editor controls that you studied in *Chapter 3, Controlling the Lamp, the Camera, and Animating Objects*:

1. Open the file that you created when you compared dollying the camera to changing the field of view.

2. In the 3D View, select the camera you dollyied into the scene. Move the cursor over the **Timeline Editor** window and go to the **Current Editor type** button in the lower-left corner of the window and click on it.

3. Select **Dope Sheet** from the menu.

4. Move the cursor to the border between the **Dope Sheet** and the **3D View** window next to it. Get the double-headed arrow, press down the *LMB* and use the mouse to make the **Dope Sheet Editor** larger.

5. You will see columns of diamonds on different layers as shown in the following screenshot. They are the keyframes.

6. Press *Ctrl+MMB* and use the mouse to spread the keyframes apart and closer together.

7. Press the *MMB* and use the mouse to move the keyframes left and right, up and down.

8. In the **Dope Sheet** header, press the arrow that is to the left of the ghost. Press it again and see how the channels displayed change. Press it until it only displays the keyframes of **Camera.Dolly**.

9. Select the triangle next to **Location**, so that the **X Location**, **Y Location**, and **Z Location** channels become visible.

10. Press *A* to deselect all of the keyframes. The diamonds will become white.

11. Press *B* and use the cursor to select the **Y Location** keyframe and the **Z Location** keyframe on frame 20, as shown in the following screenshot:

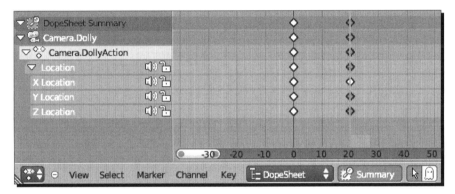

12. Press *Shift+D* to copy the keyframes and use the mouse to drag them to frame 30.

13. Press the *RMB* and select the **Y Location** keyframe at frame 30.

14. Press *G* and move the keyframe to frame 10. Press the *LMB* to release the move.

15. Select the **Current Frame Indicator** with the *LMB*. Scroll it backwards and forwards, see how moving the keyframe has affected the camera motion.

16. Press the *RMB* and select the **Z Location** keyframe at frame 30.

17. Press *X* and delete the keyframe. Choose **Delete Keyframes** from the pop-up menu.

18. Move the **Current Frame Indicator** to a frame without keyframes and press *I*. Choose **Only Selected Channels** from the pop-up menu. You've made a new keyframe.

19. You can use *Ctrl+Z* if you didn't want those changes.

What just happened?

You were introduced to the Dope Sheet. The Dope Sheet comes in handy because many times, if you have to adjust a keyframe, it's just a matter of moving the keyframe to a different frame, not changing the value of the keyframe at that frame. You also saw, when you scrubbed the animation with the Current Frame Indicator, that just moving the keyframe to a different frame can have dramatic results.

You played around with the Dope Sheet controls, so you know that they are very similar to the controls for other windows such as the **Graph Editor** window.

You may have noticed that when you copied a keyframe and moved it, there was a bar between the two diamonds. This indicates that the values of the two keyframes are the same.

Have a go hero – making corrections

One of the problems I noted when I rendered my scene was that the camera stayed on the boathouse too long. I also found that the Viking ship started too late, and you needed to be able to see a little of it as the hero runs out. I resolved the camera move by deleting some of the keyframes in the Dope Sheet to make the motion smoother. I needed to move the Viking boat closer to the shore. To do so, you can redo the keyframe in the 3D View and then move the timing of the keyframe in the Dope Sheet.

When making changes to the keyframes in the 3D View, it's good to use the keyboard commands to navigate in the timeline, rather than dragging the **Current Frame Indicator** when modifying keyframes. This way, you land exactly on the keyframe. Using the **Current Frame Indicator** could land you part of the way through a frame and you could make two keyframes in one frame, half a frame apart. It also ensures that all your keyframes are right on the frame, timewise, and this will make better looking animations.

So go to it. Look at your test animation, analyze how you can improve it, and play with the keyframes. It's an iterative cycle, change, preview, and repeat. Once you have gotten all the changes done, go back and, using your text file as a guide, undo all the changes you made for rendering and make a nice final version.

Key	Function
Ctrl+MMB	Using the mouse in the Dope Sheet, zooms in or out on a range of keyframes.
MMB	Using the mouse in the Dope Sheet, it allows you to pan the range of keyframes that are displayed.
Ctrl+MMB	Using the mouse in the Node Editor, it zooms in or out on the Node Editor window.
MMB	Using the mouse in the Node Editor, it allows you to pan the Node Editor window.
LMB	When holding down the LMB in the Node Editor you can move nodes with the mouse.

Key	Function
B	In the Dope Sheet, it lets you do a border select of keyframes.
RMB	In the Dope Sheet, it lets you select a single keyframe.
Shift+D	In the Dope Sheet, it lets you copy keyframes.
G	In the Dope Sheet, it lets you move selected keyframes.
X	In the Dope Sheet, it lets you delete selected keyframes.
I	In the Dope Sheet, it allows you to create a keyframe on the current frame.
LMB	In the Dope Sheet, it allows you to change the current frame.
Shift+B	In the 3D View and the UV/Image editor, it allows you to do a border select and zoom in to the area selected.
Shift+B	In the 3D View camera view, it allows you to select a portion of the image to render.

Summary

Well, you learned a lot, how to use a standard three point lighting system and lots of variations on it. You experimented with falloff and got the control you need to highlight the action with light and put the rest into the shadows. You studied camera work, discovering how to use wide-angle, normal, and telephoto lenses. You also created an animation and practiced making modifications and test renders.

In the next chapter you will focus on rendering and compositing. With compositing you'll learn how to use the Video Sequence Editor to edit your animation for best effects. You'll also revisit the Node Editor and learn how to create stereoscopic 3D as well as check out using the new Cycles renderer that doesn't even need lamps.

Let's go!

12

Rendering and Compositing

In the previous chapter you learned a lot about lighting; how to use a standard three point lighting system and lots of variations on it. You learned to use light to control what the viewer sees. You practiced using wide-angle, normal, and telephoto lenses. You also created an animation and practiced making modifications and test renders.

In this chapter you will focus on rendering and compositing. You will:

- ◆ Edit scenes created on the island to tell a story using the Video Sequence Editor
- ◆ Combine the stereographic views into a single 3D animation using the Node Editor
- ◆ Discover how to optimize your animations with the rendering controls
- ◆ Discover how using the Cycles renderer instead of the Blender Internal renderer can improve and alter your 3D rendering and animation

Let's get started!

Preparing for Chapter 12

You will need the following files for your work in this chapter:

- ◆ Copy `6907_12_Fields.blend` from your download pack into your `Chapter 12/Blender Files` directory
- ◆ Copy `Flashbang-Kibblesbob-899170896.mp3` in the `Audio` directory to your `Chapter 12/Audio directory`

◆ Copy `6907_12_31.png` from your download pack, into your `Chapter 12/Images` file

◆ Copy the entire `Images/Video Strips` directory from your download pack to the `Chapter 12/Images/Video Strips` directory for this chapter on your computer

◆ Get yourself a pair of red/cyan stereo glasses

Getting Red/Cyan glasses for the price of postage

If you do not have a pair of Red/Cyan glasses you can get them for the price of postage at `http://www.3dglassesonline.com/contact/free-sample-request`.

You can also buy them at `amazon.com` for a little more. Just search for anaglyph glasses.

Editing with the Video Sequence Editor

The Video Sequence Editor is similar to many standard video editors. It has channels to put video or audio strips in and allows you to mix them and create some special effects.

Time for action – dissolving with the Video Sequence Editor

Now, you're going to lay in an audio track and two video tracks, and then do a dissolve between the video tracks:

1. Open a new file in Blender.

2. In the **Dimensions** subpanel of the **Properties** window, set the **Resolution:** to **X: 512, Y: 512**, and **100%**.

3. In the Blender window header, in the seventh button from the left, just to the left of where it says **Default**, click on the button with the three boxes and choose **Video Editing** from the drop-down menu as shown in the following screenshot:

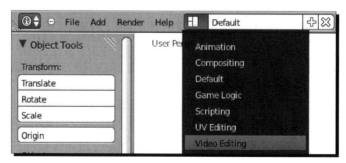

4. In the Video Editing layout, there are four windows; a **Graph Editor** window on the upper left; a **Video Sequence Editor** on the upper right, set to display the Video; a **Video Sequence Editor** in the middle row set to display the video strips; and a **Timeline** window on the bottom as shown in the following screenshot:

5. In the header of the **Video Sequence Editor – sequencer** window, in the middle, click on the **Add** button and choose **Movie** from the pop-up menu.

6. Find the `Chapter 12/Images/Video Strips/` directory in your download pack and select `Cam1_6907_12_0001-0300.avi` with the *LMB*.

7. Click on the **Add Movie Strip** button in the upper-right corner of the window.

8. Now there is a blue bar in the **Video Sequence Editor – sequencer** window. Drag the **Current Frame Indicator** over the bar and you will see the animation in the upper **Video Sequence Editor** window as shown in the following screenshot. `Cam1` shows what the observer on land sees of the scene.

9. Click on **View** in the **Video Sequence Editor – sequencer** window header. Uncheck **Show Seconds** in the pop-up menu. Now it displays the frame numbers.

10. Add the movie `Cam2_6907_12_0001-0300.avi`, from the `Chapter 12/Images/ Video Strips/` directory. They show the view from the Viking ship. Load them into the **Video Sequence Editor**, the way you loaded the first strip, to make a second strip.

11. Now click on **Add** and choose **Sound** from the pop-up menu, then select the audio strip named `Flashbang-Kibblesbob-899170896.wav` in `Chapter 12/Audio/`. Press the **Add Sound Strip** button in the upper-right corner of the window.

12. Now you have to do some things that you did in *Chapter 7, Planning your Work, Working your Plan* when you timed the animation to the music. In the **Timeline** window at the bottom, select **Playback** on the header and check the checkbox next to **Audio Scrubbing** from the top of the pop-up menu as seen in the following screenshot.

13. In the **Video Sequence Editor – sequencer** window, on the right side, is the **Properties** panel. Press *N* if you don't see it. Scroll down to the **Sound** subpanel and check the **Caching** checkbox to load the sound into RAM for smooth playback and check the **Draw Waveform** checkbox. You can now see the waveform in the audio channel.

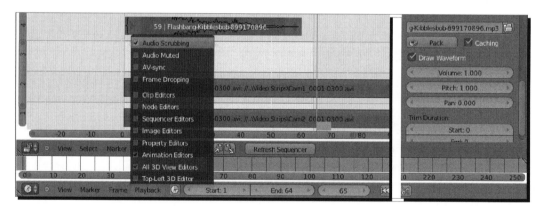

14. Move the cursor over the audio strip, press the *RMB* and hold it down to drag the audio strip to the fourth channel. Move the strip to the left so its left side is at frame 1. Press the *LMB* to release the strip.

15. Move the **Cam1** strip to Channel 3.

16. Move the **Cam2** strip to Channel 1 and put its left side at frame 1. Press the *LMB* to release the move.

17. Move the **Cam1** strip to Channel 2. Put its left side at frame 1.

18. Select the **Current Frame Indicator** with the *LMB* and scrub it back and forth with the mouse.

19. Watch the **Video Sequence Editor – preview** window as you press the *H* key to mute the **Cam1** strip. With the strip muted, its image is no longer displayed. Now as you scroll the **Current Frame Indicator**, you'll only see the **Cam2** strip in the **Video Sequence Editor – preview** window, not the **Cam1** strip above it.

20. In the **Timeline Editor** window header, set the **End:** button to **64**.

21. Press *Alt+A* to preview the beginning of your video. Press *Esc* when you have watched and listened to it several times.

22. If you cannot see to the left of frame 0, there is a light gray scroll bar on the bottom of the **Video Sequence Editor** that you can move to display different frames. Put the cursor over the scroll bar, press the *LMB* and use the mouse to move it.

23. Select the **Cam2** strip in **Channel 1** with the *RMB*.

24. Look in the **Video Sequence Editor Properties** panel. In the **Edit Strip** subpanel you will see buttons that confirm that you are working in **Channel: 1** and this strip has a **Start Frame:** of **1**.

25. Press *G, X,* and use the mouse to move the left side of the **Cam2** strip in Channel 1 to frame -3. Look in the **Video Sequence Editor Properties** panel for feedback on which frame the strip starts at. Press the *LMB* to release the move.

26. Press *Alt+A* to preview the beginning of your video. Press *Esc* when you have watched and listened to it several times. It's just three frames, but the ship seems to move in reaction to the blast now.

27. Use the scroll bar to move the display to frame 300. On the right side of the **Cam2** strip there is an arrow button. Click the *RMB*; hold it down till you start moving, then move that end to the left until the numerical indicator just above the arrow button says **58**. Press the *LMB* to release it.

28. Move the **Current Frame Indicator** to frame **47**, either dragging it in the **Video Sequence Editor** window or typing **47** in directly in the **Current Frame** button in the **Timeline** header.

29. Select the **Cam1** video strip in Channel 2 with the *RMB*. Press *Alt+H* to unmute the **Cam1** video strip. Then, press the *RMB* and hold it down while you begin moving it. Move it so the left side of the strip is at frame 47. Press the *LMB* to release it.

30. Click on the **Cam2** video strip in Channel 1 with the *RMB*. Then click on the **Cam1** video strip in Channel 2 with *Shift+RMB* to select them both.

31. In the **Video Sequence Editor** header, select **Add** then choose **Effect Strip** and **Cross** from the pop-up menus. The **Effect Strip** will appear in the overlap between the **Cam2** and **Cam1** strips as seen in the following screenshot.

32. Select the **Current Frame Indicator** and scrub across the time with the **Cross** strip to see the transition between the two strips.

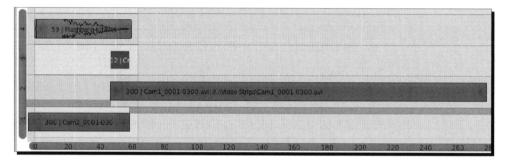

What just happened?

This is an easy method to select two video strips and put a dissolve between them. When adding an effect strip, the order that the strips are chosen in is important. In creating a dissolve, you must choose the strip that is being dissolved from first and the strip that is being dissolved into second. If the dissolve does not behave properly, you can also try changing the **Blend** mode in the Video Sequence Editor's **Properties** panel from **Replace** to **Cross** and back to **Replace**. That should reset it properly.

Editorially, the big trick here is that when the Cam1 and Cam2 strips were rendered, they actually started on the same frame, but in editing they have been staggered 50 frames. Although not literally accurate, this staggering serves to tell the story better.

Changing the Video Sequence Editor resolution

When you edit a video, you should set the **Resolution: X:** and **Y:** of your video in the **Dimensions** subpanel of the **Render** panel in the **Properties** window. Usually this might be a setting for TV, HD, or web banner. However, on some people's computers, Blender will only show an image in the Video Sequence Editor if the dimensions of the rendering resolution are powers of two; that is, **2**, **4**, **8**, **16**, **32**, **64**, **128**, **256**, **512**, **1024**, **2048**, and so on. If you have that problem, you can use the **Video Sequence Editor** at one of these power-of-two settings so you can see what is happening. Then when you are ready to render the video out you can change the rendering resolution to that of the original images. These videos were made at 512x512 just to avoid causing anyone problems.

Time for action – editing individual video strips

Now that you've gotten some video laid into the Video Sequence Editor, you'll discover how to do some soft Trims and dissolves to assemble them:

1. In the **Video Sequence Editor**, move the **Current Frame Indicator** to frame 148.

2. Select the **Cam2** video strip in Channel 1. Press *Shift+D* to make a copy. Move the copy to Channel 5.

3. Note that on the right-hand side of the new strip, there is a solid blue bar at the top, as shown in the following screenshot:

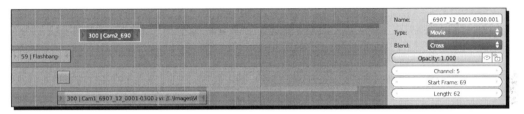

4. Use the *Ctrl+MMB* keys to scale the **Video Sequence Editor** window so you can see the entire strip and/or the blue bar.

5. On the right side of the **Cam2** strip there is an arrow button. Click the *RMB* over the arrow button on the right-hand side of the strip, hold it down while you start moving the mouse, then move that end to the right until it is even with the end of the blue bar. The bar will disappear when you reach the end. Press the *LMB* to release it.

6. In the **Video Sequence Editor**, **Properties** panel, **Strip Input** subpanel note the **Trim Duration (soft)** buttons. A soft Trim starts or ends a strip by hiding any frames beyond the Trim point, a hard Trim cuts the frames off. So if you think you might want to make changes at a later point use the soft Trim.

7. Click the *RMB* on the arrow button on the left-hand side of the strip, hold it down till you start moving, then move that end to the right until the **Trim Duration (soft)** button reads **Start: 71** as shown in the following screenshot. Press the *LMB* to release it.

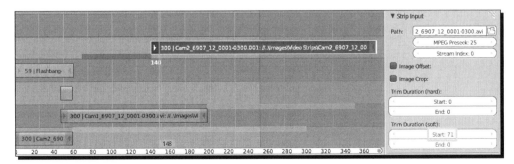

8. If you cannot get frame 71 exactly, press the *LMB* to stop changing the Trim Duration and use the *Ctrl+MMB* and *Shift+MMB* to zoom in and pan the **Video Sequence Editor** window, then resume changing the **Trim Duration:**.

9. In the **Properties** panel of the **Video Sequence Editor**, move the scroll bar up so you can see the **Edit Strip** subpanel. Note the **Length** button.

10. Click the *RMB* on the arrow button on the right-hand side of the strip, hold it down till you start moving, then move that end to the right until the **Length** button reads **90**. Press the *LMB* to release it.

11. Move the **Current Frame Indicator** to frame **148**.

12. Select the strip in its centre with the *RMB*. Press *G, X,* and move the strip so that the left-hand side of the strip is at frame **148** as shown in the following screenshot. Press the *LMB* to release it.

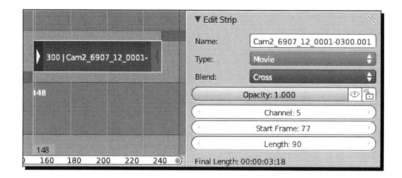

13. Press *Shift+Up Arrow* twice, then press the *Right Arrow* key once to move the **Current Frame Indicator** by 21 frames.

14. Select the right end of **Cam1** in Channel 2 with the *RMB* and move it so the strip ends at the **Current Frame Indicator**. Press the *LMB* to release the movement.

15. Select **Cam2** in Channel 5 with the *Shift+RMB* so that the strips in Channel 2 and 5 are both selected.

16. In the **Video Sequence Editor** header, select **Add** then choose **Effect Strip** and **Cross** from the pop-up menus.

17. Your channels should look like the following screenshot:

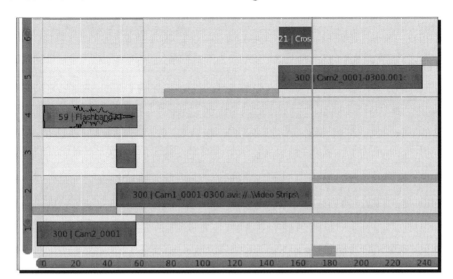

18. In the **Timeline** window header, set the **End:** value to **238**. Press *Alt+A* to preview the animation.

What just happened?

You learned how to trim video segments by modifying the length of the strip in the channel. And you now have an edited scene. Congratulations!

This part of the scene was done with just simple cuts, two strips of video, and a cross dissolve. But it tells the story. And if you watch carefully, with the camera pan and the motion of the Viking boat, the land always appears to be moving right to left, so your eye follows the flow motion from strip to strip.

Time for action – using K and Shift+K to make your trims

In addition to adjusting the ends of your strips you can use the *K* and *Shift+K* commands to shorten your film strips. The command is easy to remember, just think of the knife for cutting the strips:

1. Select the **Cam1** video strip in Channel 2. Press *Shift+D* to make a copy. Move the copy to Channel 7.

2. In the **Video Sequence Editor** header, select **Strip**. Choose **Clear Strip Offset** from the pop-up menu.

3. Scroll the **Current Frame Indicator**, move it with the mouse, and watch the **Video Sequence Editor – preview** window. Scroll until you see the Viking ship emerge from behind the pier and the last shield is visible. You can use the *Ctrl+MMB* to zoom into the preview window if you can't see the shields on the Viking boat.

4. Press *K* to do a soft Trim. Select the strip to the left of the **Current Frame Indicator** and press *X* to delete it.

5. Move the **Current Frame Indicator** to frame 227.

6. Move the strip so that the left-hand side of the strip is at frame 227. Once you start it moving, press the *MMB* to restrict the motion to that channel.

7. Scroll the **Current Frame Indicator** until you see the Viking ship touch the sloop in the **Cam1** strip in Channel 7.

8. Select the **Cam2** strip in Channel 5. Press *Shift+D* to duplicate it. Move it to Channel 8.

9. In the **Video Sequence Editor** header, select **Strip**. Choose **Clear Strip Offset** from the pop-up menu.

10. In the **Properties** panel of the **Video Sequence Editor**, scroll to the **Edit Strip** subpanel and set the **Opacity:** button to about **0.500**.

11. Press the *RMB* to start moving the strip within the channel. Press the *MMB* to lock the motion to that channel.

12. Move the strip until you see the bow of the sloop pointing right at you in the **Video Sequence Editor – preview** window. Press the *LMB* to release the strip.

13. Press *Shift+K* to do a hard Trim.

14. Select the portion of the strip to the left of the **Current Frame Indicator** with the *RMB*. Press *X* to delete it.

15. Select the portion of the strip to the right of the **Current Frame Indicator** with the *RMB*. In the **Properties** panel of the **Video Sequence Editor**, scroll to the **Edit Strip** subpanel and set the **Opacity:** button to **1.000**.

16. If you want, you can see what happens when you do a hard Trim. Press the *RMB* on the left side of the strip and move it left. It gets longer, but if you scrub the **Current Frame Indicator**, because it is a hard Trim, there are no more frames. Press *Ctrl+Z* a couple of times to put the strip back the way it was.

17. Move the **Current Frame Indicator** until you see the sloop centered between the last two shields of the Viking ship.

18. Select the **Cam1** video strip in Channel 2. Press *Shift+D* to make a copy. Move the copy to Channel 9.

19. In the **Video Sequence Editor** header, select **Strip**. Choose **Clear Strip Offset** from the pop-up menu.

20. Begin to move the strip and press the *MMB* to keep the motion within the channel. Move the strip until the stern of the Viking ship disappears behind the sloop in the **Video Sequence Editor – preview** window. Press the *LMB* to release the strip.

21. Select the strips in Channel 8 and Channel 9.

22. Press *K*. Delete the left-side strip in Channel 9 and the right-side strip in Channel 8.

23. In the **Timeline** window header, set the **End:** to **440**.

24. Grab the right end of the **Cam1** strip in Channel 9 and drag it to frame 440 as shown in the following screenshot:

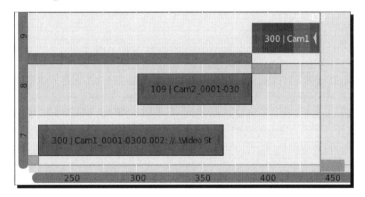

25. In the top row of the Blender window, select the button to the left of **Video Editing**. Select **Default** from the drop-down menu.

26. Click on the **Render** button in the **Properties** window header. It is the second button from the left, with the still camera on it.

27. In the **Output** subpanel, click on the folder symbol on the right side of the text input box. Find the `Chapter 12` directory on your computer. Give your output file a name. Click on the **Accept** button.

28. Click the button that says **PNG**, select **H.264** from the **Movie** menu.

29. In the **Encoding** subpanel, press the button next to **Format**. Set the format to **MPEG-4**. Select the button next to **Audio Codec:**. Set **Audio Codec:** to **MP3**.

30. If you are using a Mac, you should start with the **Quicktime** settings in the following table.

31. Press *Ctrl+F12* to render the sequence.

32. Save the file to a unique name.

33. The Blender video player does not support audio, so you will want to play the video on an external player or one of the players listed.

34. Everybody has different players on their computer. The following table has some different settings for different output types:

File Format	Format:	Codec:	Audio Codec:	Output Type	Player
MPEG	MPEG-4		MP3	`.mp4`	DivX
MPEG	Quicktime	MPEG-4	MP3	`.mov`	Quicktime
MPEG	H.264		MP3	`.avi`	Windows Media Player

What just happened?

You learned more ways to trim video segments using the *K* and *Shift+K* commands. You learned to do a soft Trim and manipulate the strip so you can use visual cues that tell you where to make a cut. You learned to expand a strip after doing a soft Trim so you can reuse a copy of it. You learned to use opacity to compare two strips at once. You learned to trim several strips with one *K* command. And you learned to set up to render a video with sound to an `.mp4`, `.mov`, or `.avi` file. As you may have guessed, you can select several strips and move them all at the same time, as you can move objects in the 3D View.

Making stereographic 3D with the Node Editor

You've already used the Node Editor when you created depth of field in the previous chapter. Now it's time to get a little bolder and use it to create stereographic 3D images which will use the Node Editor's ability to modify an image.

Since Red-Cyan anaglyph glasses are an inexpensive way to get the 3D separation when viewing an image, you are going to separate the images into a red image and a cyan image.

The stereographic images were created with the jonboat and oars that you made in Chapter 6, Making and Moving the Oars. They were recorded with a stereo rig adapted from the one you made in 6907OS_06_Using Stereoscopic Camerasl.pdf and then dropped into the world made in Chapter 10, Modeling Organic Forms, Sea, and Terrain.

Time for action – creating the red image for the left eye

You will now use the **Node Editor** to create the red channel which shows what the left camera recorded and what your left eye will see:

1. Open a new file in Blender.

2. In the **Dimensions** subpanel of the **Properties** window, set the **Resolution:** to **X: 512**, **Y: 512**, and **100%**. Set the **Frame Range: End:** to **64**. Click the **Frame Rate:** button. Select **Custom** from the drop-down menu. Set the **FPS:** to **12**.

3. In the top Blender window header, in the seventh button from the left, just to the right of **Default**, select the button with the three boxes and choose **Compositing** from the drop-down menu.

4. There are three windows, the **Node Editor** window on the top, the **UV/Image Editor** on the lower left, and the **3D View** on the lower right as shown in the following screenshot:

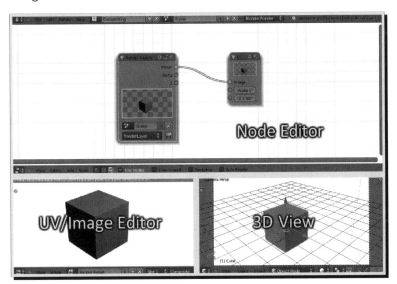

5. In the **Node Editor** window header, look at the three graphic buttons just to the right of the word **Node**. They select which Node tree type is active. Make sure the right most of the three buttons are highlighted as seen in the following screenshot. This is the Compositing: tree type. Check the **Use Nodes** checkbox as shown in the following screenshot. This creates the **Render Layer** and **Compositing** nodes.

6. In the **Node Editor** header, select **Add** and then choose **Input** then **Image** from the pop-up menus.

7. With either the *RMB* or the *LMB*, select the **Image** node you just created and hold the mouse button down while you move the node over to the upper left. Let up the mouse button to release the node. Put the cursor over the three diagonal lines in the lower-right corner of the node. Press and hold the *LMB* down and move the mouse to the right to enlarge the node.

8. Press the **Open** button at the bottom of the node and select the `boat_ stereo_6907_12_L_0001.png` file from the `Chapter 12/Images/Video Strips/` directory of your download pack. Press the **Open Image** button in the upper-right of the **File Browser** window.

9. There is now a **Source:** row in the node. Select the button that is labeled **Single Image**. Choose **Image Sequence** from the pop-up **Source** menu. Set the **Frames:** button to **64**.

10. If you need to zoom out of, or pan the **Node Editor** window, you can use the standard *Shift+MMB* and *Ctrl+MMB* commands.

11. Select the **Render Layers** node with the *RMB*. Press *X* to delete the node.

12. In the **Node Editor** header, select **Add** and choose **Color**, then select **RGB Curves** from the pop-up menus.

13. Move the new node between the **Image** node and the **Compositing** node.

14. Move the mouse over the yellow **Image** connector on the upper-right corner of the **Image** node. Press the *LMB* down and drag the connection to the **Image** connector on the lower-left corner of the **RGB Curves** node as shown in the center of the following screenshot.

15. Select the **Composite Node** with the *LMB*. Use the diagonal lines at the lower-right to make the node bigger.

16. Connect the yellow **Image** connector on the upper-right of the **RGB Curves** node to the yellow **Image** connector on the lower-left corner of the **Composite** node.

17. In the **RGB Curves** node, there are four buttons in the upper-left, labeled **C**, **R**, **G**, and **B**. Click on the **G** button. It controls the Green channel.

18. There is a diagonal line in the graph box below those buttons. Move the cursor over the upper-right corner of the diagonal line. Press the *LMB* and hold it down while you move the mouse down and drag the upper-right corner of the diagonal to the lower-right corner of the graph box so it disappears, as seen in the center of the following screenshot. Notice the color change in the **Composite** node.

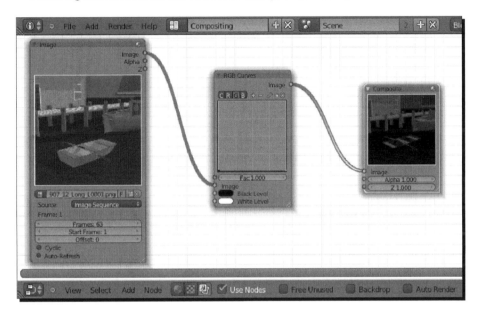

19. Click on the **B** button. It controls the Blue channel.

20. Drag the upper-right corner of the diagonal to the lower-right corner of the graph box as you did in the Green channel.

21. Note that in the **Composite** node, the image is now red as seen in the previous screenshot.

22. Save the file to a unique name.

What just happened?

You opened up Blender and chose the Compositing setup. Selecting **Use Nodes** displays the **Render Layer** and **Composite** nodes. The **Render Layer** node also links rendering and compositing.

You are not using the **Render Layer**, so its node was deleted. You loaded the images of the boat being rowed, based on the animations made in *Chapter 6, Making and Moving the Oars*. I fancied them up by dropping them into the island scene that was made in *Chapter 10, Modeling Organic Forms, Sea, and Terrain*, but the motion is the same.

You loaded in the first frame of the sequence for the left-eye view, and told Blender how many frames there were in the sequence. Then you added the **RGB Curves** node to process the images. The left channel is the Red channel. In the **RGB Curves** node, you modified the Green and Blue channels so that only the Red channel shows up. This can be seen in the **Composite** node.

Now it's time to make the Cyan channel. You will use a different method to change the image from color to a shade of cyan, but the end result is the same as the method you just did.

Time for action – making the right-eye view

This time, rather than adjust the levels of a particular channel, you will just remove the channel:

1. Zoom back in the **Node Editor** window to allow yourself some more room to work.

2. In the **Node Editor** header, select **Add** and choose **Input**, then select **Image** from the pop-up menus.

3. With the *LMB*, select the node you just created and hold the *LMB* down while you move the node over to the lower left. Let up the mouse button to release the node. Put the cursor over the three diagonal lines in the lower-right corner of the node, press and hold the *LMB* down and move the mouse to the right to enlarge the node.

4. Press the **Open** button and select the `boat_stereo_6907_12_R_0001.png` file from the `Chapter 12/Images/Video Strips/` directory of your download pack. Press the **Open Image** button in the upper right.

5. There is now a **Source:** row in the node you just made. Select the button that is labeled **Single Image**. Choose **Image Sequence** from the pop-up **Source** menu. Set the **Frames:** button to **64**.

6. In the **Node Editor** header, select **Add** and then choose **Convertor** and **Separate RGBA** from the pop-up menus. Move it below the **RGB Curves** node.

7. Move the mouse over the yellow **Image** connector on the upper-right corner of the **Image** node. Press the *LMB* down and drag the connection to the **Image** connector on the lower-left corner of the **Separate RGBA** node.

8. In the **Node Editor** header, select **Add** and choose **Convertor** and **Combine RGBA** from the pop-up menu. Move it to the right of the **Separate RGBA** node and between the **RGB Curves** and the **Composite** nodes, as seen in the screenshot after step 16.

9. Use the *Ctrl+MMB* and *Shift+MMB* controls to zoom into the **Separate RGBA** and **Combine RGBA** nodes.

10. Move the mouse over the **G** connector on the right-side of the **Separate RGBA** node. Press the *LMB* down and drag the connection to the **G** connector on the left side of the **Combine RGBA** node, as seen in the screenshot after step 16.

11. Move the mouse over the **B** connector on the right side of the **Separate RGBA** node. Connect it to the **B** connector on the left side of the **Combine RGBA** node, as seen in the screenshot after step 16.

12. Do not do this for the **R** connector or the **A** connector.

13. Zoom back out so you can see all of the nodes.

14. Look at the connection between the **RGB Curves** node and the **Composite** node. Move your mouse above the connector. Hold the *Ctrl* button and the *LMB* down, and you will see a knife cursor. With the buttons still held down, move the cursor across the connector to cut the connector, as shown in the following screenshot:

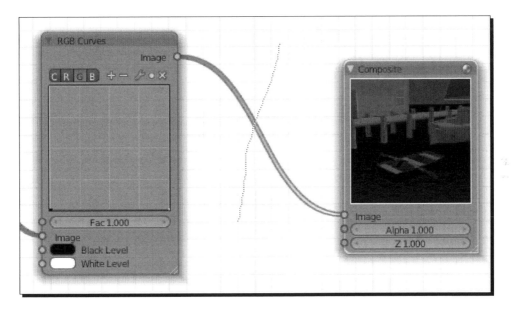

15. Connect the yellow **Image** connector on the upper-right of the **RGB Curves** node to the **R** connector on the upper-left corner of the **Combine RGBA** node as seen in the following screenshot.

16. Connect the yellow **Image** connector on the upper-right of the **Combine RGBA** node to the yellow **Image** connector on the lower-left corner of the **Composite** node as shown in the following screenshot:

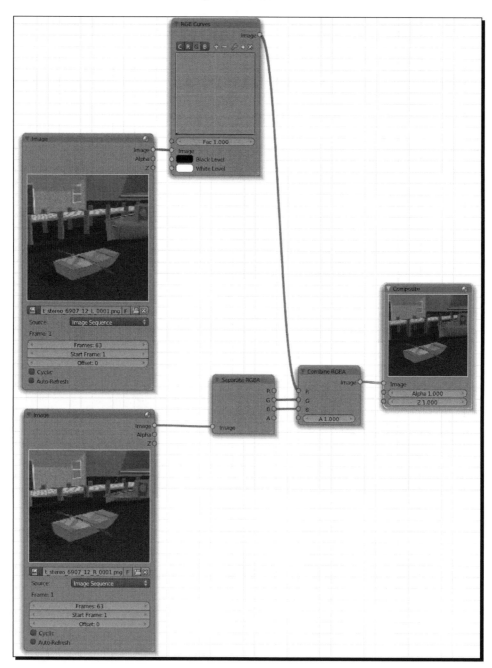

17. Press *F12*. In the **UV/Image Editor** you can see the composited image. Note that you can see how the two separate images are combined and the differences between the red and cyan channels; especially with the seats of the boat and the edges of the window of the building.

18. Save the file to a unique name.

19. Press *Ctrl+F12* and render the whole sequence.

20. When it's done, pop on your red/cyan glasses. Press *Ctrl+F11* and enjoy the animation.

What just happened?

You just composited an image with the Node Editor. The Red channel of the image was created with an RGB Curves node, and you turned the Green and Blue channels down to zero. The Cyan channel, Green plus Blue, was created with a Separate RGBA node, and the two were combined with a Combine RGBA node.

Alternatively, you could have created the Red channel by using a Separate RGBA node, or created the Cyan channel by using the RGB Curves node and turning the Red channel to zero instead of turning down the Green and Blue channels.

Have a go hero – making a cross-eye stereo image

Another way to do stereo viewing is the cross-eye stereo, like the image of the five Suzannes that we showed in *Chapter 6, Making and Moving the Oars*. You can make an animated version as well in the Video Sequence Editor.

1. Start by making a black graphic that is equal in size to both images together. For the two 512x512 images of the stereo pair, that would be a black graphic 1024x512 in size. You can use the image `6907_12_31.png` in the `Chapter 12/Images/` directory.

2. In the **Properties** window, set the resolution to 1024x512. Add the black graphic to **Channel 1** of the Video Sequence Editor.

3. Add the left-eye stereo images to **Channel 2**. The easiest way to select them is to press *B* and do a border select of the files you want. Move the left sides to frame 1 and drag the right side of **Channel 1** so it is as long as **Channel 2**.

4. Select **Channel 1** and then **Channel 2**. Add an **Effects Strip** of **Alpha Over** type and put it in **Channel 3**.

5. Add the right-eye stereo images to **Channel 4**. Check the **Image Offset** check box in the **Video Sequence Editor Properties** panel. Set the **X** offset to **512**.

6. Select **Channel 3** and then **Channel 4**. Add an **Effects Strip** of **Alpha Over** type and put it in **Channel 5**. In the timeline, set the end of the video to **63**.

7. In the **Render** panel of the **Properties** window, open the **Post Processing** subpanel and uncheck the **Compositing** checkbox. Leave the **Sequencer** checkbox checked.

8. Press *Ctrl+F12* to render a stereo animation. Then when it is rendered, press *Ctrl+F11*, sit back, cross your eyes, and watch.

9. Select **Channel 2** and in the Strip Input subpanel of the Video Sequence Editor Properties panel, check the Image Offset checkbox.

10. Save the Blender file to a unique name.

Rendering your animations

A right, you've made a scene, you've animated it, and done your fast test renders. You're ready for a final render.

Making your computer ready to render

The first thing to do when you are ready to render is open up your file manager, and make sure you have room on your computer to do it. I can't tell you how much room you'll need for a given project, and the rule of thumb is clear off as much space as you possibly can. It's a good time to save copies of all those projects you are no longer working on and then delete them from your hard drive. Back them up to:

◆ Data sticks, flash drives

◆ An external hard drive

◆ A CD or DVD

◆ Your storage on the Web

You may also want to use a program like CCleaner to clean up your computer's file registry and remove temporary files from browsers. Go into your Internet browser as well and manually delete the history if you don't have a program like that.

Use a defragmenting program to make sure that all your disk is as neat as possible and that the open spaces are as large as possible so Blender has room to move.

Making rendering more beautiful

In the last chapter, you turned off a lot of things to make the rendering faster. Now it's time to turn them back on if you need them. What do they do?

Using Anti-Aliasing for more beautiful renderings

Aliasing is a jagged line that happens at the edge between two faces when Blender tries to display them. **Anti-Aliasing** blurs this edge for a better look. It is pronounced "An Tea A Lee SS ing".

Time for action – displaying aliasing

The best way to understand aliasing is to see it:

1. Create a new file in Blender.

2. Press *F12*.

3. Press *Ctrl+MMB* and use the mouse to zoom into the rendered image so you can see only the corner of the cube closest to you. It should look like the following image on the left.

4. In the **Anti-Aliasing** subpanel of the **Properties** window, uncheck the **Anti-Aliasing** checkbox.

5. Press *F12*.

6. Now what you see looks like the right half of the image, with a jagged line where different surfaces meet.

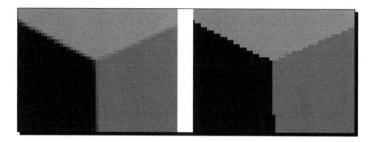

What just happened?

When you unchecked the **Anti-Aliasing** checkbox and rendered the cube, the three sides of the cube you could see were different shades, and the edge between them was jagged with no shading, as seen on the left. These jagged lines are called **Jaggies** and should be avoided. When you turned back on the Anti-Aliasing, the edges are less jagged, with lots of interim shades at the edges, as seen on the right. This looks cleaner to your eye, but it takes longer to render. That was why in previous chapter, you were instructed to turn off Anti-Aliasing to get quicker test renders.

Getting realism with subsurface scattering

If you've ever held your hand up to a strong light and seen the light shine through it, that's **subsurface scattering**. It's the light that bounces off layers below the surface of an object and is important for doing photo-realistic work. You'll learn more about it as you move on in Blender.

Putting a sparkle on your animations with ray tracing

Ray tracing is a method Blender uses to figure out which objects should get how much light. It is especially good for rendering shiny or transparent objects. You know that real light comes from the sun and bounces around. It reflects off of objects such as cars, trees, and finally comes into your eye. Whatever the light has bounced off of has colored the light. So you see the green of a leaf, or your own reflection in the hood of a car.

This is the perfect way to calculate light. It only has one problem. Most of the light doesn't go into your eye. So while it gives perfect results, it's a horribly wasteful way to calculate light for computer graphics.

To get around this, a man named *Arthur Appel* suggested doing it backwards. Follow a ray of light from your eye out into the world and see what it bounces off. You can choose how many times it bounces. If you were looking at the hood of a car, you'd see the color of the car because the light bounced off of the car, but you'd also see your own reflection because the light from the sun bounced off of you and onto the car and then into your eyes.

Ray tracing lets Blender know what should be reflected on any given surface. It gives excellent results, but it can take a long time to calculate the scene, chasing down all these light rays. So what you do is control the time required to render a scene by limiting the light to a certain number of bounces after it leaves your eye.

Time for action – seeing ray tracing

Now, you'll see ray tracing in action demonstrated with three simple spheres:

1. Open up a new file.

2. Delete the default cube.

3. Press *Shift+A*. Create a **UV Sphere** from the **Add Mesh** menu.

4. In the 3D View Tool Shelf, go to the **Object Tools** subpanel, and set **Shading: to Smooth**.

5. Press *Numpad 0* to get the Camera view.

6. Press *Shift+D* to make a copy. Move the new sphere to the right and release it next to the original.

7. In the **Properties** window, choose the **Material** button from the header. It's the ninth button from the left, with the chrome ball on it.

8. Click on the **New** button and set the color in the **Diffuse** subpanel to red.

9. Select the original sphere again.

10. Press *Shift+D* to make a copy. Move the new sphere next to the original one on the left.

11. In the **Properties** window, click on the **New** button and set the color in the **Diffuse** subpanel to blue.

12. Select the center sphere again.

13. In the **Properties** window click on the **New** button to create a new material.

14. In the **Mirror** subpanel, check the **Mirror** checkbox and set the value of the **Reflectivity:** button to **0.5**.

15. Press *F12*. You'll see the red and blue spheres reflected in the center sphere as shown in the following screenshot:

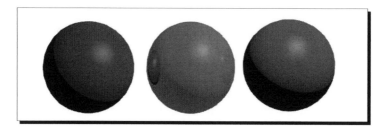

16. Select the **Render** button in the **Properties** window header. It's the second button from the left with a still camera on it.

17. In the **Shading** subpanel, uncheck the **Ray Tracing** checkbox.

18. Press *F12* to render. The reflections are gone.

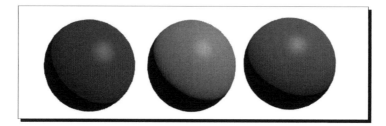

What just happened?

You created three spheres and gave the center one a mirror property. When you had ray tracing on, the spheres on either side and their highlights were reflected on the center sphere. When ray tracing was off, there was no reflection.

Choosing the proper number of tiles

The **tiles** are in your computer and refer to how the processor splits up the work of rendering. Each computer is different. The easiest way to see what works best is to render a particular frame with different tile settings and compare how long it takes. This will vary depending on your computer. Tile settings are changed in the **Performance** subpanel of the **Render** panel in the **Properties** window. My experience has been that eight tiles is about the worst setting, and that render times improve either going down to one tile or up to 32 or 64. Going down to one tile is good if all you care about is speed, but if you want speed and a quality render, more tiles may be a better choice. Do test renders with different tile settings, the times will be shown in the upper-left corner of the **UV/Image Editor**.

Using alpha channels

When Blender renders a scene, it creates four channels of image data. Three of them are the familiar Red, Green, and Blue information for each pixel. The fourth is the **alpha channel**. Instead of telling you how red, green, or blue something is, the alpha channel tells you how transparent something is.

Time for action – exploring the alpha channel

As you have shades of red, green, and blue, you also have shades of alpha channel. The darker the shade of alpha, the closer its value is to zero, the more transparent that pixel is:

1. Press *Esc* to return to the 3D View window. Select the red sphere with the *RMB*.

2. In the **Properties** window, choose the **Material** button from the header. It's the ninth button from the left with the chrome ball on it.

3. In the **Transparency** subpanel, check the **Transparency** checkbox and set the **Alpha:** to **0.4**.

4. In the 3D View, press *Shift+D* to duplicate the red sphere. Move the duplicate sphere a bit, so that both overlap but you can see more than half of each sphere as shown in the following screenshot.

5. Select the **Render** button in the **Properties** window header. It's the second button from the left with a still camera on it.

6. In the **Shading** subpanel, check the **Ray Tracing** checkbox.

7. Press *F12* and the render will look similar to the following screenshot.

8. Press *Esc* when you are done looking at it.

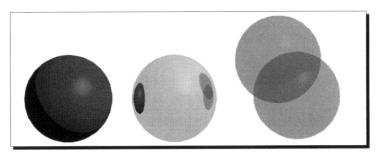

What just happened?

The alpha channel records how transparent an object is. You took one sphere and gave it a **40%** transparency setting. **100%** is solid and **0%** is perfectly transparent. Then you duplicated it and moved the copy so that the two transparent spheres overlapped and then rendered everything. Where the spheres overlap, they combine to be **80%** solid. Where they don't overlap, they are only **40%** solid. More light goes through the red spheres and doesn't bounce off. Their reflection on the center sphere is dimmer than that of the blue sphere. If you look at the glass material made for the sloop's portals and the house's windows, you will find that the transparency has been used.

Time for action – using transparency in the Video Sequence Editor

In addition to making objects transparent in relation to other objects, the transparency that you see in a scene is also used in the **Video Sequence Editor** and the **Node Editor**. Here is an example in the Video Sequence Editor:

1. Move the mouse to the border between the **3D View** window and the **Timeline** window. When you get the double-headed arrow, move the border up so that about a quarter of the screen height is filled with the **Timeline** window.

2. In the lower-left corner of the **Timeline** window, select the **Current Editor Type** menu button and choose **Video Sequence Editor** from the pop-up menu.

3. In the **Video Sequence Editor** header, select **Add** and choose **Scene** and then **Scene** again from the pop-up menus.

4. Select **Add** again, and choose **Image** from the pop-up menu. Choose any of the `boat_stereo` images from `Chapter 12/Images/Video Strips/` in your download pack. You don't need the whole strip. Just select a single frame. Click on the **Add Image Strip** button in the **File Browser** window.

5. Press on the **Scene** strip with the *RMB* and hold it down while you move it so it is above the **Image** strip.

6. Press *N* to open up the **Properties** panel of the **Video Sequence Editor**. Click on the button next to **Blend:** in the **Edit Strip** subpanel and choose **Alpha Over** from the pop-up menu.

7. Move the **Current Time Indicator** so it is within the frames covered by both strips.

8. Press *F12* and the composited render will look similar to the following screenshot:

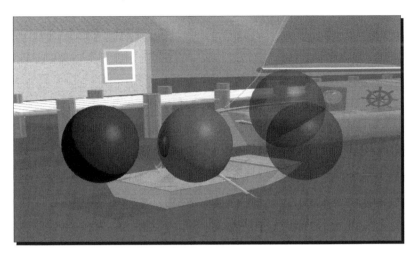

9. Save the file to a unique name.

What just happened?

Now you went into the Video Sequence Editor and laid the scene over a background image and set its **Blend:** setting to **Alpha Over**, meaning the Video Sequence Editor uses the alpha channel of the top layer in compositing the two images. When you rendered it, you got an image of the spheres over the island image. Since the left two spheres are solid, they completely cover the scene. The right-hand spheres are partially transparent so they let some of the boat scene image through.

The following are some sources for more information on the topics we just reviewed:

Anti-aliasing (`http://www.dpreview.com/learn/?/Glossary/Digital_Imaging/Aliasing_01.htm`)

Subsurface scattering (`http://en.wikipedia.org/wiki/Subsurface_scattering`)

Ray tracing (`http://en.wikipedia.org/wiki/Ray_tracing_(graphics)`)

Alpha channels (`http://en.wikipedia.org/wiki/Alpha_compositing`)

Tiles (`http://www.blender.org/development/release-logs/blender-242/render-pipeline/`)

Choosing the dimensions for your animation

It's no surprise that you have to choose the size of the image. Is this animation for a banner ad on the Web, an IMAX screen, or something in between?

That's where the **Dimensions** subpanel of the **Render** panel in the **Properties** window comes in handy. The top button is the **Render Presets** button. If you click on it, you will find a menu of common video sizes.

Time for action – selecting render presets

Render presets can save you a lot of time, make sure you don't forget to set important settings and act as a guide for what those settings should be:

1. Press *Esc* to get back to the **3D View** window. Zoom back far enough so that you can see the entire image area within the passepartout.

2. In the **Properties** window, choose the **Render** button from the header. It's the second button from the left, with the still camera on it.

3. Look at the **Dimensions** subpanel of the **Render** panel. It shows you the **X** and **Y** resolution, the range of the frame numbers, the frame rate, and the aspect ratio.

4. Select the **Render Presets** button and choose **TV PAL 4:3** from the pop-up menu as shown in the following screenshot. Watch the **3D View** window as you select it.

5. Note that the resolution, the frame rate, and the aspect ratio have changed.

6.   Now open up the **Post Processing** subpanel. Note the **Compositing**, **Sequencer**, and **Fields** checkboxes.

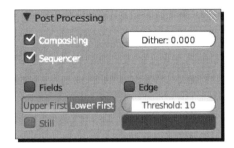

7.   Check the **Fields** checkbox.

What just happened?

The Render Presets provide you with an easy way of setting up your animation to render. Of course, you will have to know what you are creating this animation for.

For a web banner you will want to make the animation of the size requested by the webmaster, and use the slowest frame rate that still looks good. Animation, film, and video use a principle called **persistence of vision**. It means that the image is still in your brain for a short while after you see something. Bring in another image fast enough and they seem to blend together. About seven frames per second is as low as you can get and still get the persistence of vision effect that makes animation work. Film runs at 24 frames per second and Video runs at 25 or 30 frames per second.

The reason for making web graphics low speed is to make the file size smaller and also because you don't know how powerful someone's computer is. So you have to balance file size and animation smoothness.

Then there is old style TV, now known as Standard Definition (SD). The two main TV formats are **NTSC** in the U.S. and **PAL** in Europe. Early TV transmitters could only send so much of the picture in the time between the start of one frame and the start of the next one; and it wasn't enough to cover a TV screen.

So they came up with a plan where they would transmit every other line of a picture from top to bottom and then go back to the top and transmit the other lines so they could fill the screen in half the time and this would keep refreshing the picture so the image wouldn't flicker. Each one of these sets of lines was called a **field**. Blender has a **Fields** checkbox to render video that is compatible with TV signals.

When you check the checkbox, the **Upper First** and **Lower First** buttons are brightened. By default, **Upper First** is highlighted. This is for the European PAL method. The American NTSC method does Lower First.

The advent of digital cameras has made this even more muddled, many DV formats are lower first and 1080i is often upper first. So if you have any doubts, the best thing to do is create a short animation where you move a white square on a black background from left to right. Record one version Upper First, and another version Lower First. The correct one will look great on a TV monitor, the wrong one will look horrible.

When an image is made of two different fields, it is called an **interlaced** image. There can be one graphic or animation, but the system will read an interlaced image by displaying every other line of pixels or one field and then go back and display the other field of lines. The following diagram shows a TV screen. The even rows would be one field, the odd rows would be another field. The lines show the beam moving to its next location while turned off. You can see it goes from even row to even row, not straight down. At at the bottom, the beam goes up and begins the odd rows.

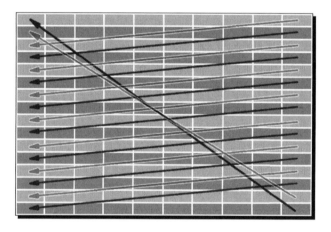

Interlacing like this is the difference between the HD formats 1080i and 1080p. 1080i is an interlaced display. With 1080p the p stands for progressive, meaning it displays the lines in order from top to bottom.

Time for action – seeing what fields look like

I made a Blender file that has the white square on the black background for you. Looking at it in action may help you get an idea of what goes on with fields:

1. Load the program `6907_12_Fields.blend` from your `Chapter 12` download pack.

2. Press *F12*. You see a white square on a black background.

3. In the **Post Processing** subpanel of the **Render** panel in the **Properties** window, check the **Fields** checkbox.

4. Press *F12*.

What just happened?

When you have fields turned on, two images are rendered and merged. One image represents the time during the first half of the frame. Every other line is rendered. The other represents the time during the second half of the frame. Then the alternating lines are rendered.

When both fields are rendered, on the computer screen, the image looks like the following screenshot. The left-hand fringe is where the square was only during the first field, the right hand fringe is where the square was only during the second field. The solid white area is where the square was during both fields.

Another thing to look out for with PAL and NTSC is the aspect ratio. There are two aspect ratios to be concerned with. One is the aspect ratio of the entire picture and the second is the aspect ratio of a single pixel as seen in the following graphic. For both PAL and NTSC the aspect ratio of the entire picture is **4** across to **3** down. Both PAL and NTSC have the same number of pixels across, but PAL has 576 lines down, and NTSC has only 486. So their pixels are different shapes to achieve the 4:3 ratio for the entire picture. You can see this in the following image.

HD screens tend to have a ratio of **16** across to **9** down and normally have square pixels.

You can see what the pixel **Aspect Ratio:** is when you select different rendering presets in the **Dimensions** subpanel of the **Render** panel. Look at the HDTV 1080p, TV NTSC 4:3, and TV PAL 4:3 settings:

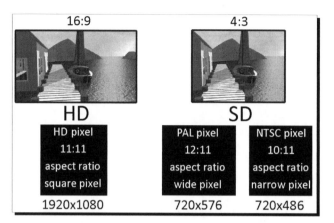

Pop quiz – rendering with fields

1. When you rendered the square without fields, it appeared square. While each field was rendering the square appeared rectangular. Why is that?

    a. A rendering bug in Blender.

    b. The image in each field is blurred because it is moving.

    c. When Blender renders a field, it's only rendering half of the rows of pixels, so what you see is only half as high. When they are interlaced, then you get the full height image.

These websites have more information on preparing your artwork for rendering.

```
http://wiki.blender.org/index.php/Doc:2.6/Manual/
Render/Output/Video
```

```
http://wiki.blender.org/index.php/Doc:2.6/Manual/
Render/Animations
```

Choosing what gets rendered

In the **Post Processing** subpanel of the **Render** panel in the **Properties** window there are **Compositing** and **Sequencer** checkboxes.

By default, both boxes are checked, but if there is nothing in the **Node Editor**, the **Compositing** does not get activated and if there is nothing in the **Video Sequence Editor**, the **Sequencer** does not get activated.

If you have used the **3D View Editor**, the **Node Editor**, and the **Video Sequence Editor**, Blender will go through them in order for each frame as shown in the next image:

- You link the render and/or the **Node Editor** with the **Video Sequence Editor** by adding a **Scene** strip in the **Video Sequence Editor** as you did earlier in this chapter. That way your render will be included in the compositing done in the **Video Sequence Editor**, as seen in the following illustration.

- You link the render to the **Node Editor** by including a **Render Layers** node in the **Node Editor**. That way your render will be included in the compositing done in the **Node Editor** as shown in the following graphic:

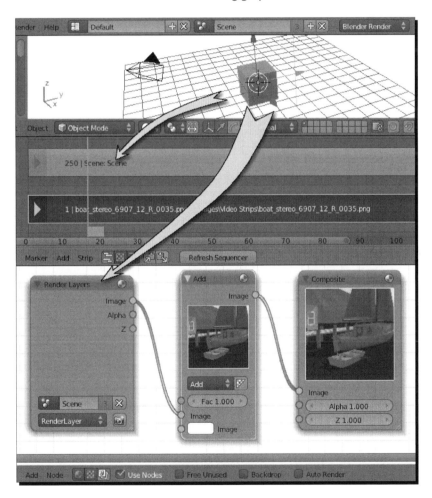

Selecting the best file format

Blender saves still images by default to the PNG format. This is a good choice. PNG files do lossless compression, so it minimizes file size while not losing any detail. The PNG file also supports an alpha channel, so you can composite the images you render. It also provides the best safety if you have problems in rendering because the entire sequence doesn't have to be re-rendered, just the few frames that have problems.

When you are ready for a final render, you need to decide what kind of output you want. That depends entirely on what you plan to do with the animation.

But in the real world, you need to consider who you are making this video for. Earlier you were given several choices to render out the sequence you edited. So the real world was that you needed to make it so it would play on whatever player was on your computer.

If it's for YouTube, then your requirements might be an .MPEG4 or MOV file, with h264, mpeg4 video codecs and AAC audio codec or an .AVI file, with an MJPEG video codec and a PCM audio codec. You'd have to check on the YouTube website to find out what size your final render should be.

If you are making an animation for TV or video, then check with the people you are making it for. When I worked for an advertising agency that did TV production, most of the time they wanted a sequence of PNG images or a MOV file, and even though their final video was output to SD, they did all their work in HD. It can vary a lot, so don't be afraid to ask. Asking good questions makes you look more professional.

Major formats for video rendering are Quicktime, AVI, H.264, and MPEG. There is more information available on the following links:

http://wiki.blender.org/index.php/Doc:2.6/Manual/Render/Output

http://en.wikibooks.org/wiki/Blender_3D:_Noob_to_Pro/Output_Formats

http://wiki.blender.org/index.php/Doc:2.6/Manual/Render/Output/Video

Rendering with the Cycles renderer

The Blender Internal renderer is only one of the many renderers available to the Blender user. The **Cycles** renderer has been incorporated into Blender in Blender 2.61, so it's worth looking at. One big difference between the Cycles renderer and the Blender Internal renderer is that you don't need lights in Cycles. Objects can be used as lights. It seems kind of strange, but we will explore it here.

This makes it easy to do cool stuff like neon lights and adding a glow to the bottom of cars. Cycles also handles glass well and creates distortions of light known as caustics, like the light patterns on the bottom of a pool.

Cycles does a style of ray tracing, bouncing the light around and following it to the source. This means that you get better shadows, lights, and reflections. It also means that rendering is never quite finished. It just gets better and better and you decide what is good enough.

Time for action – simulating the glow of a kiln

Cycles offers a lot of ways to use light. You are going to simulate the glow of a kiln as a white sphere acts as a light source and bounces light off red faces turning the light that bounces to red light:

1. Open a new file in Blender.

2. In the center of the top header, click the *LMB* over the button that says **Blender Render**, and choose **Cycles Render** from the drop-down menu as shown in the following screenshot:

3. Select the default lamp with the *RMB*. Press *X* to delete it.

4. Select the cube with the *RMB* and press the *Tab* key to get into **Edit Mode**.

5. In the **3D View** Header, click on the **Viewport Shading** menu button and choose **Wireframe**.

6. In the **3D View** Header, click on the **Face select mode** button.

7. Choose the face nearest to the camera.

8. Press *E* to extrude it, then *Enter*.

9. Press *S, 0.5,* and *Enter*.

10. Press *E, -1.7,* and *Enter*.

11. Press *A* to deselect all the faces.

12. Use the *RMB* and *Shift+RMB* keys to select only the four sides of the last extrusion you made, as seen on the left of the following screenshot.

13. Press *Ctrl+I* to select the inverse.

14. In the **Properties** window, select the **Material** button in the header. It's the ninth one from the left with the chrome ball on it.

15. If the **Material** panel looks odd, as shown in the center of the following screenshot, that's because you are now doing materials for the Cycles renderer.

16. Name the material **Outside** and assign it to the selected faces.

17. With the cursor over the **3D View** window, press *Ctrl+I* to invert the selection.

18. Press the **+** sign in the **Material** panel to make a new material. Press the **New** button.

19. Name the material **Glow**.

20. In the **Surface** subpanel, click on the button labeled **Diffuse BSDF** and choose **Mix Shader** from the drop-down menu as seen on the right of the following screenshot:

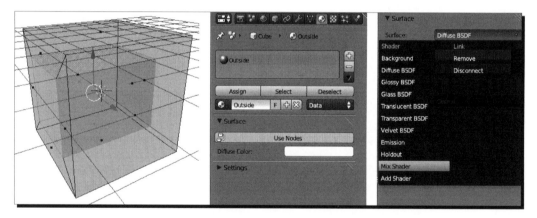

21. In the **Surface** subpanel, there are two buttons labeled **Shader:**. Click on the upper **Shader:** button and choose **Diffuse BSDF** from the drop-down menu.

22. Set the **Color** to a solid red. I used **R 0.800**, **G 0.000**, and **B 0.080**.

23. Click on the lower **Shader:** button and choose **Glossy BSDF** from the drop-down menu.

24. Set the **Color** to the same shade of red. I used **R 0.800**, **G 0.000**, and **B 0.0800**.

25. Scroll up to the **Fac:** button and set its value to **0.6**. This sets what proportion of influence each shader has.

26. Press the **Assign** button.

27. With the cursor over the **3D View** window, press the *Tab* key.

28. Press the *A* key to deselect the kiln.

29. Press *Numpad 3* and *Numpad 5* to get an **Ortho Side** view.

30. Press *Shift+A* and create a **UV Sphere** from the **Mesh** menu.

31. Scale it down so it just fits within the central cavity of the kiln.

32. In the **Materials** panel of the **Properties** window, press the **+** sign to create a new material. Click on the **New** button. Name the material **Light**.

33. In the **Surface** subpanel change the **Surface:** from **Diffuse BSDF** to **Emission**.

34. Set the **Strength:** to **60**.

35. In the **Timeline** window, select the **Current Editor Type** button, choose **Node Editor** from the pop-up menu. Cycles materials can be edited in the **Node Editor** as well as in the **Materials** panel of the **Properties** window. The nodes for the Glow texture are shown in the following screenshot.

36. Use the double-pointed arrow to move the border between the **Node Editor** window and the **3D View** window up a bit. Zoom into the nodes you see in the **Node Editor** window.

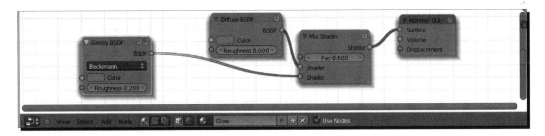

37. In the **3D View** window, press the *A* key to deselect the sphere.

38. Press *Shift+A* and create a **Plane** from the **Mesh** menu.

39. Press *G, Z,* and use the mouse to move it so it is slightly below the kiln. Press the *LMB* to release it.

40. Press *S*, *8*, and *Enter*.

41. Press *F12* to render it. It will keep rendering and getting better. Press *Esc* when you are tired of waiting.

What just happened?

That's kind of cool. There's no lamp, but you can see the glow, and not only do you see the light, but the color of the insides of the kiln gets picked up and reflected out as well. You'll notice that the materials settings are all different and can be edited in the Node Editor as well. The first image shown in the following graphic was a quick render with only 10 samples, whereas the second image had 1000 samples. That's quite a difference as you can see.

The Glow material had two portions, diffuse and glossy. Diffuse produces a flatter surface, and glossy a more highly reflective one. Using them both allowed you to tailor exactly how glossy the inner part of the cube would be, which also affects how the light from the sphere bounces off of it.

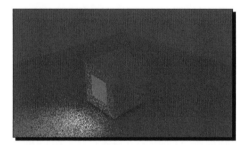 

Have a go hero – adjusting render quality in Cycles

The key to improving rendering in Cycles is in the **Integrator** subpanel of the **Render** panel in the **Properties** window. The important thing in Cycles is time. You'll have to balance quality against render time.

The controls for rendering in Cycles are in the **Integrator** subpanel of the **Render** panel in the **Properties** window. In **Samples:** try boosting the **Render:** value to **1000**, **2000**, or even **4000**. Changing the **Seed:** will change exactly which places are sampled. Changing the **Bounces:** can do a lot. The more Bounces, the more accurate the light will be. Then in the **Light Paths:** you can set the number of bounces for differing kinds of textures, though none will exceed the maximum number of bounces that you set in **Bounces:**.

Transparency? Yes, Cycles does glass very well. Note the **No Caustics** checkbox. Caustics are the patterns of light that you see in transparent objects from glass to water caused by the light bending. They add a lot to the realism of the render.

The following are some links to find out further information about Cycles:

`http://blenderartists.org/forum/showthread.php?232104-Blender-Cycles-Tutorial-Series`

`http://www.blendernation.com/2011/11/24/cycles-tutorial-a-thorough-introduction/`

`http://www.blendernation.com/2011/08/03/quick-tutorial-cycles-render-in-gpu-cpu/`

So play around with the Cycles rendering and see what you come up with.

Key	Function
*	In the **File Browser** window, the asterisk acts as a wild card allowing you to select all the images in a series if you replace the number of the frame with this in the input window.
H	Mutes a strip in the **Video Sequence Editor**.
Alt+H	Unmutes a strip in the **Video Sequence Editor**.
K	Does a soft Trim at the **Current Frame Indicator** in the selected strips. This hides the other frames in the strip in the **Video Sequence Editor**.
Shift+K	Does a hard Trim at the **Current Frame Indicator** in the selected strips. This deletes the other frames beyond the end of the strip in the **Video Sequence Editor**.
Left arrow	Moves one frame previous in the **Video Sequence Editor**.
Right arrow	Moves to the next frame in the **Video Sequence Editor**.
Shift+Left arrow	Moves to the beginning of the video in the **Video Sequence Editor**.
Shift+Right arrow	Moves to the end of the video in the **Video Sequence Editor**.
Shift+Up arrow	Jumps ahead 10 frames in the **Video Sequence Editor**.
Shift+Down arrow	Jumps back 10 frames in the **Video Sequence Editor**.
G	Lets you move the selected strip with the mouse in the **Video Sequence Editor**.
G, X	Lets you move the selected strip with the mouse, restricts it to the channel you are in in the **Video Sequence Editor**.
G, Y	Lets you move the selected strip with the mouse, restricts it to the time you are at in the **Video Sequence Editor**.

Key	Function
MMB	Press the *MMB* after starting to move a strip and it locks the motion to either the *X* or *Y* direction depending on how you started moving it in the **Video Sequence Editor**.
Alt+O	Removes offsets from a video strip in the **Video Sequence Editor**, removing any soft Trims.
X	Deletes the selected video strip in the **Video Sequence Editor**.
Shift+Ctrl+S	Saves a file.
F2	Saves a file.
Ctrl+N	Creates a new file.
Ctrl+O	Opens a file.
F1	Opens a file.
L	In **Edit Mode** selects all connected faces, edges, and vertices.
Ctrl+Tab	In **Edit Mode**, brings up the **Mesh Select Mode** menu.
Ctrl+I	In the **3D View** it inverts the selection.

Summary

You have learned to use the Video Sequence Editor to edit rendered scenes. You have used the Node Editor to create stereographic views and composite images. You have learned to use the rendering controls to create a more finished animation and explored the Cycles renderer.

I tip my hat to you. You have done very well. You got through this book and made some awesome stuff.

You are ready to go out into the wider world of Blending. While there is much to learn yet, you've reached the point where you will be comfortable modeling, animating, and creating images and you have a solid base to understand the rest of Blender. You will be comfortable on Blender websites, able to understand what people are talking about, and ready to help others. You're going to do some great work. I can't wait to see it!

Happy Blending! Let's go!

Pop Quiz Answers

Chapter 2, Getting Comfortable using the 3D View

Pop quiz – learning about Blender windows

1. **Answer**: c

   Blender window setup can be any way you want, and any window can have any kind of editor that you want. You'll be able to set it up the way that's the most efficient for you.

2. **Answer**: c

Pop quiz – learning basic computer graphics terms

1. **Answer**: b

2. **Answer**: a

3. **Answer**: c

Pop quiz – knowing how to get different views

1. **Answer**: b

2. **Answer**: c

3. **Answer**: a

Chapter 3, Controlling the Lamp, the Camera, and Animating Objects

Pop quiz – composing your scenes

1. **Answer**: The positive space is red and the colors are more saturated.

2. **Answer**: c

    Putting something in the foreground near the lower third boundary, would guide the viewer's eye between the end of the bench and the dancer's foot.

Chapter 4, Modeling with Vertices, Edges, and Faces

Pop quiz – making selections

1. **Answer**: b

2. **Answer**: a

Chapter 5, Building a Simple Boat

Pop quiz – figuring out the best way to build the boat

Answer: Yes. That would be possible. The most difficult part of that method would be scaling the bottom of the inside hull so the walls would be parallel to the outside of the hull. As with many things, one way is about as much work as another, so it's often best to just do it rather than over-think the absolute best way to do something.

Chapter 6, Making and Moving the Oars

Pop quiz – calculating how long a frame lasts

1. **Answer**: At 24 frames per second, 0.85 seconds would take 20 frames to pull the oar in the water.

2. **Answer**: At 24 frames per second, 1.08 seconds would take 26 frames to go back to the starting position, and 58 frames for the whole cycle.

Chapter 7, Planning your Work, Working your Plan

Pop quiz – organizing Blender files

1. **Answer:** b

    The relative address of the textures for the deck for `MyBoat.blend` in the `C:\NewBoat` directory is `C:\NewBoat\Images`.

2. **Answer:** c

    The more specific a file name is, the easier it is to remember. `Sloop of War_USS Constitution_1854 version.blend` is the most specific.

3. **Answer:** a

    That's right. If you want to save all the files for a certain project, it helps to start their names with common words so that the files will all be together in an alphabetical index. `Sloop_texture_deck.png`, `Sloop_texture_mast.png`, `Sloop_texture_hull.png` will all be right there together in a directory, not mixed up among other files where you will have to look at them and guess what they are.

Pop quiz – saving Blender files

1. **Answer:** c

    It's almost always a good time to save your Blender file. If you've made any significant change to it, it's time to save it and make back up copies of your files to an external hard drive, flash drive, DVD, or Internet storage daily.

2. **Answer:** c

    The file name should be incremented whenever you feel that you've made a significant change to your blender file, or if you are doing an experimental technique that you think might or might not work just the way you want it. Basically, you want to give yourself the option of going back a step, if necessary.

Chapter 8, Making the Sloop

Pop quiz – remembering Edge Tool commands

1. **Answer:** c

    Only the third answer is incorrect. You press *Ctrl+R* to start a Loop Cut.

Chapter 10, Modeling Organic Forms, Sea, and Terrain

Pop quiz – optimizing rendering times

1. **Answer**: b

   Removing the faces in the vertex group Ocean Floor is the only guaranteed method. You may have a camera angle that shows the missing backs of buildings, and you may want to sail your sloop around the Island. There is a read out of the number of vertices, edges, and faces for the entire scene in the top Info window. If you go into **Edit Mode**, it will tell you how many vertices, edges, and faces there are in a particular object.

Chapter 11, Improving your Lighting and Camera Work

Pop quiz – remembering about lighting

1. **Answer**: b

   The Sun Lamp covers the whole scene with light at the same angle.

2. **Answer**: c

   Light gets dimmer the farther away a lamp is from the object it's lighting, with both the point and spot lamps.

3. **Answer**: b

   The Spot lamp simulates a theatrical spot lamp.

Chapter 12, Rendering and Compositing

Pop quiz – rendering with fields

1. **Answer**: c

   Since each field contains only half the total lines in the picture, what you see while it's rendering is only half as tall.

Index

Symbols

0 key 55
3 button mouse 12
3D
  dimensions 49
  front view 49
3D animation
  about 22, 23
  in 1970 24
  pioneer computer animators, analyzing 23
  Triple I demo 24
3D axis indicator 46
3D cursor 46
3D manipulator 46
3D modeling
  normal, using 128
3D skills, using for
  2D animation, creating 29
  architectural walkthroughs 30
  digital signage 30
  driving simulators, creating 30
  exaggerate ideas, displaying 31
  games 29
  interactive instruction 31
  legal evidence display 30
  movie pre-visualization 29
  portfolio, creating 31
  product development 31
  scientific data, displaying 30
  Stereoscopic 3D 29
  TV 29
  video 29
  virtual reality 30
  virtual sets 30
  web animation 29
3D tools, 3D View window
  about 46
  3D axis indicator 46
  3D cursor 46
  3D manipulator 46
  reference grid 46
3D View
  angle modification, numpad used 53, 54
  back view 54
  bottom view 54
  Camera View, verifying 55
  Full Screen, displaying 60
  left side view 54
  navigating 60, 62
  numpad, using 57
  only camera view 54
  Orthographic views 59
  Perspective views 59
  Quad View, displaying 60
  Quad View, toggling 60
  rotating in another direction, numpad used 56
  rotating, numpad used 56
  scene, panning 52, 53
  scene, rotating in 51
  scene, zooming 52
  user action, recording 57
3D View window
  about 44, 384
  tools 44, 45

Tool Shelf 45
viewing, components 45
7 key 58
- key 123
+ key 123

A

absolute addressing 207
Adam Powers 25
Add Modifier button 226
Add Movie Strip button 391
Add Sound Strip button 221
A key
  about 114, 123, 296
  vertices, selecting 114
aliasing
  about 409
  displaying 409, 410
Alpha Channels
  exploring 413, 414
  sources 415
  using 413
Alt+A 224
Alt+C key 271
Alt+F key 190
Alt+H key 123
Alt key 57, 87
Alt+RMB key 271
animatics
  links 215
  using, for animation time planning 214, 215
animation
  3D animation 22
  and Blender 9

  corrections, making 383
  Dope Sheet, using 384, 385
  file, loading 86
  final render 408
  ideas, storyboarding 378
  laying out 379
  making 85
  making, keyframes used 87, 88
  motion, controlling in Graph Editor 92, 93
  planning, Charts and Guides used 215
  playing, video player used 89

previewing 88
rendering 91, 92
rendering, starting with 409
rough animation, laying out 379
storyboards, using 211
story, selecting 209, 210
time planning, animatics used 214, 215
tools, 3D View window 384
tools, Dope Sheet window 384
tools, Graph Editor window 384
tools, Timeline window 384
using 378
work, proofing 380
computers, using 21
techniques 27
animation heroes
  about 16
  folder, making 16
  history 16, 17
  in 1922 16, 17
  in 1938 20
animation planning, Charts and Guides used
  bar sheets 220
  Bounce Diagrams 218
  Eadweard Muybridge photographic series 218
  exposure sheets 219
  Lower Third 215
  Preston Blair Phoneme Mouth charts 219
  Safe Title-Action Zones 215
  Safe Title/Safe Action guide, adding 216, 217
  Safe Title Zone 215
  Standard Definition TV-High Definition TV transition 217, 218
  Walk cycle charts 219
animation production
  about 220
  audio track, adding to Blender 220-223
  boogie woogie beat, animating to 223, 224
animation, rendering
  Alpha Channels, suing 413
  Anti-Aliasing, using 409
  best file format, selecting 422
  dimensions, selecting 416
  field, viewing 418-420
  frame, choosing 421
  Ray Tracing, using 410
  render presets, selecting 416-418

starting with 409
Subsurface Scattering 410
Tile count, selecting 412
animation talents
Anticipation 21
Arcs 20
exaggeration 21
metaphors 21
secondary motion 20
animation techniques
anticipation and follow through 28
Appeal 28
Arcs 28
Contrast 28
exaggeration 28
Misdirection 28
secondary action 28
Slow in and slow out 28
Squash and stretch 28
staging 28
timing 28
animator heroes
pioneer animators, analyzing 18
anti-aliasing
about 409
sources 415
ANT Landscape generator 303
Armature 47
Assign button 150
Audio Scrubbing box 222
auto backup feature 77

B

Backspace key 296
back view 54
bar sheets 220
basic controllers
numeric keypad 35, 36
numpad 36
three-button mouse 36
using 35
basic objects, Blender
creating 117-119
beauty lighting 361
Bezier Curve
control handles, moving 99

handles, using 98
keel, making 207
modeling 200-204
motion, modifying 94
rudder object, creating 200-204
tiller cross-section, making 204-206
tiller path, making 204-206
working with 95, 96
Bezier interpolation 94
Big Buck Bunny 8
bit 48
B key
about 114, 190
border, selecting 114, 115
Blend controllers
keyboard 35
mouse 35
numpad 35
Blender
3D View window 44
about 109
advantages 8
and animation 9
basic objects, creating 117
closing 15
data block 119
first scene, rendering 12-14
information structure 120
installing 10
lamp 64
normal, uses 128
screen 10
using 12
Blender 3D
about 7
features 15
screenshot example 8
Blender 3D interface
basic controllers 35
Blender Windows, using 36
exploring 33, 34
User Preferences, setting up 34, 35
Blender files
organizing 208
saving 209
Blender Game Engine 30

Blender installation
about 10
requirements 11, 12
BlenderUser Preferences 34
Blender video player
downloading 89
Blender Windows
about 36
creating, tips 43
Header 39
joining 42
joining horizontally 42
maximizing 39
parallel edges, creating 42
playing with 36, 37
removing, tips 43
resizing 38
splitting 40, 41
tiling 39
boat
animating 179
animation cycles 184
assembling 174-178
building 125
building, methods 140
caveat 180
color, adding 147
curve, adding to hull 138
curves, adding 136-138
cycles, adding 185
forward kinematics 181
frame duration, calculating 181
gunwale 126
gunwale, coloring 147-150
height, selecting 133-136
hull 126
hull, coloring 147-150
inverse kinematics 181
keyframes, copying 184, 185
kinematics 181
length, deciding 132, 133
moving 186
moving, in sync 186-188
non-planar polygon, creating 140
object, naming 154
quadrilateral faces 140
rowing 188

seat, adding 141, 142
second seat, creating 143, 144
stroke, timing 179
texture, adding to seats 151-153
third seat, adding 144
triangles 140
width, selecting 133-136
boat tracking
camera, using 189
light, setting 189
Boolean modifiers
applying 254, 255
cabin, detailing 252-254
Difference 252
doors, creating 255
Intersection 252
portal windows, creating 255
bottom view 54
Bounce Diagrams 218
box modeling
about 126
cube, modifying into boat 126
extrusion 126
instances 126
byte 48

C

Cabin 261
Cabin/Cockpit boundary 242
Cabin Roof 261
cameo lighting 361
camera
about 363
Camera.Dolly 367
close up, using 374
Depth of Field, creating 369-372
Depth of Field, using 368
dollying 364, 365
Field of View, modifying 363
long shots 374
medium shots 374
Motion Blur, using 375, 376
perspective, using 367
rule of 180, applying 375
two shots 374
zooming 364-366

Camera 47
camera control
  global axis 78
  lens, using 79, 80
  local axis 78
  location controlling, number keys used 79
  object movement, controlling in global mode 78
  object movement, controlling in local mode 79
Camera.Dolly 367
camera moves
  Boom 84
  Dolly 84
  Pan 84
  Roll 84
  Tilt 84
  Truck 84
camera, using as canvas
  about 81
  camera, rotating 85
  camera, scaling 85
  composition guides, using 84
  composition rules 81
  moves, examining 84
Catmull-Clark button 227
C key
  about 115
  circle, selecting 115
cockpit rear
  adjusting 242
color depth 49
commands. *See* keys
components, 3D View window
  3D tools 46
  objects 45
  object types 47
  text fields 46
composition rules
  limited palette, using 83
  negative space, using 82
  positive space, using 82
  rule of thirds 81
computer
  colors, creating 48
  colors creating, specific colors used 48, 49
  using, for picture making 47, 48
cones 48

constant interpolation 93
corrections
  Dope Sheet, using 384, 385
  making 383, 386
  tools 384
Ctrl-1 54
Ctrl+Alt+LMB key 106
Ctrl + Alt - mouse wheel 53
Ctrl+Alt+Numpad 0 key 296
Ctrl+Alt+RMB key 271
Ctrl+C key 106, 296
Ctrl+F11 key 105, 380
Ctrl+F12 key 105, 381
Ctrl+G key 342
Ctrl+J command 332
Ctrl+J key 296
Ctrl key 52
Ctrl+LMB key
  about 116
  lasso, selecting 116
  warning 116
Ctrl+ M key 296
Ctrl+MMB key 105, 117, 133
Ctrl + mouse wheel 53
Ctrl+Numpad 0 key 190
Ctrl+Numpad 1 291
Ctrl+P command 332
Ctrl+P key 190
Ctrl+R key 271
Ctrl+Shift+A key 271
Ctrl+Shift-LMB key 123
Ctrl+Shift+Z key 190
Ctrl+Tab key 123
Ctrl+T key 190
Ctrl+V key 106
Ctrl-Z 57
Ctrl+Z 116, 178
Ctrl+Z key 190
Current Editor Type buttons 37
current frame indicator
  about 86
  moving, keystrokes used 96
curves
  about 47
  adding, to boat lines 136-138
cylinder, converting to oar
  blade base, creating 163, 164

blade, creating 164-168
grip, making 160-162
guard, making 160-162
shaft, making 159, 160

D

data block 119
data structures 23
Defocus node 373
Delete key 106
Depth of Field, camera
  about 368
  creating 369-373
Dope Sheet
  using 384, 385
Dope Sheet window 384
Down arrow key 296
DupliFrames
  using, for adding planks 325-327
DupliVerts 263

E

Eadweard Muybridge photographic series 218
early animators
  analyzing 19, 20
edge 111
Edge Ring 230
Edge Select Mode button 112
Edge Tools
  about 227
  bow sharpness, increasing 238, 239
  edge loops, using 230
  edge rings, using 230
  hull, finishing 239, 240
  hull shape, creating 233-236
  sloop shape, creating 231, 232
  transom, flattening 237
  using 228
  using, for Reference Block recycle 228, 229
Edit Mode 109, 110
Ekey 124
Esc key 55, 105
exposure sheets 219
extrusion
  about 122, 126
  hull internal, creating 126, 127

F

F2 key 105
F11 key 55, 105
F12 button 13
F12 key 105
face 111
Face Select Mode button 112
faces key
  E 124
  F 124
Fantasia 20
F-Curve
  about 93, 94
  Bezier interpolation 94
  Channel Selection Panel used 101, 102
  constant interpolation 93
  linear interpolation 93
FELIX TURNS THE TIDE 17
Field of View
  changing 363
file
  auto backup feature 77
  backup file, creating 77
  index, creating 208
  organizing, ways 207
  requirements 300, 345, 346, 389
  saving 76
files key
  F2 105
  Shift+Ctrl+S 105
film Noir lighting 362
F key 124
Fleischer Studios 20
fn-Down Arrow key 342
Fn+Left arrow key 296
fn-Up Arrow key 342
Focal Length 363
FR-80 graphic recorder 24
frames 85
frames per second 85
front view 54

G

Game Engine, Blender
  CrystalSpace 29

Ogre 29
Unity 29
general key
  Ctrl+Alt+LMB 106
  Ctrl+Z 106
  Home 106
  Shift+Alt+LMB 106
G key 104, 113, 296
global coordinates 50
Goonland 20
Graph Editor
  exploring 92, 93
  keyframes, adding 99, 100
Graph Editor commands
  Ctrl+C 106
  Ctrl+MMB 105
  Ctrl+V 106
  DELETE 106
  Down arrow 106
  I 106
  left arrow 105
  MMB 105
  Mouse wheel 105
  right arrow 105
  Shift+D 106
  Shift+down arrow 106
  Shift+left arrow 106
  Shift+MMB 105
  Shift+right arrow 106
  Shift+up arrow 106
  Up arrow 106
  V 106
  VA 106
  VC 106
  VF 106
  VU 106
  VV 106
  X 106
Graph Editor window 384
Greyscale button 301
gunwale
  about 126
  coloring 147-151
G X 1 key 105
G X key 104
G Y key 104
G Z key 104

H

handles
  aligned 98
  auto clamped 98
  automatic 98
  free 98
  vector 98
Header, Blender Windows 39
Height button 306
H key 123
Home key 106
HSV (Hue, Saturation, Value) 75
hull
  about 126
  coloring 147-151
  curve, adding to 138
  internal, creating 126, 127
  V-shape, adding to 139
hull modeling
  about 243
  cabin, creating 247-251
  cockpit, creating 244-247
  surface, converting to mesh 243, 244

I

I key 106, 387
INFORMATION INTERNATIONAL, INC. (TRIPLE I)
    1982 DEMO REEL 25
installing
  Blender 10
interlaced image 418
island
  ANT Landscape add-on, using 304-306
  ANT Landscape, playing with 307
  boathouse, appending 329-331
  breakwater, building 313, 314
  contours, adding to backside 315, 316
  creating 303-322
  detailing 307, 308
  modular houses, building 332
  painting 316-320
  pier, building 322
  pilings, building 329-331
  preparing, for inhabitation 322-339
  proportional editing control 308-310

proportional editing, using 310-313
rocks, creating 339
texture painting 322
trees creating, Sapling add-on used 334
Ivan Sutherland, Sketchpad☒s creator 22

J

Jaggies 410

K

key
  Shift+B key 387
keyframes
  adding 104
  copying 102
  for lights 103
  pasting 102
  using, for animation creation 87, 88
keys
  A 296
  Alt+C 271
  Alt+F 190
  Alt+RMB 271
  B 190
  Backspace 296
  Ctrl+Alt+Numpad 0 296
  Ctrl+Alt+RMB 271
  Ctrl+C 296
  Ctrl+G 342
  Ctrl+J 296
  Ctrl+M 296
  Ctrl+MMB 224
  Ctrl+Numpad 0 190
  Ctrl+P 190
  Ctrl+R 271
  Ctrl+Shift+A 271
  Ctrl+Shift+Z 190
  Ctrl+T 190
  Ctrl+V 296
  Ctrl+Z 190
  Down arrow 296
  End 296
  fn-Down Arrow 342
  Fn+Left arrow 296
  Fn+Left Arrow 224
  fn-Up Arrow 342

Home 224, 296
Left arrow 296
MMB 190
O 342
Page Down 342
Page Up 342
Right arrow 296
Shift+Alt+F 190
Shift+C 342
Shift+Down arrow 296
Shift+End 296
Shift+G 342
Shift+Home 296
Shift+Left arrow 296
Shift+Right arrow 296
Shift+Up arrow 296
Shift+X 342
Shift+Y 342
Shift+Z 342
Tab 190
U 342
Up arrow 296
V 224
Z 271
key side lighting 361

L

lamp
  about 64
  color adding, Properties window used 69-71
  light color, mixing 73, 75
  moving 64, 65
  moving, close to cube 65, 66
  moving, far away 66, 67
  multiple lamps, using 71
  scene, viewing without rendering 68
Lamp 47
Lattice 47
Layers buttons 250
layers function, Blender
  modeling 145
  using 145, 146
  using, for rendering control 146, 147
Layer Visibility Controls 145
left arrow key 105
Left arrow key 296

left mouse button (LMB) 35, 41
left side view 54
Levels of Detail
  rendering time, selecting 240-242
lighting
  about 346
  three lights, using 347
Limit selection to visible button 172
linear interpolation 93
Link/Append from Library button 275
L key 123
local coordinates 50
Loop Cut tool 233
Lower Third 215

M

MakeHuman 368
Marquee tool 114
master drawings 23
materials 147
Materials button 153
medium shot 374
Mesh 47
Meta Object 47
middle mouse button 35
MMB key 105, 190
mode keys
  Ctrl+Tab 123
  Tab 123
modeling
  templates, using 192-199
Modifiers subpanel 228
modular houses
  assembling, from kit 332-334
  building 332
Motion Blur
  about 375
  using 376
motion, controlling in Graph Editor
  about 92, 93
  Bezier curves, working with 95, 96
  channel display, controlling 102
  Channel Selection Panel, using 101
  F-Curve 93, 94
  keyframes, adding 99, 100
  keyframes, copying 102, 103

keyframes, pasting 102, 103
  modifying, Bezier curve controls used 94
  squash, adding 96, 97
  stretch, adding 96, 97
Motion Samples button 376
Mouse wheel key 105
Mouse wheel only 53
Move to Layer menu 145
MPEG file format 400
multiple lamps
  using 72
multiple vertice selection
  A key, pressing 114
  B key, pressing 114, 115
  C key, pressing 115

N

NeoGeo 29
Node Editor
  cross-eye stereo image, making 408
  red image for the left eye, creating 401-403
  red image for the left eye, using 401
  right-eye view, making 404-407
  using, for stereographic 3D creation 400-408
Node Editor window 377
Noise Size button 306
Non Uniform Rational B Spline. *See* NURBS
normal
  about 128
  displaying 129
  uses, in Blender 128
normal lens 364
NTSC 417
numeric keypad 12
NURBS 285

O

oar
  about 158
  animating 182, 183
  assembling 174-178
  blade base, creating 163, 164
  blade, creating 164-168
  cylinder, converting to 158
  grip, creating 160, 161

guard, creating 160, 161
improving 170
shaft, creating 159, 160
oarlock
about 171
animating 182, 183
assembling 174-178
blocks, adding 179
creating 171-173
oar modeling
about 158
cylinder, converting 158
scale measurements 158
surface smoothness, controlling 169, 170
object
creating, multiple Bezier Curve used 204, 206
creating, single Bezier Curve used 200-204
groups, using 341
summarizing 339-341
Object button 170
Object Data button 372
Object Manipulation key
G 104
GX 104
GX1 105
GY 104
GZ 104
R 104
RMB 104
RX 105
RY 105
RY180 105
RZ 105
S 104
Shift+A 105
Shift+D 105
Shift-RMB 104
SX 104
SY 105
SZ 105
SZ2 105
X 105
Y 105
Z 105
Object Mode 109
comparing, with Edit Mode 110
Object Mode to Edit Mode 110

objects, 3D View window 45
objects, building
reference objects 131, 132
units 130, 131
object types, 3D View window
Armatur 47
Camera 47
Curve 47
Lamp 47
Lattice 47
Mesh 47
Meta Object 47
Surface 47
ocean, creating
water surface, making 300-303
off-axis rig 190
O key 342
organic modeling 240
origin 49
Orthographic view 59
Oswald the Lucky Rabbit 18

P

Page Down key 342
Page Up key 342
PAL 417
Path Animation subpanel 327
pattern mesh object 269
Perspective view 59
pictures
creating, computer used 47, 48
pier
frame rails creating, Bezier Curves used 322-325
piling creating, arrays used 327-329
planks adding, DupliFrames used 325-327
Pivot Center button 235
Pivot Point button 293
Pixar
about 25
The Adventures of André and Wally B 26
pixels 47
Plane Crazy 18
Plateau button 306
PNG format 422
polygon 111

prerequisites
  files 273, 274
Preston Blair Phoneme Mouth charts 219
Properties panel 249
Properties window
  about 241
  using, for adding lamp color 69-71

Q

Q key 60

R

Random Seed button 306
Ray Tracing
  demonstrating 411, 412
  sources 415
  using 410
Red/Cyan glasses 390
reference blocks
  using, as reference guide 132
reference grid 46
relative addressing 207
rembrandt lighting 361
Render
  Render button 227
rendering key
  Ctrl+F11 105
  Ctrl+F12 105
  Esc 105
  F11 105
  F12 105
Render Layers node 370
Render Presets button 416
RGB (Red, Green, Blue) 75
Right arrow key 296
right mouse button (RMB) 39
right side view 54, 56
R key 104
RMB key 104
rods 48
rowing videos
  My Rowing 180
  Old Wharf Dory Rowing 1 180
  Row Exercise 180
  Tupan 180

R X key 105
R Y 180 key 105
R Y key 105
R Z key 105

S

Safe Action Zones 215
Safe Title/Safe Action guide
  adding, to Blender 216, 217
Safe Title Zone 215
Save As Blender File button 76
Shift+A 118
Shift+A command 119
Shift+A key 105, 118
Shift+Alt+F 170
Shift+Alt+ F key 190
Shift+Alt+LMB key 106
Shift + Alt - mouse wheel 53
Shift+B key 387
Shift+C key 342
Shift+Ctrl buttons 267
Shift+Ctrl key 123
Shift+Ctrl+S key 105
Shift+D 293
Shift+D key 105, 106
Shift+down arrow key 106
Shift+Down arrow key 296
Shift+End key 296
Shift+G key 342
Shift+Home key 296
Shift key 117 123
Shift+left arrow key 106
Shift+Left arrow key 296
Shift+MMB 133, 222
Shift + mouse wheel 53
Shift+Right arrow key 296
Shift+RMB 294
Shift-RMB key 104
Shift+up arrow key 106
Shift+Up arrow key 296
Shift+X key 342
Shift+Y key 342
Shift+Z key 124, 342
ship's wheel, creating
  about 263
  circle, creating 265

hub, creating 265
materials, adding 271
materials, adding to 271
parts, assembling 269, 270, 271
Spin tool, using 263, 265
spoke, making 266-268
Shutter button 376
Sintel
about 8
URL 9
Sketchpad 22
S key 104
sloop
assembling 274-278
boat name, adding 283, 284
detailing 289
door, adding 290
jib, creating 288
keel, adding 278-280
line, adding 289, 290
mainsail, creating 285-287
NURBS surface, using 285-287
portal, adding 291-293
rudder, adding 278-280
ship's wheel, adding 281, 282
tiller, adding 278-280
sloop hull
coloring 256-260
materials, reusing 261, 262
texturing 256-260
vertex groups, creating for cabin 261
Snow White and the Seven Dwarfs 20
Solid 112
Spacewar! 22
Spin button 264
Spin tool
about 263
circle, creating 265
hub, creating 265
spoke, creating 266
using, for ship's wheel rim creation 263, 265
Standard Definition (SD) 417
Standard Definition TV
transiting, to High Definition TV 217, 218
Steamboat Willie 18
stereographic 3D
making, Node Editor used 400-408

storyboards, animation
about 211
creating 211-213
creating, links 212
need for 211
own board, creating 214
Subdivisions button 306
Subdivision Surfaces
about 225
Edge Tools, using 227
making, steps 226, 227
Subsurface Scattering
about 410
sources 415
Surface 47
S X key 104
S Y key 105
S Z 2 key 105
S Z key 105

T

Tab key 113, 190
telephoto lens 364
templates
adding 194, 195
aligning 195, 196, 198
boom, creating 199
bowsprit, creating 199
gaff, creating 199
inspecting 193
mast, building 198, 199
scaling 195, 196, 198
using, for modeling 192-199
text fields, 3D View window 46
Textured display 112
texture painting
restarting 322
Textures 147
Textures button 152
The Adventures of André and Wally B
about 26
computer animation, analyzing 26
three point lighting system
about 347
back light 348
back light, using 350, 351

beauty lighting 361
cameo lighting 361
colors, using for separation 351-353
cookies, using 353, 354
Custom Curve, using 359-361
falloff, adjusting 357-359
falloff, investigating 355, 356
fill light 348
fill light, using 349, 350
film Noir lighting 362
key light 347
key light, using 348, 349
key side lighting, filing in 361
lighting intensity, changing 352
rembrandt lighting 361
using 361
Tiles
selecting 412
sources 415
Timeline Editor window 377
Timeline window 221, 222, 384
top view 54
transformation control keys
Ctrl 123
Shift 123
Shift+Ctrl 123
Shift+S 124
Transparency subpanel 413
trees
creating, Sapling add-ons used 335-338
Triple I demo 24
TRON 24

U

Ub Iwerks 18
U key 342
units, Blender
blender units 130
imperial units 130
metric units 130
selecting 130
Up arrow key 296
User Preferences 111

V

V A key 106
V C key 106
vertex 111
Vertex Select Mode button 112
vertices, for face
creating 120, 121
vertices, from edge
creating 122
Verts button 269
V F key 106
video player
installing, for Blender 90, 91
Video Sequence Editor
about 390
dissolving with 390-394
individual video strips, editing 395-397
K command, using 397-400
resolution, modifying 394
Shift+K command, using 397-400
transparency, using 414, 415
Video Sequence Editor window 222
Viewport Shading menu 112
VintageCG
computer animation titles 27
V key 106
V U key 106
V V key 106

W

Walk cycle charts 219
Walt Disney 18
water tight 140
wide-angle lens 364
Wireframe 112
work proofing
animation, proofing 383
animation with render, previewing 381
details, inspecting 381
hardware rendering, using 380
only frame part, rendering 381
preview, doing 380
render times, reducing 381-383
ways 380

X

X button 304
X dimension 49
X key 105, 106, 117, 387

Y

Y dimension 49
Y key 105
Y Location keyframe 385

Z

Z depth 121
Z-depth 368
Z dimension 49
Z key 105, 271
Z Location keyframe 385
Zooming 364

Thank you for buying
Blender 3D Basics: Beginner's Guide

About Packt Publishing

Packt, pronounced 'packed', published its first book "*Mastering phpMyAdmin for Effective MySQL Management*" in April 2004 and subsequently continued to specialize in publishing highly focused books on specific technologies and solutions.

Our books and publications share the experiences of your fellow IT professionals in adapting and customizing today's systems, applications, and frameworks. Our solution based books give you the knowledge and power to customize the software and technologies you're using to get the job done. Packt books are more specific and less general than the IT books you have seen in the past. Our unique business model allows us to bring you more focused information, giving you more of what you need to know, and less of what you don't.

Packt is a modern, yet unique publishing company, which focuses on producing quality, cutting-edge books for communities of developers, administrators, and newbies alike. For more information, please visit our website: www.packtpub.com.

About Packt Open Source

In 2010, Packt launched two new brands, Packt Open Source and Packt Enterprise, in order to continue its focus on specialization. This book is part of the Packt Open Source brand, home to books published on software built around Open Source licences, and offering information to anybody from advanced developers to budding web designers. The Open Source brand also runs Packt's Open Source Royalty Scheme, by which Packt gives a royalty to each Open Source project about whose software a book is sold.

Writing for Packt

We welcome all inquiries from people who are interested in authoring. Book proposals should be sent to author@packtpub.com. If your book idea is still at an early stage and you would like to discuss it first before writing a formal book proposal, contact us; one of our commissioning editors will get in touch with you.

We're not just looking for published authors; if you have strong technical skills but no writing experience, our experienced editors can help you develop a writing career, or simply get some additional reward for your expertise.

Blender Game Engine: Beginner's Guide

ISBN: 978-1-84951-702-7   Paperback: 220 pages

The non-programmer's guide to creating 3D video games

1. Use Blender to create a complete 3D video game

2. Ideal entry level to game development without the need for coding

3. No programming or scripting required

Blender 2.5 HOTSHOT

ISBN: 978-1-84951-310-4   Paperback: 332 pages

Challenging and fun projects that will push your Blender skills to the limit

1. Exciting projects covering many areas: modeling, shading, lighting, compositing, animation, and the game engine

2. Strong emphasis on techniques and methodology for the best approach to each project

3. Utilization of many of the tools available in Blender 3D for developing moderately complex projects

4. Clear and concise explanations of working in 3D, along with insights into some important technical features of Blender 3D

Please check **www.PacktPub.com** for information on our titles

Blender 2.5 Materials and Textures Cookbook

ISBN: 978-1-84951-288-6   Paperback: 312 pages

Over 80 great recipes to creat life-like Blender objects

1. Master techniques to create believable natural surface materials

2. Take your models to the next level of realism or artistic development by using the material and texture settings within Blender 2.5.

3. Take the hassle out of material simulation by applying faster and more efficient material and texture strategies

Google SketchUp for Game Design: Beginner's Guide

ISBN: 978-1-84969-134-5   Paperback: 270 pages

Create 3D game worlds complete with textures, levels, and props

1. Learn how to create realistic game worlds with Google's easy 3D modeling tool

2. Populate your games with realistic terrain, buildings, vehicles and objects

3. Import to game engines such as Unity 3D and create a first person 3D game simulation

4. Learn the skills you need to sell low polygon 3D objects in game asset stores

Please check **www.PacktPub.com** for information on our titles